# AT THE CROSSROADS

Nigerian Travel Writing and
Literary Culture in Yoruba and English

# AFRICAN ARTICULATIONS

ISSN 2054–5673

**The series is open to submissions from the disciplines related to literature, cultural history, cultural studies, music and the arts.**

African Articulations showcases cutting-edge research into Africa's cultural texts and practices, broadly understood to include written and oral literatures, visual arts, music, and public discourse and media of all kinds. Building on the idea of 'articulation' as a series of cultural connections, as a clearly voiced argument and as a dynamic social encounter, the series features monographs that open up innovative perspectives on the richness of African locations and networks. Refusing to concentrate solely on the internationally visible above the supposedly ephemeral local cultural spaces and networks, African Articulations provides indispensable resources for students and teachers of contemporary culture.

Please contact the series editors with an outline, or download the proposal form www.jamescurrey.com. Only send a full manuscript if requested to do so.

Stephanie Newell, Professor of English, Yale University    stephanie.newell@yale.edu
Ranka Primorac, Lecturer in English, University of Southampton    r.primorac@soton.ac.uk

Previously published volumes are listed at the back of this book

# AT THE CROSSROADS

## Nigerian Travel Writing and Literary Culture in Yoruba and English

**Rebecca Jones**

PREMIUM
**Times**
BOOKS

🔘 JAMES CURREY

James Currey
is an imprint of
Boydell & Brewer Ltd
PO Box 9, Woodbridge
Suffolk IP12 3DF (GB)
www.jamescurrey.com
and of
Boydell & Brewer Inc.
668 Mt Hope Avenue
Rochester, NY 14620-2731 (US)
www.boydellandbrewer.com

Nigerian paperback edition published 2019 by Premium Times Books, Abuja
53, Mambolo Street, Zone 2,
Wuse, Abuja, Nigeria
www.ptbooksglobal.com

British Library Cataloguing in Publication Data
A catalogue record for this book is available on request from the British Library

ISBN 978-1-84701-222-7 (James Currey hardback)
ISBN 978-1-84701-335-4 (James Currey paperback)
ISBN 978-0-9995584-5-4 (Premium Times Books Nigerian edition paperback)

# Contents

# Illustrations

The author and publisher are grateful to all the institutions and individuals listed for permission to reproduce the materials in which they hold copyright. Every effort has been made to trace the copyright holders; apologies are offered for any omission, and the publisher will be pleased to add any necessary acknowledgement in subsequent editions.

# Acknowledgements

My first thanks go to two mentors without whom this book could not have been written: Karin Barber and Insa Nolte. Their support, guidance, insight, encouragement and example has been invaluable in numerous ways, both intellectual and practical, and I could not be more grateful.

My thanks to my series editors, Stephanie Newell and Ranka Primorac, and to Lynn Taylor at James Currey, for their commitment to this book's potential and for helping me see it through to the end. It has been a pleasure to work with them, every step of the way.

In Nigeria, I owe an enormous debt of gratitude to all those who have helped with my research, offered accommodation and hospitality, helped with logistics, helped me improve my Yoruba, given their time in many ways, and much more besides, since 2009. This book could not exist without their generosity. Amongst the many people who have helped in this way, in particular, I thank Olúṣọlá, Bọ́lájí, Bísọ́lá, Tófúnmi and Samuel Ajíbádé, Joseph Oṣùọlálé and Abíọ́lá Victoria Ayọ̀dókùn, Láídé Sheba, Joshua Abíọ́dún Ògúnwálé, Adérẹ̀mí Suleiman Àjàlá, Olúwabùnmi Akíndípẹ̀, Patrick Oloko and Ọláyẹmí Ọlájídé. I thank writers Pẹ̀lú Awófẹ̀sọ̀, Joe Agbro, Chibuzor Mirian Azubuike, Emmanuel Iduma, Kọ́lá Túbọ̀sún, Fọlárìn Kọ́láwọlé, Lápé Ṣóẹ̀tán and Tọ́pẹ́ Salaudeen-Adégòkè for giving me their time for interviews, and for their continued engagement and encouragement ever since. Not all of these interviews are quoted in this book, but they have helped shape my understanding of these writers' own perceptions of travel writing. Pẹ̀lú Awófẹ̀sọ̀ has been a wonderful guide to Lagos and a patient and generous colleague throughout my research. I am also grateful to his family for hosting me in Lagos.

I thank the staff at the libraries at the University of Ibadan and Obafemi Awolowo University, and at the National Archives of Nigeria in Ìbàdàn for their assistance with my research. I am grateful to colleagues at Osun State University, the University of Ibadan and Obafemi Awolowo University for offering me the opportunity to present my research to their staff and students, and for their feedback and advice.

To all my colleagues at the Department of African Studies and Anthropology (DASA), formerly the Centre of West African Studies (CWAS), University of Birmingham, thank you for making DASA such a congenial academic home for me since 2009. This book is a product of DASA's rich interdisciplinary intellectual culture, and I hope it does it justice. My thanks to Karin Barber, Rachel Bathers, Maxim Bolt, Stewart Brown, Reginald Cline-Cole, Paulo Fernando de Moraes Farias, Juliet Gilbert, Leslie James, Jessica Johnson, David Kerr, Laura Martin, Olúkòyà Ogen, Olúfẹ́mi Ògúndayọ̀, Saima Nasar, Insa Nolte, Tom Penfold, Katrien Pype, Benedetta Rossi, David Rubyan-Ling, Jovia Salifu, Keith Shear, Kate Skinner, Elisa Tuijnder and Ceri Whatley, many of whom read and commented on drafts of parts of this book.

My dear friend and colleague Joanna Skelt sadly passed away during the time I was writing this book. She was, amongst many things, a source of constant encouragement and perspective in writing this book. She is deeply missed.

Thanks to all my colleagues at Africa in Words, particularly Katie Reid, Stephanie Bosch Santana and Kate Wallis, for many years of intellectual inspiration, new ideas and friendship.

My thanks to Kai Easton for introducing me to the study of travel writing and Africa and for her interest and support ever since. Similarly to Carli Coetzee for mentoring, inspiration, ideas and conversation, for patient discussion of the ideas behind this book, and for introducing me to the *Journal of African Cultural Studies* reading group. Thanks also to Shọlá Adénẹ́kàn, Nathan Suhr-Sytsma, Tọ́pẹ́ Salaudeen-Adégòkè and Rótìmí Fásan, who generously read or discussed sections of this book with me. And thank you to Sue Nash for helping me to see a way through for this book, many times over.

The participants in the African Travel Writing Encounters workshop held at the University of Birmingham, 9 March 2016, sparked many new ideas and conversations: Lọlá Akínmádé Åkerström, Janet Remmington, Pèlú Awófẹ̀sọ̀, Kwame Osei-Poku, Stephanie de Goeijin, Neema Ghenim, Hamza Salih, Aedín Ní Loingsigh, Ayọ̀dèjì Aláká, Alexsander Gebara, Matthew Lecznar, Abíọ́lá Victoria Ayọ̀dókùn and Humphrey Nkonde. For funding the workshop, I am grateful to the European Research Council (ERC) Starting Grant project led by Insa Nolte, 'Knowing each other: everyday religious encounters, social identities and tolerance in southwest Nigeria' (grant agreement no. 283,466), based at the University of Birmingham and Osun State University.

I am also grateful to the members of the African Print Cultures network for many new ideas and for advice in the early stages of research for this book.

My friends and family have been a constant source of support and encouragement during the long gestation of this book. I am particularly grateful to Clyde Ancarno, Rosalie Bevan, Charissa King, Catherine and Manzur Rashid, Joanna Rees, Rashi Rohatgi, Rebecca Salter and David Walker, and to my family, Jo, Mark and Andrew Jones.

My thanks to Ceri Whatley, Jo and Mark Jones, Alan Evans and Ben Holroyd for proofreading sections of this book, and Katie Van Heest for editorial support. My particular thanks to Ceri Whatley for her never-ending encouragement, understanding and sense of perspective throughout the time I was writing this book.

I cannot thank Nick Ward enough for his support, encouragement, patience and love, without which I could neither have started nor finished this book. Words cannot do justice to his willingness to help, listen to ideas, and share my enthusiasms and interests, even when they lay far from his own. This book exists partly thanks to his quiet determination to see it over the finish line, and all the many things he has done to make that possible. Thank you, from the bottom of my heart. And to our daughter, Clementine, who came into the world at the same time as this book did – this book is for you.

Although (with exceptions explained below) the translations from Yoruba – and any errors that remain – are my own, I gratefully acknowledge feedback, corrections and advice from Karin Barber, Olúṣọlá Ajíbádé, Olúfẹ́mi Ògún-dayò, Kọ́lá Túbọ̀sún and Ọláyẹmí Ọlájídé. For the translations from Yoruba used in Chapter 2, I am particularly grateful to Ọláyẹmí Ọlájídé for work-ing with me on an extended translation process: I made a first draft of these translations myself, with input from Karin Barber, and then went through the translations line by line with Ọláyẹmí Ọlájídé, who made suggestions and cor-rections. As a result, these translations should be considered a co-translation by Ọláyẹmí Ọlájídé and me. Otherwise, translations from Yoruba are my own, unless otherwise indicated in the text (e.g. in Chapter 4, in which I have used the published translations of D. Ọ. Fágúnwà's novels where available).

I gratefully acknowledge funding from the following sources: an Arts and Humanities Research Council (AHRC) Doctoral Studentship; the European Research Council (ERC) Starting Grant project led by Insa Nolte, 'Knowing each other: everyday religious encounters, social identities and tolerance in southwest Nigeria' (grant agreement no. 283,466), based at the University of Birmingham and Osun State University; and the University of Birmingham.

I thank the following editors and publishers for their permission to reproduce revised versions of parts of these chapters and articles in this book:

- 'The Sociability of Print: 1920s and 30s Lagos Newspaper Travel Writing', in *African Print Cultures*, ed. by Derek Peterson, Stephanie Newell and Emma Hunter (Ann Arbor: University of Michigan Press, 2016), 102–24. Reprinted by courtesy of the University of Michigan Press.
- 'Nigeria is my Playground: Pẹ̀lú Awófẹ̀sọ̀'s Nigerian Travel Writing', *African Research and Documentation*, 125, 2015, 65–85. Reprinted by courtesy of *African Research and Documentation*.
- 'Translation and transformation: travel and intra-national encounter in the Yoruba novel.' *Journal of African Cultural Studies*, 27.3 (2015), 98–113. © 2014 The Author(s). Published by Taylor & Francis. This is an Open Access article distributed under the terms of the Creative Commons Attri-bution-NonCommercial License (<http://creativecommons.org/licenses/by-nc/4.0/>), which permits unrestricted non-commercial use, distribution, and reproduction in any medium, provided the original work is properly cited.

- 'Journeys to the Hinterland: Twentieth-Century Nigerian Travel Writing and Local Heterogeneity in Lagos and Beyond', *Postcolonial Text*, 9.4 (2014). Warm thanks go to Chantal Zabus, Editor-in-Chief of *Postcolonial Text*, and to Sharanya Jayawickrama, Associate Editor of *Postcolonial Text,* for kindly granting permission to reprint the above article.
- 'The Benefits of Travel: Travel Writing in the Lagos Newspapers, 1912–1931', *Journal of History and Cultures,* 2 (2013), 39–56. Reprinted by courtesy of the *Journal of History and Cultures.*
- 'African Travel Writing' in *The Cambridge History of Travel Writing*, ed. by Tim Youngs and Nandini Das (Cambridge: Cambridge UP, 2019). Reprinted by courtesy of Cambridge University Press.

I also thank the following individuals and institutions for their permission to reproduce the following images: Figure 1: Page from I. B. Thomas's series 'Ero L'Ọna', published in *Akede Eko* in 1931; sourced from the National Archives, Ìbàdàn, Nigeria, reproduced with permission; Figure 2: Pẹ̀lú Awófẹ̀sọ̀'s *Tour of Duty* (2010); photograph from Pẹ̀lú Awófẹ̀sọ̀'s collection, reproduced with permission; Figure 3: *Route 234* (2016) edited by Pẹ̀lú Awófẹ̀sọ̀; photograph from Pẹ̀lú Awófẹ̀sọ̀'s collection, reproduced with permission; Figure 4: NàìjáTreks website, reproduced with the permission of Fọlárìn Kọ́láwọlé; Figure 5: 'Awọn Ẹgbẹ Oniwe-Irohin Ero L'Ọna Ilu Oyinbo' ('The Association of Newspaper Editors Travelling to the UK'), *Akede Eko*, 1 January 1944, p. 1; sourced from the National Archives, Ìbàdàn, Nigeria, reproduced with permission.

# Note on Orthography

Standard Yoruba uses diacritics: tone marks above vowels and sub-dots beneath certain letters. However, in practice, there is some variation in the ways that Yoruba speakers use diacritics in written Yoruba: some use full diacritics, some use sub-dots but not tone marks, others use them only where the meaning of a word would otherwise be ambiguous, and others use them inconsistently or not at all. Standards of orthography have also changed over time.

I have generally used full diacritics for Yoruba words in this book, including the names of people and places. However, some writers with Yoruba names, especially those who write in English, do not use tone marks on their names in their published work. In this book, for the sake of consistency, I have used diacritics on all Yoruba names where possible, but this means that in some cases I have added diacritics to names that are commonly published without them (such as Teju Cole or Adewale Maja-Pearce). Although this is an imperfect solution (and by adding tone marks to their names, I do not intend any disrespect to authors who usually choose to write their names without tone marks), I felt that this would be less inconsistent and confusing for the reader than reproducing some Yoruba names with tone marks and some without. However, to aid the reader in locating the texts cited in this book, in the references and bibliography, author names are reproduced as published in the original texts, with or without diacritics. I am grateful to the Yoruba Names Dictionary (<http://www.yorubaname.com/>), which I consulted for the tone marks for some of the Yoruba names cited in this book.

I have not used tone marks for the word 'Yoruba' itself, except where tone marks have been used in quotations, to avoid cluttering the text of the book unnecessarily. I have also not added tone marks to names of institutions or titles of texts where the institutions or texts do not use them themselves (e.g. University of Ibadan, *Akede Eko*).

For quotations from Yoruba texts, I have preserved their original diacritics, no matter how far they deviate from contemporary standard Yoruba. I have also faithfully reproduced any spelling and orthographical mistakes in the original Yoruba texts.

# Introduction

Travel writing has seemed to some critics and writers alike a genre that may have hit a dead end. Since the 1980s, studies of the genre's complicity with colonial discourse and its representation of Africa (and other non-Western regions of the world) through 'imperial eyes', in Mary Louise Pratt's famous words, have made both travel and travel writing seem irretrievably 'tainted', in some understandings, by their association with 'gendered, racial bodies, class privilege'.[1] We are all too familiar with the way Africa has been presented in travel writing as a backdrop for Western adventurers and explorers, from the early days of European exploration up to the present day, and with travel writing's continued reproduction, even in the postcolonial age, of a 'dominant Western civilisation from which travel writers emerge to document other states, cultures and people'.[2] Travel writing may also seem increasingly redundant in a globalised age of mass tourism and communication, when there are few 'unknown' places left to explore, and we can travel virtually to foreign lands at just the click of a mouse button. No wonder that the scholar of travel writing Tim Youngs has said that 'I doubt that travel writing is a genre that one would normally associate with a progressive outlook' – or that British literary magazine *Granta* devoted much of its Issue 138 in 2017 to asking nineteen contemporary travel writers 'Is Travel Writing Dead?'[3]

But travel writing is a diverse genre, and its imperial resonances, as powerful as they are, are only part of the story. Just as *Granta*'s travel writers found ways to say that there are still plenty of possibilities for travel writing in today's world, so for some African writers, too, the genre is full of potential. In 2011, I interviewed Nigerian travel writer, publisher and journalist Pèlú Awófèsò about

---

[1] Mary Louise Pratt, *Imperial Eyes: Travel Writing and Transculturation* (New York, London: Routledge, 1992); James Clifford, *Routes: Travel and Translation in the Late Twentieth Century* (Cambridge, MA; London: Harvard University Press, 1997), p. 39.

[2] Tim Youngs and Peter Hulme, *Talking About Travel Writing: A Conversation between Peter Hulme and Tim Youngs* (Leicester: The English Association, 2007), pp. 12–13; Debbie Lisle, *The Global Politics of Contemporary Travel Writing* (Cambridge: Cambridge University Press, 2006), p. 3.

[3] Youngs and Hulme, *Talking About Travel Writing*, p. 13; 'Is Travel Writing Dead?', *Granta,* 138 (2017).

his decade spent travelling around Nigeria and writing about his journeys. In the
middle of our conversation, Awófèsò proclaimed: 'Nigeria is my playground'.
With Awófèsò's implicit sense of confident entitlement to travel and to write
about Nigeria, his words seem a postcolonial challenge to the assumption that
travel writing is, at heart, a Western genre, or that it is 'inevitably one-way
traffic, because the Europeans mapped the world rather than the world map-
ping them'.[4] For many contemporary travel writers and readers, postcolonial
perspectives such as these are the much-needed fuel that is reinvigorating the
genre; they activate the potential that Youngs identifies for radical, oppositional
and subversive travel writing, and constitute what María Lourdes López Ropero
characterises as 'a powerful vehicle of cultural critique'.[5]

Indeed, travel writing by African authors has gained some visibility in recent
years. Riffing on the novel *We Need New Names* (2013) by Zimbabwean writer
NoViolet Bulawayo, in 2015 journalist Rachel Hamada published a series titled
'We Need New Stories' on the rise of African-authored travel writing in the
last decade. Hamada argues 'that the game has changed, and that the production of stories about travelling by Africans, for consumption by Africans or
indeed non-Africans but as a secondary audience, is increasing, and the genie
is never going back in the bottle'.[6] This book shares Hamada's excitement
about the new visibility of African travel writing in the anglophone West, and
its potential to redress the significant invisibility of such writing in Western
literary and publishing circles. However, travel writing by Africans is not a new
phenomenon, even though relatively few travel narratives by Africans have a
significant presence in the scholarly literature on travel writing.[7] Africa has
long been a continent of mobility, crisscrossed by traders, warriors, scholars,
religious leaders and migrants. Achille Mbembe describes centuries of African
'mixing, blending and superimposing', meaning that 'the cultural history of the
continent can hardly be understood outside the paradigm of itinerancy, mobility and displacement'.[8] Since both literal and figurative mobility are the norm

---

[4] Steve Clark, 'Introduction', in *Travel Writing and Empire: Postcolonial Theory in
Transit,* ed. by Steve Clark (London: Zed Books, 1999), pp. 1–28 (p. 3).

[5] Youngs and Hulme, *Talking About Travel Writing,* p. 13; María Lourdes López
Ropero, 'Travel Writing and Postcoloniality: Caryl Phillips's *The Atlantic Sound*',
*Atlantis* 25.1 (2003), pp. 51–62 (p. 51).

[6] Rachel Hamada, We Need New Stories – Part 2 (2015) <https://thisisafrica.me/
need-new-stories-part-2/> [accessed 27 April 2018].

[7] Literature blogger James Murua makes a similar point in his response to Hamada's
article: James Murua, *Why TIA's 'We Need New Stories' Is a Pile of Unmention-
able* (2015), <http://www.jamesmurua.com/why-tias-we-need-new-stories-is-a-
pile-of-unmentionable/> [accessed 19 January 2015].

[8] Achille Mbembe, 'Afropolitanism', in *Africa Remix: Contemporary Art of a Continent* ed. by Simon Njami (Johannesburg: Jacana Media, 2007), pp. 26–9 (p. 27).

across the African continent, such mobility has necessarily made its mark on Africa's lively and varied oral and writing cultures.

If this mobility and the literatures associated with it have not been highly visible, either in bookshops or in the scholarship on travel writing, we need new ways of encountering, reading and understanding these literatures and their representations of travel. What we need is therefore not only 'new stories' by African travel writers, but also new histories of and methodologies for the study of African travel writing – so that we are able to encompass these African stories of travel in the study of travel writing, across the many diverse modes of writing in which they can be found. This means being open to new ways of thinking about 'travel writing', and to thinking carefully about how we define the genre, particularly its complex inter-relation with 'travel writing' as it has become known in the West, but also its other locally specific historical and literary contexts and intertextual connections.

This book takes up this challenge from the perspective of Nigerian literary culture. The focus of this book is on the literary culture of southwest Nigeria, and on travel writing produced by writers from that region, writing about their travels within Nigeria. The book includes both Yoruba- and English-language travel writing, these being the two main literary languages in southwest Nigeria.[9] The main focus of this book is on texts produced during Nigeria's first century, from its amalgamation as a colony in 1914 until its centenary in 2014, although Chapter 1 and the Epilogue briefly extend this temporal focus – to look, respectively, at the nineteenth-century travel narratives of Samuel Àjàyí Crowther and at exciting new developments in travel writing since 2014 – in order to give a sense of the broader historical context for travel writing. This book is not a comprehensive history of southwest Nigerian travel writing; rather, making connections across literary genres and forms, it explores how writers have used travel writing to represent peoples and places within Nigeria at particular moments in the country's history and literary culture: from colonial encounters to the independence era, from post-civil war writing to travel blogging and the promotion of domestic tourism.

An image to which I return throughout this book is of southwest Nigerian travel writing and its writers standing at (metaphorical) crossroads: travel writing is a mode of writing that writers have used to explore different possibilities of ways of being, such as the categories of 'civilised' and 'native' that early

---

[9] Pidgin English is also widely used in everyday life in contemporary southwest Nigeria. However, very few of the texts I discuss in this book use Pidgin English, except for occasional phrases or when quoting others who speak Pidgin English. The exclusion of Pidgin English texts from this book is not a deliberate choice, but rather reflects Pidgin English's current status as primarily a spoken, rather than literary, language in southwest Nigerian literary culture.

twentieth-century travel writers often wield, to think through major moments of transition within Nigeria, such as the shift to independent nationhood, and to navigate tensions between ethnic and national identities. Travel writing has also often constituted a way for writers to test out the changing relations between reader, writer and text in the face of epistemological, social and technological change in twentieth- and twenty-first-century southwest Nigeria, and to explore the creation of new forms of selfhood.

The figure of the crossroads epitomises both the opportunity that such moments of transition and encounters with difference offer, and the confusion that they might sow. Writing of the Yoruba *òrìṣà* (deity) Èṣù, the trickster who is the guardian of the crossroads, *orita*, Moyọ̀ Òkèdìji writes that Èṣù is the only one who can 'see beyond the confusion of the crossroads, where six roads lead from the center, and the traveler does not know which one leads to good or evil'.[10] As a traveller approaches Èṣù's crossroads from a single path, according to Tóyìn Fálọlá, 'going forward becomes difficult. The traveller is confused as to the right path to the final destination, while Èṣù makes retreat an impossibility. Fear strikes the mind, irrespective of the road one takes. Èṣù occupies the space of possibilities and disruptions, leaving open-ended the resolutions to all the contradictions. The junction is a metaphor for self-doubt, anguish, and indecision'.[11] While not arguing that the writers I discuss in this book draw directly on the figure of Èṣù and the traveller at the crossroads, I gesture throughout the book to these rich metaphorical resonances of the crossroads as a figure representing both choice and indecision, possibilities and confusion. The metaphor of the crossroads is not an analytical tool in itself; rather, by being alert to these moments of both change and confusion suggested by the crossroads, I explore the varying ways that travel writers themselves characterise political, social and cultural difference, encounter and change as they travel within Nigeria, using the language and ideologies of their particular era and background: from terms such as 'civilisation' and 'development' to notions of 'hybridity' and 'detribalisation'. The power of the traveller is often imagined to reside in his or her liminality and ambivalence, in his or her ability to look in more than one direction at once, but this is not always an easy position from which to operate, as we shall see in cases where southwest Nigerian travel writers describe themselves encountering confusion, danger, despair, anxiety and incomprehension as they travel within Nigeria, alongside more optimistic

---

[10] Moyo Okediji, *The Shattered Gourd: Yoruba Forms in Twentieth Century American Art* (Seattle: University of Washington Press, 2003), p. 105.

[11] Toyin Falola, 'Èṣù: The God without Boundaries', in *Èṣù: Yoruba God, Power and the Imaginative Frontiers,* ed. by Toyin Falola (Durham, NC: Carolina Academic Press, 2013), pp. 3–37 (p. 11).

representations of translation, national unity, sociable encounter and improved knowledge of self, other and the world through travel.

I use the term 'southwest Nigeria' to refer to the Yoruba-speaking region of Nigeria, home to the cosmopolitan coastal city of Lagos and the sprawling inland city of Ìbàdàn, and most of whose inhabitants, especially outside of Lagos, claim Yoruba ethnicity. While the region has extensive connections to other parts of the country and beyond, southwest Nigeria's literary culture also has some distinctive features that make it a compelling region to study in its own right. The region can be considered a distinct, although not bounded, cultural zone informed largely but not exclusively by the culture, history, literature and language of the Yoruba people. It is home to a vital, well-established and increasingly globally renowned literary and print culture – and I am using the term 'literary culture' in its broadest sense, to encompass discursive and narrative creative non-fiction writing as well as fiction, poetry and drama – in both Yoruba and English. Writers in this region have been publishing literature in both Yoruba and English since the mid-nineteenth century, beginning with missionary endeavours to formalise Yoruba vocabularies, followed by religious, educational and historical texts.[12] The late nineteenth and early twentieth centuries saw the development of standardised written Yoruba, along with a formalised education system and print technology, which enabled the development of a distinctive print and literary culture in both Yoruba and English, fostered by a local educated elite.[13] As we will see in Chapter 2, locally owned newspapers in both Yoruba and English emerged in increasing numbers in the early twentieth century, and pamphlets, historical writing, Christian texts, poetry, plays and novels all emerged out of this energetic literary culture.

By the early twentieth century, Lagos in particular had become a lively regional hub for colonial intellectual and literary culture, growing out of the city's close interaction with Christianity, literacy and European colonial culture. As such, it was one of several early twentieth-century regional centres of literary culture across anglophone West Africa, alongside other cities such as Accra in the Gold Coast and, later, Onitsha, with its famed market literature that arose from the 1950s, and Government College Umuahia, which fostered many of the first generation of Nigerian writers, including Chinua Achebe.[14] Chapter 2 explores travel writing that arose from the distinct literary culture of colonial

---

[12] Bisi Ogunsina, *The Development of the Yoruba Novel 1930–1975* (Ibadan: Gospel Faith Mission Press, 1992), pp. 9–10.

[13] Rita Nnodim, 'Configuring Audiences in Yoruba Novels, Print and Media Poetry', *Research in African Literatures*, 37.3 (2006), 154–75 (p. 155).

[14] Philip S. Zachernuk, *Colonial Subjects: An African Intelligentsia and Atlantic Ideas* (Charlottesville and London: University Press of Virginia, 2000), p. 53; Terri Ochiagha, *Achebe and Friends at Umuahia: The Making of a Literary Elite* (Woodbridge: Boydell & Brewer, 2015).

Lagos. While many of the travel writers of later decades that I discuss in this book are also from Lagos – a place that, as a cosmopolitan megacity, has continued to view itself as somewhat distinct from the rest of Nigeria – other parts of southwest Nigeria have also made important contributions to the region's literary culture, including Abẹ́òkúta, an early seat of print culture, and Ìbàdàn, whose university has nurtured the talents of many important twentieth-century writers, such as 'first-generation' Nigerian writers Wọlé Ṣóyínká, Chinua Achebe, Christopher Okigbo, J. P. Clark and Flora Nwapa. A Yoruba-language literary tradition has developed in southwest Nigeria throughout the twentieth century, encompassing over two hundred novels as well as many other prose and poetic genres, historical writing, personal writing, religious texts, autobiographies, pamphlets and newspapers.[15] The southwest region is broadly associated with this Yoruba literary tradition, while Hausa literature has dominated in northern Nigeria, and Igbo in southeast Nigeria (and Nigeria's other less widely spoken languages across the nation have also produced their own literatures). The region is also home to a lively English-language literary tradition, including novels it is known for across the anglophone world – from *The Palm-Wine Drinkard* by Amos Tutùọlá to the contemporary fiction of authors such as Sefi Atta, Ayọ̀bámi Adébáyọ̀, Abímbọ́lá Àdùnní Adéḷẹ́kàn, A. Igoni Barrett and Lọlá Shóné̩yìn – as well as poetry and drama, such as that of Wọlé Ṣóyínká, Níyì Ọsúndáre and Fẹ́mi Ọ̀ṣọ́fisan. Travel writing, as we shall see, also plays a role in the literary and cultural history of this region.

## Border-crossings: ways of reading southwest Nigerian travel writing

If travel writing is so closely associated with imperialism, colonialism and the Western gaze on the rest of the world, why would southwest Nigerian travel writers choose to adopt the genre? Travel writing is a notoriously difficult genre to define. Some critics have sought to define travel writing fairly narrowly, based on its history in the anglophone West, in terms of what Jan Borm refers to as the 'travel book' or 'travelogue': 'any narrative characterized by a non-fiction dominant that relates (almost always) in the first person a journey or journeys that the reader supposes to have taken place in reality while assuming or presupposing that the author, narrator and principal character are but one or identical'.[16] Other critics consider the 'travel book' just one form of travel

---

[15] Lérè Adéyẹmí, 'Magical Realism in Contemporary Yoruba Novels', in *Texts and Theories in Transition: Black African Literature and Imagined Tradition,* ed. by Charles Bodunde (Bayreuth: Eckersdorf, 2010), pp. 91–102 (p. 92).

[16] Jan Borm, 'Defining Travel: On the Travel Book, Travel Writing and Terminology', in *Perspectives on Travel Writing,* ed. by Glenn Hooper and Tim Youngs (Aldershot: Routledge, 2004), pp. 13–26 (p. 17).

writing and define the genre in such a way that it embraces a much wider range of texts, taking in memoir, scientific description, historical accounts, exploratory narratives, reportage, fiction and more; Jonathan Raban writes that the genre 'accommodates the private diary, the essay, the short story, the prose poem, the rough note and polished table talk with indiscriminate hospitality'.[17] Borm characterises this latter, more expansive sense of the genre defined not formally but thematically, as texts in which travel is the 'main theme', and which embraces fiction as well as non-fiction, as 'travel writing' or 'travel literature', as distinct from the more narrowly defined 'travelogue' and 'travel book'. Travel writing as defined in this broad sense is thus a hybrid, appropriative genre, which has taken many forms over its long history.

Travel writing's hybridity, ambiguity and slipperiness as a genre is only amplified if we try to apply the many definitions of travel writing that have developed in relation to Western travel writing to forms of writing produced in African contexts. Studies of travel writing from the non-Western world, including China, Russia and the Islamic world, demonstrate the widespread nature of writing about travel, and remind us that it is not inherently and necessarily a Western genre. A rich body of scholarship on Islamic narratives of travel, from North Africa to the Middle East, for example, has shown the importance of the *riḥla* – the journey after Islamic knowledge – in the tradition of Islamic travel narratives.[18]

Southwest Nigerian travel writing, however, takes a somewhat different route from some of these non-Western travel writing traditions that have long histories in their own right. With the region's pre-colonial verbal cultures being centred on oral rather than written arts, writing and literary culture in southwest Nigeria have been, in their early days especially, closely associated with the colonial encounter and with literary forms generally thought of as Western in origin, some of which – such as the novel – the region's writers have adopted, adapted and shaped into new forms, as well as creating new forms that speak to the circumstances of the twentieth and twenty-first centuries. Travel writing is not considered a 'traditional' or canonical southwest Nigerian or Yoruba genre in the vein of established Yoruba oral genres such as *oríkì* (praise poetry), *odù Ifá* (divination verses), *òwe* (proverbs) or *ìtàn* (narrative), or newer oral and semi-oral genres such as *ewì* (media and print poetry) and the travelling theatre. Although numerous tales of travel appear or are alluded to in several Yoruba oral genres such as *ìtàn*, *oríkì*, *ìjálá* (hunters' chants) and *àlọ́* (prose tales) (and I discuss examples of this in Chapters 1 and 4), there is no particular oral

---

[17] Jonathan Raban, *For Love and Money: Writing, Reading, Travelling, 1968–1987* (London: Collins Harvill, 1987), p. 253.

[18] Houari Touati, *Islam and Travel in the Middle Ages* (Chicago and London: University of Chicago Press, 2010).

genre that has become renowned exclusively for tales of travel.[19] Therefore, the writers discussed in this book are not usually writing with a sense of a single established 'indigenous' genre dedicated to travel to write into, although some writers may selectively adapt and transform oral tales of travel in their written texts, as we will see in Chapters 1 and 4. However, the texts discussed in this book, many of which focus on moments of epistemological, social and political change in twentieth and twenty-first century Nigeria, are generally less interested in transforming oral tales of travel within written texts than they are in using travel writing itself as a way to investigate the role of the written text and its relationship with its readers in twentieth and twenty-first century Nigeria.

A question of definition therefore immediately arises when we attempt to study 'travel writing' in this region. Is the study of 'travel writing' in this context the study of how a Western genre (in all its ambiguity and diversity) has been adopted and reshaped by the region's writers? Or is it rather a thematic study of writing about travel, which may include the 'travel writing' genre as it has become known in the West, but which also explores other modes of writing about travel that may be specific to African contexts? In other words, in African contexts, are we interested in tracing the history of 'travel writing' as a genre that we consider to have its origins in the West, to which we are adding an African history, or are we expanding the notion of 'travel writing' itself to include both forms of travel and ways of writing about travel that have African histories that may differ from those of the West?

While both approaches have their merits, this book takes the latter approach, in agreement with Aedín Ní Loingsigh's contention that the 'generic boundaries of travel writing need to be probed and tested' in any reading of African travel writing, in order not to transpose assumptions about genre derived from Western literary cultures to African literary cultures, and in order to recognise the many forms that travel and writing about travel have taken in southwest Nigeria, as I discuss in more detail in Chapter 1.[20] Therefore, in selecting the varied texts I discuss in this book, I have chosen to adhere to Jan Borm's expansive, theme-based definition of travel writing: 'a collective term for a variety of texts both predominantly fictional and non-fictional whose main theme is travel'.[21] The term 'travel writing' as used in this book therefore refers both to texts that may be recognisable as 'travel writing' as we have come to know it in the West, and to texts more broadly that have travel as their 'main theme'; the two often, but do not always, overlap, and are held in productive tension

---

[19] Karin Barber, *The Anthropology of Texts, Persons and Publics* (Cambridge: Cambridge University Press, 2007), pp. 46–58.

[20] Aedín Ní Loingsigh, *Postcolonial Eyes: Intercontinental Travel in Francophone African Literature* (Liverpool: Liverpool University Press, 2009), p. 17.

[21] Borm, 'Defining Travel', p. 13.

throughout this book, keeping these ambiguities and difficulties of definition in view.

The texts I discuss range from missionary journals and historical writing to serialised newspaper travel narratives, memoirs, conventional 'travel books', fiction and online writing, including blogs. While some of these texts appear to adopt particular forms of Western travel writing fairly uncritically, but adapt them to suit new purposes and the southwest Nigerian context, others address Western audiences or imagine themselves to be writing in Western travel writers' footsteps but seek to subvert the genre's traditions; this rewriting of the travel writing genre is sometimes called 'countertravel writing', which 'pits itself against the dominant Eurocentric model'.[22]   In other cases, however, writers have written about travel in ways that do not accord so closely with Western notions of travel writing, reflecting locally significant forms of travel, that draw on conventions of local literary culture, experiment with new forms of writing, or address particular local political, social and cultural concerns. Where the texts I discuss in this book accord with the definition of the 'travelogue' or the 'travel book' as discussed above, and particularly where they clearly intersect with Western travel writing traditions, I refer to them as 'travel books' or 'travelogues', whereas for other texts I use the more expansive terms 'travel writing' and 'travel narrative'.

There are a wealth of representations of travel in other forms of Nigerian cultural production, from poetry, drama and oral genres to music and Nollywood movies, but in this book I have limited my selection of texts to prose fiction and non-fiction. The broad definition of travel writing I have adopted allows the book to explore the boundaries between travel writing and other related genres, such as autobiography and self-development literature, and also between fiction and non-fiction as forms of travel writing. As Morádéwún Adéjùnmòbí suggests, it is important to avoid artificially detaching literary fiction from the rest of Africa's large, vibrant, locally produced and circulating textual ecology, which includes non-fiction texts as well as popular, locally circulating literary texts, and to recognise the extent to which literary fiction and other textual forms share social concerns, textual conventions and readerly expectations.[23] Indeed, scholars of travel writing have frequently identified a significant overlap between fact and fiction, even in apparently non-fiction

---

[22]   Patrick Holland and Graham Huggan, *Tourists with Typewriters: Critical Reflections on Contemporary Travel Writing* (Ann Arbor: University of Michigan Press, 2000), p. 21.

[23]  Moradewun Adejunmobi, 'Provocations: African Societies and Theories of Creativity', in *Rethinking African Cultural Production,* ed. by Kenneth W. Harrow and Frieda Ekotto (Bloomington, IN: Indiana University Press, 2015), pp. 52–77 (pp. 55–7)

travel narratives, and a shared history between the novel and the travel narrative, both in Europe and in Africa.[24] In Chapter 4, I consider the quest narrative in novels by D. Ọ. Fágúnwà, Amos Tutùọlá, Ben Okri and J. Akin Ọmọ́yájowó as a form of travel writing. The danger is, of course, that very broad definitions of 'travel writing' have the potential to expand almost infinitely to encompass almost any text that includes episodes of travel, rendering them less analytically meaningful. I have therefore focused on those texts that, in accordance with Borm's definition, have travel as their 'main theme', although I recognise that, even so, the boundaries around 'travel writing' still remain blurred. Chapter 1 discusses these challenges of definition in more detail, looking at where the boundaries around 'travel writing' may lie through the example of historical writing about migration in southwest Nigeria.

Echoing the movement that southwest Nigerian travel writers often picture themselves making across borders and between different ways of being, this book also makes several movements of its own across and between literary forms, languages and regions of Nigeria, reading southwest Nigerian travel writing through local and transnational texts, 'popular' and 'literary' texts, and Yoruba and English, as well as through the lens of travel writing's ambivalent articulations with both local genres and Western travel writing. Postcolonial criticism of African texts has been criticised for privileging what Eileen Julien has called the 'extroverted African novel': transnational and diasporic texts and those that seem to 'write back' to the West or speak to Western discourses about Africa. This emphasis on such novels has, Evan Mwangi argues, come at the expense of recognition of the 'internal heteroglossia' within Africa and intertextuality between African texts.[25] While southwest Nigeria has produced a number of internationally read and renowned writers, it also has, in common with many West African countries, a vibrant literary and print sphere that has often been characterised as 'local' by scholars, referring to those texts that do not necessarily gain international visibility, but that circulate widely within Nigeria. This book explores a number of forms of travel writing that have circulated primarily within Nigeria, such as newspaper serials, local historical writing, and memoirs and novels about Nigeria's National Youth Service Corps (NYSC). In order to locate such texts I conducted archival research in southwest Nigeria (at Obafemi Awolowo University, the National Archives of Nigeria in Ìbàdàn, and the Kenneth Dike Library at the University of Ibadan),

---

24 Ní Loingsigh, *Postcolonial Eyes*, pp. 16–20; Percy Adams, *Travel Literature and the Evolution of the Novel* (Lexington, KY: University Press of Kentucky, 1983).

25 Evan M. Mwangi, *Africa Writes Back to Self: Metafiction, Gender, Sexuality* (Albany, NY: Suny Press, 2009), pp. 1–4; Eileen Julien, 'The Extroverted African Novel', in *The Novel,* ed. by Franco Moretti (Princeton, NJ: Princeton University Press, 2006), pp. 667–700.

as well as seeking out texts in the bookshops of Ìbàdàn, Ilé-Ifẹ̀ and Lagos and directly from their authors, since many of the self-published books that populate the contemporary Nigerian literary landscape are sold directly by the author and their friends, rather than being distributed to bookshops. Reading locally circulating texts as well as internationally circulating texts is important in order to offer readings of travel writing that are embedded within southwest Nigeria's literary culture. Moreover, the sense amongst scholars of a paucity of travel writing by African writers, which I discuss in Chapter 1, can be traced at least partially to a focus on African travel narratives published by major publishers and readily available in the West, of which there are relatively few. Focusing on genres of writing less familiar as travel writing, on forms of travel that are locally significant, and on texts that circulate locally reveals a greater wealth of Nigerian travel writing than the scholarship on travel writing has previously tended to recognise.

Locally circulating texts often, although not always, overlap with what has been labelled Africa's 'popular literature', referring to 'non-elite, unofficial and urban' texts, usually locally published and often self-published, cheaply priced and sold in local bookshops and market stalls or directly by the author, without the distribution networks commanded by major literary publishers and mass market texts. Such texts, of which the best known example in Nigeria is the Onitsha market literature that arose in the 1950s, are popular both in the sense of commanding significant local readerships, feeding what Stephanie Newell identifies as the 'voracious book-hunger' of urban school leavers in Africa, and in their adoption of genres such as the thriller or romance and their constant reworking of 'ubiquitous character types and plots'. Popular texts, both fiction and non-fiction genres such as self-help or advice pamphlets, often offer 'symbolic resolutions to the everyday problems of non-elite readers', and 'never fail to generate debate amongst readers on moral and behavioural issues'.[26] While the distinction between 'popular' and 'elite' or 'high' literary texts may, in practice, be blurred, nonetheless these two forms of literary production have often been analysed separately.

However, this book seeks not to reify such distinctions between 'local' and 'transnational', 'popular' and 'literary', but to cross between them, putting them into dialogue with each other. Reflecting the common perception that travel writing itself is often a middlebrow genre that sits somewhere between 'high' and 'popular' literatures, this book encompasses texts that could be considered popular, such as newspaper serials, novels, self-development literature, spiritual autobiographies, self-published memoirs and blogs, alongside 'high' literary texts by canonical Nigerian authors such as Isaac Délànọ̀, D. Ọ.

---

[26] Stephanie Newell, 'Introduction', in *Readings in African Popular Fiction*, ed. by Stephanie Newell (London: International African Institute, 2002), pp. 1–10.

Fágúnwà, Amos Tutùọlá and Téjú Cole, and a number of texts that might be considered to sit somewhere in between. The book also considers the points of articulation between 'local' literatures and internationally renowned texts, as well as intersections with Western travel writing and literature, exploring the ways they both draw on and generate varied locally and internationally circulating discourses about both travel and text. Thus as well as tracing connections between travel narratives *within* southwest Nigeria – such as those between the Yoruba newspapers of the 1920s and Yoruba novels from the 1920s to the 1950s, including the novels of D. Ọ. Fágúnwà – I also explore points at which transnational connections are considered to have more weight than local connections. Chapter 7 in particular explores the question of the space for transnational texts within southwest Nigeria's literary culture by looking at diaspora return travel narratives and criticism of some of these texts as overly alienated or extroverted.

This book also crosses back and forth between Yoruba and English. Both Yoruba and English are spoken to varying degrees within southwest Nigeria; some people speak only or mainly Yoruba, while for others, in the region's cities especially, English or Pidgin English may be the main languages of daily interaction (especially in Lagos, home to people from all over Nigeria), and many people navigate life through a mixture of Yoruba, English and Pidgin English. Yet the Yoruba and English literatures produced in this region – novels in particular – have sometimes been viewed as distinct literary traditions; Nigerian English literature has been depicted as being at first imitative and colonial, then either popular and urban, or transnational, postcolonial and elite. Yoruba (or other African-language) literature, meanwhile, is often represented as local, traditional, oral and under pressure from both English and the dwindling of a Yoruba-reading public.[27] Wendy Griswold's study of 'the Nigerian novel', its readerships and publishing, suggests that 'full novels' in Yoruba and other Nigerian languages are 'few and far between'.[28] Griswold is interested in Nigeria's 'national' literature and, for her, this means novels that can potentially be read throughout the nation, beyond any one ethnolinguistic region; therefore, she claims, 'only novels written in English can truly be called *Nigerian* novels'.[29] Griswold implicitly limits Yoruba to being regional or ethnic, while imagining English as a supra-regional, 'national' language.

English has become widespread in Nigeria as a language of education and business, and many Yoruba intellectuals are concerned about a loss of Yoruba

---

[27] Karin Barber, 'African-Language Literature and Postcolonial Criticism', *Research in African Literatures,* 26.4 (1995), pp. 3–11.

[28] Wendy Griswold, *Bearing Witness: Readers, Writers, and the Novel in Nigeria* (Princeton, NJ: Princeton University Press, 2000), p. 31.

[29] Ibid. p. 32; original emphasis.

reading and writing skills amongst young Yoruba speakers, who may prioritise what they see as more immediately useful English language skills. However, while certainly not everyone in contemporary southwest Nigeria speaks English, and those who do not may face certain disadvantages, nonetheless the region is in many contexts a bilingual culture in which many people, especially school leavers, do not so much translate between Yoruba and English as work with both of them, switching between them as necessary. This dialogue between the two languages has also been the case in the region's literature. Even at the beginning of the twentieth century, when English was much less widely spoken than it is today, both languages were used in the local press. Pamphlets, historical texts and educational tracts by Lagosian writers were also published in both Yoruba and English.[30] Writers of local town histories often published one version of their history in one language, and then a later version in the other language, usually a retelling rather than a direct translation. Writers in the Yoruba- and English-language newspapers at the turn of the twentieth century commented on each other's publications, and even occasionally reprinted each other's articles across the language divide. Moreover, throughout the twentieth century, Yoruba print and literary culture has had a considerable interaction with both locally and internationally published English-language texts, as we will see in the case of the many English-language influences on D. Ọ. Fágúnwà's writing, for instance.

Nonetheless, the two literatures are not interchangeable; English and Yoruba texts often draw on different references and imagine different readerships, particularly in an age of global readerships for Nigerian anglophone literature; the relationship between the two languages is one of 'kiss and quarrel', as Níyì Ọsúndáre evocatively puts it, recognising the challenges of translation between the two languages, whose epistemological, linguistic, ontological and socio-cultural frameworks do not always neatly align.[31] As Karin Barber argues of the Yoruba and English newspapers in early twentieth-century Lagos, '[s]ome things were said in one language, other things in the other'.[32] English and Yoruba texts often imagine their reading publics in different ways, and draw on a different range of linguistic and cultural resonances.[33] The distinctiveness of

[30] Karin Barber, 'Translation, Publics, and the Vernacular Press in 1920s Lagos', in *Christianity and Social Change in Africa: Essays in Honour of J. D. Y. Peel*, ed. by Toyin Falola (Durham, NC: Carolina Academic Press, 2005), pp. 187–208.

[31] Niyi Osundare, 'Yorùbá Thoughts, English Words: A Poet's Journey through the Tunnel of Two Tongues', in *Kiss & Quarrel: Yorùbá/English Strategies of Mediation,* ed. by Stewart Brown (Birmingham: Centre of West African Studies, 2000), pp. 15–31.

[32] Barber, 'Translation, Publics, and the Vernacular Press', p. 189.

[33] Karin Barber, 'I. B. Akinyele and Early Yoruba Print Culture', in *Recasting the Past. History Writing and Political Work in Modern Africa,* ed. by D. Peterson and G. Macola (Athens, OH: Ohio University Press, 2009), pp. 31–49 (pp. 43–7).

Yoruba texts often comes from their authors' playing with the Yoruba language and its tonal quality, the multiple resonances contained within many words and phrases, and on textual resources such as metaphors, òwe (proverbs), oríkì (praise or attributive poetry) and ìtàn (historical narratives and stories). Concepts such as ọ̀làjú or 'civilisation' that we will encounter in this book often have slightly different resonances in each language.

The relationship between English and Yoruba can therefore be characterised more as one of affiliation, interchange and translation than of hierarchy, and so in this book, I read the two languages and their literatures together, recognising their differences but also tracing their interactions. Sometimes I put them directly into dialogue with each other: in Chapter 2, I read Yoruba- and English-language travel narratives alongside each other, and in Chapter 4, I explore how English-language texts such as Amos Tutùọlá's *The Palm-Wine Drinkard* can be read in the light of D. Ọ. Fágúnwà's Yoruba-language novels. In several chapters we will see how travel writers represent themselves as doing the work of translation between Nigeria's many languages. In other chapters, my focus is more on English-language writing (although even in these texts, we will see how Yoruba words often intrude), but my overall contention is that reading these two languages alongside each other over the course of this book not only gives a fuller picture of the region's travel writing, but also allows us to see the way ideas move back and forth between the two languages.

This book also explores the way literature from southwest Nigeria makes links back and forth into the rest of Nigeria and beyond. When I began research for this book, as a scholar with a background in Yoruba studies, I had originally conceived of the book as a study of Yoruba travel writing, and I therefore sought to confine my study strictly to southwest Nigeria, comparing Yoruba-language travel writing from this region with its English-language counterpart from the same region. However, as I wrote the book, it became ever clearer that a strictly ethnolinguistic approach to this subject would be less fruitful than one that maintained a focus on southwest Nigeria, but that also acknowledged the region's complex linkages with the rest of Nigeria, and the way the region's relationship with the nation has changed across the twentieth and twenty-first centuries. The region now known as southwest Nigeria has defined and continues to define itself variously through ethnic, regional and national identities, including being defined in largely ethnic terms as the Yoruba region, but also understanding itself as partaking – if still sometimes sceptically – in a Nigerian national identity in the post-independence era, while nonetheless maintaining a strong sense of a distinctive Yoruba culture and history. It is not possible to conceive of either 'Yoruba' or 'southwest Nigeria' as a bounded unit, since there are constant flows of people, ideas and texts into and out of the region; Mbembe's claim for the African continent that its cultural history cannot be understood outside the paradigm of mobility is also true for this region. Moreover, ideas of what 'Yoruba', 'southwest Nigeria' and 'Nigeria' mean are all perpetually in flux and under discussion. Travel writing itself enables southwest Nigerian writers to play with categories such as 'Yoruba' and 'Nigeria', and has both reflected and contributed to changes in the ways that the people of this region relate to ideas of 'Yoruba' and 'Nigeria' in unstable, fluid ways.

Southwest Nigeria's literary culture, too, stretches out beyond the region itself, particularly in the case of English-language writing, for which texts, especially novels, are commonly read as part of a national Nigerian literary culture rather than as belonging to southwest Nigeria more exclusively. Writers themselves often travel across the nation during the course of their education and literary careers, and are not necessarily confined to the regions in which they grew up or claim their ethnic origin. This is not to deny the role that geographies and ethnolinguistic histories may play in shaping literary works, nor the role of particular regions of Nigeria in producing clusters of writers. Nonetheless, many Nigerian literary works in English tend to be published and read within the context of a national literary culture and in dialogue with other Nigerian texts, across but not ignoring ethnolinguistic and regional differences, making it difficult to define a text as either strictly 'Nigerian' or strictly 'Yoruba' or 'southwest Nigerian'.

Therefore, while this book retains an overall focus on the history and literary culture of southwest Nigeria, it adopts an open-ended approach to the notion of 'southwest Nigeria' and its literary culture; it also considers the region's literary connections beyond this region, and moreover recognises the ethnic diversity of the southwest region. For instance, in Chapters 4 and 7 I put texts by Ben Okri and Noo Saro-Wiwa, who both claim their heritage elsewhere in Nigeria and who have both lived for significant periods of time in the UK, into dialogue with southwest Nigerian texts, in order to make cross-Nigerian comparisons and to reflect the way they write into a shared anglophone Nigerian literary culture. In Chapter 5, I discuss an English-language memoir by Chibuzor Mirian Azubuike, who identifies as Igbo. Azubuike grew up in and continues to live in Lagos, attended university in Benin and Ìbàdàn, and her memoir contrasts her life in Lagos with her experiences in Bauchi. Lagos, in particular, is a cosmopolitan city that is home to people of many different ethnic origins, not just Yoruba. To exclude Lagosian or other southwest Nigerian writers from this study on the basis of ethnicity or ancestry when their texts circulate in the same sphere as those of Yoruba authors would be to essentialise ethnicity to an unviable degree.

Reading southwest Nigerian travel writing through questions of genre and through its local history, as well as its ambivalent, unstable and fluid relations with Western forms of travel writing and with national and transnational literary cultures, enables us to position such travel writing amid broader questions about 'local' and 'global' ways of reading: is travel writing a recognisable

global genre, albeit one that has local inflections? Can we compare manifestations of 'travel writing' around the world, or should we read them as separate
(if sometimes comparable) genres? How do genres emerge within local literary ecologies? And how do we examine how such 'local' literary ecologies
are linked to the world, while still placing local subjectivities at their heart?
Finally, how do we trace histories of genres that undeniably have Western
roots or prominent Western histories, but also have numerous other histories
elsewhere in the world? These questions are of crucial importance as scholarship increasingly reads literary genres through the lens of 'world literature',
tracing global articulations between texts and genres.

As well as the novel, other literary genres that, in common with travel writing, appear to have strong roots in Europe and its imperial ambitions are also
now being read through their complex African histories. Within the genre of
science fiction, for instance, Africa has been not only a backdrop to European
fantasies of the future but has also, since the early decades of the twentieth century, produced its own science fiction. In reading such texts as science fiction,
Mark Bould asks, '[c]an we move beyond European models of fiction, without
neglecting the long history of interactions and influences between continents?'[34]
In other words, to what extent is it useful to apply a genre category that has
such a long Western history to African texts? Alena Rettová argues that it can
be illuminating to do so: there has been a critical reluctance to apply the label
'science fiction' to African texts about the future, which have often instead been
read as utopian/dystopian, or as forms of magical realism, emphasising their
'folkloric' or 'mythological' elements rather than their orientation to the future.
Yet reading these texts as science fiction (or as Afrofuturist, which Rettová
sees as a sub-genre of science fiction) reveals their connection to 'the future
not only of Africa, but indeed of the planet and beyond'.[35]

This book explores equivalent questions for travel writing, examining the
extent to which it is useful and necessary to trace African texts' interactions
with Western texts and textual histories. Eileen Julien argues that rather than
situating the rise of the novel as 'one episode in a multi-layered narrative of
European modernity's sweep of the globe', the novel can be located within a
broader African literary landscape, as one form of discursive self-representation
among many, amidst an interpenetration of global and local forms.[36] In this
book I am similarly interested in ways of reading travel writing not as a genre
'imported' to a southwest Nigerian periphery from the West and infused with

[34] Mark Bould, 'Africa Sf: Introduction', *Paradoxa*, 25 (2014), pp. 7–15.
[35] Alena Rettová, 'Sci-Fi and Afrofuturism in the Afrophone Novel: Writing the Future and the Possible in Swahili and in Shona', *Research in African Literatures*,
48.1 (2017), pp. 158–82 (pp. 160–2).
[36] Julien, 'The Extroverted African Novel', pp. 669, 683.

Nigerian content, but as a body of writing that can be read through both its southwest Nigerian history and its connection to Western forms of travel writing and a global history, operating alongside each other and interpenetrating one another rather than in hierarchy.

## Standing at the crossroads: writing Nigeria from 1914 to 2014

The methodological border-crossings this book makes are echoed by those the travel writers themselves make as they travel within Nigeria. This book's focus is on travel writing about Nigeria (including the southwest region, but also beyond, into the rest of Nigeria) rather than on Nigerian writing about travel overseas. This focus on intra-Nigerian travel – on what, in other contexts, has been called the 'home tour' – is not meant to suggest that southwest Nigerian travel writing is limited to writing about Nigeria; Nigerians have also produced a significant amount of overseas travel writing, which offers exciting material for a study in its own right.[37] However, my interest in this book is in the ways that southwest Nigerian writers have used travel writing to represent their encounters with Nigeria's heterogeneity, to explore connections, commonalities and difference within Nigeria, and to create new forms of knowledge about Nigeria. Nigeria is heterogeneous enough to have provided fertile ground for travel writers seeking encounters with difference and strangeness within national borders – to the extent that we cannot in fact take it for granted that travel within Nigeria constitutes a 'home tour' for all the writers I discuss in this book, some of whom consider parts of Nigeria they encounter through travel to be very distinct from their home. In her study of nineteenth-century domestic travel writing by Mexican writers, Thea Pitman shows how such travel narratives maintain both the imperial rhetoric that distinguishes between the travel writer and those '"others" who live in unfamiliar, *exotic* terrain', and a nationalist view of the space travelled in as familiar territory. This book explores, though in a different historical and geographical context, a similar tension between viewing Nigerians as 'others' and as compatriots in some of the travel writing I discuss.[38] Southwest Nigerian travel writers often describe themselves crossing not only physical borders between regions of Nigeria, but also metaphorical borders such as those constituted by differences of language, class, gender, ethnicity and notions of 'civilised' or 'developed' regions of Nigeria, particularly the difference between Lagos and elsewhere in Nigeria.

---

[37] On the 'home tour' in the English and postcolonial travel writing traditions, for instance, see Barbara Korte, *English Travel Writing: From Pilgrimages to Postcolonial Explorations* (Basingstoke and New York: Palgrave, 2000), pp. 66–81, 170–8.

[38] Thea Pitman, *Mexican Travel Writing* (Bern: Peter Lang, 2008), p. 48; original emphasis.

As such, travel writing constitutes a way they are able to picture themselves standing at a crossroads between different ways of being Yoruba or Nigerian, showing their readers differences of language, culture and ways of life.

The reasons that these differences within Nigeria are so pertinent in southwest Nigeria's travel writing are related to complex histories of and relations between towns, regions, ethnicities and nation in Nigeria. Nigeria's genesis as a nation has not been straightforward. The region that is now known as the Nigerian nation was, in the pre-colonial era, home to numerous distinct but connected kingdoms, city-states and other regional communities based upon ties of politics, history, kinship and language, now usually understood as ethnicity. As well as established trading links across the Sahara, the region has a long history of contact with Europe – particularly with the Portuguese, who set up trading posts, including slave trading, across the West African coast from the sixteenth century, and were later joined by other European slavers, traders, missionaries and explorers, including the British. British influence over the region rapidly increased from 1851, when they shelled Lagos and deposed its ruler. In 1861, the British annexed Lagos, and they gradually claimed rights to larger areas of Nigeria until in 1914, the colony of Nigeria was formed when Britain amalgamated the Northern and Southern Protectorates of Nigeria, with Lagos then the capital of the new Colony and Protectorate of Nigeria. This colony became home to people from more than 250 ethnic groups, speaking over four hundred languages, spread across regions with significant political, historic and religious differences, and British colonial divide-and-rule policy emphasised those differences, particularly between northern and southern Nigeria.[39]

After Nigeria gained its independence in 1960, this young nation retained its vast heterogeneity, and suffered several periods of major political instability and volatility. The three main regions – northern, western and eastern, dominated by the Hausa-Fulani, Yoruba and Igbo respectively – engaged in a struggle for power in the new nation.[40] From 1967–70, in particular, the nation was in crisis as the Igbo region attempted to secede as the independent nation of Biafra, resulting in three years of devastating civil war. While the federal state won the civil war and the Igbo region has remained part of Nigeria, tensions continue to rumble between Biafran secessionists and the state. After a period of relative wealth in Nigeria's oil boom years of the 1970s, a period of austerity and the introduction of the International Monetary Fund's structural adjustment program (SAP) in the 1980s led to an economic crisis from which Nigeria

---

[39] Efurosibina Adegbija, *Multilingualism: A Nigerian Case Study* (Trenton, NJ: Africa World Press, 2004), pp. 3, 8.

[40] Wale Adebanwi, *Nation as Grand Narrative: The Nigerian Press and the Politics of Meaning* (Rochester, NY and Woodbridge: University of Rochester Press/ Boydell & Brewer, 2016), p. 15.

has not yet fully recovered. While Nigeria's years of military rule following the civil war are now over, high rates of poverty and youth unemployment continue to trouble Nigerians across the nation. Simultaneously, Nigeria's oil wealth is unequally distributed, environmental degradation in the southern oil-producing regions causes continual unrest, Islamist groups such as Boko Haram are on the rise in northern Nigeria, and there are concerns in both northern and southern Nigeria about the distribution of political power. However, there is no immediate likelihood of the break-up of the Nigerian nation, and there are also significant forms of inter-ethnic interaction and mixing across the nation, such as the growth of ethnic 'diaspora' communities in most of Nigeria's major cities.[41] Nonetheless, some Nigerians are convinced that Nigeria is not a viable or legitimate entity (or not, in fact, a nation but a 'mere geographical expression') and may feel more loyalty, both politically and culturally, to ties of ethnicity and region than to Nigeria, or may only infrequently come into contact with Nigerians from other distant parts of the country.

Consequently in Nigeria, as in many postcolonial African nations, while the state is relatively well established, if patchy, the idea of the nation as a social identity has remained, as Amina Mama writes, 'poorly established, continuously contested, and less successfully hegemonic in the face of the multiethnic, multilingual, and multireligious clamour of life on the continent', and thus, 'national identities have remained very much in the making, less homogeneous, less *clearly imagined*, more precarious than, say, "Englishness" or "Germanness"'.[42] Until roughly the 1930s, Tóyìn Fálọlá and Matthew Heaton suggest, few Nigerians regarded themselves as 'Nigerians', considering their loyalties to lie with regional or African identities, and the British colonial state to be illegitimate.[43] As nationalist politics began to emerge in the late colonial era, national consciousness was fostered through the production of 'Nigerian-ness', including in print and literary culture. In his book *Nation as Grand Narrative*, Wálé Adébánwí writes of the critical role of the twentieth-century Nigerian press in creating competing 'narratives of what constitutes a nation and how to understand and relate to the idea and practices of such a "nation"' in a multi-ethnic colonial and then independent state, in which there were competing claims to nationhood. Adébánwí shows how the Nigerian press constantly gestured towards a 'nation of aspiration' that would surpass the many different

---

[41] See, for instance, Rasheed Olaniyi, *Diaspora Is Not Like Home: A Social and Economic History of Yoruba in Kano, 1912–1999* (Muenchen: Lincom Europa, 2008).

[42] Amina Mama, 'Is It Ethical to Study Africa? Preliminary Thoughts on Scholarship and Freedom', *African Studies Review,* 50.1 (2007), pp. 1–26 (p. 16); original emphasis.

[43] Toyin Falola and Matthew M. Heaton, *A History of Nigeria* (Cambridge: Cambridge University Press, 2008), p. 137.

regional and ethno-national interests in Nigeria and, crucially, in doing so they created a 'grand narrative' of the Nigerian nation, an idea of what a nation could and should be.[44]

Adébánwí's concern is chiefly with the role of narratives of nation and nationalism in the 1950s, as Nigerians agitated for independence, and in the volatile postcolonial era. However, ideas about what both the colony of 'Nigeria' and forms of 'nationhood' might mean were circulating in southwest Nigerian print and literary culture in earlier decades too; in this book I show how travel writing was used to map shifting relations between locales in colonial Nigeria in the 1920s and 1930s, and to suggest ideas about particular kinds of 'nations' or other forms of collective identity that writers and their readers might want to establish, which did not always correspond with the colony of Nigeria. In the postcolonial era, efforts have been made at federal level to try to consolidate the Nigerian nation, including, as we will see in Chapter 5, the establishment of a National Youth Service Corps (NYSC) in 1973, which sought, in the wake of the civil war, to bring together Nigeria's youth to serve the nation. The work of imagining the postcolonial nation in its 'precariousness' is also the task undertaken by some of the texts I examine in this book. In Chapters 5 and 6 I discuss travel narratives by writers who have self-consciously produced travel writing that traverses the Nigerian nation in the hope of creating better knowledge of each other amongst Nigerians and thereby engendering greater national unity.

The Yoruba region has similarly undergone a process of imagining, as J. D. Y. Peel showed in his influential study of the 'cultural work of Yoruba ethnogenesis' through which nineteenth- and early twentieth-century Yoruba intellectuals contributed to the idea of a unified Yoruba people.[45] While today there may be considered to be a group of people called 'the Yoruba', prior to the late nineteenth century, the region now recognised as the Yoruba region consisted of towns and city-states that had shared histories and cultures, but also a wide variety of linguistic, political and historical differences, including distinctive dialects of what has now become standard 'Yoruba' (which is in fact based on the dialect of the Ọ̀yọ́ region). The nineteenth-century wars between towns in this region, and the resulting interference in trading activities within the region, helped create a desire for a pan-Yoruba identity that would overcome sub-regional interests.[46] But even today, many Yoruba speakers claim loyalty

---

[44] Wale Adebanwi, *Nation as Grand Narrative*, p. 5.

[45] J. D. Y. Peel, 'The Cultural Work of Yoruba Ethnogenesis', in *History and Ethnicity*, ed. by Elizabeth Tonkin, Maryon McDonald, and Malcolm Chapman (London: Routledge, 1989), pp. 198–215.

[46] Toyin Falola, *Yoruba Gurus: Indigenous Production of Knowledge in Africa* (Trenton: Africa World Press, 1999), p. 6.

to a particular town, sub-group and/or dialect of Yoruba, perhaps as well as to being 'Yoruba'. Peel and subsequent scholars have argued that Yoruba subjectivity is in fact a modern historical phenomenon consciously produced or 'made' through 'cultural work', including written texts such as Yoruba historian Samuel Johnson's seminal work *The History of the Yorubas* (1921), which sought to establish a common history for the 'Yoruba' people.[47] Although not all scholars agree that the 'Yoruba people' were 'created' in the nineteenth century – some argue that the notion of a Yoruba people has longer roots – it is certainly clear from the travel writing discussed in this book that 'being Yoruba' is something that travellers and writers, amongst others, have worked on throughout the twentieth century, with changing meanings.

Indeed, Yoruba literary scholarship has shown that numerous literary texts can be considered part of this 'cultural work', not only in their direct interventions in imagining 'Yoruba-ness', but also in the way they imagined readerships on changing scales throughout this period. As relations between Yoruba towns and sub-groups, as well as with the rest of Nigeria, changed rapidly across the late nineteenth and early twentieth centuries, Yoruba-language writers sought new ways of conceptualising relations and encounters between peoples within those spaces. In the 1920s, poets and novelists imagined audiences centred on particular towns or regions; they used sub-group dialects of Yoruba, and made reference to local settings and concerns. From the 1930s onwards, they 'not only began to reach out to more encompassing audiences, but also to inscribe their texts with imaginings of larger social formations, such as publics, ethnic communities or nations'.[48] Importantly, it is not the case that Yoruba-language texts, with Yoruba-language readers in mind, cannot write of 'Nigeria' and Nigerian nationalism as well as 'Yoruba'. The Yoruba term for nation, *orílè-èdè*, which refers to both an ancestral home and place of origin in *orílè* and a shared language in *èdè*, can in fact be used by Yoruba speakers to refer to both the Yoruba 'nation' and the Nigerian nation. The polysemous nature of the term is indicative of some of the different strategies Yoruba writers have used to represent Nigeria: some use Yorubaland as a synecdoche for the Nigerian nation, while others have sought to create microcosms of the Nigerian nation, representing individuals from Nigeria's numerous ethnic groups encountering one another.[49] Karin Barber and Rita Nnodim have shown how Fágúnwà's

---

[47] Peel, 'Yoruba Ethnogenesis'; see also Adélékè Adéèkó, *Arts of Being Yorùbá: Divination, Allegory, Tragedy, Proverb, Panegyric* (Bloomington, IN: Indiana University Press, 2017).

[48] Nnodim, 'Configuring Audiences', p. 157.

[49] Kole Omotoso, 'The Nigerian Federation in the Nigerian Novel', *Publius,* 21.4 (1991), pp. 145–53; Karin Barber, 'Time, Space, and Writing in Three Colonial Yoruba Novels', *The Yearbook of English Studies*, 27 (1997), pp. 108–29; Nnodim, 'Configuring Audiences'.

novels imagine themselves to be convening audiences simultaneously composed of individual Yoruba towns, all black people, even the whole world, and
often many different senses of *orílè-èdè wa*, 'our nation'.[50] Senayon Ọláolúwa,
meanwhile, has demonstrated that while some contemporary Yoruba poetry
addresses primarily the Yoruba 'nation', treating Nigeria as what Ọbáfẹ́mi
Awólọ́wọ̀ called a 'mere geographical expression', in other cases contemporary
Yoruba poetry explicitly addresses 'national concerns and the imagination of
the Nigerian nation', decrying ethnic essentialism.[51]

Southwest Nigerian travel writers have similarly used travel narratives to
construct ideas about such communities, regions and the Nigerian nation, often
depicting themselves crossing borders within Nigeria, or standing at crossroads
between ethnic and national affiliations. In Chapter 3, I show how the production of knowledge about the Yoruba region can be read as part of the ongoing
'cultural work of Yoruba ethnogenesis'. More recently, travel writers have seen
themselves creating knowledge of Nigeria amongst Nigerians – the 'cultural
work of Nigerian national genesis', perhaps. In these travel narratives, knowledge of other people, places and languages within Nigeria is often positively
valued as a form of *ọ̀làjú* (enlightenment or civilisation – a term I discuss in
more detail in Chapter 1), or intra-Nigerian cosmopolitanism. Thus although
not straightforwardly a study of 'nation and narration', since it reads the many
different scales of collectivities, readerships and zones of travel that these writers imagine and work with, this book contributes to the growing literature on
the ways that writers have used travel narratives not only to represent places as
they encounter them on their journeys, but also to attempt to create new forms
of 'imagined community', including the nation.[52]

Southwest Nigerian travel writers deploy numerous strategies in representing other parts of Nigeria: from their strikingly frequent representations of
cannibals, to depictions of networks of contacts spreading across Nigerian
space, contrasts of 'civilisation' and 'native' ways or of the 'modern' and the
'traditional', and representations of fear of other parts of the nation together
with ways of overcoming that fear. Travel writers also, by virtue of their position at the crossroads of cultures, languages, and ways of being within Nigeria,

---

[50] Barber, 'Time, Space and Writing', pp. 123–4; Nnodim, 'Configuring Audiences',
pp. 160–4.

[51] Senayon Olaoluwa, 'Ethnic; or National: Contemporary Yoruba Poets and the Imagination of the Nation in *Wa Gbo ...*', *Journal of Literary Studies*, 28.2 (2012),
pp. 37–57 (pp. 42–4); Obafemi Awolowo, *Path to Nigerian Freedom* (London:
Faber & Faber, 1947), pp. 47–8.

[52] Homi K. Bhabha, 'Introduction: Narrating the Nation', in *Nation and Narration*,
ed. by Homi K. Bhabha (London: Routledge, 1990), pp. 1–7; Benedict Anderson,
*Imagined Communities: Reflections on the Origins and Spread of Nationalism*, 3rd
edn (London: Verso, 2006 [1983]).

sometimes imagine themselves to be engaging in both interlinguistic and intercultural translation, as they both literally and metaphorically translate for their readers different ways of being, or one part of the nation to another. Kwaku A. Gyasi, drawing on postcolonial translation theories, has pointed to the ways that in African literary contexts the concept of translation can include intercultural translation as well as linguistic translation. African writers in European languages, he argues, necessarily engage in 'creative translation' at the intersemiotic level, translating African cultural forms such as oral genres into forms of European origin such as the novel and, relatedly, at an intercultural level, conveying 'concepts and values', 'communicating ideas and meanings of several cultural artifacts in a given society' and explaining the 'the norms of his or her society'.[53] As such, translation is a means through which, in African novels, African cultures are interpreted for Western audiences.

Some of the works of travel writing I discuss in this book can also be considered to be engaging in a related, although not identical, kind of intercultural translation in a dual sense: firstly, in some cases, in their adoption of forms of travel writing associated with the West, which they then have to make work within an African context, bringing with them resonances of both travel and text in that context in ways that may differ from the expectations commonly attached to Western manifestations of the genre. Secondly, they may consider themselves to be translating for their readers aspects of the people and places they encounter as they travel, not only for Western readerships, as in the examples Gyasi discusses, but also within Nigeria, as they strive to make readers understand other parts of Nigeria, and therefore know each other better. In this latter sense, writers sometimes envisage translation – both linguistic and cultural – in a utopian sense, which they imagine to create a 'third space' or 'in-between' space of mingling and hybridity that often coincides with the nation and with the English language. At the same time, however, they also sometimes gesture to moments of incomprehension and mistranslation as they travel, or translate only very minimally. Thus the crossroads at which they picture themselves can be, as both Òkèdìji and Fálọlá highlight in their discussion of the figure of the crossroads, a point of confusion as well as encounter.

## The plan of this book

Chapter 1 of this book explores questions of forms of travel and genres of travel writing in southwest Nigeria in more detail. It discusses the varied ways that the genre of 'travel writing' has developed in the Western canon and in the scholarship on travel writing about Africa, and tackles the question of what

---

[53] Kwaku A Gyasi, 'Writing as Translation: African Literature and the Challenges of Translation', *Research in African Literatures,* 30.2 (1999), pp. 75–87 (pp. 80–2).

'travel writing' may mean in southwest Nigerian literary and print culture, as well as what 'travel' itself means in this region. As examples, it looks at the travel narratives of Samuel Àjàyí Crowther as an instance of African travel writing that appears to intersect very closely with the Western missionary travel narrative, and Yoruba- and English-language historical writing as a form of writing about travel in southwest Nigeria that stands outside the traditional limits of the genre 'travel writing'.

Subsequent chapters each discuss a text, or set of texts, located at a particular moment within southwest Nigeria's history. Chapters 2 and 3 both examine texts published in the early twentieth century, in the decades after Nigeria had been founded as a colony but before it gained independence, and continue the focus, established in my discussion of Crowther's travel writing in Chapter 1, on the way travel writing was adopted by colonial intellectuals in southwest Nigeria. Chapter 2 focuses on travel narratives published in the Yoruba newspapers of Lagos in the 1920s and 1930s. As well as examining the relationship between these texts, the colonial travel writing tradition and southwest Nigerian print and literary culture, I explore the ways the writers depicted other regions of Nigeria, and their insistence on travel as a sociable act that allowed them to generate and display their networks of friends, family and acquaintants.

Chapter 3 centres on a discussion of Yoruba novelist Isaac Délànọ̀'s non-fiction book *The Soul of Nigeria*, published in 1937. The book is a mix of travel narrative, ethnography, memoir and anecdote, focusing on Délànọ̀'s experience of the Yoruba region. I consider why Délànọ̀ used the travelogue framing for his book, and how it enabled him to contribute to debates of the era about the relationship between African and European forms of 'civilisation', with Délànọ̀ picturing himself as a traveller at a crossroads in both space and time.

Chapter 4 looks to the late colonial era of the 1930s to the 1950s, and turns its sights to fiction to consider the motif of the journey, and the quest in particular. Focusing on the renowned Yoruba novels of D. Ọ. Fágúnwà, I show how the quest motif in his novels can not only be read as drawing on 'traditional' or oral motifs, and as an allegory for life and its challenges, but can also be understood as intervening in a moment of what critic Adélékè Adéẹ̀kọ́ identifies as epistemological change in southwest Nigeria. I read Fágúnwà's novels together with his own non-fiction travel narrative, *Irinajo*, which describes his visit to the UK in the late 1940s, and with other Yoruba and English-language texts that revolve around the quest motif, to explore how textual representations of the quest have been transformed by writers over the course of the twentieth century and across the two languages.

Chapters 5 and 6 shift their focus to the postcolonial era. Chapter 5 examines texts produced in Nigeria's independence era, in the wake of the focus on nation-building that emerged in the long aftermath of Nigeria's civil war of

1967–70. Introducing a greater focus on Nigeria as a nation than in previous chapters, and pointing to new ideas of what Nigerian nationhood might mean in the post-independence, post-civil war era, the first text I discuss in this chapter is surveyor Babátúndé Shàdẹ̀kọ̀'s *The Magic Land of Nigeria*, a travel memoir in which Shàdẹ̀kọ̀ attempts to enable readerly knowledge of Nigeria's heterogeneity and to produce what he idealises as the 'detribalized Nigerian'. The second set of texts I discuss in this chapter are narratives produced by participants in the NYSC, which was formed with the hope of promoting national cohesion after the civil war. Looking at novels and memoirs produced by former Corps members, I examine their portrayal of their often fearful encounters with unfamiliar places in Nigeria during their service year, and particularly their representation of the dangers and temptations of female sexuality away from home. I show how they combine the development of new national subjectivities with the development of new personal subjectivities, putting their texts into dialogue with Nigeria's burgeoning popular self-development and motivational publishing industry. While previous chapters of this book have focused on male authors, who tended to dominate literary and print culture in the early twentieth century, in this chapter I introduce travel writing by women writers, and subsequent chapters all similarly feature texts by female authors.

Chapter 6 turns to the decades since the millennium, and the work of a new generation of Nigerian travel writers writing up to roughly the year 2014, who have used self-publishing and the online space to experiment with travel writing, and who often emphasise Nigeria's potential as a tourist destination. I focus in particular on the work of Pèlú Awófẹ̀sọ̀, one of contemporary Nigeria's most prolific travel writers, but I also discuss the work of fellow travel bloggers Kọ́lá Túbọ̀sún, Lápé Ṣóètán and Fọlárìn Kọ́láwọlé, who were amongst the most prominent of southwest Nigeria's travel bloggers in 2014. Drawing on interviews with the writers as well as readings of Awófẹ̀sọ̀'s and Ṣóètán's travel narratives, I show how they attempt to foster new types of travellers and readers for travel writing and new ways of being a knowledgeable Nigerian, and I examine how they position themselves in relation to Western travel writing traditions.

Chapter 7 discusses late twentieth-century and early twenty-first century travel writing by Nigerian diasporic writers who have returned to Nigeria, focusing on non-fiction travel narratives by Adéwálé Májà-Pearce and Noo Saro-Wiwa, and a fictional travel narrative by Téjú Cole. I explore the ways such writers represent both alienation from Nigeria and new ways of relating to Nigeria, beyond the ties of family. I examine the continuities and divergences between travel writing by writers of the Nigerian diaspora and that produced by writers based within Nigeria, and the viability of categories such as 'southwest Nigeria' in the face of the emphasis on hybrid and national identities in diaspora travel writing.

The final chapter of the book, the Epilogue, brings the story of travel writing in southwest Nigeria up to the present day, touching on new directions in both literary travel writing and tourism-focused blogging and social media use. In particular, I discuss the work of Invisible Borders, one of the most significant contemporary African travel writing projects, suggesting that their experiments with form and their use of the visual image as a counterpart to travel writing may be seen as characteristic of the new directions some of southwest Nigeria's travel writers are taking. The Epilogue also brings together the motifs of crossroads and border crossings that have emerged repeatedly throughout the book, examining the stories that travel writing has been able to tell about Nigeria, and also the ambivalent relationship between Nigerian and Western travel writing.

# African travel writing: genres of writing and forms of travel

Travel writing about Africa by Western writers has produced enduring images of the African continent. In 2006, Kenyan writer Binyavanga Wainaina published his now renowned piece 'How to Write about Africa', a satire of Western writing about Africa. 'Always use the word "Africa" or "Darkness" or "Safari" in your title', Wainaina begins:

> Never have a picture of a well-adjusted African on the cover of your book, or in it, unless that African has won the Nobel Prize. An AK-47, prominent ribs, naked breasts: use these. If you must include an African, make sure you get one in Masai or Zulu or Dogon dress.

> In your text, treat Africa as if it were one country. It is hot and dusty with rolling grasslands and huge herds of animals and tall, thin people who are starving. Or it is hot and steamy with very short people who eat primates.[1]

Wainaina suggests that Western writing about Africa is a literature of repetition, filled with recycled stereotypes of the continent. Certainly, the images of Africa that Europeans produced in travel writing from over several centuries have coalesced into some of the authorising images of the African continent in Western eyes. As European powers raced to 'discover' Africa from the seventeenth century, explorers such as Mungo Park and David Livingstone wrote accounts of their travels across Africa, often commissioned by European exploration societies such as the African Association, founded in 1788.[2] Scientific, naturalist and ethnographic expeditions also began to proliferate from the eighteenth century, as Africa became the object of an Enlightenment-era desire to classify the living world. Travel narratives describing such expeditions often positioned themselves as establishing objective truth about the world through faithful eyewitness observation and evidence.[3] Yet these seemingly disinterested, not explicitly imperial expeditions nonetheless often mobilised rhetorical

---

[1] Binyavanga Wainaina, 'How to Write About Africa', *Granta*, 92.1 (2005), pp. 92–5 (p. 92).

[2] Pratt, *Imperial Eyes*, p. 74.

[3] Larissa Viana, 'The tropics and the rise of the British Empire: Mungo Park's perspective on Africa in the Late Eighteenth Century', *História, Ciências, Saúde-Manguinhos*, 18.1 (2011), 33–50 (p. 39); Pratt, *Imperial Eyes*, pp. 38–68.

figures that manifested mastery and conquest of the landscape, such as the commanding gaze from a vantage point through which travellers represent themselves as the 'monarch-of-all-I-survey'.[4] This leads Mary Louise Pratt to term such narratives 'anti-conquest' narratives, in which 'European bourgeois subjects seek to secure their innocence in the same moment as they assert European hegemony'.[5] Missionary travel accounts also sometimes adopted this position by taking a benevolently paternalistic attitude towards the peoples they encountered on their African journeys. For instance, the mid-nineteenth-century North American Baptist missionary William H. Clarke was pleasantly surprised to find the Yoruba region 'fair, productive, beautiful and healthy'.[6] Nonetheless, he maintained a hierarchy between the Yoruba people and the 'civilized and enlightened nations of Europe and America'.[7] The sentimental 'non-hero' figure of the traveller who focuses on personal adventure, danger and tribulation also emerged during this era, thrilling readers with tales of daring and peril.[8]

Meanwhile, in the high imperial era of the late nineteenth century, some travel writers sought to affirm supposed European cultural superiority by representing Africans in explicitly hostile and racist terms of 'technological deficiency and mental incapacity', as Tim Youngs puts it, and denouncing scenes of apparent witchcraft, savagery and cannibalism.[9] The notion of Africa as 'heart of darkness', as it was memorably framed by Joseph Conrad in his novella *Heart of Darkness* (1902), gripped the Western imagination. By the twentieth century, this 'heart of darkness' seemed to have faded away in a geographical sense, now that Africa was mostly mapped and known to the West. Yet the legacy of travel writing from earlier eras has lingered. Some writers who have travelled in postcolonial Africa – including Africans themselves – have nostalgically retraced canonical journeys or routes, with varying degrees of self-reflexivity.[10] Others have sought to engage directly with the continent's colonial and postcolonial history and politics, and with travel writing's complicity in that history, seeking to re-imagine travel writing as a literature of

[4] Pratt, *Imperial Eyes*, pp. 38–85, 201–8.
[5] Pratt, *Imperial Eyes*, p. 7.
[6] William H. Clarke, *Travels & Explorations in Yorubaland (1854–1858)* (Ibadan: Oxford University Press, 1972), p. 35.
[7] Letter from Clarke quoted in J. A. Atanda, 'Editor's Introduction', in *William H. Clarke, Travels & Explorations in Yorubaland (1854–1858)* (Ibadan: Oxford University Press, 1972), pp. xi–xxxvii (p. xxii).
[8] On the 'anti-conquest', the sentimental 'non-hero' and the rhetorical figures of 'imperial eyes' and 'monarch-of-all-I-survey', see Pratt, *Imperial Eyes*, pp. 38–85, 201–8.
[9] Tim Youngs, *Travellers in Africa: British Travelogues 1850–1900* (Manchester: Manchester University Press, 1994), p. 65.
[10] L. Nas, 'Postcolonial Travel Accounts and Ethnic Subjectivity: Travelling through Southern Africa', *Literator*, 32.2 (2011), pp. 151–71.

genuine cultural encounter and exchange.[11] Nonetheless, as Carl Thompson argues, while contemporary Western travel writing about Africa now generally (although not always) avoids explicit racism, and is sometimes celebrated for its cosmopolitan ethos, it has nonetheless been criticised for continued assumptions of authority to represent Africa, and use of tropes of power, paternalism and darkness.[12]

The sheer weight of the tropes and images of Africa that emerged from such travel writing – and the growing body of scholarship on these works of travel writing – gives the impression that Africa is saturated with European or Western imagery of the continent, at the expense of African voices. In 2007 Zimbabwean writer Petina Gappah observed that '[m]issing from the bestseller lists, from any list, is the internal gaze, a book about travel in Africa by a black African'.[13] Indeed, except for medieval Moroccan traveller Ibn Battuta, scholarship on travel writing has tended to paint Africans as the 'travellees', in Mary Louise Pratt's term, rather than the travellers – or as the backdrop to European adventures in Africa, rather than as the authors of travel writing and the creators of images of Africa in their own right.[14] Tabish Khair et al. note that 'the feeling grew – and it persists in the present – that until recently non-Europeans did not travel or hardly travelled', attributing this notion to a perceived absence of travel writing by Africans and other non-European travellers. Consequently, they argue, '[t]he travels of entire peoples [...] have been erased', primarily because African and other non-European travellers 'often *appear* to have left nothing or little in writing', and especially did not do so in forms that were familiar or accessible to the West.[15] As such, Aedín Ní Loingsigh shows, African travel writing has often been thought an 'underdeveloped' and 'meagre' tradition in comparison to the vast corpus of Western travel writing.[16]

This sense of Westerners as the travellers and Africans as the travellees, both in travel writing itself and in the scholarship on travel writing, sustains a binary between the two that echoes such binaries between Westerners and Africans within imperial discourse about Africa itself. Yet some of the most effective scholarship on travel writing destabilises imperial discourse, and particularly

---

[11] López Ropero, 'Travel Writing and Postcoloniality'.

[12] Carl Thompson, *Travel Writing* (London: Routledge, 2011), pp. 154–5; Lisle, *The Global Politics of Contemporary Travel Writing*.

[13] Petina Gappah, *Not yet Uhuru* (2008) <http://www.african-writing.com/holiday/webpages/petinagappah.htm/> [accessed 18 March 2014].

[14] Pratt, *Imperial Eyes*, p. 136.

[15] Tabish Khair et al., *Other Routes: 1500 Years of African and Asian Travel Writing* (Bloomington, IN: Indiana University Press, 2005), pp. 5–6; original emphasis.

[16] Aedín Ní Loingsigh, 'African Travel Writing', in *The Routledge Companion to Travel Writing,* ed. by Carl Thompson (London: Routledge, 2016), pp. 185–95 (p. 185).

the coloniser/colonised dichotomy at the heart of many travel narratives. Since the 1990s, for instance, scholarship on travel narratives by women travel writers in Africa has sought not only to recuperate these women's voices in the archive, and to explore the ways travel enabled women to escape the restrictions of Victorian-era femininity at home, but also to recognise the complex gendered, racialised and class-bound subjectivities and discourses produced by travel writing. Sara Mills has shown how some British women travel writers struggled with some aspects of imperialism, and adopted an ambivalent, 'tentative' voice, while upholding other aspects of imperial discourse.[17] Such scholarship seeks not simply to insert marginalised voices into hegemonic discourses of imperialism, but to avoid reproducing the binaries of self/other, male/female, coloniser/colonised that imperial discourse itself often produced. The apparent divide between Western travellers and African travellees is another such binary that requires careful interrogation in order to avoid simply reproducing imperial claims to power over the representation of Africa.

Indeed, the notion of Africans as primarily travellees rather than travellers would be hardly recognisable in other disciplines concerned with the study of Africa, where Africans' mobility within and beyond the African continent has long been a subject of research. Migration has been a particular focus of a wealth of studies focusing on the omnipresence of such mobility in both past and contemporary African societies.[18] Historical scholarship has also documented the changes in mobility brought about by the colonial era and its emphasis on infrastructure such as railways, roads and canals. This scholarship has shown how Africans themselves, and not just European colonial powers, experienced mobility and developed local transport infrastructure and regimes.[19]

African travellers' own experiences and accounts of travel, and the creativity with which they narrate such accounts of travel, are increasingly coming to the fore within anthropological and other social scientific studies of Africa as, for instance, in Mbugua wa Mungai and David A. Samper's account of Kenyans' personal experiences of travelling by *matatu*, or Alessandro Triulzi

---

[17] Sara Mills, *Discourses of Difference: An Analysis of Women's Travel Writing and Colonialism* (London: Routledge, 1991), p. 3.

[18] See, for instance: Olaniyi, *Diaspora Is Not Like Home*; Lillian Trager, *Yoruba Hometowns: Community, Identity, and Development in Nigeria* (Boulder; London: Lynne Rienner Publishers, 2001).

[19] In Nigeria, see, for example, Ayedele Olukoju, 'Maritime Trade in Lagos in the Aftermath of the First World War', *African Economic History*, 20 (1992), pp. 119–35; Francis Jaekel, *The History of the Nigerian Railway* (Ibadan: Spectrum Books, 1997); Lisa A. Lindsay, *Working with Gender: Wage Labor and Social Change in Southwestern Nigeria* (Portsmouth, NH: Heinemann, 2003). Elsewhere in West Africa, see Jennifer Hart, *Ghana on the Go: African Mobility in the Age of Motor Transportation* (Bloomington, IN: Indiana University Press, 2016).

and Robert Mackenzie's research on migrant narratives.[20] David Coplan and Nhlanhla Maake have both shown how Sotho migrant workers in the mines of South Africa created a new oral genre, *lifela*, that drew on traditional values of 'eloquence' and cultural knowledge while narrating their (often very difficult) contemporary experiences of migrant life.[21] Literary scholarship on the novel, meanwhile, has pointed to the importance of exile, diaspora, transnationalism, migration and, more recently, Afropolitanism in contemporary African experiences of travel – to the extent that critics have argued that a new generation of African writing of the early twenty-first century is characterised by being transnational, located betwixt and between, in a 'borderless, global, textual topography', concerned with migration and 'multiple worlds and languages'.[22]

However, non-fiction writing about travel by Africans has enjoyed markedly less critical theorising and attention. Aedín Ní Loingsigh's ground-breaking work on francophone African intercontinental travel literature represents one of the first scholarly monographs to consider 'the important contribution of Africans themselves to the development of the genre'.[23] Ní Loingsigh examines travel literature by francophone Africans travelling to Europe and America, as students, tourists, 'citizens of the world' and migrants. Such travel can be understood as initially a continuation of the 'voyage à l'envers' [inverted voyage] of Africans to colonial metropoles, especially Paris, although recent travel literature inverts and subverts these centres and peripheries. Ní Loingsigh highlights the 'split readership' of both metropolitan European and African readers of these texts, and explores how the writers often use the travelogue to critique Western culture.

---

[20] Mbugua wa Mungai and David A Samper, '"No Mercy, No Remorse": Personal Experience Narratives About Public Passenger Transportation in Nairobi, Kenya', *Africa Today*, 52.3 (2006), pp. 51–81; Alessandro Triulzi and Robert McKenzie, *Long Journeys: African Migrants on the Road* (Leiden and Boston, MA: Brill, 2013).

[21] David B. Coplan, 'Eloquent Knowledge: Lesotho Migrants' Songs and the Anthropology of Experience', *American Ethnologist*, 14.3 (1987), pp. 413–33; Nhlanhla Maake, '"I Sing of the Woes of My Travels": The Lifela of Lesotho', in *The Cambridge History of South African Literature*, ed. by David Attwell and Derek Attridge (Cambridge: Cambridge University Press, 2012), pp. 60–76.

[22] Mildred P. Mortimer, *Journeys through the French African Novel* (Portsmouth, NH: Heinemann, 1990); Brenda Cooper, *A New Generation of African Writers: Migration, Material Culture and Language* (Woodbridge: James Currey/Boydell & Brewer, 2008), p. 1; Pius Adesanmi and Chris Dunton, 'Nigeria's Third Generation Writing: Historiography and Preliminary Theoretical Considerations', *English in Africa*, 32.1 (2005), pp. 7–19; Pius Adesanmi and Chris Dunton, 'Everything Good Is Raining: Provisional Notes on the Nigerian Novel of the Third Generation', *Research in African Literatures*, 39.2 (2008), pp. vii–xii (p. ix).

[23] Ní Loingsigh, *Postcolonial Eyes*, p. 2.

Ní Loingsigh's study also crucially highlights how the work of 'unt[ying] travel writing from its Western moorings and open[ing] up a space for African representations of travel' must necessarily provoke questions about forms of travel and genres of travel writing.[24] As Ní Loingsigh remarks, scholarship on non-Western travel writing, which often comes under the rubric of postcolonial travel writing, has tended to examine how non-Westerners have 'written back' to Western travel writing. In doing so, it has challenged the dominance of Western travellers and travel writing by recognising 'the agency of non-Western subjects' as travellers. However, such scholarship has nonetheless tended to focus on the ways in which these subjects 'participate in, and reconfigure, eurocentric modes of travelling, seeing and narrating'.[25] For instance, non-Western or postcolonial travel writing has often been read through the lens of 'countertravel writing', a term used by Patrick Holland and Graham Huggan in their study of texts such as Antiguan writer Jamaica Kincaid's *A Small Place* (1988) to characterise travel writing that 'pits itself against the dominant Eurocentric model' of travel writing and tourism.[26] Understood in this sense, countertravel writing subverts Western forms of travel writing, but nonetheless takes Western travel writing as the originator of the genre.

Trailblazing anthologies by Khair et al. and Alasdair Pettinger move beyond the 'eurocentric modes of travelling, seeing and narrating' that Ní Loingsigh identifies by examining '1500 years of African and Asian travel writing' and Black Atlantic travel writing, respectively. Their anthologies include not only writers fairly well known in the West, but also the writings of more obscure traders, monks, pilgrims, slaves and aristocrats, although Khair et al. focus mostly on Asian travel writing, with only a handful of accounts from African writers such as Moroccan traveller Ibn Battuta, Omani-Zanzibari princess Emily Said-Ruete and the freed slave and abolitionist Olaudah Equiano.[27]

The focus on the ways that Africans have written within or back to European discourses and modes of travel writing means that African accounts of travel that do not conform to Western critical expectations of the genre have often been passed over in the scholarship on travel writing.[28] Drawing on Mary Louise Pratt's notion of 'critical mimesis', Ní Loingsigh argues that critics of travel writing 'return repeatedly to the same narrow canon of accounts' and to the assumption that travel involves the metropolitan subject being sent forth to 'know the world'. This narrow focus produces 'a self-referential deadlock that ignores the ways alternative traditions of travel and travel writing challenge

---

[24] Ibid. p. 3.
[25] Ibid. p. 2.
[26] Holland and Huggan, *Tourists with Typewriters*, p. 21.
[27] Khair et al., *Other Routes*, pp. 13–14.
[28] Ní Loingsigh, 'African Travel Writing', pp. 185–7.

prevailing understandings of the form'.[29] African accounts of travel that are framed within other genres may not be recognised as travel writing. Marion Frank-Wilson makes a similar point in her preliminary bibliography of African travel writing, as she explains how categorisations of genre affect the accessibility of travel writing by African writers:

> The main reason for the poor accessibility of the genre is that there are no bibliographies or anthologies on the topic. The shorter texts are hidden away in journals. The longer ones are published as novels or historical, anthropological, or missionary accounts and are catalogued under different, fairly general subject headings, such as the various subject headings for 'missionaries – Africa', 'Africa – fiction', 'Africa – history'.[30]

The challenge, then, is to place African experiences, textual cultures, modes of writing and forms of travel at the heart of the study of travel writing, while also recognising the ways in which some African writers have manoeuvred within the genre in its Western manifestations. To do so involves examining interlinked assumptions about both forms of travel and the 'travel writing' genre in African contexts. As Ní Loingsigh argues, 'the process of determining the generic identity of travel writing is inextricably bound up with privileged European figures and practices of travel'.[31] The 'travel' in 'travel writing' thus often signifies forms of travel that belong to a specific historical moment and social category. James Clifford argues that 'travel', and especially what Clifford calls 'good travel' – the kind of travel highly valued in the West, 'heroic, educational, scientific, adventurous, ennobling' – has long been marked by gender, race, class, culture and privilege, to the point where it can be difficult to conceptualise 'travel', in its privileged form, outside 'a history of European, literary, male, bourgeois, scientific, heroic, recreational meanings and practices'.[32] Travel for discovery and exploration, and recreational travel or travel for its own sake are particularly easily recognised as the subject of the genre 'travel writing', while other forms of travel lend themselves less easily to expectations of the genre. Scholar of British travel writing Paul Fussell, for instance, distinguishes 'real travel' from tourism but also from many other forms of mobility when he writes that '[t]ravel implies variety of means and

---

[29] Ibid. p. 186; see Mary Louise Pratt, 'Modernity, Mobility and Ex-Coloniality', in *Travel Writing: Critical Concepts in Literary and Cultural Studies,* ed. by Tim Youngs and Charles Forsdick (London and New York: Routledge (2012 [2002]), pp. 118–33 (p. 122).

[30] Marion Frank-Wilson, 'African Travel Writing', *African Research and Documentation,* 92 (2003), pp. 27–38 (p. 28).

[31] Ní Loingsigh, 'African Travel Writing', p. 187.

[32] Clifford, *Routes,* pp. 31–5.

independence of arrangements'.[33] As Carl Thompson notes, for Fussell, 'real travel' seems to have existed only in the nineteenth and early twentieth centuries, 'when people began to have the leisure to undertake travel simply for travel's sake', but before the emergence of mass tourism.[34]

By contrast, Clifford asks what would make it possible for the journeys of servants accompanying Victorian bourgeois travellers to be considered 'travel'.[35] Indeed, some of the first studies of travel narratives by Africans focused on recentring the voices of African servants who had previously been marginalised in the accounts of European explorers. Antony Kirk-Greene and Paul Newman, for instance, published an edited version of two Hausa-language narratives by colonial-era African travellers: Dorogu, a Hausa boy who accompanied Heinrich Barth in his West African expeditions in the 1850s, and Maimaina, who worked for the Royal Niger Company at the turn of the twentieth century.[36] The accounts of African former slaves, too – most notably, Olaudah Equiano – have also been read as a form of travel writing.[37] Although the veracity of *The Interesting Narrative of the Life of Olaudah Equiano* (1789) has now been challenged by some historians (as, of course, has the veracity of many other travel accounts), reading slave narratives such as Equiano's as travel writing challenges us to rethink the history and significance of 'travel' in contexts of forced, violent travel, and moreover highlights, as Paul Gilroy has shown, the centrality of mobility in an alternative modernity of the black Atlantic more broadly.[38]

New ways of thinking about travel and travel writing also necessarily emerge when we consider contexts in which Africans' travels were restricted by colonial states. This was the case in apartheid South Africa, for instance, where black South Africans faced both legal and economic barriers to free

[33] Paul Fussell, *Abroad: British Literary Traveling between the Wars* (Oxford: Oxford University Press, 1982), p. 39–41.

[34] Thompson, *Travel Writing*, p. 22.

[35] Clifford, *Routes*, pp. 33–4.

[36] Anthony Kirk-Greene and Paul Newman, *West African Travels and Adventures* (New Haven: Yale University Press, 1971).

[37] Claudia Gualtieri, *Representations of West Africa as Exotic in British Colonial Travel Writing* (Lewiston: Edwin Mellen Press, 2002), p. 197; Philip D. Curtin, *Africa Remembered: Narratives by West Africans from the Era of the Slave Trade* (Madison: University of Wisconsin Press, 1967); Adélékè Adéèkó, 'Writing Africa under the Shadow of Slavery: Quaque, Wheatley, and Crowther', *Research in African Literatures*, 40.4 (2009), pp. 1–24.

[38] Vincent Carretta, *Equiano the African: Biography of a Self-Made Man* (Athens: University of Georgia Press, 2005), Alasdair Pettinger, *Always Elsewhere: Travels of the Black Atlantic* (New York and London: Weidenfeld & Nicolson, 1998); Paul Gilroy, *The Black Atlantic: Modernity and Double Consciousness* (London, Verso, 1993).

movement.[39] Janet Remmington shows how Solomon Plaatje's *Native Life in South Africa* (1916) and *Mhudi* (1930) – more typically examined through the lens of literary, political and historical studies – can be read through the nexus between travel and writing, as a means of 'political assertion' and 'creative expressions of agency' for Plaatje in the years of white rule in South Africa.[40]

Recognising the significance of forms of travel that do not accord with 'real travel' or 'good travel' as defined in the West, and being open to the genres of writing associated with such forms of travel, is not to say, however, that travel for its own sake has not formed part of the history of travel in Africa, nor that African writers have not also adopted, and adapted, the Western genre of 'travel writing'. Perhaps one of the best known examples of an African account of travel for its own sake is Tété-Michel Kpomassie's *L'Africain du Groenland* (1981), which traces its Togolese author's travels of adventure and curiosity in Greenland.[41] Fellow francophone writer, Ivorian poet and novelist Véronique Tadjo uses travel writing to reflect on her position as a tourist in Rwanda in her book *L'ombre d'Imana: Voyages jusqu'au bout du Rwanda* (2000).[42] *L'ombre d'Imana* is an account of Tadjo's journey to Rwanda in 1998 as part of a group of African writers commissioned, as part of the Fest'Africa project, to write about the Rwandan genocide. Tadjo reflects on the experience of being part of what Nicki Hitchcott characterises as an 'unconventional set of visitors in a far from typical tourist destination', and Hitchcott shows how Tadjo's travel narrative encourages the reader to think about the ethical possibilities and dilemmas of (African) travel and travel writing, especially in countries such as Rwanda that have a troubled history and that demand empathy from the traveller.[43] The text thus challenges the reader to consider the many forms that voluntary travel and tourism may take in Africa, including accounts of 'dark tourism', which I discuss in Chapter 7. *L'Ombre d'Imana* is also formally innovative, written through fragments of stories of those Tadjo encountered on her journey, and thus demonstrates the extent to which the adoption of the genre by African writers may demand or benefit from experiments with form, in order to make a genre often associated with a Western literary history suited to a new context.

---

[39] David Newmarch, 'Travel Literature (South Africa)', in *Encyclopaedia of Post-Colonial Literatures in English*, ed. by Eugene Benson and L. W. Conolly (London: Routledge, 1994), pp. 1595–8.

[40] Janet Remmington, 'Solomon Plaatje's Decade of Creative Mobility, 1912–1922: The Politics of Travel and Writing in and Beyond South Africa', *Journal of Southern African Studies*, 39.2 (2013), pp. 425–46 (p. 426).

[41] English version: *An African in Greenland*.

[42] English version: *The Shadow of Imana*.

[43] Nicki Hitchcott, 'Travels in Inhumanity: Véronique Tadjo's Tourism in Rwanda', *French Cultural Studies*, 20.2 (2009), pp. 149–64 (p. 152).

## Travel and travel writing in southwest Nigeria – from migration to missionary Christianity

Southwest Nigeria has its own long and varied history of travel that we must therefore take into account when seeking to define 'travel writing' in the region. *Ìrìn-àjò* (journeys) and *ìdálẹ̀* (travelling) have taken numerous different forms in the region's history. In the pre-colonial era, the region now known as Nigeria was traversed by traders travelling on foot, canoe and pack animals, who exchanged items across the region, often ignoring ethnolinguistic boundaries as we know them today, and carrying 'ideas and cultural complexes' as well as goods to trade.[44] In the nineteenth century, for example, the Ọ̀yọ́ people (one of the most powerful Yoruba kingdoms) purchased goods from Borno, Nupe and across the Sahara, as well as re-exporting European goods.[45] Diasporas of migrant traders and merchants grew up across the region, such as the Hausa diaspora in Lagos.[46] Travel was woven into the fabric of professional life for some: from itinerant traders (*alájàpá*) to masqueraders – the precursors to the twentieth century's travelling theatre tradition – and hunters (*ọdẹ*), who travelled into the bush on what were often long, perilous journeys. Journeys were also part of everyday life for some people, such as farmers who regularly travelled between home and farmstead.[47]

A form of travel that has been particularly important in southwest Nigeria is migration, which is imagined in both oral and written histories of the region as the foundations of nearly all the region's towns and cities. Nearly all Yoruba towns have a founding story that authorises the town's existence by claiming its origins elsewhere; many towns claim the Yoruba town of Ilé-Ifẹ̀ as their *orísun* (source), but this claim is also sometimes made of other Yoruba towns, Egypt, the Arab world, or the Sudan. Most Yoruba towns are associated with oral historical narratives called *ìtàn,* which tell the story of a great migration and subsequent founding of the town, often, although not always, located in a distant era, possibly several centuries ago. *Ìtàn* is the Yoruba word for history or narrative in general, and it is also more specifically the name of a Yoruba oral genre concerned with the narration of stories and histories. *Ìtàn* as historical narratives are 'straightforward and direct' sources of information about the past: 'Their subjects include the acts of the *òrìṣà* and great men; the origins of peoples, lineages, and towns; battles lost and won; and the establishment

[44] Elizabeth Isichei, *A History of Nigeria* (Harlow: Longman, 1983), p. 89.
[45] Ibid. p. 88.
[46] Ibid. pp. 88, 117.
[47] Niara Sudarkasa, *Where Women Work: A Study of Yoruba Women in the Marketplace and in the Home* (Ann Arbor: University of Michigan, 1973), p. 122; Jeremy Eades, *The Yoruba Today* (Cambridge: Cambridge University Press, 1980), p. 38; Olaniyi, *Diaspora Is Not Like Home*, p. 24.

of religious or political institutions'.[48] *Ìtàn* place travel – especially, but not only, migration – at the heart of their ideas about history, narrative, home and personal and communal identities.

Although *ìtàn* was originally an oral form, in the early decades of the twentieth century, intellectuals in Lagos and elsewhere in the Yoruba region began to publish written histories of Yoruba towns, known as *ìwé ìtàn ìlú* (town histories), in both Yoruba and English.[49] These texts share the name *ìtàn* and similarly document history, but they are not simply written versions of the oral historical form *ìtàn*. These local historians drew extensively on *ìtàn* in writing their histories, but they also moulded their new genre by making use of their own research, colonial records, treaties, petitions and letters, colonial and missionary travel accounts, eyewitness accounts and life stories, anecdotes, popular sayings and the work of other historians, and drew on the methods of classical European historiography.[50] Between the 1850s and 1940 at least sixty-nine such histories were published, and by 1999 they were estimated to number over one hundred.[51] Such histories lie far from what we conventionally consider travel writing. They are not first-person narratives, and they trace other themes besides travel as they narrate the histories of towns. But reading them as a potential form of travel writing in its broadest sense, while not making claims that they should necessarily be considered in dialogue with the genre in its conventional sense, allows us to consider the relationship between travel and narrative in these foundational narratives of Yoruba history, and to ask where the limits of the genre may lie in terms of both forms of travel and genres of writing in the southwest Nigerian context.

Many of the earliest Yoruba histories, most famously Samuel Johnson's *History of the Yorubas* (1921), were general Yoruba histories rather than histories of individual towns. Johnson narrates the mythical origins of the Yoruba people as a whole, which he locates in Nubia or Arabia. He describes how Ọ̀rànmíyàn,

---

[48] Deirdre LaPin, 'Story, Medium and Masque: The Idea and Art of Yoruba Storytelling' (unpublished PhD thesis, University of Wisconsin-Madison, 1977), p. 31. *Òrìṣà* are Yoruba deities.

[49] They were also published, to a much lesser extent, in Arabic scripts, in a tradition centred on the town of Ìlọrin in the late nineteenth and early twentieth centuries. The principal Arabic history of Ìlọrin dates from 1912: *Ta'lif akhbar al-qurun min umara' bilad Ilúrin* [*Book of information about (past) centuries, concerning the Emirs of Ìlọrin*], by Ahmad bin Abi Bakr. Few Arabic histories were published in Ìlọrin after this time. Robin Law, 'Early Yoruba Historiography', *History in Africa* 3 (1976), 69–89 (p. 70). See also H. O. Danmole, 'The "Ta'līf Akhbār Al-Qurūn Min Umarā' Bilad Ilūrin": A Critique', *History in Africa*, 11 (1984), pp. 57–67.

[50] Michel Doortmont, 'Recapturing the Past: Samuel Johnson and the Construction of the History of the Yoruba' (unpublished PhD dissertation, Erasmus Universiteit Rotterdam, 1994), pp. 9–17; Barber, 'I. B. Akinyele', p. 31.

[51] Doortmont, 'Recapturing the Past'; Falola, *Yoruba Gurus*, p. ix.

generally thought of as the child or grandchild of Odùduwà, the mythical
progenitor of the Yoruba people, travelled from Ilé-Ifẹ̀ to found Ọ̀yọ́, from
where his descendants 'spread East, West, and South-west'.[52] Subsequently,
as Johnson describes it, the Yoruba people dispersed across the region through
migration as well as war, founding new towns over the centuries. Johnson thus
controversially locates Old Ọ̀yọ́ as the centre of Yoruba political history rather
than Ilé-Ifẹ̀, as is more usual. Nonetheless, by insisting on Yoruba history being
told through a unifying *orísun* (source), Johnson imagines Yoruba history as a
story of travel and dispersal.

Many subsequent authors wrote histories focused on one town – usually
the historian's own town – rather than echoing Johnson's attempt to create a
pan-Yoruba history. But in these histories, too, migration from elsewhere is the
way that a town is able to claim legitimacy as a truly Yoruba town, whether
semi-mythical origins in Ọ̀yọ́ or, more usually, Ilé-Ifẹ̀, or a more recent migration from elsewhere.[53] In Ìmẹ̀sí-Ilé, for instance, the historian Ọlábísí Adékanlá
reports that after the original Nupe settlers left, a diversity of Yoruba peoples
moved in:

> From the beginning of time, Imesin-Ipole (Imesi-Ile) had been a convergence
> of many diverse clans and communities. There were people from Ara, Ijero,
> Otun, Akoko, Ido, Mosi, Ila and many others living together as Imesi-Ile citi-
> zens long before the Kiriji War.[54]

In addition, Adékanlá mentions 'individuals who came from neighbouring
towns like Otan-Ile, Ibokun, Ipetu and Ekiti lands to seek their fortunes at
Imesi-Ile' (12), and 'other settlers [who] had come from as many as twenty
different Yoruba and Nupe countries' (2), to the extent that '[f]or all we know,
every family at Imesi-Ile migrated to the place from somewhere' (11).

What is significant in the way these Yoruba historians tell the histories of
their towns is not simply that they depict towns as being made up of people with
ancestral origins elsewhere, which is surely the case the world over. Rather,
their significance lies in the way they place the town's origins in travel insistently at the heart of the stories they tell about the town and its inhabitants, and
in the ways they imagine the towns' settlements, their inhabitants' relationships,
even people's bodies, to be structured and marked by mobility. The towns'

[52] Samuel Johnson, *The History of the Yorubas* (Lagos: CMS (Nigeria) Bookshops, 1921), pp. 10–11.
[53] Doortmont, 'Recapturing the Past', p. 62; Falola, *Yoruba Gurus*, p. 11.
[54] Olabisi Adekanla, *Imesi-Ile: The Ancient Kiriji Camp* (Ibadan: Peetee Nigeria, 1999), p. 18. Subsequent references are to this edition and will be given in parentheses in the text.

diversity of origins, with each *ilé* (compound, lineage) coming from elsewhere, are emphasised and imagined to make the town strong and prestigious.

An evocative discussion of *ìtàn* by Ọlábìyí Yai illuminates this centrality of migration to Yoruba history as it is constructed in both the oral genre and in written town histories. Yai describes how in *ìtàn*, 'history is viewed as expansion [...] of individuals, lineages, races beyond their original cradle'. For this reason, he argues, 'the Yoruba have always conceived of their history as diaspora.' Diaspora, 'viewed and perceived in certain cultures (Greek, Jewish) as either necessity or lamented accident, is rationalized in Yorubaland as the normal or natural order of things historical'.[55] Thus in *ìtàn*, history is constituted by stories of what Yai characterises as 'spreading'; as Moses Bótù Okùbọ́té's history of Ìjẹbu, *Iwé Ìtàn Ìjẹbu* (2009), puts it: 'ìwé yìí ṣàlàyé ìtàn orírun àti bí àwọn ènìyàn ṣe rìn títí wọn fi wà níbi tí wọn dó sí títí di òní yìí' ('this book explains the history of origins and how people journeyed until they were in the place where they settled until today').[56] Journeying, travelling – 'ṣe rìn' – is not an aberration or exceptional, as it is seen in many conventional travel narratives, but rather is the way that history is created.

This centrality of mobility to history also reaches further, into the nature of narrative itself. The noun *ìtàn* is derived from the verb *tàn*, whose meaning encompasses 'spread, reach, to open up, to illuminate, to shine'.[57] The word *ìtàn* can thus also be read as 'spreading, reaching, opening up, illuminating, shining', as well as its more common meanings of 'history' and 'story'. Yai further argues that this 'spreading' has three axes: chronological, spatial and discursive or reflexive. The second axis, *ìtàn* as spatial or geographical spreading, we have already encountered. The chronological axis of *tàn*, Yai argues, refers to the spread of human generations and their deeds, while the discursive or reflexive dimension focuses on the 'illuminate' sense of *tàn*, meaning 'to discourse profoundly' on the other two dimensions.[58] Thus, according to Deirdre LaPin, bearing in mind this sense of *tàn* as both spatial and discursive spreading, *ìtàn* not only narrate history-as-travel, but in some parts of the Yoruba region, narratives are conceptualised as a metaphorical journey themselves:

> Tradition in many Yoruba speech areas conceives the experience of hearing a story as a journey which the storyteller once embarked upon and which his listeners now share vicariously with him. If the performer wishes to prepare

[55] Olabiyi Babalola Yai, 'In Praise of Metonymy: The Concepts of "Tradition" and "Creativity" in the Transmission of Yoruba Artistry over Time and Space', *Research in African Literatures*, 24.4 (1993): 29–37 (p. 30).

[56] Moses Bótù Okùbọ́té, *Iwé Ìtàn Ìjẹbu* (Ibadan: Third World Information Services, 2009), p. xi.

[57] Yai, 'In Praise of Metonymy', p. 30.

[58] Ibid. p. 31.

his audience for a long tale, he might warn them: *Ìtàn yí, ó jìnnà*: 'now this ìtàn is going along a long way' [...] Often the close of his venture into the lives of the characters is marked by an implied 'return'. A storyteller may conclude his performance with the statement: *Ibí mo bá ọn dé kí mo sèyìn 'o*: 'And that's how far I went before I turned back.' The same idea may be expressed in a reduced formula: Abọ̀ rèé ni, 'That's where I came back'. Frequently, audiences greet the performer with the cry '*E káàbò!*' 'Welcome!': a standard formula for noting someone's arrival.[59]

To consider Yoruba town histories a form of travel writing maybe a stretch too far, even in terms of the most expansive definitions of the genre such as Jan Borm's definition of travel writing as a text 'whose main theme is travel', since they have other 'main themes' besides travel.[60] At the same time, in many town histories, it is impossible to imagine the histories of the towns without a story of travel and, as Yai and LaPin both suggest, the notion of travel is placed at the heart of understandings of what *ìtàn* or narrative is. Thus travel can in fact be understood as in some senses a 'main theme' of town histories, even if the texts are not solely about travel. Furthermore, they indicate how forms of travel beyond 'good travel' or 'real travel', as discussed above, may be written into the fabric of narrative form, histories and textual cultures in ways that ask us at least to question the limits of the genre 'travel writing' through examining the particular relationships between travel and text in the southwest Nigeria. They also demonstrate the ways in which understandings of travel and narrative generated in oral forms have been, in some cases, brought to bear on written texts, in conjunction with other forms of written text and with contemporary understandings of travel. We will see a similar relationship between orality and travel writing played out in the novels of D. Ọ. Fágúnwà discussed in Chapter 4, which draw on tales of travel established in oral forms but also meld them with numerous other influences, such as European literature and contemporary ideas about the value of travel, to create new ways of writing about travel that themselves investigate the relationship between orality and writing.

However, if town histories and *ìtàn* sit far outside Western forms of travel writing, the region's turbulent nineteenth century also gave rise to travel writing by early Yoruba missionaries, such as writer and scholar Samuel Àjàyí Crowther, which was so closely linked to British missionary travel writing that Crowther has been retrospectively characterised as having a 'colonial mentality' and as having collaborated with colonial discourse. As town histories

---

[59] LaPin, 'Story, Medium and Masque', pp. 160–1. *Ìtàn* is not the only oral genre associated with travel or wandering. *Oríkì* can also be ended with a formulation imagining the telling as a journey (Karin Barber, personal communication, 1 August 2013).

[60] Borm, 'Defining Travel', p. 13.

themselves often recall, the nineteenth century was a time of great upheaval in the Yoruba region. Wars between towns and city-states across the region caused refugees, prisoners of war and warriors to flee their towns of origin, resulting in political, cultural and linguistic mingling and the formation of new towns, such as the great city of Ìbàdàn.[61] In addition, people who had been taken as slaves or captives to the New World but then freed began returning to towns such as Lagos and Abẹ̀òkúta, often via Sierra Leone or Liberia, sometimes with new ideas and with regional, pan-African and transatlantic associations. The *Sàró* and *Àgùdà*, as these returnees from Sierra Leone and Brazil respectively became known, played a particularly important role in Lagos's intellectual, print and literary culture, as we will see in Chapter 2, contributing to the creation of what has been characterised as a Lagosian creole culture that combined African and Western perspectives and ways of life.[62]

It was from this background that Samuel Àjàyí Crowther emerged, before going on to become 'one of the most distinguished West African Christians of the nineteenth century'.[63] Born in Òṣoògùn, Crowther was captured as a slave in the 1820s, but was then recaptured during a British anti-slavery raid and settled in Sierra Leone.[64] There he was baptised, quickly learnt to read and write in English at Fourah Bay College, and became a Church Missionary Society (CMS) teacher and missionary. Convinced by the European policy of 'native agency', and agreeing that 'the evangelisation of the interior of Africa must be carried out by Africans themselves', Crowther travelled extensively around present-day Nigeria for missionary work where, together with fellow missionaries, he established the first Anglican church in what would become Nigeria at Badagry in 1845, the Ẹ̀gbá mission at Abẹ̀òkúta in 1846, and the Niger Mission in 1857.[65] He became a Bishop in 1864, with his pioneering efforts as a missionary giving him renown as 'the father of modern missionary enterprise in the Nigerian mission field'.[66]

---

[61] Isichei, *A History of Nigeria*; Falola and Heaton, *A History of Nigeria*, p. 77.

[62] Zachernuk, *Colonial Subjects*, pp. 19–46; Karin Barber, *Print Culture and the First Yoruba Novel: I. B. Thomas's 'Life Story of Me, Ṣẹgilọla' and Other Texts* (Leiden: Brill, 2012), pp. 13–15; Olakunle George, *African Literature and Social Change: Tribe, Nation, Race* (Bloomington, IN: Indiana University Press, 2017); Adéẹ̀kọ́, 'Writing Africa'; J. Lorand Matory, *Black Atlantic Religion: Tradition, Transnationalism, and Matriarchy in the Afro-Brazilian Candomblé* (Princeton, NJ: Princeton University Press, 2009).

[63] P. R. McKenzie, *Inter-Religious Encounters in West Africa: Samuel Ajayi Crowther's Attitude to African Traditional Religion and Islam* (Leicester: University of Leicester, 1976), p. 11.

[64] Duke Akamisoko, *Samuel Ajayi Crowther in the Lokoja Area* (Ibadan: Sefer Books, 2002), p. vii.

[65] Ibid. p. viii; George, *African Literature*, p. 69.

[66] Akamisoko, *Samuel Ajayi Crowther*, pp. vii–viii.

Crowther took part in expeditions up the River Niger in 1841, 1854, 1857–59 and 1862 as well as journeys of his own, during which he produced journals and letters describing his travels that were published as part of CMS reports also containing the accounts of fellow European missionaries and explorers.[67] The CMS also published a letter Crowther wrote in 1837 describing his capture as a slave in the 1820s.[68] Crowther and his fellow travellers – who included fellow Africans as interpreters – engaged in missionary activity on their journeys, but also other exploratory activities, such as charting the River Niger, finding missing fellow explorers, and looking for areas suitable for commercial activity along the River Niger: 'a crucial role of missionaries like Crowther', Ọlákúnlé George reminds us, 'was to pave the way for the incursion of European capitalist interests into the interior of West Africa'.[69] Crowther resigned from the CMS in 1890, following disagreements with the CMS head office in Britain over his administration abilities and his 'dabbling in trade and politics' in the Niger valley. He died in 1891.[70]

A number of African ex-slaves and missionaries in this region kept journals.[71] However, Crowther's journals have received a particular amount of scholarly attention, especially as historical sources for the region's nineteenth-century wars, missionary history and African intellectual and religious history.[72]

---

[67] Samuel Crowther, *The Gospel on the Banks of the Niger: Journals and Notices of the Native Missionaries Accompanying the Niger Expedition of 1857–1859, by Samuel Crowther and John Christopher Taylor* (London: Church Missionary House, 1859); Samuel Crowther, *Journals and Notices of the Native Missionaries on the River Niger, 1862* (London: Church Missionary House, 1863); Samuel Crowther, *Niger Mission: Bishop Crowther's Report of the Overland Journey: From Lokoja to Bida, on the River Niger, and Thence to Lagos, on the Sea Coast, from November 10th, 1871, to February 8th, 1872* (London: Church Missionary House, 1872); Samuel Crowther, *Journal of an Expedition up the Niger and Tshadda Rivers Undertaken by Macgregor Laird in Connection with the British Government in 1854*, 2nd edn (London: F. Cass & Co, 1970); Samuel Crowther, *Journals of the Rev. James Frederick Schon and Mr. Samuel Crowther, Who, with the Sanction of Her Majesty's Government, Accompanied the Expedition up the Niger, in 1841, on Behalf of the Church Missionary Society*, 2nd edn (London: F. Cass & Co., 1970).

[68] Reproduced in Curtin, *Africa Remembered*, pp. 298–316.

[69] Akamisoko, *Samuel Ajayi Crowther*, p. 9; George, *African Literature*, p. 73.

[70] George, *African Literature*, p. 70.

[71] Doortmont, 'Recapturing the Past', pp. 19–24. See, for instance, Curtin, *Africa Remembered*; J. D. Y. Peel, 'For Who Hath Despised the Day of Small Things? Missionary Narratives and Historical Anthropology', *Comparative Studies in Society and History* 37.3 (1995), pp. 581–607; J. D. Y. Peel, *Religious Encounter and the Making of the Yoruba* (Bloomington, IN: Indiana University Press, 2000).

[72] See J. F. A. Ajayi, *Christian Missions in Nigeria: The Making of a New Elite, 1841–1891* (London: Longman, 1965); J. Page, *The Black Bishop* (London:

But alongside offering these insights into the region's history, these African missionaries' journals, along with accounts of their capture as slaves, can also be considered currently the earliest known travel writing by people who claim their origins in this region, and reading them as such gives us an important indication of how and why African writers might adopt a form of travel writing that has been closely associated with the West.

Much of the scholarship on Crowther's journals has centred on Crowther's subject position as an African Christian, with many scholars agreeing with Michel Doortmont that Crowther's journals were written 'in the tradition of early nineteenth-century travellers'[73] – that is, the tradition of European exploratory and colonial travel writing, aimed, as George puts it, at 'the Victorian bourgeoisie' as an instance of an 'African voice' that appeared to suit Victorian values.[74] Crowther's reports were published by the CMS, many of them in conjunction with Seeley's, a British publishing house that published travel accounts and adventure books from across the British colonies.[75] The market for such travelogues was 'the [British] home-front, important for financial and moral support of the mission', as distinguished from Yoruba vocabularies and practical books for use in the field.[76] Crowther was thus writing to a British audience, and he also appears to write with a sense of a lineage of Western travellers and explorers – not only missionaries – into which he can insert his own expeditions: 'The exploration of the Niger by different travellers, namely Mungo Park, Clapperton, the Landers, Messrs McGregor Laird, Lander, Old-field, and Lieut. W. Allen', he writes, 'had prepared the way for Trotter's Great Expedition of 1841', of which Crowther was a part.[77]

Bearing in mind Crowther's place in missionary history and his compliance with the expectations of missionary travel writing, it is perhaps not unexpected that history has not always been entirely kind to Crowther. Wọlé Ṣóyínká condemned Crowther's 'colonial mentality', excoriating him for his collaboration with missionary Christianity and his admiration of European values: Crowther, Ṣóyínká writes, 'grovelled before his white missionary superiors in a plea for

Simpkin, Marshall, Hamilton, Kent & Company, 1910); R. W. July, *The Origins of Modern African Thought* (London: Faber & Faber, 1968); Peel, *Religious Encounter*.

[73] Doortmont, 'Recapturing the Past', p. 39.
[74] George, *African Literature*, p. 71.
[75] Doortmont, 'Recapturing the Past', pp. 41–2.
[76] Ibid. pp. 42–3.
[77] Unpublished manuscript by Crowther dated 17 August 1876 (MS CA3/04/554) held at Church Missionary Society Archives, University of Birmingham, cited in George, *African Literature*, p. 88.

patience and understanding of his "backward, heathen, brutish" brothers'.[78] Indeed, it is possible to read Crowther's travel journals as an African iteration of a Western genre – and not a subversive iteration, as in the case of the 'counter-travel writing' highlighted by Holland and Huggan, but rather something closer to an 'autoethnographic' take on the genre.[79] 'Autoethnography' is the term used by Mary Louise Pratt to describe instances in which 'colonized subjects undertake to represent themselves in ways that engage with the colonizer's terms [...] in response to or in dialogue with [...] metropolitan representations', producing new representations of peoples or communities in response to colonial narratives, but doing so through 'a selective collaboration with and appropriation of idioms of the metropolis or the conqueror', which are 'merged or infiltrated to varying degrees with indigenous idioms to create self-representations intended to intervene in metropolitan modes of understanding'.[80] Echoing this sense that Crowther was drawing on the idioms of colonial travel writing and addressing British understandings of Africa, Claudia Gualtieri focuses on Crowther's 'in-between position' to explore how his diaries 'collaborate' with colonial discourse. In common with other 'Afro-Englishmen', she suggests, Crowther 'endorsed the perspective of liberal Englishmen, used colonial stock images of the African, showed a strong adherence to the Bible, and took great care with writing in English for a British audience'.[81] Gualtieri suggests that Crowther's 'colonial associations' result in mutual incomprehension in his encounters with Yoruba people. Noting that Crowther draws on the discourse associated with imperial travel writing about Africa, such as wonder and disgust, she surmises that Crowther's 'discourse is clearly addressed to his British audience and the CMS, and in so doing he distances himself from local non-westernised people who are said not to understand him'.[82] However, she suggests, Crowther's role was not 'totally "western and colonial"'; he also portrays himself acting as a hybrid intermediary or mediator between missionary and Yoruba, thus infusing his writing, to a limited degree, with the 'indigenous idioms' that Pratt points to as characteristic of autoethnographic travel writing.[83]

Indeed, the possibilities of readings of Crowther's position as that of the intermediary point to the significance of travel writing in the creole intellectual culture of the late nineteenth century and early twentieth century West

---

[78] Wole Soyinka, *Myth, Literature and the African World* (Cambridge: Cambridge University Press, 1976), p. xii.

[79] Holland and Huggan, *Tourists with Typewriters*, p. 21.

[80] Pratt, *Imperial Eyes*, p. 7 (original emphasis); Mary Louise Pratt, 'Arts of the Contact Zone', *Profession* (1991), pp. 33–40 (p. 35).

[81] Gualtieri, *Representations of West Africa*, p. 205.

[82] Ibid. pp. 228–9.

[83] Ibid. pp. 191, 227, 231–2.

African coastal region.[84] As Ọlákúnlé George describes, 'a class of Western-ized blacks' emerged in the wake of the Atlantic slave trade, composed of freed slaves and their descendants and typically known as 'native agents' by British missionaries and 'black whitemen' by Africans.[85] They operated with-in what George characterises as an 'ambivalent location' – they were central to the spread of Christianity in West Africa, and were inextricably linked to the slave trade, owing to connections to Freetown and Liberia, as well as their own or their ancestors' histories as slaves. At the same time, in the late nineteenth and early twentieth centuries, they saw themselves as part of a 'transatlantic "Negro" collective', as George characterises it.[86] Discursively, Crowther and his fellow 'black whitemen' operate within the same 'Victorian ideology of Christian superiority' as their white missionary counterparts. But they 'occupy a different subject position' because of the 'simultaneous ideol-ogy of racial hierarchy' of the age. Thus, not European and yet also seeing themselves as distinct from fellow Africans, Crowther and his fellow 'black whitemen' can be understood, George argues, as beginning to articulate a new sense of 'collective subjects-in-formation' as 'enlightened Africans' or 'black patriots', conceived against the 'pagan native'. Therefore, George suggests, 'Crowther is condescending toward traditional African entrenched values, but it is precisely in this wholesale acceptance of a eurocentric perspective that he complicates European missionary writing', through his 'drama of cul-ture and subject positioning' that ensues precisely because of his ambivalent position.[87]

Crowther's attention to cannibalism in his travel writing, in particular, points towards a figure epitomising this crossroads position that is of importance in many southwest Nigerian travel narratives. Crowther repudiates human sac-rifice and cannibalism. As such, it is easy to read him as falling into line with missionary discourse and its representation of such practices as evidence of African 'pagan' savagery. And yet, George points out, Crowther argues that cannibalism is used by Africans as a 'tactic' to intimidate opponents, not sim-ply as a debased cultural practice. He renders cannibalism not as culture but as politics, reminding his readers that the African is 'a fallen mortal like all non-Christians, pushed to the extremities of politics and war. On these terms, cannibalism turns out to testify to the African's membership in, not distance from, the community of fallen man.' Thus rather than stressing 'primitive dif-ference' and 'racial hierarchy', Crowther, George argues, relocates the figure

---

[84] Julien, 'The Extroverted African Novel', p. 675.
[85] George, *African Literature*, p. 62; see also Michael Echeruo, *Victorian Lagos: As-pects of Nineteenth Century Lagos Life* (London: Macmillan, 1977).
[86] George, *African Literature*, pp. 62–3.
[87] Ibid. pp. 102, 83, 65.

of the cannibal into 'unchristian worldliness', and therefore one who might be saved.[88] As we shall see, throughout the twentieth century, Nigerian travel writers have returned repeatedly to this figure of the cannibal used as a marker of intra-Nigerian difference – sometimes representing this potential for being saved at the hands of more 'enlightened' Nigerians, sometimes representing the fear of the intra-Nigerian other, and sometimes a more ironic trope, used to mock Nigeria's own 'consumption' of itself through the discourse of ethnicity or 'tribalism'.

Although often renowned primarily as a missionary, Crowther was, George suggests, 'first and foremost a reader and a thinker', whose pioneering intellectual work included his studies of the Yoruba, Igbo and Nupe languages and Yoruba translations of several books of the Bible, which rendered him, according to Michel Doortmont, 'the father of Yoruba as a modern (written) language'.[89] At the same time, Crowther wrote his journals and reports principally in English, demonstrating how Yoruba intellectuals were working with both languages from the beginnings of Yoruba print and literary culture. As George remarks, '[a]s a reader and a translator, Crowther recognizes his task as resting at some level on language, on the inventiveness needed to translate between languages' – but also, I suggest, between cultures.[90] In acting as a 'mediator' or 'intermediary' as well as a linguistic translator, Crowther can be pictured as standing at a crossroads, engaged in a form of both linguistic and cultural translation between missionary and Yoruba, Britain and Africa – a position we will see adopted by several of the travel writers discussed in this book.

George locates Crowther amid a wider context of 'diasporic investment in African letters', ranging across 'such other black whitemen as Tiyo Soga, Thomas Birch Freeman, Kwegyir Aggrey, Magema Fuze, Charles Reindorf, Samuel Johnson, Aaron Sibthorpe, and Sol T. Plaatje'.[91] This context for Crowther's writing suggests the possibilities of reading travel writing within a broader African diasporic framework of writing by authors with dual perspectives – to which we will return in Chapter 7 in the form of travel narratives of 'return' by authors living in the Nigerian diaspora in the UK and the US. In some cases their writing has been criticised for articulating overly 'Western' or extroverted viewpoints. The presence, however, of both this viewpoint and criticism of the author's overly 'Western' stance in this earlier form of travel writing by Crowther and other such missionaries suggests a way of reading contemporary diaspora writing as part of a longer discourse about Nigeria's literary, cultural and social relation with its diaspora and with the West.

---

[88] Ibid. p. 74.
[89] Ibid. p. 81; Doortmont, 'Recapturing the Past', p. 48.
[90] George, *African Literature*, p. 82.
[91] Ibid. p. 67.

Crowther's travel writing also contributes to a wider body of Yoruba literature produced through encounters with Christianity.[92] Crowther writes of his
travels within a framework of divine direction – 'O Lord, I know that the way
of man is not in himself, it is not in man that walketh to direct his steps!'[93] His
journeys themselves are structured around mission stations, baptisms, preach-
ing and evangelising. Even his travels as a slave are re-imagined through the
metaphor of a divine journey; the day he was captured as a slave is later
recalled as an 'unhappy day' but also a 'blessed day', 'being the day which
Providence had marked out for me to set out on my journey from the land of
heathenism, superstition, and vice, to a place where His Gospel is preached'.[94]
Indeed, J. D. Y. Peel suggests that one of the ways in which Yoruba missionaries ascribed narrative form to their diaries was to understand their journeys as
divinely directed. Peel argues that Crowther and fellow Yoruba missionaries
used the grand narratives offered by Christianity – especially the 'great Ur
narrative of the Bible' but also the collective history of Christianity, and the
promise of 'a new narrative in which Christianity would resolve the problems
of the age' – to create larger narratives out of their chronicles of everyday life
in their journals.[95] After Crowther, Yoruba missionaries continued to produce
reports on their travels for missionary work, such as Yoruba Baptist Minister
Mọjọlá Agbẹ̀bí's *An Account of Dr Mojola Agbebi's Work in West Africa, Com-
prising Yorubaland, Fantiland, the Ekiti Country, Central Nigeria, Southern
Nigeria and the Cameroons* (1904), published in New Calabar.[96] Later in this
book, we will encounter other forms of travel narratives mediated through the
relationship between Christianity and travel, such as the travel narratives of
Lagos newspaper editors who often signalled their Christianity as they travelled, and narratives of Nigeria's NYSC, in which Christianity constitutes a
guiding framework for the writers – and often their readers.

Yet while Crowther's journals can certainly be understood as writing within the Christian missionary travel writing tradition, they can also be read as
a contribution to a different, if not unrelated, intellectual project that had a
greater attachment to Yoruba intellectual concerns than to those of the West:

---

[92] Adéẹ̀kọ́, 'Writing Africa'; Stephen Ney, 'Ancestor, Book, Church: How Nigerian
Literature Responds to the Missionary Encounter' (unpublished PhD thesis, University of British Columbia, 2010).

[93] Crowther, *Niger Mission*, p. 31.

[94] 'Letter of Mr. Samuel Crowther to the Rev. William Jowett, in 1837, then Secretary
of the Church Missionary Society, Detailing the Circumstances Connected with
His Being Sold as a Slave', reproduced in Curtin, *Africa Remembered*, p. 299.

[95] Peel, 'For Who Hath Despised', pp. 595, 605.

[96] See Nara Muniz Improta França, 'Producing Intellectuals: Lagosian Books and
Pamphlets between 1874 and 1922' (unpublished PhD thesis, University of Sussex, 2013), p. 78.

the 'creation' of the notion of the Yoruba people through writing, as part of the 'cultural work of Yoruba ethnogenesis', as J. D. Y. Peel has called it.[97] Crowther is thought to have been one of the first people to write of 'the Yoruba'.[98] Simultaneously, however, his travel journals speak of his sense of strangeness as a traveller in the Yoruba region.[99] In his letter describing his travels as a slave, he recounts how he was taken to the town of Ìtokò, in the Ẹ̀gbá region. 'I was a perfect stranger', he writes, 'having left the Oyo country far behind'.[100] He recalls his inability to comprehend the Lagos dialect of Yoruba – 'Here we got once more into another dialect, the fourth from mine; if I may not call it altogether another language, on account of now and then, in some words, there being a faint shadow of my own' – and his great surprise at seeing the lagoon around Lagos Island: 'The sight of the river terrified me exceedingly, for I had never seen anything like it in my life.'[101] Throughout the twentieth century, Nigerian travel writers have similarly sought to produce collective identities, such as the Yoruba region or Nigeria, through travel writing, while at the same time seeing these places as full of strangeness or, at least, heterogeneity.

Moreover, Crowther's journals also point towards the significance of diary-keeping as a local intellectual practice in southwest Nigeria in the nineteenth and twentieth centuries. The practice of diary keeping often coincided with the influence of missionary Christianity and colonial education, but also developed as part of local intellectual culture and created what George calls 'narrative[s] of independent subjecthood', that is, the 'unfolding of a specific interiority, separate from the surface layering of official Christian intention'.[102] P. R. McKenzie's detailed readings of the inter-religious encounters in Crowther's journals emphasise Crowther's increasing knowledge of the great variety of religious and social practices within Yorubaland. McKenzie acknowledges the limits that Crowther's position as a missionary imposed on his understanding, but also points to the importance of his subjective experience of travel as a source of knowledge: 'he was not, nor did he regard himself as a kind of proto-anthropologist or historian of religions. He did not strive above all else after scholarly objectivity, or even necessarily towards a vantage point of sympathetic understanding.'[103] Thus Crowther's travels, even though circumscribed in particular ways by his position as a missionary, also contributed to his own interior formation of experience and subjectivity.

---

[97] Peel, 'Yoruba Ethnogenesis'.
[98] Doortmont, 'Recapturing the Past', p. 60.
[99] Ibid.
[100] Curtin, *Africa Remembered*, p. 307.
[101] Ibid. p. 309.
[102] George, *African Literature*, p. 77.
[103] McKenzie, *Inter-Religious Encounters*, p. 95.

Although Crowther is one of the best known of those who kept journals of their travels, the early twentieth-century 'explosion of writing and print' in Nigeria and elsewhere in Africa meant that diary keeping and other forms of personal writing were also adopted by other literate southwest Nigerians, including clergy, politicians, clerks, artisans, teachers and intellectuals, amongst whom they became an important form of self-documentation. Many of these diaries were preserved for occasional reading to the author him- or herself or in the presence of others.[104] While it is unlikely these diarists thought of themselves as travel writers, many documented their travels in their journals, amongst other details of everyday life. Such diaries, Karin Barber suggests, were not simply documentations of comings and goings, but were also ways in which their authors imagined 'new kinds of personhood, new ways of being social, and new ways of relating to the world of officialdom'.[105]

Thus while both Crowther's travel writing and diary keeping in southwest Nigeria have been closely associated with the West in the form of missionary Christianity and literacy, they have simultaneously provided scope for the creation, through writing, of what George identifies as a new sense of 'collective subjects-in-formation', or what Barber characterises as 'new kinds of personhood', amongst both writers such as Crowther and those who adopted such forms after him. Crowther's adoption of travel writing in a way that has been characterised as both 'collaborating with' and 'complicating' the Western missionary travel narrative and colonial discourse demonstrates the way that he was writing at the crossroads of Western and Yoruba cultural concerns, languages and histories, and adopting a Western genre of travel writing while also making it speak to his own intellectual concerns, in ways that, as we shall see, have reverberated in southwest Nigerian literary culture in the century since then.

## Travel, *òlàjú* and leisure in twentieth-century Nigeria

New forms of travel within southwest Nigeria and beyond became possible in the era of technological change that characterised the twentieth century. In 1901, the British colonial government opened the 123 miles of track between Lagos and Ìbàdàn, which signalled the beginnings of a railway network that would grow rapidly over the next few years to connect Lagos, Abẹ́òkúta, Òṣogbo, Kaduna and Kano, eventually stretching all the way to faraway Nguru in northern Nigeria, built to aid colonial exploitation of Nigeria. Cars, trains, trams, bicycles and steamers were introduced into Lagos over the first years

---

[104] Karin Barber 'Introduction – Hidden Innovators in Africa' in *Africa's Hidden Histories: Everyday Literacy and Making the Self,* ed. by Karin Barber (Bloomington: Indiana University Press, 2006), 1–21 (pp. 1–2).

[105] Barber, 'Introduction – Hidden Innovators in Africa', pp. 3–4.

of the twentieth century and were rapidly taken up by those Lagosians who could afford them. In 1907 there were just two cars on the streets of Lagos.[106] By 1920, there were six hundred, and by the 1930s there were around five hundred to eight hundred new cars being registered in Nigeria each year.[107] The first lorry was introduced by the colonial government in 1906, but over the next decades lorries and buses were increasingly run by private businesses, and as well as transporting goods they became an important means by which Nigerians were able to travel on the growing road network.[108] The railways also became increasingly popular with private passengers. By 1913 they were handling 1.16 million passenger journeys per year (over a million of whom were third-class passengers). This had tripled to 3.8 million passenger journeys per year by 1929–30.[109]

By the 1950s and 1960s, travel had become even more widely possible and desirable for the elites. Cars, buses and motorcycles were now common-place enough for advertisements for them to proliferate in newspapers, and in the 1960s newspapers such as the *Morning Post* published regular motoring pages. The buzz surrounding the railways in the 1920s and 1930s had by now diminished, and the press excitement had shifted instead to the launch of the country's first airline, Nigeria Airways, in 1958.[110] By the last decades of the twentieth century, mass travel had become a reality. The railways had by this time gone into decline, accounting for less than 0.25 per cent of passenger journeys in 2003.[111] However, road travel had boomed; there were estimated to be 920,000 people travelling by road within Nigeria per day in 1981, with a million vehicles on the roads by 1984, and 2.2 million vehicles by 2004.[112]

New forms of overseas travel, too, gained traction in the late nineteenth and early twentieth centuries as new routes between Nigeria and the rest of the world, particularly Britain, became increasingly important. The *Eagle and Lagos Critic* in 1886, for instance, published reports on a trip to England by

[106] 'A Motor Car Incident', *Lagos Standard*, 2 January 1907, p. 3.
[107] Olukoju, 'Maritime Trade', 122; Francis G. I. Omiunu and Andrew Godwin Onok-erhoraye, *Transportation and the Nigerian Space Economy* (Benin City: University of Benin, 1995), p. 110.
[108] Ayodeji Olukoju, *The 'Liverpool' of West Africa: The Dynamics and Impact of Maritime Trade in Lagos, 1900–1950* (Trenton, NJ: Africa World Press, 2004), p. 18.
[109] Jaekel, *The History of the Nigerian Railway* (Vol. 3), p. 209.
[110] 'Our Plane Arrives', *Daily Service*, 3 October 1958, p. 12.
[111] H. Gujba, Y. Mulugetta, and A. Azapagic, 'Passenger Transport in Nigeria: Environmental and Economic Analysis with Policy Recommendations', *Energy Policy*, 55 (2013), pp. 353–61 (p. 354).
[112] P. Chukwuemeka Ezeife and A. Tunji Bolade, 'The Development of the Nigerian Transport System', *Transport Reviews*, 4.4 (1984), pp. 305–30 (p. 321); Gujba et al., 'Passenger Transport in Nigeria', p. 321.

prominent Lagosian J.A. Payne and his wife, via Sierra Leone, Senegal, South America and Europe, for the Colonial and Indian Exhibition of 1886. Nozomi Sawada suggests that Payne broadcast his experiences of travel through letters to the press to 'confirm his elite position and respectability' in Lagos society.[113] As the rapid growth of the steamer network in the early twentieth century made travel across the West African coast, as well as to elsewhere in Africa and to Europe, quicker and easier than ever, the newspapers frequently printed lists of names of both European and African passengers who were travelling back and forth across the West African coast and to Europe. Overseas travel had become a matter of public record and social prestige.

As was also the case in other African countries, southwest Nigerians were recruited by the European powers as soldiers during the twentieth century, and accounts of their travels at war can be read as a significant genre of African travel writing.[114] Nigerians also continued to travel overseas as a matter of social prestige, and to seek new educational, economic and professional opportunities throughout Africa and especially in Britain, but also increasingly elsewhere in the English-speaking world and beyond. A rich seam of scholarship on Nigerian travel writing has centred on accounts of overseas travel: Kwame Osei-Poku has shown how travelogues published in *West African Review* in the 1930s to the 1950s, for instance, included accounts by newspaper editors, civil servants, students, soldiers, teachers and other intellectuals. In the postcolonial era, travels to the US and the UK have also been recounted in both non-fiction prose and poetic form in J. P. Clark's *America, Their America* (1964), Nnamdi Azikiwe's *My Odyssey* (1970), Dèjì Haastrup's *Eavesdropping* (1992), Rèmí Rájí's *Shuttlesongs. America: A Poetic Guided Tour* (2001), and Odia Ofeimun's *London Letter and Other Poems* (2000).[115]

---

[113] Nozomi Sawada, 'The Educated Elite and Associational Life in Early Lagos Newspapers: In Search of Unity for the Progress of Society' (unpublished PhD thesis, University of Birmingham, 2011), p. 234.

[114] Isaac Fadoyebo, *A Stroke of Unbelievable Luck* (Madison: African Studies Program, University of Wisconsin-Madison, 1999); Oliver Coates, 'Narrative, Time, and the Archive in an African Second World War Memoir: Isaac Fadoyebo's *A Stroke of Unbelievable Luck*', *The Journal of Commonwealth Literature* 51.3 (2015), pp. 371–86; David Killingray, *Fighting for Britain: African Soldiers in the Second World War* (Woodbridge: Boydell & Brewer, 2010).

[115] Kwame Osei-Poku, 'African Authored Domestic Travel Writing and Identity: A Returnee Soldier's Impressions of Colonial Life in Takoradi (Gold Coast)', *Coldnoon: International Journal of Travel Writing and Travelling Cultures*, 6.4 (2018), pp. 22–48; Tony E. Afejuku, 'J. P. Clark's Romantic "Autotravography"', *Literature Interpretation Theory*, 4.2 (1993), pp. 137–44; Obododimma Oha, 'The Rhetoric of Cross-Cultural Engagement and the Tropology of Memory in Remi Raji's America-Travel Poetry', in *Iba: Essays on African Literature in Honour of Oyin Ogunba*, ed. by Wole Ogundele and Gbemisola Adeoti (Ile-Ife: Obafemi

Some forms of travel, both within Nigeria and overseas, became associated with modernity and the notion of 'civilisation', although sometimes ambivalently. At the turn of the twentieth century, the Lagos press was sometimes full of celebration and wonder at the new forms of transport and opportunities for travel; its writers marvelled at the speed of the trains, and the way journey times had been sliced and new routes opened up. As the *Lagos Standard* proclaimed in 1907, 'the Iron Horse [the railway] is conceded to be a great civilising agent'.[116] But 'civilised life' was not always a welcome arrival:

> Railways, tramways, motor waggons, electric light, water rates, and all the accessories of European civilised life are introduced and follow each other with a rapidity that takes away one's breath and in the presence of which the unsophisticated Native stands bewildered and dumbfounded.[117]

Few of the newspapers' Lagosian writers are likely to have thought of themselves as an 'unsophisticated Native' standing 'bewildered and dumbfounded'; this is likely a paternalistic reference to 'natives' from the Yoruba 'hinterland', rather than to Lagosians, which emphasises by contrast the Lagosian writer's greater familiarity with 'civilised life'. Nonetheless, the newspapers complained that the 'Europeanised' life in Lagos had become too stressful, too frantic, and was unsuited to 'African' ways of life:

> All the hurry, bustle and activity of modern civilised life, the railroad pace at which everything moves, the high pressure state of existence, the dress, the food, and other acquired tastes are, it will be confessed, but ill-adapted to local requirements. The African was not made for such a life [...] A return to the simple life is the urgent call to the educated Native in West Africa.[118]

At the same time, though, travel was valorised by some southwest Nigerians as improving and edifying. The Yoruba notion of *ọlàjú*, meaning 'enlightenment' or 'civilisation' (literally, 'the splitting (open) of eyes') is, J. D. Y. Peel argues, often associated with 'education, the world religions, external trade and travel'.[119] Particularly since the colonial era, it has been closely aligned

---

Awowlowo University Press, 2003), pp. 137–50; Oyeniyi Okunoye, 'The Margins or the Metropole? The Location of Home in Odia Ofeimun's *London Letter and Other Poems*', *Tydskrif vir letterkunde,* 43.2 (2006), pp. 107–21; Ayodeji Isaac Shittu and Anya U Egwu, '"Third-Worlding" the Colonial Metropolis: Post-Colonial Travelogue, Identity and a Tale of Two Cities in Odia Ofeimun's *London Letter and Other Poems*', *Covenant Journal of Language Studies,* 2.1 (2016).

[116] 'Lagosian on Dits', *Lagos Standard*, 11 September 1907, p. 4.

[117] 'The Tendency to Rush', *Lagos Standard*, 3 March 1909, p. 4.

[118] 'A Serious Problem', *Lagos Standard*, 13 February 1907, pp. 4–5.

[119] J. D. Y. Peel, 'Olaju: A Yoruba Concept of Development', *Journal of Development Studies*, 14.2 (1978), pp. 139–65 (p. 139).

with openness to external knowledge, exposure to the outside world, and new ideas and ways of living. Though connected to colonialism and education, *òlàjú* stresses more broadly the value of travel, openness to the outside world and new ideas that engender individual and communal 'enlightenment'. Peel cannot say whether this word was used before European contact, but he notes that as well as referring to education and missionary Christianity, *òlàjú* is also linked with knowledge of 'distant places' through trading, as in his description of *òṣómàáló* (long-distance traders) as bearers of *òlàjú*: '[t]hey had travelled [...] they introduced new tastes, costumes and habits, as well as ideas for how things at Ilesha might be improved after the model of things abroad'.[120] As one of Peel's respondents said, 'Ọlaju ni fi aiye dara ju ti atijọ; awọn enia nṣe irin ajọ gbogbo ohun ti awon si ri l'ọhun ni nwọn mu wa sibi. [It's *òlàjú* makes the world better than it was before. People travel, and everything they see abroad, they bring here.]'[121] Further glossing *òlàjú* as 'the Yorùbá concept of historical timeliness', Adéèkọ́ elaborates that the concept refers to 'the placement of discursive bodies in their time and space', so that one who is 'properly placed' takes 'optimal advantage of the particular social environment', both spatial and temporal. Thus, he suggests, '[d]efinitely, "*òlàjú*" involves newness. But it also involves promptness and propriety (in the sense of appropriate responsiveness or responsibility to social stimuli)'.[122] The term suggests an ability to take proper advantage of all that is offered by the world – including, potentially, through travel.

Lisa Lindsay adds that while colonial notions of 'modernisation' were based on industrialisation, labour, regulation of time and the nuclear family, *òlàjú* suggested a different conception of 'enlightenment', used to describe 'those who were not necessarily well educated, but who gained worldly knowledge by pursuing trading opportunities away from the hometown'.[123] Lindsay points out that when the colonial authorities in the 1950s introduced a free travel allowance for Nigerian railway workers, workers often split their travel allowances between their hometowns and elsewhere, 'visiting friends or exploring unfamiliar parts of the country'. One of the train drivers with whom Lindsay spoke described his travels to faraway places in the north and east of the country, both in the course of his work and on annual leave, in terms of knowledge and self-improvement: 'I can tell more of these places than someone who has not travelled.' Such travel, Lindsay argues, contributed to the railway workers' image of themselves as 'modern, cosmopolitan' men.[124]

---

[120] Ibid. p. 153.
[121] Ibid. p. 142.
[122] Adéèkọ́, *Arts of Being Yorùbá*, pp. 49, 69.
[123] Lindsay, *Working with Gender*, p. 14.
[124] Ibid. p. 156.

Despite such notions of the value of travel, the twentieth century has not necessarily heralded an age of leisure travel within Nigeria, particularly since Nigeria's economic decline since the 1980s. In his research on Nigerian tourism,
Musisi Nkambwe describes how there was some development of the domestic
tourism industry in Nigeria during the early 1980s.[125] However, participation
in domestic tourism was still low, owing principally to the majority of Nigerians' lack of time or money for leisure travel, poor transport infrastructure and
lack of awareness of tourist attractions.[126] Indeed, Nkambwe, writing in 1985,
describes his respondents' 'surprise at the idea of spending money to visit,
purely for pleasure, places where they know nobody':

> Although these same people indicate they wish to travel, tourism for its own
> sake has little value to them. Most people who have this view of tourism con-
> sider travelling in terms of going to see relatives and friends.[127]

Nonetheless, the relatively limited practice of leisure travel within Nigeria,
and the frequent association of the terms 'travel' and 'tourism' with Western
travel practices, compared to the travel for social reasons that Nkambwe identifies as more typical of his respondents' experience of travel, does not mean that
leisure travel has not sometimes been promoted as an ideal or an aspiration in
southwest Nigeria, especially amongst the region's elites. In 1940, for instance,
the *Nigerian Observer* published a three-part narrative of a journey 'From Port
Harcourt to Lagos' by 'A Holiday-Maker', describing the writer's journey by
train to Lagos, via Kaduna: 'It was with feverish excitement that I left my little
home-town one Thursday morning for Port Harcourt', the piece begins.[128] The
confident independence-era press of the 1950s and 1960s published a number
of intra-Nigerian travel narratives addressed to children, advising them that
'without any hesitation, travelling is a sort of education', and that reading
about travel 'will have great educational value for your studies'.[129] Even in the
straitened economic circumstances that have plagued Nigeria since the 1980s,
international travel and tourism, too, continued to be promoted in the press. An
article in the *National Concord* of 1992, for instance, describes the pleasures
of Dakar for the tourist: its history, its beaches, its arts and crafts, 'fascinating

---

[125] Musisi Nkambwe, 'Intranational Tourism in Nigeria', *Canadian Journal of African Studies* 19.1 (1985), pp. 193–204 (pp. 193–4).

[126] Ibid. p. 201.

[127] Ibid. p. 196.

[128] 'A Holiday-Maker', 'From Port Harcourt to Lagos', *Nigerian Observer,* 16 March
1940, p. 18.

[129] 'A Visit to Important Towns', *Daily Service*, 7 November 1958, p. 9; 'Ekiti Visit –
then "tour of the world"', *Independent*, 4–11 March 1961, p. 6.

curiosities', its nightlife and the 'smiling and hospitable people'.[130] Tourism has become part of the Nigerian state's repertoire, as a source of potential economic benefit, and a Nigerian travel and tourism journalism industry has steadily grown, as I discuss further in Chapter 6.

The promotion of travel and tourism in the Nigerian press is also echoed by the idealisation of the value of travel through the figure of some individual Nigerian travellers who have taken on a metaphorical quality through their association with it. The most pertinent example is Ọlábísí Àjàlá, an 'indomitable and daring globe-trotter'[131] who became renowned between the 1950s and the 1970s for having travelled 'all over the world', and particularly for his claim to be the first man to circumnavigate the globe on a Vespa. Àjàlá, who published a book about his travels called *An African Abroad* (1963), was praised in a song by Chief Ebenezer Obey, and 'Àjàlá' remains a popular nickname for anyone who loves to travel.[132] The traveller thus has the potential to become a celebrity; indeed, as I discuss in the Epilogue, tourism has become an aspirational practice for many elite Nigerians, who value tourism and travel for its own sake as a performative gesture, particularly in the age of social media in which images of travel become highly valuable forms of social capital.

The diversity of forms of travel in southwest Nigeria discussed in this chapter demonstrates not only the necessity of taking locally specific forms of travel into account when determining what constitutes 'travel writing' in the region, but also the intimate connection between forms of travel and genres of writing: Crowther's writing for the CMS unsurprisingly took the journal form associated with missionary Christianity and adopted many of its tropes, while *ìtàn* conceive of narrative and travel as interrelated through the trope of 'spreading'. The rest of this book will take into account further locally significant forms of both travel and travel writing, including newspaper editors' travels to promote their newspapers, a Yoruba intellectual's tour of the Yoruba region, which he published as a form of autoethnography, fictional tales of hunters' travels, and accounts of young Nigerians' travels as part of the country's National Youth Service Corps. These take their place alongside forms of travel and travel writing that, like Crowther's missionary journals, are more familiar to the genre in the Western sense, but still nonetheless often 'complicate' the genre, such as a travelogue recounting the author's work as a surveyor, and more recent narratives of travel for travel's sake.

---

[130] 'Dakar: City Ready to Entertain Its Guests', *National Concord*, 10 January 1992, p. 19.
[131] 'Travelling via hell's highway', *Daily Service,* 31 December 1958, p. 4.
[132] Oluwaseun Adeniyi Abimbola, 'The Legend of Ajala's Travels and Transnational Backpacking in Africa' (unpublished MA dissertation, University of Ibadan, 2016).

In his discussion of Nigerian domestic tourism, Musisi Nkambwe points to the importance of travel for social purposes, to visit family and friends.[133] In the next chapter, we will see how travel was intensely associated with sociality by the writers of travel narratives in the 1920s' Yoruba-language press in Lagos. This chapter explores a form of travel writing that owes much to the journal form, the *Sàró* culture of Lagos and the sense of standing at a cultural crossroads discussed in this chapter, which develops an even more intense interest in new forms of personhood and subject formation through literacy and the written text. As such, we will see how these travel narratives opened up space for exciting new experiments with literary genre and style in early twentieth-century Nigeria.

[133] Nkambwe, 'Intranational Tourism in Nigeria', p. 196.

In the 1920s, colonial Lagos was home to a rapidly developing literary culture centred on the city's locally owned press. The 'foundations of one of the African continent's largest and most dazzling modern literary traditions', Karin Barber argues, referring to Yoruba literature, developed out of 'profuse and innovative experimentation' in the pages of the newspapers.[1] Indeed, this was a particularly important era for Yoruba print and literary culture. Newspapers had been published in Lagos since the 1860s, but the 1920s were a vibrant decade for the Lagos press. Five new Yoruba newspapers were founded in Lagos in the 1920s, joining a larger range of English-language newspapers: the new Yoruba newspapers were *Eko Akete*, founded in 1922, *Eleti-Ọfẹ* in 1923, *Iwe Irohin Ọsọṣẹ* in 1925, *Eko Igbẹhin* in 1926, and *Akede Eko* in 1928.[2] These new Yoruba newspapers were small operations; editors often wrote much of their content alongside reader contributions and the output of a small team of writers. Although generally referred to as 'Yoruba newspapers', these newspapers in fact often featured some English-language pieces alongside their Yoruba-language content. In common with their longer-established English-language counterparts in Lagos, they published political news and reports on day-to-day life, as well as lengthy opinion pieces and comments on the long-running debates of the age, alongside advertisements for modish products such as refrigerators, cars and medicines.[3]

The establishment of these newspapers also marked an inventive phase in Yoruba literary creativity, particularly with regard to literary genre. As well as publishing news and political opinion, the newspapers made space for literary

---

[1] Karin Barber, 'Experiments with Genre in the Yoruba Newspapers of the 1920s', in *African Print Cultures: Newspapers and Their Publics in the Twentieth Century*, ed. by Derek Peterson, Emma Hunter, and Stephanie Newell (Ann Arbor: University of Michigan Press, 2016), pp. 151–78 (pp. 151–3).

[2] Barber, *Print Culture*, pp. 27–34. Although Yoruba-language newspapers had been published before (beginning with *Iwe Irohin*, established by missionary Henry Townsend in 1859), the new generation of newspapers published in the 1920s were, with the exception of the short-lived *Iwe Irohin Ọsọṣẹ*, the longest-running to date: the first set of newspapers to last for more than eight years. A new Yoruba newspaper was also established in Ìbàdàn in 1924: the *Yoruba News*.

[3] Barber, 'Experiments with Genre', p. 151.

and creative texts ranging across genres, from *oríkì* to satire, philosophy, advice columns, biography, historical narratives, poetry and plays.[4] As Barber describes, 'several new genres were first tried out in the newspapers' pages, and subsequently consolidated by republication as books: among them, the novel and new styles of modern written poetry'.[5] The Yoruba print culture that gave birth to these major new genres was one of constant experimentation with genre and with forms of writing and addressing readers, with some innovations being adopted for years to come, while others were discarded when they did not catch on.[6]

Travel writing was also one of the genres that found a home in this open, innovative print culture, and while not as wildly successful as the Yoruba novels that were later republished as books, it became a feature of the Yoruba press for years to come. Within these newspapers' pages, a group of writers and editors, members of Lagos's up-and-coming cultural elite, creatively described their journeys across the newly established colony of Nigeria – their playful serialised narratives often lasting for several weeks. These travel narratives ranged from a twelve-part account of a journey across southern Nigeria to shorter one- or two-part accounts of journeys to nearer towns and cities in the Yoruba region. While some of their authors were pseudonymous, others were prominent intellectuals in early twentieth-century colonial Lagos who wrote under their own names: newspaper editors Isaac Babalọlá Thomas and Emmanuel Awóbọ̀ Akintán, and historian Àjàyí Kọ́láwọlé Ajíṣafẹ́. In their personal, lively and idiosyncratic travel narratives, some of these travel writers sought to help connect their Lagosian readers to the Yoruba-speaking hinterland, and to convince them of its intellectual, social and political significance to Lagosians. Others sought to make sense of their relationship with places beyond the Yoruba-speaking region in the nascent colony of Nigeria, where they encountered 'civilisation' in the form of Yoruba-speaking, Christian Lagosian migrants, but also strangeness in the form of local people who spoke different languages and with whom they felt they had little in common.

Accounts of journeys were not a new phenomenon in the Lagos press; as we shall see in Chapter 3, a small number of English-language travel narratives were published in Lagos newspapers in the earliest decades of the twentieth century, focusing either on short accounts of elite Lagosians' journeys for work and leisure or on descriptions of other regions of Nigeria, current affairs and the perceived connections between Lagos and the towns of the Yoruba 'hinterland'. However, the travel narratives in the Yoruba press of the 1920s offered something unique in their intensely personalised tone, their experiments with

---

[4] *Oríkì*: Yoruba oral praise poetry. Barber, 'Experiments with Genre', p. 156.
[5] Ibid. p. 151.
[6] Ibid. p. 153.

literary style, and their emphasis on the writer's subjectivity. While the writers of these travel narratives were likely to have been familiar with British travel writing about Africa, travel writing in these newspapers seems not to have been linked particularly closely to the British tradition. Instead, it both reflected and encouraged the spread of print culture itself across Nigeria, helped shape ideas of what Lagos, Yoruba and Nigeria might mean to Lagosians in the earliest decades of the colony of Nigeria, and was a product of the experimental, innovative print culture of 1920s Lagos.

Travel narratives continued to be published intermittently in the Yoruba press in subsequent decades, joined by an increasing number of accounts of journeys overseas as travel abroad became more accessible. This chapter, however, focuses on travel narratives published in the first ten years of this new wave of Yoruba newspapers, from 1922 to 1932. At least eleven travel narratives of this kind were published in the Yoruba newspapers *Akede Eko*, *Eleti-Ọfẹ* and *Eko Akete* in this decade, and they were a feature of the Yoruba press of the 1920s from almost its beginnings. In 1923, a writer calling himself (for it seems highly likely it was a 'he') 'Ajeji', a Yoruba word meaning 'stranger' or 'foreigner', set out from Lagos to Cameroon. He published an account of his journey in a five-part serial called 'Irin-Ajo Lati Eko Lọ Si Kamerun' ('A Journey from Lagos to Cameroon') in the newly established newspaper *Eko Akete*. In the narrative, Ajeji describes various towns and sights he encounters, along with his responses to them and the history and society of each place. Despite his use of a pseudonym – a common rhetorical feature of the West African press in this era – Ajeji's travel narrative adopts a personalised, conversational tone, focused on his own experience.[7] Thus although the narrative begins with a formal announcement of the ship's itinerary, the tone shifts into a personalised account as Ajeji describes the departure rituals on board the ship: the Captain rings the bell, while 'olukuluku ero ni funfun ati dudu si nju aṣọ funfun si awọn ojulumọ ti o sin wọn wa si Ebute' ('each passenger, white and black, waved white handkerchiefs to their loved ones who had come to see them off at the harbour') all the while 'nfi ọwọ kan jẹun' ('using one hand to eat') afternoon tea while running to wave to their loved ones on the shore.[8] This conversational, anecdotal tone based on Ajeji's own experiences persists throughout the series. Describing Calabar, for instance, Ajeji frames his impressions of the city through his body; he describes walking until he was tired, and the darkness that prevents him from viewing the city any further:

[7] Stephanie Newell, *The Power to Name: A History of Anonymity in Colonial West Africa* (Athens: Ohio University Press, 2013).
[8] Ajeji, 'Irin-Ajo Lati Eko Lọ Si Kameroon', *Eko Akete*, 17 February 1923, p. 7.

mo rin titi o rẹ mi, mo kuro ni agọ ti awọn enia dudu, o di adugbo ti awọn oyinbo. Owo ti nwọn na sibẹ ko kere, ilu nlanla pẹlu ogba jankan-jankan – gbogbo rẹ tẹ lọ bẹrẹbẹ – koriko daradara si hu lọ salalu bi ti ọdan [...] mo gba ọna Marina mo rinrin titi mo de ibi *Shop* awọn oyinbo, o pọ lọ sua l'oniruru bẹ si ni awọn enia dudu pagọ bẹrẹbẹ lọ niwaju nwọn bi ti Ẹhingbẹti l'Eko, işu nla-nla, ati oniruru nkan ni jijẹ mimu ati wiwọ lo kun ile ọja wọnyi, igbati ilẹ şu şa ti nko riran mọ ni mo wa pada sinu ọkọ ka wa lọ sinmi.[9]

I walked until I was tired, I left the African quarter, and headed into the European neighbourhood. The money they had spent here wasn't small; it was a very big town with noteworthy gardens – which were all very extensive – and fine grass grew all over like on a grassy plain [...] I set out on the way to the Marina, and I walked until I got to the place where the white people's shops were, they were very varied and extensive, and also Africans had set up extensive rows of stalls in front, as in Ẹhìngbẹtì in Lagos. Huge yams, and all kinds of things to eat, drink and wear filled these shops, and only when it was dark such that I could not see any more, did I return to the boat to relax.

Ajeji's narrative was one of the first of a small but quite extraordinary trend for the publication of travel narratives in the Yoruba press in the 1920s. The chief pioneer of this Yoruba-language travel writing was the journalist and newspaper editor Isaac Babalọlá Thomas. Thomas, a Christian Lagosian of *Sàró* descent (the *Sàró* were former slaves and their descendants, often educated Christians, who had returned to Lagos via Sierra Leone and formed the city's intellectual and cultural elite; see Chapter 1), had previously been a schoolteacher, but he turned to Yoruba-language journalism in the 1920s, first as a writer for *Eko Akete* and *Eleti-Ọfẹ*, then as proprietor and editor of the newspaper *Akede Eko*, which he founded in 1928 and edited until 1958.[10] Thomas, along with many of his newspaper contemporaries, was interested in Yoruba and Nigerian history; he wrote a biography of Nigerian nationalist Herbert Macaulay and newspaper columns on other politicians and nationalists. He is best known, however, for *Ìtàn Ìgbésí Ayé Èmi Sẹ̀gilọlá Ẹléyinjú Ẹgẹ́ Ẹlẹ́gbẹ̀rùn Ọkọ L'áiyé*, generally recognised as the first Yoruba novel, which he published to great popular acclaim as a serial in *Akede Eko* in 1929–30.[11]

---

[9] Ajeji, 'Irin-Ajo Lati Eko Lọ Si Kamerun II', *Eko Akete*, 3 March 1923; 17 February 1923, p. 5.

[10] Barber, *Print Culture*, pp. 34–6; Adeboye Babalọla, 'Yoruba Literature', in *Literature in African Languages: Theoretical Issues and Sample Surveys,* ed. by B. W. Andrzejewski, S. Piłaszewicz, and W. Tyloch (Cambridge: Cambridge University Press, 1985), pp. 157–89 (p. 187).

[11] 'The Life-story of Me, "Sẹgilọlá of the fascinating eyes", she who had a thousand lovers in her life' in Barber's translation. For brevity I refer to it henceforth as *Sẹ̀gilọlá*; Barber, *Print Culture*, pp. 34–65.

*Sègilolá* was not Thomas's only literary innovation. In 1926, the author published what appears to have been his first serialised travel narrative in the newspaper *Eleti-Ọfẹ*. Adopting the serial format that was already common in the Yoruba press, Thomas's series 'Ero L'Ọna' or 'The Traveller' describes his three-month long journey on newspaper business from Lagos to Sapele, in present-day Delta State.[12] Thomas continued to publish 'Ero L'Ọna' travel narratives in his new newspaper, *Akede Eko*, with three further series appearing between 1929 and 1931 (and further into the 1930s, including series in 1934 and 1937), describing journeys to the nearby Yoruba-speaking region as well as to southeast Nigeria.

Each individual narrative in Thomas's series was usually one to two pages long. Many of the narratives were presented as a first-person journal entry, dated according to individual days and tagged with the town Thomas was in at the time, and often printed while Thomas was still on his travels, although usually with a lag of several weeks, reflecting the time it would have taken to get his copy back to Lagos while he was on the road. But these were journal entries clearly designed for publication, without offering any pretence at being private reflection only later published; they often addressed newspaper readers directly within the text, with Thomas asking readers to keep him in his prayers, or giving them a cliff-hanging preview of next week's instalment, while some of them were written in the format of letters addressed to the newspaper readers.

These humorous and idiosyncratic travel narratives tell of Thomas's experiences of travelling by steamer, train and lorry, his encounters with friends old and new, and his impressions of the towns and people he visits. They revel in a lively, personable Yoruba, abounding with stories, jokes, songs and proverbs: 'A ki nṣe ọrẹ ero, ka yọ, ero nre ile rẹ l'ọla' ('we don't make friends with a traveller in order to be happy, because the traveller will return home tomorrow') runs one proverb he uses several times.[13] As was commonly the style in the Yoruba-language newspapers of the 1920s, they are bombastic, emotional, and often full of hyperbole. Thomas's rhetorical set-pieces include proverbs, quotations from the Bible, panoramas, melodramatic depictions of sorrow at leaving his family, effusive declarations of the wonders of travel, praise of his hosts and the delicious food they served him, greeting readers with Itsekiri and Igbo words he had encountered on his travels, and onomatopoeic descriptions of the sights and sounds of travel. 'Fo o o o o!!!' cries a ship's horn, while a train makes the sound 'Fakafiki-fakafiki!' and cockerels crow 'Kekereke e e e!!' ('Cock-a-doodle-do!'), 'omije anu' ('tears of sorrow') roll down Thomas's face as he leaves home, and he often reports crying out in amazement at the wonders he encounters: 'Emi kẹ! Emi kẹ! Emi kẹ!' ('Me! Me! Me!'), he exclaims

[12] On the serial format, see Barber, 'Experiments with Genre', p. 155.
[13] Thomas, 'Ero L'Ọna', *Akede Eko*, 14 March 1931, p. 6.

on being picked up by a dazzling car.[14] While the travel narratives would sometimes finish with a joyful return to Lagos, in other cases they petered out towards the end of the journey as if the writer had become tired of writing about a journey that had ended several weeks ago, or perhaps more urgent matters had taken up space in the newspapers instead.

Although Thomas was the most prolific of the Yoruba-language travel writers of the 1920s, fellow newspaper editor E. A. Akintán also experimented with the genre. Akintán was, like Thomas, a former schoolteacher, and he was the editor of the Yoruba newspaper *Eleti-Ọfẹ*, which he established in 1923. When the newspaper closed in 1932, he returned to teaching as one of the founders and the Principal of Lagos Public School.[15] Akintán also published a serialised novel, *Ìtàn Èmi Ọmọ-Orùkàn*, in *Eleti-Ọfẹ* in 1926–30 and, in common with Thomas, published travel writing alongside his novel (although Akintán's novel has received less critical interest than Thomas's *Sẹ̀gilọlá* and is often regarded as a novella or a less successful attempt at the novel form). Akintán's long series 'Irin Ajo Lati Eko Lọ si Ileṣa, Lati Ọwọ Oniwe Irohin' ('A Journey from Lagos to Ilẹ̀ṣà, by the Newspaper Editor') was published in *Eleti-Ọfẹ* from November 1926 to February 1927, and two shorter series, one in English and one in Yoruba in 1928 and 1930. Akintán's fourteen-part narrative 'Irin Ajo Lati Eko Lọ si Ileṣa' followed the form established by Thomas as Akintán travelled across the Yoruba-speaking region and wrote of the people he met, his impressions of the towns, and the changes he noticed. Akintán did not explicitly use the epistolary form, but he nonetheless addressed readers within his narratives, and his weekly instalments were written as if they had been sent to the newspaper for publication while Akintán was in the midst of his journey.

A third travel writer, A. K. Ajíṣafẹ́, was not a newspaper editor but a historian. Ajíṣafẹ́ was born Emmanuel Olympus Moore to a Christian *Sàró* family of Ẹ̀gbá origin in Lagos, although he adopted the Yoruba name Àjàyí Kọ́láwọlé Ajíṣafẹ́ in 1921 amid the era's cultural nationalism (the *Sàró* were the descendants of former slaves, often educated Christians, who had returned to Lagos via Sierra Leone; see Chapter 1).[16] Ajíṣafẹ́ was a central figure in early Yoruba print culture, a prolific historian and chronicler of Yoruba law, religion and customs, and a poet, writer and journalist who published at least eighteen works, many connected with Ẹ̀gbá history.[17] Amongst these, Ajíṣafẹ́ published his English-language *History of Abeokuta* in 1916, and the Yoruba-language version *Ìwé Ìtàn Abẹ̀òkúta* at an unknown later date. In 1930 (and again in

---

[14] Thomas, 'Ero L'Ọna', *Akede Eko*, 18 April 1929, p. 7; 14 February 1931, p. 6; 14 March 1931, p. 7; 18 April 1929, p. 6; 16 May 1929, p. 7.

[15] Babalọla, 'Yoruba Literature', p. 179.

[16] Ibid. p. 178. Ẹ̀gbá is a Yoruba sub-group, based largely in Abẹ̀òkúta.

[17] Doortmont, 'Recapturing the Past', p. 52.

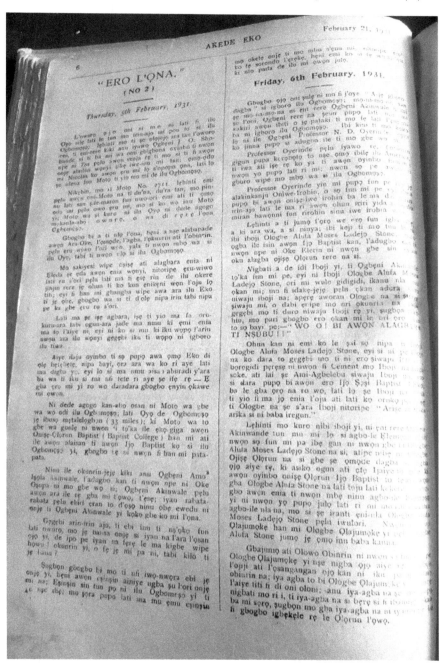

**Figure 1** Page from I. B. Thomas's series 'Ero L'Ọna', published in *Akede Eko* in 1931; sourced from the National Archives, Ìbàdàn, Nigeria, reproduced with permission

1934), he published narratives describing his travels for a slightly different purpose from those of the other newspaper travel writers: 'lati tubọ wadi aṣa ati ofin ati awọn ọgbọn aṣiri ilẹ Yoruba daradara ki mba tubo le mọye si i fun ṣiṣe iwe ọgbọn ati iṣesi ilu wa fun aiye lati mọ' ('in order to do further thorough research into the culture, laws and secret wisdom of Yorubaland, so that I could increase my understanding of it for the work of writing a book of the wisdom and characteristics of our towns for the world to know').[18] In his 1930 series, Ajíṣafẹ́ describes the people and towns he visits in the course of this research for his historical writing, and recounts his audiences with Yoruba ọbas (rulers), who shared with him their knowledge of the history of their towns.

Alongside the long, personalised narratives by these writers, other writers also published shorter, less idiosyncratic accounts of visits by their hometown associations to towns in the Yoruba hinterland, such as Adélaní Gbogboadé, clerk of the Owu Association of Lagos, who published in the newly established *Eko Akete* in 1922 a Yoruba-language account of the Owu Association's visit to Abẹ́òkúta, and Ọmọ Ẹgbẹ ('Association Member') who similarly described a hometown association visit to Ìkòròdú in *Eko Akete* in 1924.[19] Another pseudonymous writer called Gay – a regular contributor to *Eleti-Ọfẹ* – published his English-language narrative 'A Travellers' Obsevations' [sic] in *Eleti-Ọfẹ* from June to September 1926, which described a trip to Ìbàdàn, Ìkòròdú and Badagry, and focused on distinctions between Lagos and surrounding towns, particularly in terms of their 'modernity'.

## The spread of Yoruba print culture

These travel narratives form an important part of the story of the experimental Yoruba print and literary culture in the 1920s, in that they provided space for the experiments with genre, form and audience that subsequently led, in particular, to the development of the serialised newspaper novel in Yoruba. Alongside his travel writing, I. B. Thomas also published historical and biographical pieces, but he is now best known for his serialised novel *Sẹ̀gilọlá*, published to great popular acclaim in *Akede Eko* in 1929–30. *Sẹ̀gilọlá* is the life story of Sẹ̀gilọlá, a former prostitute who spent her life being chased by the men of Lagos and now, on her deathbed, appears to repent of her past life, telling it – in cliff-hanging instalments – to *Akede Eko* readers as a cautionary tale.

Travel is not particularly a theme of *Sẹ̀gilọlá*, beyond a trip the protagonist takes to Sekondi in the Gold Coast when she elopes with a lover. Nonetheless,

---

[18] A. K. Ajiṣafẹ, 'Irin-Ajo Kakiri Ilu Oke', *Akede Eko*, 28 June 1930, p. 5.

[19] A. Gbogboade, 'Irohin Ikọ Ti Ẹgbẹ Owu Eko Ran Si Ọba Olowu Ni Abẹokuta', *Eko Akete*, 26 August 1922; Ọmọ Ẹgbẹ, 'Irohin Ṣoki Nipa Irin Ajo Lọ Si Ikorodu', *Eko Akete*, 2 February–1 March 1924.

what is striking about reading *Sègilọlá* in the light of Thomas's travel writing, which he published in the same newspaper, *Akede Eko*, both before and after he published *Sègilọlá*, is how similar they are stylistically and formally. As Karin Barber describes, *Sègilọlá* was written as if it were a pseudonymous autobiography, without being attributed to Thomas, and it was so lifelike and so emotionally affecting that many readers were convinced that Sègilọlá was indeed who she said she was. While Sègilọlá claims to be sorry for her life of sin and urges her readers not to make the mistakes she did, the novel also revels in the detail of Sègilọlá's many lovers and her outrageous lifestyle.[20] Barber's description of Sègilọlá's letters to *Akede Eko* readers could equally be applied to Thomas's travel narratives:

> Sẹgilọla's letters looked real. They were written in a fluent, colloquial, conversational style – often repetitious and sometimes verging on incoherence, they overflowed with emotion, mixing pious exhortations with knowing and nostalgic allusions to the shared popular culture of Lagos, past and present. They were addressed directly to the editor and readers of *Akede Eko*, buttonholing them insistently and demanding attention and response.[21]

The travel narratives, too, are suffused with 'pious exhortations', quotations from the Bible, especially the Psalms, and with thanks to God. They also 'overflow with emotions': Thomas gives melodramatic depictions of sorrow at leaving his family: 'mo bu s'ẹkun ramuramu bi ọmọde ti a na' ('I burst into tears, roaring like a child who had been beaten'). When his family turned their backs to go home, he tells us, 'otutu nla kan fi da bo mi lojiji. Fun odidi abọ wakati ni mo fi nikan daduro laisọrọ' ('a great coldness covered me suddenly. For a whole half hour I did nothing but stand still without speaking').[22] And the travel narratives are 'repetitious', repeating tropes and forms of address from one series to another, and are addressed directly to readers, in common with *Sègilọlá*.

This stylistic crossover between the travel narratives and the serialised novel suggests that Thomas was re-using and testing rhetorical strategies between one narrative form and another, retiring those that did not work, and repeating those that did. In fact, Thomas's 1929 'Ero L'Ọna' stops abruptly mid-journey and is followed six weeks later by *Sègilọlá*, as if the travel narrative and the serialised novel were competing for space with one another (*Sègilọlá* appears to have been more popular, provoking numerous appreciative letters from readers). Thus, although Bísí Ògúnsínà has suggested that *Sègilọlá* was 'written in a hitherto unprecedented style in Yoruba literary history, the epistolary

---

[20] Barber, *Print Culture*, p. 3.
[21] Ibid. p. 5.
[22] Thomas, 'Ero L'Ona', *Eleti-Ọfẹ*, 28 April 1926, p. 8.

technique', in fact by tracing the development of travel narratives that also used the epistolary form, we can see this technique being finessed very shortly before being deployed in *Sẹ̀gilọlá*.

Akintán, too, published a serialised novel called *Ìtàn Èmi Ọmọ-Orùkàn*. This was the story of the orphan Bánwò who was forced to leave home to seek her fortune, and it was published intermittently in *Eleti-Ọfẹ* between 1926 and 1930. Akintán's narrative is, in common with *Sẹ̀gilọlá*, a first-person narrative, though Karin Barber writes that it 'lacked *Sẹgilọla*'s characteristics of episto-larity, confessional mode and realistic urban setting', and its status as fiction was not concealed, as was the case for *Sẹ̀gilọlá*.[23] Ògúnsínà points out that no 'creative story' had appeared between the publication of Akintán's *Ìtàn Èmi Ọmọ-Orùkàn* and Thomas's *Sẹ̀gilọlá*.[24] However, seen as part of this tradition of creative writing, the continuities between *Ìtàn Èmi Ọmọ-Orùkàn*, *Sẹ̀gilọlá* and the travel writing come to the surface, suggesting that although no novels were published in this intervening period, the writers' experiments with genre and literary style did not stop. Although *Sẹ̀gilọlá* may have been 'new in both content and form', as Ògúnsínà puts it, it was not entirely new in terms of experimentation with form, genre, creative writing and address to readers, all of which Thomas and Akintán had also played with in their travel narratives.

Beyond this use of travel writing to experiment with genre, for Thomas and Akintán, however, there was also an eminently practical reason for travelling: their desire to spread their newspapers beyond Lagos. In the opening instalment of his 1929 'Ero L'Ọna', Thomas informed his readers that he was travelling 'fun ire ati ilọsiwaju iwe irohin mi yi' ('for the good and the progress of this, my newspaper') and he reminisced about a previous journey to Minna, Jos, Kaduna and Kano.[25] Indeed, throughout the 1920s, Lagos newspaper editors embarked on publicity tours of Nigeria, during which they 'establish[ed] agents and generally ma[de] themselves known to as many people as possible'.[26] In the late nineteenth and early twentieth centuries, the worldview of the Lagos newspapers had been insular; they were '[q]uite unabashedly [...] specifically concerned with Lagos affairs. Lagos was their point of ultimate reference'.[27] Readerships for these newspapers were typically composed of elite Lagosians, alongside a smaller number of readers scattered across southwest and south-east Nigeria, particularly in towns with a Christian or *Sàró* population. These were small, intimate, but not always reliable readerships; many issues of these

---

[23] Barber, *Print Culture*, p. 7, note 2.

[24] Ogunsina, *Yoruba Novel*, p. 14.

[25] Thomas, 'Idagbere "Ero L'Ọna"', *Akede Eko*, 11 April 1929, p. 7.

[26] F. I. A. Omu, *Press and Politics in Nigeria, 1880–1937* (London: Longman, 1978), p. 84.

[27] Echeruo, *Victorian Lagos*, p. 6.

newspapers appealed to their readers to pay their subscriptions so the newspapers could stay afloat.

However, by the 1920s, the scope, orientation and audiences of the Lagos newspapers were broadening. By 1929, *Akede Eko* had around eight hundred regular readers: small enough to foster what Barber describes as an 'intensely personal and addressive style', but large enough that the editor would not have known all of his readers personally.[28] Although the newspapers continued to address their readers as Lagosians, and filled their pages with reference to Lagos politics and popular culture, hints of readerships beyond Lagos – in the Yoruba hinterland and elsewhere in the colony of Nigeria – began to creep into their pages. The spread of Lagos's newspapers into the Yoruba hinterland and across the southern Nigerian coast in particular reflected the growth of communities of educated migrants from Lagos and the hinterland towns, who were taking advantage of new road, rail and steamer networks to seek new commercial opportunities elsewhere in Nigeria.[29] The newspapers were increasingly read by, and published news about, these communities across Nigeria, often tracing the routes of the rail network as it expanded and enabled the distribution of newspapers and news.

It was in part through personal contact with readers that newspaper editors were able to establish their newspapers amongst new Yoruba-reading readerships beyond Lagos. Thomas represented himself as especially successful in establishing his newspaper beyond Lagos in this way. In 1929, *Akede Eko* boasted in English that 'There is hardly any town in the Province where the *Akede Eko* cannot now be bought. The ambition and energy of this enterprising Editor is well known to many in this community'.[30] Thomas's descriptions of his personal endeavours in the service of his newspaper remind us that, as Karin Barber points out, Yoruba print culture was not an inevitable consequence of the arrival of printing technology, but rather it was 'a creation, an innovation that participants consciously worked on'.[31] These travel narratives play out in front of our eyes one of the forms of work that newspaper editors undertook in order to develop this print culture, as Thomas recounts:

> bo ti jẹ pe irohin 'Akede Eko' yi ti fi ẹsẹ mu'lẹ to ni igboro ilu Ilesha, okiki iwe irohin 'Akede Eko' yi ko ni ẹgbẹ ni igboro ilu Ilesha; ẹnu ya emi papa [...] mo ti tun gbiyanju lati fi ẹsẹ iwe irohin mi 'Akede Eko' na mu'lẹ ninu awọn ilu titun wọnyi bi: – Ọyọ, Awẹ, Ogbomọshọ, Akurẹ, Ondo, Ọwọ, Benin City,

---

[28] Omu, *Press and Politics*, pp. 261–62; Barber, 'Experiments with Genre', p. 174.
[29] See Zachernuk, *Colonial Subjects*, p. 91.
[30] 'News and Notes', *Akede Eko*, 9 May 1929, p. 8.
[31] Barber, 'I. B. Akinyele', p. 47.

Onitsha, Ẹnugu, Aba, laiṣọ ti ilu Port Harcourt to jẹ pe iwe irohin 'Akede Eko' ti di onile ati ọlọna ni igboro ilu na.[32]

since this newspaper Akede Eko has become established in Ilẹ́ṣà, the fame of this newspaper Akede Eko has no competitor in Ilẹ́ṣà; I myself was very surprised [...] I also tried to establish my newspaper Akede Eko amongst these new towns: Ọ̀yọ́, Awẹ́, Ogbómọ̀ṣọ́, Àkúrẹ́, Oǹdó, Ọ̀wọ̀, Benin City, Onitsha, Enugu, Aba, not to mention Port Harcourt, where the Akede Eko newspaper has become a well-established presence in that town.

*Akede Eko*'s circulation did indeed increase from eight hundred to a thousand readers weekly from 1929 to 1930, a period that coincided with some of Thomas's promotional tours, suggesting that his tours may have borne fruit.[33] Travel was thus vital in expanding the readership and scope of the Lagos newspapers, helping sustain them beyond the relatively small audiences that Lagos could offer, and these travel narratives can therefore be understood as the product of the geographical spread of Lagos's print culture.

The publication of travel narratives about those travels therefore became important not only as a literary experiment, and as a way to keep readers hooked, awaiting the next instalment of the series, but as a way to imagine, represent and address these changing readerships established through the editors' travels. Thomas's travel narratives were often addressed directly to readers, as was the custom of the newspapers of the 1920s.[34] He addresses his farewell letter in his 1929 series, for instance:

si ẹnyin ẹbi on ara mi olufẹ, si ẹnyin ọkawe mi, si ẹnyin ọrẹ mi olufẹ, si ẹnyin alabaṣiṣẹ mi ọwọn, ati si olukuluku ẹnyin enia ti ẹ o da mi l'ọla lati ka iwe idagbere mi yi

to you my beloved family and relatives, to you my readers, to you my dear friends, to you my dear colleagues, and to each of you who will do me the honour of reading this farewell letter of mine.[35]

Readers also found their way into the travelogues themselves. Contrary to the emphasis on the landscape common in many colonial travelogues in the British tradition, Thomas's travel narratives are intensely peopled: they display an exuberant sociability centred on the writer, his hosts and his readers. Thomas's representation of his fellow Yoruba migrants who had settled across the southern Nigerian coast is informed not by the travel writer's gaze, but by

[32] Thomas, 'Ero L'Ọna', *Akede Eko*, 14 March 1931, p. 6.
[33] Omu, *Press and Politics*, pp. 261–2.
[34] Barber, *Print Culture*, pp. 42–8.
[35] Thomas, 'Idagbere "Ero L'Ọna"', *Akede Eko*, 11 April 1929, p. 7.

dialogue, interactions and social relationships, to the extent that some of the most sociable of his travel narratives are almost overwhelmed by the author's namedropping. For instance, Thomas's 1931 travel series encompasses more than seventy named people, friends, business contacts and important local figures, alongside many unnamed 'friends and acquaintances' and townspeople, and numerous newspaper readers. In his 1926 series 'Ero L'Ọna', Thomas mentions meeting 'ọrẹ ati ojulumọ' ('friends and acquaintances') in Forcados, while in Warri he meets a friend, Joseph Akiwowo, whose brother knew Thomas's father-in-law.[36] In Sapele, friends and acquaintances host a ball for him. In Koko, he meets 'Ọgbẹni M. T. Clarke, ojulowo ọmọ Eko ti o nṣe Postmaster ilu na, Ọgbẹni na yọ gidigidi lati ri mi nitoripe a jumọ ṣe ọmọde pọ ni *School* Faji, nigba ọdun gbọrọ' ('Mr. M. T. Clarke, a true Lagosian who is working as the Postmaster of this town, and this gentleman was full of joy to see me, because we were together as children in Faji School very many years ago'), while in Ijerimi, near Warri, he comes across 'awọn ọmọ ilu wọnyi diẹ ti mo ti kọ l'ẹkọ ni ile-iwe' ('a few of the townspeople whom I taught in school').[37] Thomas also cements new connections he has made on his journey (although again without naming non-Yoruba Nigerians) thanking 'awọn Jẹkiri lọkunrin ati lobinrin ti nko fi igbakan mọ tẹlẹ ri' ('the Itsekiri men and women whom I hadn't known previously').[38]

Thomas's hosts and contacts were from literate and professional circles: clerks, traders, teachers, shop owners, pastors, postmasters, a produce buyer and a medical officer. Although most of his encounters are with people bearing Yoruba or *Sàró* names, he describes occasional meetings with other members of the local elite, Gold Coasters and Europeans, whom he mentions by name – but not with Igbo-, Ijaw- and Itsekiri-speakers, with whom he rarely represents substantial encounters. Those people whose religion he mentions were almost entirely Christians, many of whom had migrated from Lagos or had family connections there. Thomas's frenetic sociability even encompasses deceased ancestors, so that his networks spread across time as well as space; he describes a meeting with Archdeacon D. C. Crowther in which Crowther was delighted to discover that Thomas was 'okan ninu awọn ọmọ-ọmọ Daddy-Ẹlẹkun ni igboro ita-Balogun' ('one of the grandchildren of Daddy-Ẹlẹkún in the town of Ìta-Balógun').[39] Thomas thus uses his travel narratives to reinforce social and business ties with Lagosians and other readers and acquaintances across the region.

---

[36] Thomas, 'Ero L'Ọna', *Eleti-Ọfẹ*, 12 May 1926, p. 7.
[37] Thomas, 'Ero L'Ọna', *Eleti-Ọfẹ*, 16 June 1926; 30 June 1926, p. 8.
[38] Thomas, 'Ero L'Ọna', *Eleti-Ọfẹ*, 23 June 1926, p. 7.
[39] Thomas, 'Ero L'Ọna', *Akede Eko*, 9 May 1929, p. 4.

Akintán and Ajíṣafẹ́, too, depicted the Yoruba region as permeated with friends, colleagues and acquaintances. E. A. Akintán's fourteen-part series 'Irin Ajo Lati Eko Lọ si Ileṣa' ('Journey from Lagos to Iléṣà', 1926–27) documents Akintán's journey from Lagos to Iléṣà via Ìbàdàn, Ọ̀yọ́ and Ilé-Ifẹ̀. Akintán does not state any explicit interest in knowing about the Yoruba region, or re-acquainting Lagosians with the hinterland. Rather, his narrative describes his own relationships with the Yoruba-educated elite. Print culture and Christianity maintain many of Akintán's relationships, as he encounters editors, priests, writers and schoolteachers, and even 'Ọgbẹni Alagba kan' ('one elder gentleman') selling newspapers who knows Akintán's work:

> O ni gbogbo iwe irohin Eko li on nka; mo juwe ara mi fun u pe Oniwe-irohin *Eleti-Ọfẹ* ni mi; ẹnu ya a inu rẹ si dun lati ri mi; ọkan ninu awọn ọrọ rẹ niyi: '*Are you the Editor? I have read of your tour in your paper, I am pleased to meet you.*'[40]

> He said he read all the Lagos newspapers; I introduced myself to him as the editor of the *Eleti-Ọfẹ*. He was surprised and happy to see me. One of the things he said was: 'Are you the Editor? I have read of your tour in the paper, I am pleased to meet you.'

A. K. Ajíṣafẹ́'s travels, meanwhile, were concerned not with the spread of the newspapers but with his own research for his historical writing. Nonetheless, his travel narrative centres on accounts of social contacts, in his case with *ọba*s and other rulers who helped him with his research, as well as colonial officials who helped arrange his visits, and also over twenty relatives and friends, clerks, pastors, church congregations and the Ẹ̀gbá Association of Ifẹ. Thus even where this sociability is less connected to the newspapers' own spread, travel narratives allow the writer to constitute his social self in print, establishing Ajíṣafẹ́'s wealth in people and his connections to the elites of the Yoruba hinterland through the written word.

The writers' displays of sociability were accompanied by ritualised representations of their hosts' hospitality, to the extent that sometimes the travel narratives read as vehicles for displays of gratitude and connectedness. They praise qualities of their hosts, especially their hospitality – they welcome Thomas 't'ọwọ t'ẹsẹ' ('with open arms') or 'gẹgẹbi ọba ti nṣe enia l'alejo' ('in just the way a king treats a visitor') – as if the narratives are *oríkì* (praise poetry) transformed into writing.[41] It is also possible that Thomas was aware of libel cases increasingly landing at the feet of newspaper editors, and was careful to avoid

---

[40] E. A. Akintan, 'Irin Ajo Lati Eko Lọ Si Ileṣa', *Eleti-Ọfẹ*, 9 February 1927, p. 4.
[41] Thomas, 'Ero L'Ọna', *Akede Eko*, 9 May 1929, p. 7; thanks to Kelly Askew (personal communication, 23 April 2012) for this observation.

anything but assertions of his hosts' good character.[42] But in a piece called 'Irin-Ajo' ('Travelling') which prefaces his 1929 travel narrative, Thomas outlines a distinctively Yoruba travelling sociability based on *ìwà* (character):

> Bi o ti le wun ki awọn Yoruba tabi ọmọ Eko meji ma rẹ pọ to ni ile, ṣugbọn nigba nwọn ba f'oju ganni arawọn ni idalẹ, bi ọmọ iya ni nwọn mba arawọn lo pọ; iwa yi dara pupọ, o si yẹ fun wa gẹgẹbi ọmọ Yoruba lati ṣ'ogo le iwa rere na l'ori; ẹ jẹ ki gbogbo wa papa awọn enia wa ti nwọn mbẹ ni idalẹ tubọ ma tẹ siwaju nipa titẹle iwa rere na.[43]

> However much Yorubas or two Lagosians may not be on good terms at home, when they run into each other in a distant land, they get on like children of the same mother. This behaviour is very good. And it is befitting for us as Yorubas to boast about this good character. Let us, especially our people abroad, increasingly make progress in following this good character.

The travel narratives can be read as an opportunity for Thomas to portray both himself and his hosts as *ọmọlúwàbí* – people of good character – amid webs of reciprocated welcome and hospitality.

What is so important about the hospitality that Thomas encounters is, therefore, that it is recorded in print for readers to see. A power play of reciprocity is enacted through the printed text; his hosts' hospitality puts Thomas in their debt, so in return he offers a display and archiving in print of his hosts' generosity. When Thomas encounters a car belonging to his hosts in Aba he stresses the spectacle of the resplendent car and its driver's splendid uniform. This is so, Thomas jokes, because the driver had been told that if he did not impress Thomas, the *Akede Eko* 'yio kede rẹ fun araiye gbọ' ('would proclaim it for the world to hear').[44] Thomas represents his own power as generating the owner's light-hearted but calculated display of hospitality; that power is produced by Thomas's ability to broadcast the printed word to a wider readership. Thomas generates a form of authorship centred on his ability to write about others. His praises of his hosts are performative and generative; by holding out the possibility of naming someone publicly as a generous host, it makes future hosts generous, reminiscent of the way *oríkì* are imagined to actualise the latent qualities of a person that they name.[45]

---

[42] Accusations of libel were an ever-present threat for colonial West African newspapers; see Ayo Olukotun, 'At the Barricades: Resurgent Media in Colonial Nigeria, 1900–1960', in *The Foundations of Nigeria: Essays in Honour of Toyin Falola,* ed. by Adebayo Oyebade (Trenton: Africa World Press, 2003), pp. 237–9.

[43] Thomas, 'Irin-Ajo', *Akede Eko*, 11 April 1929, p. 6.

[44] Thomas, 'Ero L'Ọna', *Akede Eko*, 16 May 1929, p. 7.

[45] Karin Barber, *I Could Speak until Tomorrow: Oriki, Women and the Past in a Yoruba Town* (Edinburgh: Edinburgh University Press, 1991), pp. 75–8.

Thomas's textual representations of encounters with readers and patrons as he travelled moreover allowed him to claim that his readers were not rhetorical, imagined audiences, but actual readers, named and co-opted into the text. Just as Thomas depicts his network of acquaintances stretching beyond Lagos, so too he imagines readers of *Akede Eko* permeating the towns to which he travels. In 1929, Thomas reports an encounter with a prominent newspaper reader in Port Harcourt:

> inu mi si dun pupọ lati gbọ wipe ẹni're Lọya Lucas jẹ ọkan pataki ni ilu Pọta yi to nka iwe irohin (Akede Eko) nigbagbogbo; ẹnu kekere kọ lo si ya mi nigbati Lọya Lucas ba 'Kudi' (owo) lu mi wipe on fi ṣe iranl'ọwọ fun mi ninu iṣẹ iwe irohin na.[46]

> I was very pleased to hear as well how the good Lawyer Lucas was one of the important people of this Port Harcourt who reads the newspaper (*Akede Eko*) all the time; I was greatly surprised when Lawyer Lucas gave me 'Kudi' (money) to assist me in the enterprise of the newspaper.

Thomas was using the travel narratives to bolster the newspaper's reputation in the eyes of its existing and potential readership, by representing its eminent and growing readership. In the midst of his 1931 'Ero L'Ọna' series, Thomas printed a separate article in which he named seventeen men whom he thanked for hosting him on his journey.[47] It is not clear whether these hosts were actual readers of the newspaper; the list of names can be read as a rhetorical gesture designed to advertise Thomas's connectedness. Nonetheless, the text implies or even conscripts these hosts as readers – in Garrett Stewart's sense of the reader 'conscripted' or 'deliberately drafted' by the text to play particular roles, as 'part of the script' – and in doing so it marshals them as evidence of the newspaper's readership beyond Lagos.[48]

But it is also possible that readers may have 'rebelled against, complied with or simply ignored' textual instructions, conventions or attempts to control reader responses.[49] In his study of early 19th-century British readerships, Jon Klancher attributes writers' increasingly conscious creation of readerships to the uncertainty of the eighteenth century when 'no single, unified "reading public" could be addressed' and writers 'carved out new readerships and

---

[46] Thomas, 'Ero L'Ọna', *Akede Eko*, 9 May 1929, p. 6.

[47] Thomas, 'A Lọ Were! A Bọ Were!! Oju T'ẹni Ti Ko Lọ!!!', *Akede Eko*, 21 March 1931, p. 8.

[48] Garrett Stewart, *Dear Reader: The Conscripted Audience in Nineteenth-Century British Fiction* (Baltimore: John Hopkins University Press, 1996), pp. 6, 8.

[49] Stephen Colclough, *Consuming Texts: Readers and Reading Communities, 1695–1870* (Basingstoke: Palgrave Macmillan, 2007), p. 15.

transformed old ones'.[50] In the Lagos newspaper travel narratives we read the authors' attempts to suggest how readers should respond to a growing print sphere, as the newspapers' readerships were similarly no longer necessarily just Lagosians, but could rather potentially be convened across Nigeria. Thomas depicts himself addressing and meeting his readers, but simultaneously he represents the expanding scope of the newspapers, such that the newspaper editor could no longer know all his readers. We could therefore read in the travel narratives what Patrick Brantlinger describes as 'the nervousness of authors about how their stories may be misinterpreted by readers whom they have no way of knowing.[51]

By encountering and naming his readers and potential readers, Thomas develops a sense of a sociable print culture based on displaying and addressing friends and readers in an apparently intimate tone, while also aspiring towards ever greater readerships. The travel narratives thus textualise their writers' own importance as social actors, and the newspapers' growing local, regional and, implicitly, Nigerian readerships. Their emphasis on dialogue and sociability is a function not only of the writers' relationship with their Lagosian migrant and other elite 'travellees' – as partners in 'civilisation', rather than the coloniser–subject relationship of much contemporaneous European travel writing about Africa – but also of their addressive print culture, which enabled and expected the incorporation of readers, patrons and 'travellees'.

## Cannibals and 'civilisation' in the world beyond Lagos

However, not all the people they encountered were represented as readers or fellow elites. These writers travelled with a characteristically colonial Lagosian sense of themselves as distinct from other Nigerians, including fellow Yoruba speakers from the hinterland, in their claims to 'civilisation'.[52] These Lagosian writers, many of whom were *Sàró*, were familiar with both European and African ways of life. The educated elite amongst the *Sàró* dominated the professions and commerce in colonial Lagos. Together with the *Àgùdà* (also descendants of former slaves, but who had returned from Brazil and Cuba rather than Sierra Leone), what J. Lorand Matory has characterised as their 'creole' culture, which revolved around their diasporic connections, literacy and Christianity, meant that they were initially quite separate from both Lagos's indigenes, who were,

[50] Jon P. Klancher, *The Making of English Reading Audiences, 1790–1832* (Madison: University of Wisconsin Press, 1987), p. 3.
[51] Patrick Brantlinger, *The Reading Lesson: The Threat of Mass Literacy in Nineteenth-Century British Fiction* (Bloomington, IN: Indiana University Press, 1998), p. 19, cited in Colclough, *Consuming Texts*, p. 21.
[52] Echeruo, *Victorian Lagos*, pp. 29–49.

as Karin Barber writes, 'predominantly non-literate, pagan or Muslim, and organised in traditional kinship groups', and also from the Yoruba hinterland, in which many of the Sàrós' origins lay but to which they did not always have direct links, kinship ties having been disrupted by their own or their ancestors' capture as slaves.[53] Even in the 1920s, when many of the Sàró had lived in Lagos for several generations, and when more Lagosians had attended school and were therefore beginning to take lower-level white-collar jobs, the Sàró maintained their distinct culture; as Karin Barber writes, they referred to themselves in the Yoruba newspapers as 'the onìṣòkòtò gbòọrọ – the long-trousered ones – as distinct from the alágbádá, those who wear traditional robes'.[54] These Lagosians were thus 'cultural brokers' who celebrated their ability to stand at a crossroads between 'European' and 'African' culture, who saw themselves as having a distinct role in translating what they perceived as 'civilised' life into local circumstances, but who were also not afraid to speak out from time to time about the failings of British colonial culture and politics.[55]

In accordance with this sense of their distinctiveness as Lagosians, the travel writers represented themselves as first and foremost Lagosians in their travel narratives. Lagos was the place from which all of their journeys started, and to which other places were compared. According to Ajeji, for instance, the trains in Victoria were 'dabi eyi ti o ti wa larin Eko ri' ('like those in Lagos before'), while the yams in Calabar were much cheaper than those of Lagos. Gay, meanwhile, tells readers that Badagry is 'one-eighth of Lagos in size'.[56] Thomas writes of Lagos as the known place that could be compared with the unknown and the strange, and as an emblem of the fast-moving pace of modern life: 'nigbati mo wo irisi ilu Sapẹlẹ lọ garaga, a le fi we gẹgẹbi Ebute Mẹta ti ri niwọn ọdun mẹdogun sẹhin' ('when I extensively viewed the city of Sapele, we were able to compare how Èbúté Mẹ́ta looked fifteen years previously').[57] After making several similarly unfavourable comparisons between Sapele and Lagos, he concludes 'anu nla ṣe mi lọpọlọpọ pe: "KO SI IBIKAN TO DABI ILE"' ('I was very sorry indeed that, "THERE'S NO PLACE LIKE HOME"').[58]

The result of this focus on Lagos as the centre of their world was a stratified representation of other Nigerians, based on perceived differences of

---

[53] Barber, *Print Culture*, p. 14; Matory, *Black Atlantic Religion*, p. 51.
[54] Ibid. p. 15.
[55] Paulo Fernando de Moraes Farias and Karin Barber, 'Introduction', in *Self-Assertion and Brokerage: Early Cultural Nationalism in West Africa*, ed. by Paulo Fernando de Moraes Farias and Karin Barber (Birmingham: Centre of West African Studies, 1990), pp. 1–10 (p. 1).
[56] Ajeji, 'Irin-Ajo Lati Eko Lọ Si Kamerun', *Eko Akete*, 16 June 1923, p. 4; Gay, 'A Travellers' Obsevations', *Eleti-Ọfẹ*, 1 September 1926, p. 10.
[57] Thomas, 'Ero L'Ọna!', *Eleti-Ọfẹ*, 26 May 1926, p. 8.
[58] Thomas, 'Ero L'Ọna!', *Eleti-Ọfẹ*, 2 June 1926, p. 8.

'civilisation'. Thomas was the Yoruba newspaper travel writer who travelled most frequently to the south and southeast of Nigeria. In his accounts of these journeys, while he celebrates the acquaintance of both Lagosian migrants and the local elites, when describing other non-Lagosian, non-elite peoples he sometimes uses tropes of exoticism and disgust, comparing the region and its people unfavourably with Lagos. Thomas did not avoid the exoticising metaphors and rhetoric characteristic of colonial travel writing simply because he was writing about fellow Africans. He writes of distinctions of class, 'civilisation' and, implicitly, ethnicity – rather than race, as was often the case in colonial travel writing – premised on the perceived difference between the *Sàró* culture of Lagos and the other places to which he travelled, especially those beyond the Yoruba region. Thus, he describes a market in Burutu as making him feel sick:

> mo ṣakiyesi kokoro yiyan kan ti a sin wọn sinu igi ti o dabi idin nla ni wiwo, ti awọn Jẹkiri npe ni 'Ogongo', a sọ fun mi pe ohun ti nwọn fi njẹ koko-gari niyẹn, wiwo lasan ti mo wo kini na nrin mi laiya ambọtori jijẹ.[59]

> I noticed a roasted insect which they thread on skewers and which looked like a huge maggot, which the Itsekiri call 'Ogongo'. I was told that they eat them with coarse gari – just looking at it made me feel nauseous, not to speak of eating it.

Even more explicitly, he describes nakedness and animalistic behaviour, and invokes fears of cannibalism as he travels between Port Harcourt and Onitsha: on seeing people walking naked by the side of the road, Thomas asks 'awọn enia ha ni wọnyi tabi ẹranko igbẹ?' ('are these people or wild animals?'), and comments that he hopes missionaries will visit them soon to 'kọ awọn onihoho wọnyi ki nwọn le di afin'ju lati le ma fi aṣọ bo ibi aṣiri wọn' ('teach these naked people, so that they can become civilised, so that they can wear clothes to cover their private parts').[60] Thomas reports that when he previously came across the 'Dewo' people in 1913, 'oju nwọn ran'ko bi ẹranko inu igbe' ('their eyes were fierce, like those of animals in the bush') and, he alleges, they were cannibals who specialised in eating Yoruba people:[61]

> Oju awọn Dewo wọnyi ran'ko tobẹgẹ ninu odun 1913 fun ẹran-enia ni jijẹ, papa nwọn fẹran ẹran-ara awọn yoruba lati fi lo igba tabi duniyan nipa fifi se iṣu jẹ de ipo wipe gbogbo awa ara-Eko to wa ni ilu na lasiko yi kun fun ibẹru nla gidigidi.

[59] Thomas, 'Ero L'Ọna', *Eleti-Ọfẹ*, 12 May 1926, p. 7.
[60] Thomas, 'Ero L'Ọna', *Akede Eko*, 23 May 1929, p. 8.
[61] 'Dewo', which is taken from the Igbo greeting 'ndewo', is Thomas's name for the local people, probably corresponding to the Igbo or Ikwerre people.

Bi a ba wa l'ọja won, ti nwọn ba ṣakiyesi pe ara Eko tabi yoruba kan nla-ogun-ara, ni ṣe ni awọn Dewo wọnyi yio ma f'ọwọ wọn tọ ogun-ara oluwarẹ la s'ẹnu wọn; nwọn yio sin ma fi ede ilu wọn sọ bayi pe: – 'Ora lo pọ l'ara eleyi bayi!'

Ṣugbọn l'oni, awọn Ijoba Gẹsi ti gba'na oju awọn Dewo na nipa ọna bayi; ṣugbọn bi enia ba lọ jẹ alejo ni ilu na, ti oluwarẹ ba lọ rin irin-kurin lati lọ bọ s'ọwọ awọn enia na; bi idan ni nwọn yio fi oluwarẹ p'ata sinu iṣasun wọn.[62]

These Dewo were so avid for human flesh in 1913, they especially liked Yoruba flesh to eat with boiled yam for enjoyment or at festivities, to the extent that all we Lagosians who were in the town at that time were greatly afraid.

When we were at their markets, if they noticed that a Lagosian or a Yoruba was sweating, these Dewo would actually use their hands to touch the person's sweat and put it into their mouths; and they would use their language to say: 'This one is good and fat!'

But today, the English rulers have put an end to this habit of the Dewo people, but if anyone goes to be a visitor in the town, and that person falls, on his ill-fated wanderings, into these people's hands, like magic they will devour the person in their soup-pots.

Thomas's rhetoric of disgust, exoticism and cannibalism is similar in tone to colonial discourse about Africa, with which the Lagos newspaper writers are likely to have been familiar. The anglophone Lagos newspapers occasionally printed foreign-authored travel writing about West Africa, such as the *Lagos Weekly Record*'s publication in 1910 of 'Impressions of Lagos' by Frank Voce, and 'Lagos Through Foreign Eyes' by 'A Traveller'.[63] However, Lagosian readers of European travel accounts did not simply absorb the imperial rhetoric that such travel accounts often wielded. Reviews of European travel writing about Nigeria in the anglophone newspapers suggest a familiarity with the conventions of travel writing that verged on contempt for their imperial rhetoric. The *Lagos Standard* gives a sardonic account of a talk by 'Captain E. A. Steel R.F.A. who is reported to be an officer who took part in "the expedition which explored the previously unpenetrated area in Southern Nigeria"'. Deploring Steel's stereotyped account of his travels – claiming to be the first to encounter 'tribes' who had never left the village eking out an existence with bows and arrows, along with tales of human sacrifice, polygamy and fattening ceremonies – the *Standard* retorts, '[i]t is surprising that at this enlightened day, any one should be found bold enough to try to palm off such tales upon

---

[62] Thomas, 'Ero L'Ọna', *Akede Eko*, 2 May 1929, p. 4.
[63] Frank Voce, 'Impressions of Lagos', *Lagos Weekly Record*, 14 May 1910, p. 5; A Traveller, 'Lagos through Foreign Eyes', *Lagos Weekly Record*, 6 August 1910, p. 3.

the public, and more surprising still that people are to be found who are simple enough to listen to, and receive them in all seriousness'. Seeking to undermine the colonial explorer posture, the *Standard* concludes:

> The fact of the matter is that there is no part of Southern Nigeria that has not been explored over and over by the white man during the last twenty years. It is therefore remarkable, to say the least, that it should be left to Captain STEEL to be the first to observe and report upon these characteristics of the people.[64]

While Thomas does not make explicit reference to European travel writing, it seems likely he would have been familiar with its conventions. In particular, he may have had access to missionary travel reports via Lagos's well-established CMS Bookshop.[65] Thomas also may have known Samuel Àjàyí Crowther's work (see Chapter 1): he was acquainted with Crowther's son (Archdeacon D. C. Crowther, whom Thomas reports meeting on one of his journeys) and grandson, Herbert Macaulay, whose biography Thomas wrote. The trope of cannibalism could therefore have drawn on depictions of cannibalism familiar to these writers from both African and European missionary travel writing about West Africa, as a way of representing the supposed danger of the 'other'. The trope was also circulating in the Lagos press in the early twentieth century; the *Lagos Standard* newspaper, for instance, reported in 1909 on an account of the 'degenerate tribes of the south' engaging, like their counterparts in the Congo, in cannibalism and human sacrifice, although it also noted that such reports 'may be regarded as a sort of salve to the European consience [sic] for the iniquitous wars waged upon unarmed and defenceless natives from time to time', and was sceptical about the truth of such reports: 'If human life were held in such cheap estimation by the Native, and so wantonly destroyed as is reported, Southern Nigeria would by this time have been a wild waste of country, instead of containing the teeming millions it possesses.'[66]

Thomas's supposed fear and disgust, and his appeal to missionary enlightenment, surely owe something to what the *Standard* characterises as imperial rhetoric, of the kind that David Spurr identifies as debasement.[67] Moreover, they constitute an attempt to distance his Lagosian self from other regions of the colony, to reinforce his status as part of the Lagosian cultural elite, the 'cultural brokers' between Nigeria and the British. At the same time, his invocation of cannibalism also seems designed to tease his readership, to heighten the drama

---

[64] 'Lagosian on Dits', *Lagos Standard*, 10 March 1909, p. 4.
[65] Doortmont, 'Recapturing the Past', pp. 41–7.
[66] Janus, 'Lagosian on Dits', *Lagos Standard*, 5 May 1909, p. 4.
[67] David Spurr, *The Rhetoric of Empire: Colonial Discourse in Journalism, Travel Writing and Imperial Administration* (Durham, NC: Duke University Press, 1993), pp. 76–91.

and to enhance Thomas's self-presentation as an adventurer, particularly in the 'Dewo' people's preference for Yoruba flesh: the only demographic likely to be reading this Yoruba-language narrative.

But the trope of cannibalism also seems related to this particular moment of intra-Nigerian encounter, deploying its power as a 'key metaphor for the threat of incorporation into savagery' that Kelly Watson identifies in the context of imperial encounters in the North Atlantic; here, Thomas may be read as gesturing not to the imperial encounter, but rather to his fear of being incorporated, consumed or swallowed up by Nigeria, which encompasses these non-Christian cannibals whom he presents as so distinct from his Lagosian sensibilities, and who continue to threaten to 'devour' Lagosians and Yorubas who leave their home regions to approach them.[68] Elsewhere in Africa, at least four late nineteenth-century travelogues by Swahili authors also refer to African cannibalism, with one of the authors doing so as a metaphor for the way that the people of Zanzibar will 'eat' a traveller's money 'when they see that someone does not know the language of Zanzibar'.[69] I. B. Thomas's reference to cannibalism is not explicitly metaphorical in this way; nonetheless it may also draw on this potentiality of cannibalism as a metaphor for the vulnerability of the traveller away from home, unable to speak the languages of southeast Nigeria and encountering a colony full of as yet little-known others.

For Thomas, therefore, the intra-Nigerian otherness he encounters on his travels is structured by the contrast between Lagosian and colonial, missionary norms and people who are Nigerian subjects, and yet, to his eyes, are not like him: they are not Christian, they do not speak English, and their bodies are not presented in the 'civilised' fashion. And yet, simultaneously, in calling for them to be taught to wear clothes, Thomas suggests that these people's otherness could be transformed into familiarity, as fellow partners in civilisation, if they had access to the accoutrements of civilisation such as clothing and Christianity. In doing so, he echoes some more paternalistic forms of nineteenth-century humanitarian and Christian missionary travel writing by Europeans, which represented Africans as either innocent children or noble savages ripe for being redeemed through Christianity. Simultaneously, though, in a striking echo of Samuel Àjàyí Crowther several decades earlier (see Chapter 1), Thomas turns the figures of the cannibal and the naked Nigerian into one who might be saved, rendering them a 'fallen mortal', as Ọlákúnlé George writes, rather

---

[68] Kelly L. Watson, *Insatiable Appetites: Imperial Encounters with Cannibals in the North Atlantic World* (New York and London: NYU Press, 2015), p. 170.

[69] Thomas Geider, 'Early Swahili Travelogues', *Matatu – Journal for African Culture and Society,* 9 (1992), pp. 27–65 (p. 52).

than an irredeemable savage.[70] He thus emphasises the performative rather than essentialised or race-based nature of 'civilisation'.

Moreover, in the very same Burutu market in which he describes being repulsed by maggots, Thomas also gives the Yoruba names for several varieties of fish available, as if to stress the commonalities between Lagos and this market in faraway Burutu. He depicts himself enjoying interactions with some local people, and he learns a few phrases of Itsekiri and Igbo:

> bi mo ti duro l'ẹnu ọna ile mi, bẹni mo ngbọ: – Ndo, ado! ndo, ado!! ndo, ado!!! eyi ni ede ti awọn Ṣẹkiri fi nki enia; ko si ede miran fun nwọn mọ lati fi ki enia bikoṣe awọn ede yi nikan; bi nwọn ma ki ọ ku owurọ tabi ku asan ati ku alẹ, tabi bi nwọn yio ba ọ kẹdun fun ohunkohun laiye yi, ko si ede miran fun nwọn mọ bikoṣe:- *Ndo, ado! ndo, ado!! ndo, ado!!!*

> As I stood at the doorway of my house, I heard: *'Ndo, ado! Ndo, ado!! Ndo, ado!!!'* This was the language that the Itsekiri were using to greet people. There are no other words for them to use to greet each other except for this alone. If they greet you for the morning, or the afternoon, or the evening, or if they offer condolences for anything in life, there are no other words for them except *'Ndo, ado! Ndo, ado!! Ndo, ado!!!'*[71]

Thomas also takes pleasure in the strangeness of these places beyond Lagos – and in their potential to make good stories – and he envisages his travel narratives helping readers know these places better, forming a textual and linguistic connection with them through the possibilities of translation across ethnolinguistic boundaries, through the pages of the newspaper.

Others of the Lagos newspaper travel narratives were concerned not so much with strangeness within other parts of Nigeria, but rather with the nearby Yoruba region in which the writers claimed their ancestry. E. A. Akintán's fourteen-part travel narrative, 'Irin Ajo Lati Eko Lọ si Ileṣa' (1926–27), emphasises the cohesiveness of the Yoruba region. The series documents Akintán's journey from Lagos to Ilẹ́ṣà via the Yoruba towns of Ìbàdàn, Ọ̀yọ́ and Ilé-Ifẹ̀. In each town, Akintán writes of the people he meets, his impressions of the town and the changes he has noticed. The overriding impression produced by Akintán's narratives is that he is visiting different but comprehensible places within the same Yoruba cultural and social world. Indeed, although Akintán describes the geographies of the towns he visits, his narratives do not in fact particularly distinguish these towns from one another; he visits the same types of churches and schools, meets the same types of people and receives the same hospitality everywhere he goes.

---

[70] George, *African Literature*, p. 74.
[71] Thomas, 'Ero L'Ọna!', *Eleti-Ọfẹ*, 26 May 1926, p. 8.

Over the course of his series, he produces a sense of the region as a whole, comparing Yoruba towns to one another: 'Ọna Motọ lati Ilẹṣa lọ si Oṣogbo dara pupọ ju lati Ile-Ifẹ lọ si Ilẹṣa lọ; ko si iyọnu kankan, tarara ni ọkọ nlọ lori rẹ' ('The motor road from Iléṣà to Òṣogbo is much better than the road from Ilé-Ifẹ̀ to Iléṣà. There was no trouble at all, the vehicle went smoothly on it').[72] He discusses the commonalities between towns, with his experience as a traveller seemingly giving him a panoramic sense of the Yoruba region as a whole: 'Ohun ti o wọpọ larin awọn ara ilu oke ni pe ibikibi ti Afin Ọba wọn ba gbe wa, ọja ko nṣai si nibẹ; bayi ni mo ri i l'Ọyọ, Ibadan, Ile-Ifẹ, Oṣogbo ati Ilẹṣa' ('The thing that is common amongst the people of the hinterland is that wherever the Palace of their King is, there could not fail to be a market there. That is how I saw it in Òyọ́, Ìbàdàn, Ilé-Ifẹ̀, Òṣogbo and Iléṣà').[73] For Akintán, the Yoruba-speaking region is heterogeneous, but he emphasises its shared features more than its differences.

Writers of accounts of visits by their hometown associations to towns in the Yoruba hinterland, such as Adélaní Gbogboadé and 'Ọmọ Ẹgbẹ', similarly proclaimed the close links between Lagos and towns in the Yoruba hinterland, often representing themselves as having prestigious social links in the hinterland, but also established their distance from these regions as visiting Lagosians rather than residents of the towns. Meanwhile, the pseudonymous writer Gay's English-language narrative 'A Travellers' Obsevations' [sic] in *Eleti-Ọfẹ* from August to September 1926, which described a trip to Ìbàdàn, Ìkòròdú and Badagry, offered an alternative approach, focusing less on sociability and networks and more on distinctions between Lagos and surrounding towns, particularly in terms of their 'modernity'. Gay explains that he travelled partly in order to 'increase my stock of knowledge of the custom, language and views of the various countries with which Lagos is surrounded.' In doing so, he suggests that the 'countries with which Lagos is surrounded' are distinct from Lagos, but nonetheless significant enough to Lagos that he ought to know them better. His travel narrative makes a further distinction between Badagry and the Yoruba cities of Ìbàdàn and Abẹ́òkúta, assessing them in terms of their achievement of the 'modern'. 'Speaking from the standpoint of modern development', Gay writes, Badagry is 'very, very backward, she lacks almost everything modern. There are no metalled roads, and no means of communication, consequently there is no means of carrying on trade advantageously.' The piece ends with a discussion of Christianity in Badagry to further cement the writer's sense of its backwardness: he tells readers that though Badagry was 'the first country in Nigeria to embrace Christianity [...] speaking of the religious activity in

---

[72] Akintan, 'Irin Ajo Lati Eko Lọ Si Ilẹṣa', *Eleti-Ọfẹ*, 5 January 1927, p. 5.
[73] Akintan, 'Irin Ajo Lati Eko Lọ Si Ilẹṣa', *Eleti-Ọfẹ*, 29 December 1926, p. 5.

Badagry to-day is simply to admit that the passage in the Scripture which says – The first shall be the last and the last shall be the first is true.'[74]

In Ìbàdàn, Gay similarly paints a picture of what he perceives as 'modern', but in contrast to Badagry this is pictured through presence rather than absence: Ìbàdàn has new 'splendid roads', along with 'decent houses and Offices', and '[n]ew trading firms.' 'Educationally Ibadan is undoubtedly progressing most wonderful', he reports; 'there are besides day schools of different denominations, Roman Catholic and C.M.S. Grammar Schools and the Wesley College', whose Principals 'are said to be managing the institutions in such a scientific manner that nothing could be desired to make the students more efficient'. Gay also describes an interview with D. A. Ọbasá, editor of *The Yoruba News*, a newspaper established in Ìbàdàn in 1924.[75] Ọbasá, Gay remarks approvingly, has 'great interest in the development of the country and the welfare of his race.' Ìbàdàn, Gay determines, again gesturing to the notion of progress, is 'decidedly making great stride [sic] in almost all directions'.[76] Thus Gay, like Thomas, offers a sense of hierarchies of civilisation and progress in the region beyond Lagos, assessing these regions on how far they match up to his own ideals of modernity, but also imagining that these places can make progress, even if currently 'backward', through the active work of intellectuals such as Ọbasá to maintain 'development' and the advantages that Christianity and other forms of perceived 'modernity' confer.

Therefore, despite the differing relations to the regions beyond Lagos that they encountered on their journeys, a sense of exceptionalism pervades most of these travel narratives, as their Lagosian writers imagine themselves to have a special role to play in translating 'civilisation', the Yoruba hinterland and other places in the region to one another, while still revelling in their own distinct Lagosian social and intellectual world. Although the writers represent difference, this is often centred on bodies and on differences of 'civilisation'. Where they face differences of language and culture, they find it sometimes relatively straightforward to translate them into something recognisable, either through literal translation of language, as in Thomas's case, or by appealing to a broader shared sense of being Yoruba or sometimes of being 'African' – though never 'Nigerian' – which makes comprehensible things that might otherwise seem strange. Indeed, although some of these writers travelled beyond Lagos and the Yoruba region to other parts of Nigeria, and nationalist ideas were starting to take shape in Lagos's political culture and in its newspapers in the 1920s – particularly Herbert Macaulay's *Lagos Daily News* – neither the word 'Nigeria' nor explicit discussions of the Nigerian nation appear in these travel narratives,

[74] Gay, 'A Travellers' Obsevations', *Eleti-Ọfẹ*, 1 September 1926, p. 10.
[75] Falola, *Yoruba Gurus*, pp. 21–2.
[76] Gay, 'A Traveller's Observations', *Eleti-Ọfẹ*, 18 August 1926, pp. 8–9.

with the exception of Gay's English-language account of Ìbàdàn and Badagry.[77] Thus although the Yoruba newspaper travel writers of the 1920s are writing within the region we now conceive of as Nigeria, and in retrospect we can read their writing as seeking to orient themselves, their values and their newspapers within that nation, their travel narratives do not explicitly create Nigerian subjectivities, but rather focus on the writers' varying senses of themselves as both Lagosians and Yoruba speakers, and as simultaneously both strangers and people with connections within the spaces in which they travel. The writers are not necessarily refusing the notion of Nigeria, but rather are more interested in the interaction between other regions and communal formations: Lagos and the Yoruba hinterland, elite Lagosian migrant networks, and the interaction between individual spheres such as Lagos and the southeast region.

## Knowledge, authority and textual travels

In both writing of their own social relatedness and representing spaces within Nigeria, the travel writers were engaged in a form of self-writing: as Lagosians in distinction to other Nigerians they encountered, or as people with connections to, and knowledge of, the Yoruba hinterland. Another form of self-writing that some of these writers engaged in was as cosmopolitan, experienced and knowledgeable travellers, which they offered as a justification for both their travels and their travel writing. This also functioned as a justification for print culture and the written text itself in an era when, as Karin Barber has shown, some of the Yoruba intellectual elite were making claims for the necessity of preserving history and culture (including oral culture) through writing.[78] Preceding his 1929 'Ero L'Ọna' series, Thomas published an article titled 'Irin-Ajo' ('Travelling'), in which he encouraged 'enia wa' ('our people') to travel more 'kakiri-aiye gẹgẹbi ẹkọ' ('around the world as an education'). Gay, writing in *Eleti-Ọfẹ* in 1926, claims that his motivations for travelling are to experience and gain knowledge of other places:

> It is often said that to be able to acquire a wide knowledge and experience of the world, one must be a traveller, it is therefore advisable for anyone who wishes to know something beyond his place of birth to avail himself of the opportunity of travelling to anywhere under the sun or as far as his purse could carry him as soon as the opportunity offers itself.[79]

---

[77] Luke Uka Uche, *Mass Media, People and Politics in Nigeria* (New Delhi: Concept Publishing Company, 1989), p. 23.

[78] Barber, 'I. B. Akinyele', p. 37.

[79] Gay, 'A Travellers' Obsevations', *Eleti-Ọfẹ*, 1 September 1926, p. 9.

It was not only the writers themselves, however, who were envisaged as becoming knowledgeable people through travel. Writing at a time in which print was making claims to preserve the past as a form of permanent written archive, these travel writers also suggested that their travel narratives were valuable in being able to offer textual knowledge of other places for readers who could not travel themselves. Thomas in particular claimed that readers of his travel narratives would gain *ẹ̀kọ́* (lessons, knowledge) and *ọgbọ́n* (wisdom) through reading them. In his 1926 'Ero L'Ọna', Thomas entreated his readers, 'ẹ jọwọ ẹ ma ka irohin mi wọnyi gẹgẹ bi ẹkọ' ('please read my news as a lesson'), and explained that he was writing 'fun anfani ẹnyin ọkawe wa lọkunrin, lobinrin, lọmọde ati lagba ti ẹ ko yi ti ni anfani lati rin irin-ajo lẹkan ri yala l'ori omi-okun tabi nipa Motọ l'orilẹ' ('for the benefit of you our readers, men and women, children and elders, who have not yet had the opportunity to travel on the sea or around the land by car').[80] In 1929, he similarly advised the reader: 'Ẹ mura lati ri ọgbọn kọ ninu awọn arẹwa irin-ajo gbajumọ Editor na' ('Be prepared to learn wisdom from the beautiful journeys of the distinguished Editor').[81]

In common with descriptive travel accounts by Lagosian writers about the Yoruba region in the Lagos anglophone press in the 1910s (see Chapter 3), some of the Yoruba-language travel narratives of the 1920s and 1930s claimed to offer objective knowledge of other places to their readers. A. K. Ajíṣafẹ́ explains the importance of first-hand experience of a place, combined with research, in the creation of knowledge that others may read about in his book:

> Ko si tabitabi pe Ile-Ifẹ jẹ ilẹ iyanu. Ẹniti o ba le rin de ibẹ, ti o ba si le ri ọna de'bi awọn nkan ti mo nwi yi ni yio mọ pe ohun iyanu ni Ile-Ifẹ jasi. Mo de ibiti Ọpa Ọranyan ati Igbo Ọranyan mbe. A mu mi de igbo Oduduwa, ati ọpọlọpọ ibimiran ti nkoiti ri aye lati rohin. Ki iṣe eyi nikan, mo wadi itan ati aṣa ibẹ kinikini gẹgẹbi ọgbọn mi ti mọ.[82]

> There is no doubt that Ilé-Ifẹ̀ is a wondrous land. Anyone who travels here and can see the things of which I am speaking shall know that Ilé-Ifẹ̀ is a wonder. I came to the site of Ọ̀ránmíyàn's Staff and Ọ̀ránmíyàn's Forest. They took me to the forest of Odùduwà, and many other places which I have not yet had the opportunity to tell you about. It was not just this alone; I thoroughly investigated the customs and the history of the place, as far as my wisdom would allow.

Thomas, too, represents himself substantiating the non-Yoruba world beyond Lagos for his readers:

---

[80] Thomas, 'Ero L'Ọna', *Eleti-Ọfẹ*, 28 April 1926, p. 8.
[81] Thomas, 'Irin-Ajo', *Akede Eko*, 11 April 1929, p. 6.
[82] A. K. Ajisafe, 'Irin-Ajo Kakiri Ilu Oke', *Akede Eko*, 19 July 1930, p. 7.

Bo ti jẹ pe mo ni anfani lati lọ mọ awọn ilu pataki to jẹ ilu awọn Ṣekiri ati Ijọ papa, eyi yio fun mi laye dada lati fun nyin ni irohin aladun nipa iṣesi ati ilo awọn enia wọnyi ni ilẹ ti a bi wọn si.[83]

Since I have the opportunity to go and know these important Itsekiri and Ijaw towns themselves, this will give me a great chance to give you interesting news about the characteristics and the ways of these people in their place of birth.

Akintán also describes local foods and other idiosyncrasies of the Yoruba towns he visits, and Thomas recounts details such as dressing up for photographs in Warri wearing 'aṣọ ni ti aṣa ibilẹ awọn ọmọ Ṣekiri' ('the native clothing of the Itsekiri'), and the 'aṣọ kijipa dudu' ('black kijipa cloth'[84]) he saw the Yoruba locals wearing.[85] These writers describe themselves coming to knowledge through experience, through 'investigation', as Ajíṣafẹ́ puts it, and also through observation. Thomas in particular frequently deploys panoramas, depicting himself gazing at towns from the sea in order to encompass them in their entirety. Thus he describes Lagos as if from the sea:

> wo o, bi a ti nwo ẹwa ilu Eko lọ l'oju omi, wo ile Elerin ati Tower rẹ l'Olowogbowo bo ti l'ẹwa to, wo oriṣiriṣi awọn arẹwa ile ti nwon gbe ilu wa niyi nla lokere ani awọn bi: *Colonial Bank, Post Office, Glover Hall, Elder Dempster*, ile *Lawyer* Alákijà kekere ti awọn Oyinbo oniṣowo Sick haya, *Bank of British West Africa*; wo bi ile isin *Christ Church Cathedral* ti l'ẹwa to lokere, wo awọn *Towers African Bethel Church* titun bo ti tan ẹwa rẹ to; wo ọgba ibiṣẹ Ọba (*Secretariat*) wo ile Ọba papa bo ti tan rakafo (*Government House*) gbogbo iwọnyi fi iyi nlanla fun ilu wa ti a si le ṣe igberaga le l'ori.[86]

See our observation of the beauty of Lagos from the sea, look how beautiful the Elephant House and its Tower in Olówógbowó are, see all kinds of beautiful houses in the distance which give great distinction to our town, such as: Colonial Bank, Post Office, Glover Hall, Elder Dempster, the house of the Lawyer Alákijà the younger, which the European trader Sick rents, Bank of British West Africa, come and see how beautiful the Christ Church Cathedral is in the distance, see how complete the beauty of the new Towers African Bethel Church, see the Secretariat, see how perfect the Government House itself is: all of these bring great honour to our town which we can be very proud of.

Thomas views towns from the sea in this way throughout his travel narratives; on arriving at Forcados in the Niger Delta, he notes that 'Ilu Forcados

---

[83] Thomas, 'Ero L'Ọna', *Eleti-Ọfẹ*, 2 June 1926, p. 8.
[84] *Kijipa* is a coarse rural cloth.
[85] Thomas, 'Ero L'Ọna', *Akede Eko*, 11 April 1931, p. 8; 14 February 1931, p. 7.
[86] Thomas, 'Ero L'Ọna', *Eleti-Ọfẹ*, 28 April 1926, p. 9.

dun nwo lokere lati inu ọkọ, irisi ilu na lokere dabi igbati enia duro leti ebute Ẹhingbẹti, ki oluwarẹ ma wo Apapa lọkankan' ('Forcados looked lovely from a distance inside the ship; from a distance, the town looked as if one were stand-ing at the edge of Ẹ̀hìngbẹtì harbour, looking out at Àpapá straight ahead').[87] His gaze from the sea again emphasises his exceptionalism as a traveller, tak-ing advantage of this coastal perspective that the inauguration of the steamer routes offered. Even on land, Thomas emphasises the value of observing new places, often through depicting himself wandering: 'mo fi ẹsẹ ṣa diẹ ni ilu Warri, nitori aibamọ nko ṣa tun mọ ọjọ ti mo tun le ni anfani lati de ilu na mọ' ('I walked around Warri a little, because I do not know when I will next have the opportunity to come to that town again').[88] On the road to Warri, he surveys Itsekiri houses as they pass on the road, while in Sapele, one of his first actions on arriving is to look for the view: 'Mo tete ji l'owurọ kutukutu oni, mo jade si iwaju ile ti a fi mi wọsi, lati wo bi orere ilu Sapẹlẹ ti ri si' ('I got up very early in the morning today, I went out to the front of the house in which I was lodging, in order to see what the view of Sapele was like').[89]

However, overall, with the exception of Gay's narratives describing Ìbàdàn and Badagry, the travel writers do not systematically or extensively document the world beyond Lagos; they tend to wield details of the places they encounter as local colour, or evidence of a lack of 'civilisation', rather than attempting to build a full picture of those towns. These travel narratives are rooted in the writers' own itineraries and experience, rather than making more universal claims about the places to which they travel. Yet the writers nonetheless en-visaged themselves passing numerous other forms of knowledge onto their readers through their experience of travel. The travel writers often described for their readers their experiences of being a traveller in this age of novelty, as Thomas puts it:

> Pupọ enia yio ranti pe lasiko lailai o ni iye ọjọ ti awọn Arin-irin-ajo ni lati gba l'ọna ki nwọn to ti Eko de ilu Abẹòkúta, ṣugbọn l'oni, bi enia dide l'Eko lati lọ si Abẹòkúta l'owurọ, oluwarẹ yio jẹun ọsan l'Abẹòkúta; awa kan ṣe eyi ni apẹrẹ kekere ṣa ni, nitoripe pupọ ẹnyin ọkawe wa yio ranti awọn nkan miran bawọnyi nipa anfani ti gbogbo wa ni l'aiye l'oni nipa irin-ajo-ririn.[90]

> Many people will remember that in the olden days travellers had to spend sev-eral days on the road to get from Lagos to Abẹòkúta, but today, if one leaves Lagos for Abẹòkúta in the morning, that person will eat lunch in Abẹòkúta. We give this as a small example, because many of you our readers will remember

[87] Thomas, 'Ero L'Ọna', *Eleti-Ọfẹ*, 12 May 1926, p. 7.
[88] Thomas, 'Ero L'Ọna', *Eleti-Ọfẹ*, 19 May 1926, p. 8.
[89] Thomas, 'Ero L'Ọna', *Eleti-Ọfẹ*, 26 May 1926, p. 8.
[90] Thomas, 'Irin-Ajo', *Akede Eko*, 11 April 1929, p. 6.

other things like this about the advantages that all of us have in today's world regarding travelling.

Their experiences of travel did not always, however, celebrate colonial travel infrastructure, as a form of the 'colonial sublime', as Brian Larkin identifies it, and the potential for travel that it offered.[91] In one of his travel narratives, for instance, Thomas describes his outrage at how African steamer passengers had to undergo humiliating quarantine procedures.[92] However, the travel writers generally revelled in recounting their experiences of travel for their readers, and teaching them how to travel. While Akintán, unlike Thomas, did not openly state a desire to educate his readers, his travel narratives were nonetheless suffused with snippets of information about places, people and events derived from his own experience and observation, and with descriptions of his experience of travel. He opens his 1926 travel narrative by describing his trip from Lagos to Ìbàdàn by train. He describes the train unfurling its flag before setting off, its 'faka-fiki-faka-fiki' sound as it sets off, and his surprise at the way the passengers greet each other on boarding and leaving the train, as if they are greeting 'ọmọ titun: "Ẹ ku abọ, alafia kọ ni ẹ de bi?"' ('a newborn child: "Welcome, did you come well?"').[93] The greeting ritual that Akintán observes on the train to Ìbàdàn strikes him so much that he is able to 'yọ ẹkọ kekere kan lati inu rẹ' ('pull a little lesson out of it'), turning the journey, the tickets and the greeting into a simile for life and death:

> Loju mi ọkọ Reluwe dabi aiye ti a wa yi; nigbati a bi wa sinu rẹ awa pẹlu Ticket wa lo wa; ẹlomiran nlọ si ọna ajo ti o kuru boya lati Eko de Agege; awọn ẹlomiran wa lati lọ si irin ajo ti o gun diẹ, bi Alagbado titi de Lafẹnwa; awọn ẹlomiran si wa lati rin ọna ajo gigun, bi Ifọ lọ si Ibadan tabi Kano; bayi ni mo bẹrẹ si ro nkan wọnyi lọkan ara mi. Gẹgẹ bi olukuluku ti nfi Ticket rẹ fun Ọgakọ nigbati o ba to ati bọ silẹ; bẹ gẹgẹ ni awa ẹda nfi Ticket wa silẹ ki a to le kuro laiye; gẹgẹ bi ọna ajo awọn ẹlomiran ko ti gun bẹ gẹgẹ ni ọjọ ori awọn ẹlomiran ki ipọ laiye ki nwọn to lọ.
>
> Mo si tun nro lọkan mi wipe bi nwọn ti nfi tayọ-tayọ ki awọn ti o bọ silẹ, bẹ gẹgẹ ni nwọn yio ma fi tayọ-tayọ gba awọn ti o ba ku lọhun; bi nwọn ti nfi tayọ-tayọ ki awọn titun ti o ṣẹṣẹ wọ inu ọkọ, bẹ gẹgẹ ni awa papa ma nfi tayọ-tayọ ki ọmọ titun ti a ṣẹṣẹ bi sinu aiye; bayi ni mo joko ni kọrọ kan ninu ọkọ ti mo si nro gbogbo nkan wọnyi.[94]

---

[91] Brian Larkin, *Signal and Noise: Media, Infrastructure and Urban Culture in Nigeria* (Durham, NC and London: Duke University Press, 2008), pp. 35–43.

[92] Thomas, 'Ero L'Ọna', *Eleti-Ọfẹ*, 28 April 1926, p. 8.

[93] Akintan, 'Irin Ajo Lati Eko Lọ Si Ileṣa', *Eleti-Ọfẹ*, 24 November 1926, pp. 8–9.

[94] Ibid. p. 9.

In my view, the train resembled this world in which we live: when we are born into it, we come with our Tickets; some were going on short journeys, perhaps from Lagos to Agége; others have to go on a journey which was a little long, such as Alágbàdo to Láfẹ́nwá, and others have to go on a huge journey, from Ifọ̀ to Ìbàdàn or Kano, thus I started to think these things to myself. As each one was producing his Ticket for the conductor when he was ready to get down, so we humans leave our tickets before we can leave the world; as the journeys of some are not far, so the days of some people are not many in the world before they go.

I thought again to myself, just as they happily greeted those who got off, so they will welcome with happiness those who die there; as they happily greeted those new ones who just entered the train, so we ourselves will happily greet newborn children who have just come into the world; thus it was that I sat in a quiet corner of the train where I was thinking all these things.

Akintán characterises his extended metaphor about the nature of life and death as a 'lesson' or 'education' (ẹ̀kọ́) for both himself and his readers; he envisages his narrative educating readers about both the literal and metaphorical significance of travelling.

As well as teaching readers about the nature of travel in the early twentieth century, the travel narratives also implicitly transmitted knowledge about the writers and the authority they gained through their experience of the world. Although the Lagos travel writers of the 1920s did not make an explicit connection between their travels and ọ̀làjú ('civilisation' or 'enlightenment' – see Chapter 1), they describe a similar sense of the value of seeing the world to that embodied in the notion of ọ̀làjú, taking advantage of their travels for their newspaper business or research to also become more 'enlightened' through experience of the world. During his stay in Sapele, Thomas describes himself taking a trip on the water for 'itura ati orun aladun' ('a refreshing rest and relaxation'), and exploring a nearby town.[95] Describing another journey on foot from Asagba to Ogele, Thomas dramatises the danger of the trip and his suffering, writing it as an adventure narrative with himself as the unlikely Lagosian anti-hero:

bo ti jẹ pe a ni lati rin ni, mo ri iya, mo pe e ni baba l'ọjọ yẹn, larin igbo didi birabira ati papa gbalasa ni a ngba kọja; ojo gbe'bẹ o ni ọjọ yẹn ni on nrọ boto, ati oyinbo ati gbogbo wa lo wọji ninu ojo, mo tun pada ke abamọ wipẹ kini mo tilẹ wa fi ara mi ṣe bayi; gbogbo ibadi mi mọ ọrun ẹsẹ mi lo kurẹ patapata gba [...] Nikẹhin a de ilu Ogele, nibẹ ni a gbe ba oyinbo ti a npe ni Ọgbẹni G. S. Hughes, District *Officer* ilu Warri; oyinbo yi ṣe idaro wa pupọ nigbati o ri itu ti ojo fi wa pa; o si sọ pe anu emi nikan ni o ṣe on julọ nitoripe awa ọmọ Eko ko nṣe ohun ti o ni ipa bi eyi lẹhin gbẹfẹ; eyi jẹ ki ẹrin pa mi.[96]

since we had to walk, I was totally confused that day, we were passing through a dense forest and boundless open plains, the rain took charge of the place and decided to rain heavily. Not only the Europeans but all of us were soaked in the rain. I came to regret having come, wondering why I was treating myself like this; my waist right down to my ankles were completely soaked. […] In the end we came to Ogele, there we met a European called Mr G. S. Hughes, District Officer of Warri; this European comforted us very much when he saw the mischief that the rain had done to us, and he said that it was I that he pitied the most, because we Lagosians don't do hard things like this except for fun. This made me laugh.

The supposed exceptionalism of Thomas's expedition through the forest suits his vision of himself as an unusually intrepid traveller. As well as European travel narratives, adventure novels such as H. Rider Haggard's *King Solomon's Mines* were circulating in early twentieth-century West Africa, and Thomas's wilder descriptions of perilous adventures could owe something to these stories.[97] Nonetheless, they also suggest his own desire to represent himself as a particularly intrepid traveller taking full advantage of the opportunities for travel he encountered on his journeys and, again, emphasise the particular character of the Lagosian, as one who, accustomed to the comforts of Lagos, does not usually endure hardships such as rain and forest treks.

In such travel narratives, the implicit notion of *ọlàjú* is often individualised: the benefits of travel are conferred on the travelling individual, who becomes an enlightened person. But travel writing becomes a way of broadcasting the experience of travel to a wider readership. Thus as well as being self-aggrandising, Thomas's emphasis on the wisdom an individual gains through travel is also a way of justifying the value of the printed word itself, by suggesting that second-hand experience gained through reading rather than through travelling itself nonetheless has value. In his preface to his 1929 travel narrative, Thomas justifies the publication of his travel narrative by explaining that it is a pity that many Lagosians who have travelled 'ni nwọn ti ṣe awun nipa pe nwọn ko ṣe irin ajo wọn na l'anfani gbogbo enia lẹhin anfani ti ara wọn nikanṣoṣo iyẹn ni pe nwọn ko sọ gbogbo ohun ti oju wọn ba pade ninu irin ajo na fun awọn ọmọ ẹlẹgbẹ wọn gbọ' ('are miserly in that they don't put their travelling to the benefit of everyone, just to the benefit of themselves alone; they don't say all

---

[96] Thomas, 'Ero L'Ọna', *Eleti-Ọfẹ*, 30 June 1926, p. 8.
[97] Stephanie Newell, 'An Introduction to the Writings of J. G. Mullen, an African Clerk, in the *Gold Coast Leader*, 1916–19', *Africa,* 78.3 (2008), pp. 384–400 (p. 390).

the things that their eyes met on the journey for their associates to hear').[98] If travellers do not *sọ* (tell) their journeys for their acquaintances to *gbọ́* (hear), readers might still benefit from reading about them instead. Thomas posits print as a potential counterpart to oral narrative – not necessarily a replacement for orality, but a way of spreading these stories more widely. Yet Thomas does not claim to be able to replicate entirely mimetically the experience of travelling; in one of his travel narratives, he uses a proverb to remark on the impossibility of verbally communicating first-hand experience: 'ohun t'oju ri ni mẹkun, ko ṣe de'le wi' ('the mysterious things I see on journeys, I can't recount them at home').[99] Thomas and his fellow travel writers thus explore, somewhat ambivalently and inconclusively, the limits of the emerging print culture of the 1920s, and the relationship between writerly experience, oral and written narrative, and readerly knowledge.

Along the West African coast, a richly creative print culture was experimenting in similar ways with travel writing: travel narratives by Gold Coast clerk J. G. Mullen describing travels in Cameroon and by a pseudonymous author called 'Rambler', 'describing rambles around the Gold Coast countryside in an epic, rambling tone', were published in the Gold Coast press in 1916–18 and 1919 respectively, and travel narratives were also published in the francophone Cameroonian press in the early twentieth century.[100] Mullen's narrative was, Stephanie Newell argues, 'without precedent' in the colonial Gold Coast: an early attempt at 'writing the self' made possible by the 'open, experimental space of the Gold Coast newspapers'.[101]

Thus across West Africa, print was making space for new ways of writing about communities and about the self, through writing about travel, experimenting with literary genres, and establishing and re-establishing relationships between readers and writers through the written text. The Yoruba travel narratives in the press in the 1920s emerged in the context of colonialism, and as a product of the perception amongst Lagos's elite that they stood at the crossroads between European and Yoruba culture, but were also a product of demands of the city's print culture and display of a sociable self. Even though they may appear to have borrowed some aspects of the rhetoric of the missionary or colonial travelogue of the late nineteenth and early twentieth centuries – or, at least, shared a worldview with such travelogues, particularly in their view

[98] Thomas, 'Irin-Ajo', *Akede Eko*, 11 April 1929, p. 6.
[99] Thomas, 'Ero L'Ọna', *Akede Eko*, 23 May 1929, p. 8.
[100] Newell, 'J. G. Mullen', Newell, *The Power to Name*, p. 8; Emma Hunter, personal communication, 23 March 2014.
[101] Stephanie Newell, 'Newspapers, New Spaces, New Writers: The First World War and Print Culture in Colonial Ghana', *Research in African Literatures* 40.2 (2009), pp. 1–15 (pp. 5, 11).

of other, non-Christian Nigerians – and they were a product of a flourishing and dynamic local literary culture that centred on the newspapers. They also both reflected and contributed to changing relations across the space that was now known as Nigeria, and simultaneously changing newspaper readerships. This was a nascent genre that grew out of a particular kind of travel, in the service of the newspapers or other personal interests. It was also stimulated by a desire to write the self as a sociable, known and knowledgeable person. This genre therefore emerged from a particular crossroads in the history of Lagos and of Nigeria, as the inhabitants of this colony considered their relations to one another. It furthermore grew out of a particular kind of Lagos print culture that also stood at a crossroads, as it intimately addressed its readership of mostly Lagosian readers, while also seeking to expand that readership within the colony of Nigeria.

In the next chapter, we turn to another example of travel writing being used to think through a sense of a culture and society standing at a crossroads; to create forms of subjectivity while writing about place; and to play with genre, but centred on a different kind of travel and a different kind of writing, more for the purposes of apparent 'autoethnography' than in the service of a growing print culture and a desire to display one's social connections.

# Isaac Délànọ's *The Soul of Nigeria*, at the crossroads of 'civilisation'

'You are entering a new world', Isaac Délànọ tells readers of his book *The Soul of Nigeria* (1937), as he takes them, in the first chapter of the book, on a textual journey through the rapidly developing Lagos cityscape.[1] This chapter explores this 'new world' that Délànọ describes in *The Soul of Nigeria*. It shows how Délànọ, a Lagosian intellectual with roots in the Ẹ̀gbá region of Yorubaland, used travel writing ostensibly to document long-held Yoruba 'customs' and 'native ways', but also to chart a path for the Yoruba region's future, in this 'new world' full of competing claims to 'civilisation'. In doing so, Délànọ aligned himself with other intellectuals of the era who saw themselves as faced with the task of selecting the best forms of 'civilisation' as they stood at the crossroads of Yoruba, Lagosian and European ways of life and intellectual cultures.

In Chapter 2, we saw how the Yoruba travel writers of the 1920s and 1930s, I. B. Thomas in particular, created a genre of travel writing that both illustrated and generated their own social connectedness, and the spread of Lagosian migrant communities and print culture beyond Lagos. Their writing was often more concerned with the creation of the writer's subjectivity and a display of sociability than with documenting the places to which their writers travelled. This chapter, reading Délànọ's book from 1937 alongside earlier travel narratives from the 1910s and 1920s published in the Lagos press, examines how a different type of travel narrative, more focused on documenting other people and places, became a way for Lagosian and Yoruba intellectuals to establish narratives of 'civilisation' within Nigeria, to orient themselves within the new colony of Nigeria, and to claim particular regional identities. The travel narratives I examine in this chapter also continue to reveal some of the ways in which southwest Nigerian writers conceived of the various communities that were already available to them in public discourse, and that were constructed and reconstructed through travel narratives. Such communities included the 'nation', used in complex ways to refer to the Yoruba nation, the Nigerian nation, and overlaps between the two.

---

[1] Isaac Delano, *The Soul of Nigeria* (London: T. Werner Laurie, 1937), p. 14. Subsequent references are to this edition and will be given in parentheses in the text.

## Writing culture through travel

In the 1930s, Lagos's political and intellectual elite found themselves beginning to give way to incomers from the hinterland as education took root more
widely across the provinces. A period of political, civic and intellectual change
and uncertainty ensued as a more populist, nationalist politics, moving towards
pro-independence rhetoric, began to challenge the patrician civic values of the
old elite.[2] It was against this background of shifting political values and the
beginning of discussions about the prospects of an independent Nigeria – and
Lagos and the Yoruba region's place in that Nigeria – that Isaac Délànọ̀ published his book *The Soul of Nigeria*.

*The Soul of Nigeria*, published in 1937, is in some senses a conventional
travel book, appearing to offer a first-person, non-fiction account of the author's
travels in Nigeria, but it is also a mélange of memoir, history and ethnography,
framed as an account of Yoruba ways of life. Alongside descriptions of his life
in Yaba Garden City, then on the outskirts of Lagos, most of the places Délànọ̀
describes travelling to are in Abẹ́òkúta and its environs, the Ẹ̀gbá region in
which Délànọ̀ claimed his own origins, although he also relates anecdotes
from a period when he lived in Ìbàdàn, and in the ethnographic sections of the
book, describes things he encountered in Ìjẹ̀bu-Òde, Ilé-Ifẹ̀ and Ilẹ́ṣà. However,
Délànọ̀ also implies that he has travelled more widely in the Yoruba region, and
moreover that his findings from his travels can be generalised to the whole Yoruba region; although, as we shall see, the book slips unstably between 'Yoruba',
'African', 'Nigerian' and 'native', it is also framed resolutely throughout as an
account of 'Yorubaland', 'Yoruba people' and the 'Yoruba countries'. Written
in a conversational tone, it is presented as a meandering, personal account of
what Délànọ̀ describes as ten years of 'watching and studying the natives'
ways, life and customs at close range' (102), as well as anecdotes drawn from
his own and his father's life, and stories told to him by others. Many of the
book's short chapters are presented as mini-ethnographies of subjects typical
of ethnographic enquiry of the era: death, marriage, divorce, customs, religion,
hunting, dance, medicine, names, the *ìwọ̀fà* (pawn labour) system, charms
and witchcraft. Other chapters are concerned with the impact of colonialism
and 'civilisation', contemporary education and government, and the 'English
official at work', and take diversions into Délànọ̀'s own opinions on British rule
and 'civilisation'. The book is illustrated with twenty-three photographs, many
of them of 'native' social institutions, such as 'a typical native hut', 'a Yoruba
bride on her wedding day' and 'native dress', but also some of contemporary
life, such as a view of 'Denton Crossway from Iddo Island' and bird's eye
views of Abẹ́òkúta and Ìbàdàn.

---

[2] Zachernuk, *Colonial Subjects*, pp. 85–94.

Délànọ̀'s book appears curiously without reference to or quotation from antecedents, despite the publication of similar works of history and cultural documentation, such as the 'ethnographic' sections of Samuel Johnson's renowned *History of the Yorubas* and historical works by fellow Ẹ̀gbá intellectual A. K. Ajíṣafẹ́, with which Délànọ̀, as a prominent Ẹ̀gbá intellectual himself, must surely have been familiar. Instead, the text is presented as if it arose spontaneously from Délànọ̀'s curiosity, memories and wanderings, rather than being written into an existing Yoruba genre. Unlike those more conventional historical works, he does not present written versions of oral texts such as *oríkì* or *ìtàn* relating to the places he writes about, and the book is also substantially more subjective and personalised; while some historical works were produced at least in part from research the writers carried out by travelling within the Yoruba region (as we saw in Chapter 2 in the case of A. K. Ajíṣafẹ́), the author's travel itself was not usually described within town histories, as it is in *The Soul of Nigeria*. The overall effect is to render *The Soul of Nigeria* more a socio-political commentary and travel narrative than historical writing, and closer in tone to the travel narratives published in the Yoruba press in the 1920s and 1930s (see Chapter 2), with their emphasis on the travelling author's personality and encounters with others, although with a greater focus on documenting places and culture than in those travel narratives.

The book's publisher, too, positions *The Soul of Nigeria* closer to travel writing than any other genre; the book was published in 1937 by British publisher T. Werner Laurie, which published travel writing by mainly British and other European writers describing their adventures in the colonies as well as middlebrow novels, historical works, biographies and other miscellaneous texts. *The Soul of Nigeria* contains an advertisement for *A Frenchman in Japan* (1936) by the best-selling French travel writer and novelist Maurice Dekobra, also published by T. Werner Laurie. T. Werner Laurie thus positions *The Soul of Nigeria* amid a wider field of interwar travel writing published in Europe, offering to take the reader on exotic adventures around the world.

Although Délànọ̀ includes some reminiscences of his childhood, particularly his schooldays, much of the book focuses on his findings from his more recent travels around the Yoruba region, spurred by his curiosity and his research for this book. 'A man seeking information must expect adventure', Délànọ̀ explains, recounting his travels to an unnamed town (55). Arriving in the town a stranger, with nowhere to stay and no way of obtaining food except through the kindness of strangers, he describes how 'I went straight to a house close by, introduced myself as one who came to learn something about the history of the village, a man looking for adventure' (55). Offered food and a bed for the length of his stay in the town, Délànọ̀ recounts episodes from his time there, including the simplicity of its church service and his host's views on Nigeria's current affairs.

This episode epitomises the method behind the book, in its presentation of Délànọ̀ as a stranger in the Yoruba region, seeking both knowledge and adventure, and in Délànọ̀'s use of his own experiences to narrate both the past and the contemporary Yoruba region and its people. Délànọ̀'s stated reason for writing the book is to document Yoruba customs for posterity: 'Old customs and laws are fast dying out', he explains in the introduction to the book, 'and in the following pages I have attempted to record in plain and readable form some of the details concerning our origin before they die out altogether' (7). In order to gain access to these '[o]ld customs and laws', Délànọ̀ must travel, to both experience and hear about such customs first-hand. Thus '[f]or ten years', Délànọ̀ explains, 'I devoted such spare time as I have to finding out how our ancestors lived, governed themselves and enjoyed things, before the advent of the white man' (7). The book's framing as a travel narrative is important in allowing Délànọ̀ to authorise his observations about the Yoruba region by claiming that they are derived from intimate, first-hand experience.

Travel is also important for engendering an encounter with the pre-colonial past. 'To learn about the past', Délànọ̀ explains, 'I discovered that one has to dig deep, so I went to Abeokuta' (46). The combination of the spatial metaphor of 'digging deep' with Délànọ̀'s enquiry into 'the past' is characteristic of Délànọ̀'s distinctive sense that travel in the Yoruba region is a way of moving through both space and time. The Yoruba region is represented as a place where the past can be encountered through the present through two means: through the continued existence of 'customs' that are presumed to provide an enactment of the past, the ways of 'our ancestors' and 'our origin'; and through orality, the stories of the past that Délànọ̀ is able to hear only by travelling and encountering people who know about the 'our ancestors' and 'our origin'. 'The past', *The Soul of Nigeria* suggests, is accessible in Yorubaland and in the cultural memory that the region's orality contains, in a way that it implicitly is not in Lagos. Lagos, with its creole colonial culture, was frequently denounced by the educated elite as a place of corruption and shallowness, lacking the cultural depth and respect for the 'old ways' seen as characteristic of the hinterland – a view that found expression, as Karin Barber shows, in the representation of the seamy life of the city in the 1920s through the figure of the wayward prostitute Sẹ̀gilọlá in I. B. Thomas's novel *Sẹ̀gilọlá*.[3]

This accessibility of the past in the Yoruba region is linked to the distinction that Délànọ̀ draws between 'natives' and those who might offer knowledge that is 'tainted'. In order to record the true 'old customs and laws', Délànọ̀ considers that he must observe the ways and stories of the 'natives', rather than the literate ruling elite: during the course of his research, he explains, he

---

[3] Barber, *Print Culture*, p. 21.

'particularly avoided Obas, chiefs and people in high office in order to obtain my information at first hand, untainted by present civilization and ideals which are stoutly pushing our native methods of doing things into the corner' (7). To get away from knowledge 'tainted' by 'civilization' or by politics, Délànǫ proclaims that he must travel: therefore, '[o]n train, canoe and lorry, I gathered my information from the rank and file of the people of Nigeria' (7). 'There is no other way open to me', he explains, 'to obtain the information I desire than by journeying to our more important towns for the purpose of meeting people, asking their views, and making observation' (46). Travel enables not only geographical movement between city and hinterland, but also social movement between elite and 'rank and file', historical movement between past and present, and cultural movement between 'native' and 'civilised'.

In 1944, Délànǫ published another travel narrative: *Notes and Comments from Nigeria*.[4] This shorter, pamphlet-length travel narrative was published by the United Society for Christian Literature in its series 'Africa's Own Library'. The series was designed, according to its British publishers, to 'stimulate Africans to take an interest in reading of the great tribes and personalities of their continent' and featured mainly texts by 'African of education' who 'as far as possible, are left to express their views in their own words'. It featured texts from across the British colonies in Africa, including Jomo Kenyatta's *My People of Kikuyu* (1944) as well as other texts by Délànǫ and similar semi-ethnographic accounts such as *My Ngoni of Nyasaland* (1942) by Y. M. Chibambo and *Our People of the Sierra Leone Protectorate* by Max Gorvie (1944). Like *The Soul of Nigeria*, *Notes and Comments* mixes accounts of people and places that Délànǫ encountered on his travels with ethnographic description, historical narrative and anecdote, and opinion on current affairs. In thirteen short chapters, most of them just a few pages long, the pamphlet follows Délànǫ as he travels on train and lorry, horseback and donkey, again in the Yoruba region but also to parts of central and northern Nigeria, from Lagos to Ìkòròdú, Ìbàdàn, Ọ̀yọ́, Ìlọrin, Kano and the land of the Gwari people (today known as Gbagyi, in central Nigeria).

While *Notes and Comments* took Délànǫ into northern Nigeria, *The Soul of Nigeria,* despite its title, focuses exclusively on the Yoruba region, barely mentioning any of the other regions of colonial Nigeria. This conflation of 'Yoruba' with 'Nigeria' was possibly the decision of the British publisher rather than Délànǫ himself, but it is also perhaps less surprising if read in the light of Délànǫ's later career in Yoruba literature and cultural production, and his subsequent reputation as a Yoruba cultural nationalist. Isaac Olúwọlé Délànǫ

---

[4] Isaac Delano, *Notes and Comments from Nigeria* (London and Redhill: United Society for Christian Literature (Lutterworth Press), 1944). Subsequent references are to this edition and will be given in parentheses in the text.

was born in 1904 into the Ẹgbá sub-group of the Yoruba, a group with its ori-gins in Abẹ́òkúta that had a particularly long association with education and Christianity and had been an independent kingdom until it was incorporated into the Colony and Protectorate of Nigeria in 1914, and which produced many early twentieth-century Yoruba intellectuals. Délànọ̀'s father was a priest and a judge in the native courts. The young Délànọ̀ received an elite education at Lagos Grammar School and then King's College, Lagos, before becoming a civil servant in 1924.[5] He was, at the time of writing *The Soul of Nigeria*, an up-and-coming member of Lagos's literate elite, well-acquainted with the dual pillars of colonial 'civilisation': Christianity and education. Simultaneously, though, he also had a somewhat more immediate connection to the Yoruba re-gion through his childhood than some of the *Sàró* intellectuals of Lagos whom we encountered in Chapter 2.

In later years, Délànọ̀ published two important Yoruba novels: *Aiyé d'Aiyé Òyìnbó* (1955) and *L'ọ́jọ́ Ọjọ́ Un* (1963). In common with *The Soul of Nigeria*, these historical novels trace the changes that the colonial era and 'civilisation' brought to the region, the effects of Christianity, colonial laws and indirect rule on 'traditional' ways. *Aiyé d'Aiyé Òyìnbó* employs a narrative style 'fashioned on the characteristic mode of Yoruba elders' delivery of their recollections', suffused with proverbs, idioms and 'deep' Yoruba, marking Délànọ̀'s concern with Yoruba modes of expression and changing ways of life.[6] Throughout his career, Délànọ̀ was concerned with the Yoruba language and intellectual tradi-tions; alongside his novel writing, he also held academic posts, and published biographies of prominent Ẹgbá men including the Reverend J. J. Ransome-Kútì and *Ọba* Adémọ́lá II, the *Aláké* (ruler) of Ẹgbá; works on the Yoruba language including a dictionary, grammar and compilation of proverbs; and commentary on contemporary life, such as his pamphlet 'An African Looks at Marriage' (1944), also published by the United Society for Christian Literature. Reflecting the era's growing cultural nationalist politics, from 1948, Délànọ̀ was Secretary of the *Ẹgbẹ́ Ọmọ Odùduwà*, the Yoruba political and cultural society founded in 1945 by Ọbáfẹ́mi Awólọ́wọ̀ and other leading Yoruba cultural nationalists and politicians as Nigeria agitated for independence from Britain. Délànọ̀ became an established member of the Yoruba political and intellectual elite, reflected in the award of a chieftaincy title in Aké, Abẹ́òkúta in 1955, and he was associated with a form of Yoruba cultural and political nationalism that proclaimed the distinctiveness and validity of Yoruba intellectual traditions and ways of life.[7]

Despite being written in English rather than Yoruba, Délànọ̀'s book *The Soul of Nigeria* can be seen as an early attempt to establish what Délànọ̀ viewed as

[5] Babalọla, 'Yoruba Literature', p. 180.
[6] Ibid. p. 169.
[7] Ibid. p. 180.

distinctive and worthwhile in the Yoruba region. Délànǫ was not the first Yoruba author to attempt to document the Yoruba region in this way. As Karin Barber has shown, the Lagos and broader Yoruba intellectual elite of the 1880s to the 1930s saw itself as producing an archive; it valorised the production of town histories (see Chapter 1) and other written texts, including historical texts published in the newspapers, as repositories of both history and culture, in the form of heritage and language, because culture was viewed as 'fast disappearing' in the colonial era, and hence in need of preservation in writing for the benefit of future generations.[8] However, *The Soul of Nigeria* does not explicitly address fellow Lagosians, Yorubas or Nigerians, and its often simple explanations of the ways of life of the 'natives', along with a chapter that outlines the easy, leisured lifestyle of the colonial officer in Nigeria, and occasional comparisons to British life, read as if intended to make Nigeria attractive to prospective British colonial officials. The book opens by characterising Nigerians as loyal subjects of empire: 'The people of Nigeria are very proud of the British Empire to which they belong, and of British statesmanship and British equity.' Nigerians realise, Délànǫ continues, 'that they cannot safely become independent of the British Government as things are to-day in the world', and '[w]e live quite contentedly under British rule, and we are proud to confess that we know of no better government than the British' (8).

The text could thus be situated within a literary field of empire, or texts that explain the empire and the rest of the world to Britain, rather than within a Yoruba or Nigerian print sphere. As such, it invites reading as autoethnography, to use Mary Louise Pratt's term for a text in which 'colonized subjects undertake to represent themselves in ways that engage with the colonizer's terms […] in response to or in dialogue with […] metropolitan representations'.[9] *The Soul of Nigeria* can be read as co-opting the travel book genre, situating itself within the field of imperial representation of the world, speaking in terms that the British can understand, while writing 'in response to' British notions of 'civilisation'. It is a translation of 'native' ways into terms that the coloniser can understand, while retaining an 'authentic' sense of the 'native', positioning the author both inside and outside his or her own culture. This, indeed, was how the book was received by 'W. F.', a reviewer for *The Geographical Journal* in 1937, who emphasised the value of its 'native' voice, despite its shortcomings as a work of geography:

> its pages will be read with interest, because the author is a native of West Africa. Our knowledge of the people of this region has been, until recently, dependent upon the writings of European visitors who, whatever their oppor-

---

[8] Barber, 'I. B. Akinyele', p. 37.
[9] Pratt, *Imperial Eyes*, p. 7; original emphasis.

tunity or ability, have generally proved unable to free themselves from the prejudices of an intellectual environment far removed from that of the African; and the time has come to allow the African to speak for himself in the simple and direct manner which is characteristic of him.[10]

Here the 'African' is presumed free of European intellectual modes and therefore authentically 'native', and yet his African-ness is also imagined as enabling him to speak in a 'simple and direct' manner that is implicitly intelligible to Europe. Délànọ̀ is positioned by this reviewer, in the condescending tone of the era, as the 'cultural broker' whom Karin Barber and Paulo Fernando de Moraes Farias describe as characteristic of Lagos's educated elite in the early twentieth century, who translated 'civilised' life into local circumstances and vice versa.[11] In common with several contemporaneous works of southwest Nigerian historical writing, and the Lagos press itself, *The Soul of Nigeria* could be read as an 'extended memo to the colonial government', or even a counter-intelligence report, as Karin Barber writes of historian I. B. Akínyẹlé's *Outlines of Ibadan History* (1946) – written with the hope of influencing colonial authority, by writing in a language and genre they can understand.[12]

However, Délànọ̀'s presentation of the book should not necessarily be taken at face value; his proclamation of loyalty to the British can also be read as a discursive manoeuvre that creates space for criticism. While writing of Nigerian loyalty to Britain, he adds that Nigerians 'have their complaints against the white man's government, but they prefer him to any other white men in the world' (8). These 'complaints' were eagerly recounted to him by some of the Nigerians he encountered on his travels; while many of those he encountered 'were unwilling to voice their opinions; others were over anxious to express themselves' he recalls, 'especially concerning the white man's government' (8). As the book progresses, criticisms of British rule emerge. A chapter on the lifestyle of British colonial officials turns the tables on the British, making them the subject of the African travel writer's gaze. It begins by describing the beauty of Lagos's colonial residential areas, their good infrastructure, European clubs, sports facilities, imported foodstuffs and short working hours: 'duty is not too arduous for the European official, who has many African subordinates in his charge', Délànọ̀ notes (224). But then a faintly ironic tone intrudes, as if mocking the European's indolence: the British colonial official comes to work in his car, takes a 'brief glance at the local daily paper' and then starts work, which 'is not very arduous, but it is responsible'. He leaves the office

---

[10] W. F., '*The Soul of Nigeria,* by Isaac O. Delano', *Geographical Journal*, 90.2 (1937), p. 177.
[11] Farias and Barber, 'Introduction', p. 1.
[12] Barber, 'I. B. Akinyele', p. 46.

at 12.30 pm and drives home for lunch, followed by a nap, two more hours' work and then an afternoon of sports, followed by 'the club, the library or a dance', where he meets fellow Europeans and 'enjoys himself to the fullest extent' (226). British women's lives in the colony are even emptier, according to Délànò: 'I cannot imagine what they find to do at home with a staff of servants at their command' (226). The contrast between the colonial British and the Yoruba is drawn even more starkly when juxtaposed with the book's chapters on Yoruba farming, hunting and war, in which the Yoruba people are depicted as industrious and productive.

## Travel as a lens on 'civilisation'

Délànò's ironically complimentary description of the ease of the British colonial lifestyle is indicative of his interest in the present, as well as the 'old ways': in particular, the moment of social, cultural and epistemological rupture that colonialism represented, and the ways in which Yoruba society should respond, especially in its negotiation of 'civilisation'. Délànò's interest in the present 'civilisation' as well as the past is where he differs from many of his predecessors amongst the Yoruba intellectual elite, who tended to focus their energies on documenting what they perceived as the cultural richness of the past, located in the culture of the Yoruba hinterland.[13] Throughout the book, Délànò critiques British 'civilisation' in Nigeria, particularly its education system, which he says has produced literate but alienated subjects. In response to this issue, he identifies aspects of 'native' life and of pre-colonial African 'civilisation', along with selected aspects of European 'civilisation', that would, in his opinion, constitute a better basis for the Yoruba region's development. This stance irritated reviewer Charles Kingsley Meek (a British anthropologist and former Resident of Nigeria), who asserted that Délànò's 'picture of the past is purely fanciful', and accused Délànò of 'quite forgetting that until the assumption of effective government by the British less than fifty years ago the greater part of present-day Nigeria, which is now a land of general prosperity and contentment, was one of wholesale rapine and disorder'.[14]

However, the book's contrast of an idealised past with the colonial era can also be related to a broader Lagosian and Yoruba intellectual and political project of assessing the use and validity of different forms of 'civilisation' for the Yoruba region in the dawn of Nigeria's nationalist era. Since the late nineteenth century, intellectuals from this region had criticised aspects of colonial rule, drawing on an intellectual culture that scholar Philip Zachernuk characterises

---

[13] Barber, 'I. B. Akinyele', p. 37.
[14] C. K. Meek, '*The Soul of Nigeria* by Isaac O. Delano', *Journal of the Royal African Society,* 37.146 (1938), pp. 119–22 (p. 120).

as 'critical adaptation of the ideas available to them from the Atlantic world'.[15] By the 1930s, Nigerian intellectuals, along with British colonialists, scholars and others interested in Nigerian colonial politics, were entangled in debates about whether Africans should adopt European ways or preserve what was seen as 'African' culture, and in particular about what character Nigeria's education system should take: European or 'indigenous'.[16] Zachernuk reads *The Soul of Nigeria* as a 'cultural nationalist plea for development on indigenous lines', linking it to a larger argument amongst some colonial-era intellectuals about the value of 'African civilisation', embodied in Edward Blyden's notion of the 'African personality', and popularised in Britain by British traveller and ethnographer Mary Kingsley's argument that African cultures were 'vital and valuable in their own place' (if nonetheless, in Kingsley's account, inferior to those of Europe).[17]

In particular, the book was written amid debates about a shift in colonial education policy in the 1930s towards vocational and vernacular education for Nigerians, rather than the academic education in English that had produced the region's literate elite. This shift was epitomised by a controversial proposal that the new Yaba Higher College in Lagos, which opened in 1934, should offer mainly vocational training rather than academic subjects.[18] J. D. Y. Peel suggests that '[f]ew issues united Nigerians of all shades of opinion in the late 1930s' as much as opposition to this proposal, and indeed, Délànọ̀ notes that 'I joined with those who chastised the Government on Yaba Higher College' (18).[19] But *The Soul of Nigeria* is also sympathetic to the need for a 'vernacular education' at primary and secondary level, which promotes both the Yoruba language and an education suitable for the Yoruba context and lifestyle. While noting that schools had improved since his childhood, and approving a shift to teaching in Yoruba, Délànọ̀ was concerned about both the former system's over-production of clerks and of semi-literate English speakers, and the possibility that the new system, with its emphasis on vocational education, would curtail Nigeria's prospects: 'We have seen where the early system of education has placed us. Where will the present system lead our own children? Will it enable them to take an intelligent part in international affairs?' he asks (31). Délànọ̀'s

---

[15] Philip S. Zachernuk, 'Critical Agents: Colonial Nigerian Intellectuals and Their British Counterparts', in *Agency and Action in Colonial Africa*, ed. by Chris Youé and Tim Stapleton (Basingstoke: Palgrave Macmillan, 2001), pp. 156–71 (p. 163).

[16] Ibid. p. 165.

[17] Ibid. pp. 163–4.

[18] A. Babs Fafunwa, *History of Education in Nigeria* (London: George Allen & Unwin, 1974), pp. 132–4, 141–3; Timothy Livsey, 'Imagining an Imperial Modernity: Universities and the West African Roots of Colonial Development', *Journal of Imperial and Commonwealth History*, 44.6 (2016), pp. 952–75 (pp. 955–8).

[19] Peel, 'Olaju', p. 150.

position on education is indicative of his stance towards British colonial rule throughout the book; his criticism is not necessarily of colonialism itself, but rather of aspects of colonial rule he finds unsatisfactory, and he is concerned to sift and mediate these aspects of colonial 'civilisation', as well as Yoruba ways of life, to find the best way forward for Nigeria.

While the intellectual debate that Zachernuk describes was primarily concerned with the perceived contrast between African and European civilisation, the African-owned Lagos press sometimes used travel writing to investigate perceived hierarchies of 'civilisation' within Nigeria, although still often in relation to their closeness to 'African' or 'European' ways of life. In the early decades of the twentieth century, the anglophone Lagos press published a small but steady trickle of travel narratives that described towns and cities both within the Yoruba region and elsewhere in the colony of Nigeria, based on the writers' impressions of those places as they travelled to them. One of the differences of 'civilisation' that the press of this era was interested in was that between Lagos and the Yoruba 'hinterland'. Many literate Lagosians were Yoruba speakers, with their origins in the Yoruba region (although in the case of those writers of *Sàró* background, those origins may have been some generations previous). Reacting to the elite, anglicised culture of late nineteenth and early twentieth-century Lagos, some Lagos intellectuals sought to distinguish themselves from European forms of 'civilisation', and to valorise Yoruba or African ways of life, reconnecting with their Yoruba heritage. Some, for instance, reclaimed Yoruba names, rejecting their anglicised Christian names.[20]

A three-part travel narrative called 'A Tour to the Hinterland', published in the *Lagos Weekly Record* in 1912, can be read in the light of this movement amongst Lagosian and Yoruba intellectuals towards reclaiming 'African-ness' and distinguishing it from European ways. In this series, a pseudonymous writer called 'Our Special Correspondent' travels to the Yoruba-speaking towns of Abẹ́òkúta, Ìbàdàn, Ọ̀yọ́, Òṣogbo, Ẹdẹ, Iléṣà, and Ifẹ̀, where he comments on political institutions, rulers, roads and industry. Although based on the writer's own experience, his narratives are less interested than the Yoruba-language travel narratives of the 1920s were in narrating the subjectivity of the traveller and his sociability (see Chapter 2). Instead, their focus is on documenting the places to which 'Our Special Correspondent' travels and offering commentary on matters of contemporary political and social significance. In particular, the writer explores the impact of the British colonial era on the Yoruba region. He reports approvingly on some of the infrastructural change he encounters, comparing it to his previous experiences of Yoruba towns. He discusses the

[20] Newell, *The Power to Name*, p. 18; Echeruo, *Victorian Lagos*, pp. 36–8; Emmanuel Ayankanmi Ayandele, *The Missionary Impact on Modern Nigeria, 1842–1914: A Political and Social Analysis* (London Longmans, 1966), pp. 257–8.

development of roads and railways in each town; the 'whole face' of Abẹ́òkúta has been changed by roads being 'opened up in every direction', which he judges to be a great improvement, while he explains that Ìbàdàn has changed immensely since the opening of the railways in 1901: 'What was called the Iddo gate or Iddo road and which was then a bare expanse is now covered with commercial houses on both sides of the roadway which surpasses even the Marina at Lagos.'[21]

However, the writer also seeks to distinguish between the infrastructural and technological changes of colonial modernity, and the potentially damaging intellectual and social change that he perceives colonial 'civilisation' to bring. On meeting *Balógun* Sówẹ̀mímọ́ in Ìbàdàn, 'Our Special Correspondent' remarks approvingly that he is not 'an Anglicised African': 'Here was indeed a lesson for the African and an example which if he had followed would have saved him from the contempt and the ridicule of the European.'[22] 'Our Special Correspondent' uses his travel narrative to emphasise the value of the 'African' and the danger of 'Anglicisation', perhaps imagining that this untainted African-ness can be more easily found in the Yoruba region than in anglicised Lagos.

This concern with the ways that the Yoruba region and Lagos are differentially negotiating African-ness and the European colonial era is connected with the writer's rationale for his travel narrative. The series is couched in terms of the need for Lagosians to align themselves with the Yoruba-speaking region: 'To the African who knows that his life is bound up with that of his people, a tour to the Hinterland at the present time is fraught with no little interest.' The writer argues that the '[f]oreign influence' of religion serves to 'divorce' 'the African' in Lagos 'from his own people and life and sends him out a segregated unit whose ideas [sic] of national life is a nationality built up without a nation'. This account of his tour of the hinterland is designed to (re)acquaint Lagosians with their 'nation', filling the emptiness of the abstract concept of 'nationality' with symbolic meaning through contact with others who are more 'national', less subject to 'foreign influence'.[23] The 'nation' that the Lagosian is lacking is ambiguous, but implicitly it is the Yoruba region; although this is not spelt out, it is implied in the scope of the series, in which the writer travels to a number of major Yoruba towns. The 'nation' is created for the Lagosian through travel, by connecting him to 'his people' – by implication, the travel narrative can connect the similarly alienated Lagosian reader to 'his people', creating a 'nation' where once there was only an empty category. Both travel and the travel narrative are imagined as mediating the effects of colonial modernity, allowing

---

[21] 'A Tour to the Hinterland by Our Special Correspondent', *Lagos Weekly Record*, 19 October 1912, p. 5.
[22] *Balógun* is a title given to a town's senior warrior; ibid.
[23] Ibid.

the writer to select the best parts of both 'civilisation' and 'his people' to create a new 'nation', just as the writer himself admires technological change in the Yoruba region, but rejects 'Anglicisation'.

In 1913, on the eve of the colonial amalgamation of Nigeria in 1914, 'Our Special Correspondent' – presumably the same writer, judging by similarities of tone – published another travel narrative, 'A Trip to Northern Nigeria and Back', which details his travels in northern Nigeria: Kaduna, Zaria, and Kano. Contrasting with the sense of connection and shared 'nationhood' established in his tour of the Yoruba region, this northern Nigerian tour glories in a depiction of northern Nigeria as both exotic and primitive:

> Scanning the plains to the right and left one sees a network of mud huts, grass-roofed, conical in shape and suggestive of Primitive men emerging from the dawn of civilisation [...] Your first impression of these huts is to view them with indifference and scorn since they present a striking contrast to the massive structures of the more progressive towns of Southern Nigeria [...] Philosophically considered, they inspire you with a sublime love for the Simple Life and attune your soul to the plain melodies of mother Nature.[24]

This depiction of the 'primitive' men of mud huts and the 'Simple Life', closer to nature than the 'civilised' Lagosian, suggests a desire to distinguish 'progressive' Lagos from the 'primitive' northern provinces on the eve of Nigerian unification, establishing the intellectual and social primacy of Lagos and the Yoruba region in this new colony. 'Our Special Correspondent' has a second, apparently contrasting weapon in his rhetorical arsenal to draw readers' attention to the sharp distinction between Lagos and northern Nigeria; he describes 'heavily turbaned and gorgeously attired' Hausas 'zarkiing'[25] to the

---

[24] 'A Trip to Northern Nigeria and Back by Our Special Correspondent', *Lagos Weekly Record*, 2 August 1913.

[25] The adoption of the custom of the 'zarki' by British colonial officials in northern Nigeria was described by the *Nigerian Chronicle* in 1912 as follows: 'it is the custom of the Fulani Conquerors whenever the Emir is out, for some of his retinue to precede him shouting ZARKI! ZARKI! ZARKI!!! all the way, – a sort of announcement that the Emir is on his way out through that street. At this notice, people either clear out of the road or stoop down as a sign of respect while the Emir passes. Whenever he passes through the market and this announcement is made business is for that moment suspended and every individual is under obligation to pay obeisance – the women kneeling and the men stooping down until he passes away. When the British Government took up control of Northern Nigeria it is said that officials adopted this Fulani custom under the pretext of it being native custom; but, in reality, as a means of enhancing their personalities before the subject races'. 'Zarki! Zarki!! Zarki!!! A Sidelight into the Zaria incident', *Nigerian Chronicle*, 13 September 1912, p. 2.

Resident.[26] The exotic spectacle reminds readers that this is a strange place, not like home, and not easily conflated with the Yoruba region, even if the British were seeking to create a colony out of these disparate places. In doing so, 'Our Special Correspondent' contributes to a narrative of southern Nigeria as 'the solid antithesis of a monolithic and backward north' and of the north as overly acquiescent to British imperialism that Wálé Adébánwí identifies in the 1950s press as, at least in part, a reaction to Frederick Lugard's proclamation that the Fulbe (Fulani) emirs of northern Nigeria were 'born rulers'. This narrative of 'constant condescension' to northern Nigeria would continue to circulate in the Lagos press in later decades as southern Nigerian intellectuals and politicians expressed their concern about the potential power of northern Nigeria in an independent Nigerian state.[27] But we can see here, in earlier decades, how narratives of 'Nigeria' were already circulating, even if they were very sceptical about the conjoining of south and north of this colony.

As well as distancing himself from northern Nigeria, 'Our Special Correspondent' also gently criticises the colonial state: he sarcastically describes a visit to the notoriously harsh and racist British Residency in Kano as likely to be 'regular rollicking fun'.[28] As he also did in his travel narrative describing the Yoruba region, 'Our Special Correspondent' uses his northern Nigerian travel narrative to judge and establish hierarchies of 'civilisation' within Nigeria, and to select aspects of ways of life and political regimes, both Nigerian and colonial, that he wishes to reject or distance himself from.

First-person travel narratives of this kind continued to be published into the 1920s in the anglophone Lagos press, as Nigeria adjusted to its colonial statehood, and as intellectuals increasingly questioned the ways in which Nigeria's elite should relate to colonial forms of 'civilisation'. Délàṇọ's *The Soul of Nigeria*, too, can be read as a later contribution to this aspect of Yoruba intellectual and literary culture as Nigerian nationalism began to gain strength in the late 1930s, calling into question the relation between Lagos, the Yoruba region and the rest of Nigeria. Délàṇọ uses travel to select aspects of colonial 'civilisation' with which to make progress, while asserting the need to retain 'African-ness', and establishing hierarchies of 'civilisation' within Nigeria, with Lagos at the centre. Indeed, the opposition that Délàṇọ sets up in this book is often not that between 'native' and coloniser, but a binary between 'native' and the literate Lagosian and Yoruba elite. While the book was hailed by reviewer 'W. F.' as offering an 'African' voice, Délàṇọ distances himself

---

[26] 'A Trip to Northern Nigeria and Back by Our Special Correspondent', *Lagos Weekly Record*, 9 August 1913.

[27] Adebanwi, *Nation as Grand Narrative*, pp. 56–7.

[28] 'A Trip to Northern Nigeria and Back by Our Special Correspondent', *Lagos Weekly Record*, 9 August 1913.

from the African 'natives' that he describes. 'I confess I have been surprised', he writes, 'during the ten years I have been watching and studying the natives' ways, life and customs at close range, at the seriousness and solemnity attached to the dead which these ceremonies evince' (102). Délànọ̀ here is the observer, not a 'native' himself.

Délànọ̀ plays out this distinction between 'native' and 'civilisation' through literacy in particular. It is 'illiterate natives' from whom he envisages himself gaining his most valuable knowledge because, as he puts it in his chapter on death, they 'still uphold the traditional ceremonies' (110). In a chapter on the *ìwọ̀fà* system, Délànọ̀ explains how he especially seeks out illiterate knowledge: 'My stay in this village was particularly interesting, for as a result of my talks with some of the people, and especially with illiterate natives, I was able to gain enlightenment upon a phase of local life in which I was very interested. I refer to the subject of the Iwofa system, about which I was anxious to obtain reliable and untainted information' (70).[29] The 'natives' are imagined as closer to 'tradition' and the past, 'untainted' by book knowledge and religion.

The literate Yoruba elite are most frequently referred to through the figure of the 'clerk', a term used in this era to describe not only a literal clerk, but also someone who had passed through the colonial education system to at least primary school level and taken up a job that required the use of literacy. Despite epitomising this figure himself, and being identified as a clerk by a lorry driver he encounters on his travels (48), Délànọ̀ is critical of the value of the clerk: 'A civilization that ties our hands, prevents us doing manual labour, and simply places a pencil behind our ears is useless', Délànọ̀ writes. 'People say it is so intentionally designed. I don't know' (44), he adds, confirming the implicit criticism of British colonialism and its destruction of African ways of life that runs throughout the book. Délànọ̀ describes how, under the previous education system, becoming a clerk removed a boy from his home both spatially and culturally: 'When the boy left school he became a clerk, and was a man of influence when next he visited his village or town'; the 'clerk' invariably leaves home, returning only for visits. The 'clerk' is transformed physically: his hair becomes 'wild and bushy', he carries pens and pencils, and dresses in knickers, stockings, a khaki helmet and brown shoes. He would 'go round the village or neighbourhood from door to door':

> people received him cordially or otherwise, as their feelings dictated. Those whose children were still experiencing stormy weather, saw in the young man the goal they were aiming at, the destination their dear ones were making for. (23)

---

[29] A system of pawn labour, in which the labour of a bondman or -woman (*ìwọ̀fà*) is given for a set period of time in exchange for a loan.

The clerk is a symbol of aspiration but also dislocation, taking on the status of a visitor in his own village, and physically marked out as different.

Délànọ's sense of the difference that 'civilisation' produces between Nigerians is played out in a scene in the beginning of the book in which he describes his daily journey into Lagos from his home in Yaba, now a suburb of mainland Lagos, but then a new, planned development at the far edge of the city. Délànọ describes how he encounters a 'strange, overpowering sense of the wonder of existence, rendered conspicuous by the new Carter Bridge. Here indeed is an engineering feat which has gained complete ascendancy over nature' (13–14). Délànọ's description of the Carter Bridge, built by the British in 1901, could be considered a manifestation of what Brian Larkin terms the 'colonial sublime': the 'use of technology to represent an overwhelming sense of grandeur and awe in the service of colonial power'.[30] However, Délànọ's description of the significance of the bridge rests not on the distinction between coloniser and colonised that Larkin identifies in the colonial sublime, but in distinctions of wealth between Lagosians: 'On the bridge one feels more secure than on land, and has an utter disregard of the water below, whilst the poor folks, day in and day out, find their livelihood upon it' (14). Colonial technology produces distinctions and stratifications not only between coloniser and colonised, but also within Lagos, between the elite who can walk on the bridge feeling 'secure', having an 'utter disregard' for that which is beneath them, and those whom they watch below, the 'poor folks' dwarfed by the scale of the bridge. Délànọ, and implicitly the reader travelling with him, are imagined to be 'on the bridge', for without having walked 'on the bridge' Délànọ would not be able to describe how 'secure' it makes him feel.

Délànọ is so successful in making a claim to his apparent distance from 'native' life that reviewer Charles Kingsley Meek remarked that 'Mr. Delano frequently expresses amazement at customs which even a European with slight acquaintance of Africa would consider merely commonplace', and suggested that Yoruba life constituted 'a culture with which [Délànọ] has clearly, at many points, completely lost contact.'[31] However, Délànọ's claim to 'clerkly' distance from the 'natives' should not always be taken at face value. Throughout *The Soul of Nigeria*, Délànọ grapples with the 'contestation of identities' that Paulo Fernando de Moraes Farias and Karin Barber identify as characteristic of the lived culture of Lagos's cultural brokers, as Délànọ explores his own relation to the Yoruba people who are the subject of the book.[32]

The complexities of the multiple forms of 'civilisation' on offer are played out through slippages and contradictions in the position of Délànọ himself. The

---

[30] Larkin, *Signal and Noise*, p. 7.
[31] Meek, '*The Soul of Nigeria* by Isaac O. Delano', pp. 119, 21.
[32] Farias and Barber, 'Introduction', p. 1.

most revealing of these slippages can be found in the frequent shifts of pronouns used to refer to Délànǫ and to 'natives', which underscore the difficulty that Délànǫ encounters in occupying a single subject position as a literate Yoruba in this rapidly changing age. Describing his surprise at a conversation with his host in an unnamed village about the past, current affairs and 'the present political and economic difficulties of the world', Délànǫ writes:

> I had certainly thought I might find among these impoverished natives a re-awakening interest in our own affairs; I might hear varnished or unvarnished tales of the past; gain a knowledge of their heroes and heroines and their old tribal warfare. I might gather information regarding their native laws and customs; hear their views on the white man's government; perhaps something about our local Samuel Pepys or Mark Twain. These things I expected to come across and enjoy, but I never seriously thought I should glean a crystallized opinion on modern affairs and world events from a native, whose only claim to a knowledge of modern civilization is the fact that he is a Christian! (58)

Délànǫ initially distinguishes himself from 'these impoverished natives', whom he expects to be able to recount oral tales of the past and 'native' customs but not 'modern affairs', which are Délànǫ's concerns. Yet despite making this sharp distinction of 'civilisation', the pronoun 'our' also enters the paragraph, as Délànǫ envisages a hybrid, a literate writer who is nonetheless 'local'. The reference to Pepys and Twain indicates Délànǫ's imbrication with the literary cultures of the anglophone West, but it is nonetheless 'our local' Pepys or Twain to whom he refers, as if envisaging someone who could bridge the gap between 'I' and 'they' to create 'our' storytellers. Moreover, it is 'our own affairs' that he imagines the 'natives' might be interested in; with his use of the first person pronoun, Délànǫ momentarily aligns himself, however condescendingly, with the 'impoverished natives'.

Délànǫ uses 'we' and 'us' to align himself directly with 'natives', usually when making a civilisational distinction: 'Natives never kiss', he claims, for instance. 'Kissing was imported with the Western civilization. It is foreign to us' (121). He particularly claims a sense of 'we' when it links him to the 'natives' of the past, rather than the present. In the pre-colonial past, Délànǫ claims, '[w]e spoke the truth always and acted upon it. It is deplorable, however, that many of the principles of our great-grandparents have been discarded' (204). 'Our great-grandparents' provide a genealogical link between past and present, between 'civilised' and 'native', as if the 'clerk' and the 'illiterate native' are cousins with the same ancestors, but are no longer the same people. Thus even within the same chapter, when he returns to discussing the present day, Délànǫ writes of how, having lost the values of honesty that he locates in the past, 'We have ceased to be African and we can never be European. Our minds are hybrids of black and white. Isn't it a pity?' (205). Here, 'we' is the 'hybrid', the 'clerk', not the 'illiterate native' who can give Délànọ the way back to his origin. So 'we' functions in both senses: the pre-colonial 'native' and the 'hybrid' Euro-African.

A scene in which Délànọ describes an instance of 'native surgery' epitomises Délànọ's unstable narratorial position with regard to the 'natives'. When reporting on the 'natives', Délànọ typically occupies the stance of either an observer or a listener. In a scene in which he describes a 'native surgeon' treating a man with a severe abscess, Délànọ initially occupies his customary observer stance: 'His groaning reached me outside, and sheer humanity prompted me to enter. The odour of gin filled the air. The medicine was mixed with gin. I sat down. When my eyes became used to the prevailing darkness, I began to study the room in detail' (84). As Délànọ studies the scene, he occupies his characteristic position of surprise, describing his 'curiosity' as he sees '[s]mall knives, big knives, curved knives, knives of many kinds and shapes', and then 'amazement' as he realises the patient is about to be cut open with a 'red hot' knife that is resting in the fire: 'I was surprised', he explains. 'I knew something about native medicines and other relative things, but I had never heard of native surgery' (84).

But Délànọ is then asked by the surgeon to assist in the operation, revealing the instability of his attempts to position himself on the outside of 'native' ways, as perhaps the surgeon does not perceive Délànọ as so distant from participation in 'native ways' as Délànọ himself might imagine. Délànọ describes this shift from observer to actor as producing anxiety about the consequences of his participation: 'My heart leaped within me. If the man died under this crude operation, was I not a participant in an act of murder and an accomplice?' (85). But the operation is a success. Describing his return that evening to the home of his host – a station-master in an unnamed small town near Abẹ̀òkúta – Délànọ returns to his position as narrator, retrieving his distance from the scene by again recalling his surprise, and contrasting it with his host's lack of surprise:

> I returned to the house with the full intention of giving the inmates an account of an event which would surprise them. The women had returned, but I was not yet sufficiently free to spin the yarn. When the station-master arrived he came straight to my room and inquired after my welfare. I told him how I had spent the morning, and how the surgeon had performed the operation. He did not appear surprised, for the man had circumcised his baby a few months before, and he spoke lightly of his ability. (86)

Délànọ is once again the Lagosian shocked at 'native' ways, while the station-master, despite his imbrication in 'civilisation' through his job working on the railways, is positioned as more of a 'native' than Délànọ, an actor in commissioning 'native ways' such as surgery.

These slippages of position are echoed by the book's generic instability. The book moves back and forth between personal anecdotes from Délànọ̀'s childhood, observations implicitly from his travels, accounts of Yoruba history and politics, stories he has been told either on his travels or at other times in his life, and attempts to generalise about Yoruba customs. In the second half of the book, Délànọ̀ moves from personal accounts of specific journeys to an attempt at a more generalised ethnographic mode, with travel still the implicit method behind his observations but no longer the subject of his narrative. Neither one thing nor the other, the book resists being tied down to any of these modes of narration about 'customs' and 'civilisation'. Charles Kingsley Meek remarks that 'although the book contains many crudities and contradictions it is interesting and readable throughout'.[33] I would, however, suggest that rather than being 'interesting' *despite* its 'contradictions', it is *The Soul of Nigeria*'s many 'contradictions' that make it so interesting. These slippages, the tussle back and forth between knowledge of 'the native way' and claiming distance from it, is emblematic of the book's greater overall tussle between ways of being during a perceived moment of rupture. If Délànọ̀ is sometimes more 'surprised' by 'the native way' than Meek would expect, it is not simply because he has 'lost contact' with Yoruba culture, but because the narrative itself is enacting the process of being in a moment of change, standing at a crossroads between worlds.

In her history of pseudonymity in the colonial anglophone West African press, Stephanie Newell argues that through the use of pseudonyms, new modes of subjectivity were established in colonial West African print culture that radically decentred the author from his or her textual persona. Newell shows how authors used the power of print and pseudonymity to detach the individual author from the sometimes playful subjectivities created in print, 'complicat[ing] the selves that were expressed' and allowing authors to experiment with 'voices, genders, genres, and opinions'.[34] A model of subjectivity emerged that was not fixed, with one author constituting one subject, but rather it was 'disconnected from the writing body' and enabled the birth of a notion of print as 'existing beyond the subject, conveying a public voice and public opinion'.[35]

Much of the travel writing examined so far in this book differs from the pseudonymous writing Newell discusses in that it appears to attach itself insistently to an individual author, their physical self, their travelling body and their anecdotes, whether to stress their sociability and reputation, or their authority and experience, as in the case of Délànọ̀. Yet reading Délànọ̀'s travel writing through Newell's model, we can see a similar instability in authorial

[33] Meek, '*The Soul of Nigeria* by Isaac O. Delano', p. 119.
[34] Newell, *The Power to Name*, pp. 2, 5.
[35] Ibid. pp. 22, 121.

subjectivity, even if it less overtly claimed than in the case of the pseudonymous writers Newell describes. Délànọ̀, the narrator, is not just a 'clerk' and he is also not just a 'native', although both of these are positions he claims in the book. He is not just living 'quite contentedly under British rule' nor is he simply decrying the 'present civilization'. He embodies all of these positions, and sometimes slips between them in ways that leave the authorial presence behind the text unstable, challenging 'imperialist modes of labelling and containing Africans', as Newell puts it, in this case as either 'native' or 'civilized'.[36] Rather than rigidly occupying one position or another, as Délànọ̀'s British reviewers would have it, Délànọ̀'s narrative can be read as shifting back and forward, unstable and uncentred.

## Shifting ideas of community

The slippages in Délànọ̀'s own position – the play between 'civilised' and 'native' – are echoed by slippages between 'Yoruba', 'Nigeria' and 'Africa' that reveal similar instabilities in the ways that these communal identities were conceived in this era. Although the book is entitled *The Soul of Nigeria*, it focuses exclusively on the Yoruba region. Délànọ̀ does not elaborate on whether the Yoruba region is the 'soul' of Nigeria, or whether he is claiming to provide an insight into the 'soul' of all of Nigeria through his travels in just the Yoruba region, although he does claim that the Yoruba region contains 'all the largest and most important towns in Nigeria', and that the Yoruba are 'the most advanced of all the tribes in Nigeria' (210–11). This sense that Nigeria can be described by describing the Yoruba region is sometimes echoed by a flattening of difference within the Yoruba region. Many of the villages and towns to which Délànọ̀ travels are unnamed, and he tends not to refer to customs belonging to particular places, but rather to homogenise them as 'Yoruba' or 'native' customs. He makes this homogenisation of the Yoruba explicit as he describes the characteristic hospitality that he received throughout his travels:

> If I do not refer again to my generous host, it is not because I am ungrateful or do not appreciate all he did for me. It is that I am unwilling to create a precedent I may not be able to follow, for such kindness is the rule rather than the exception throughout the country. The comfort provided, the home life, the rations supplied without charge, and the words of encouragement, were the same everywhere. I would be accompanied half a mile on my journey when leaving them; their wives were kind; their children amusing and friendly. To describe all this and how I distributed my parting presents among the wives and moth-

---

[36] Ibid. p. 8.

ers would prove monotonous, as all Yoruba tribes are one and spring from the same origin – the same father who lived and died at Ile Ife. (78)

Délànọ̀ connects his homogenising project to the notion of a unified Yoruba identity that, as we have seen in previous chapters, has been understood as a product of the late nineteenth century onwards, produced by the 'cultural work' of Yoruba intellectuals.[37] Délànọ̀'s unnamed hosts and villages are unified by being 'one' and from the 'same origin' at Ilé-Ifẹ̀ – thus, he suggests, although travel is crucial in providing evidence for his observations, individuation within the Yoruba region is not essential, so names of hosts and their towns are not necessary, and it is not necessary for Délànọ̀ to recount his travels to individual places. Délànọ̀'s emphasis on the hospitality he received throughout his travels recalls I. B. Thomas's emphasis on hospitality as a defining characteristic of the Lagosian and Yoruba migrants who welcomed him throughout his travels in Nigeria (see Chapter 2), and it similarly points to the imagination of an essential 'Yoruba' character, the ọmọlúwàbí (person of good character), as one who is hospitable to travelling strangers.

Délànọ̀'s insistence on the unity of the Yoruba region provides a justification for his overall method of writing ethnography through travel. Thus, he claims, he has no particular method for selecting the places to which he travels: 'I returned to Abeokuta and continued my rambling, moving about the country without any special programme and without itinerary. I went a few miles up-country by rail and here I alighted, although there was nothing much of interest' (78). Sometimes he encounters things of interest, and sometimes he does not, but there is no need to tie knowledge to particular places; it is all the same Yoruba region, so can be encountered through 'rambling' and will eventually produce generalisable knowledge.

Yet later in the book, Délànọ̀ does acknowledge significant differences within the Yoruba region. He explains that 'There is one language spoken in different dialects throughout the length and breadth of Yorubaland. The dialects vary considerably, so much so that if one does not study a particular dialect it is almost impossible to understand it when it is spoken by the people' (194). He gives numerous examples of the extent of the difference encapsulated in these dialects, to the point, he says of the Iléṣà dialect, that 'You can hardly repeat intelligibly after a real native. I tried and failed, and I am a Yoruba man!' (197). Délànọ̀'s comment here is indicative of the sense that local specificity belongs to the 'real native', but at the same time, such a person is a 'Yoruba' just like Délànọ̀. Similarly, Délànọ̀ remarks with surprise on the dialects of Abẹ́òkúta, the town in which Délànọ̀ himself claimed ancestry, as an Ẹ̀gbá: 'I found it difficult to understand the dialect of an elderly Toko man with whom

[37] Peel, 'Yoruba Ethnogenesis'.

I talked, and had I not met him at Abeokuta I would have declared he was not speaking an Egba dialect' (197). Délànò's admission of incomprehension even in those places such as Abẹ̀òkúta, where he feels he should be most familiar, and of intra-Yoruba incomprehension more generally, is a surprising jolt to his insistence elsewhere on the generalisability of 'Yoruba' and 'native' ways.

But Délànò frames this contrast between local specificity and generalis-ability again as a product of 'civilisation', as he remarks on the development of standard Yoruba, 'the written Yoruba of our Bible' (194). Thus what is originally discussed as a marker of difference is again homogenised as part of the 'cultural work of Yoruba ethnogenesis'; there is again a turn from local specificity to what Délànò characterises as 'pure Yoruba, which is understand-able by any Yoruba man' (195). Délànò's attribution of 'purity' to standard Yoruba is surprising, given standard Yoruba's origins in nineteenth-century missionary endeavour and its assemblage out of particular dialects of what has now become unified as 'Yoruba', but perhaps refers to standard Yoruba's lack of local embeddedness. Regardless, Délànò's discussion of dialect and local specificity reminds us that the 'cultural work of Yoruba ethnogenesis' was by no means finished by the 1930s, and the category 'Yoruba' remained open to contestation. No wonder that Délànò is sometimes 'surprised' at things he encounters in the Yoruba region; while Meek may implicitly insist on the homogeneity of the customs of 'Africa', Délànò shows that the Yoruba region is heterogeneous and the 'cultural work of ethnogenesis' is ongoing.

There was an even greater sense of the instability of 'Nigeria' as a category during this era, and this creeps into the way Délànò inconsistently frames the difference between 'Yoruba' and 'Nigeria' in the book. Sometimes, Délànò conflates Yoruba and Nigeria, as in a chapter on 'the marriage system in Nigeria' that describes Yoruba marriage practices (121). Elsewhere, Délànò acknowledges the difference between Yoruba and Nigeria: in discussing naming practices, he mentions that '[e]very tribe in Nigeria attaches great importance to names, and the Yoruba people are no exception to this rule' (146). But his comparative reference point in this book is not usually other Nigerians – who are rarely acknowledged, with only one mention of the Igbo people in the whole book – but the British. For instance, writing of naming practices, he asserts that '[w]ith Yoruba people, one's name is one's name. We do not attach our father's name to our own' (146); the implicit comparison is with British surnames (and with the British-influenced naming practices adopted by educated Lagosians), not with the naming practices of 'every tribe in Nigeria'. Again, Délànò's 'we' is implicitly the Yoruba 'native' rather than the Lagosian.

Later in the book, Délànò also identifies the Yoruba people as Africans, in order to strengthen the perceived contrast between 'African' and 'British' civili-sation: 'During a tour of the country I heard the African point of view', Délànò writes (220). This 'African' perspective is identified both as an upstanding contrast to British civilisation, and in opposition to both colonialism and hybridity: 'Honesty, fair dealing and straightforwardness were our virtues in the olden days', Délànǫ claims. He continues: 'When Africans cease to be Africans in mind, in thought and sometimes in appearance, then they degenerate and become dishonest' (205). Elsewhere, he slips between 'Nigerian' and 'African' as he writes of attitudes towards colonialism: 'The African was not certain of the Englishman's motive. He admitted the lofty ideal placed before him, but he required proof of the white man's sincerity. He wondered if there would ever be a Nigerian Government controlled by Nigerians' (220). Délànǫ writes of 'Nigeria' here as perhaps not yet realised, as long as the 'Nigerian Government' is not 'controlled by Nigerians'. By contrast, the 'African' is written as a viable mode of subjectivity, understood in contrast to the 'Englishman': the African, he writes, is 'contented to remain an African'; he is 'not anxious to become a European' (220).

Yoruba novelist D. Ǫ. Fágúnwà, whose first novel was published just a year after *The Soul of Nigeria* in 1938, similarly moved fluidly between categories such as Yoruba, Nigeria and Africa in his writing, so that, as Karin Barber puts it, 'the Yoruba are the Egba writ large, Nigeria is Yorubaland writ large, and Africa, perhaps, is Yorubaland writ even larger'.[38] Délànǫ's own unstable shifts between categories such as Yoruba, Nigerian and African, and the way he sometimes, but not always, attempts to make his travels largely in the Ègbá region stand for Yoruba and Yoruba for Nigeria, may thus reflect a broader literary moment of communal identity-making in mid-twentieth-century Nigeria, as writers sought to make sense of the multiple categories of communal identity that were available to them, the emerging cultural and nationalist politics, and the multiple allegiances they could claim. We saw in previous chapters how Crowther, Thomas and Akintán imagined themselves, in different ways, as both distant from and linked to the Yoruba people and to other Nigerians, again, often in terms of perceived civilisational difference. These writers of the late nineteenth and early twentieth centuries were writing in an age when the boundaries within the region and, in the 1920s and 1930s, within colonial Nigeria, were in flux. As Délànǫ shows in his investigation of the Yoruba region, it can be claimed as both unified and highly heterogeneous, a 'nation' in itself and, ostensibly at least, a region within a not-yet-fully realised nation of Nigeria. Charles Kingsley Meek and 'W. F.' criticise the 'contradictions' within the book and Délànǫ's apparent distance from the Yoruba people, but the book suggests that Délànǫ's sense of potential estrangement within the Yoruba region is also attributable to the shifting boundaries, the heterogeneity, of the Yoruba region and the upheaval that 'civilisation' produces.

[38] Barber, 'Time, Space and Writing', pp. 123–4; Nnodim, 'Configuring Audiences', pp. 160–4.

By 1944, when Délànọ̀ published his second travelogue, *Notes and Comments on Nigeria*, his view of Nigeria had widened beyond Yoruba-speaking Nigeria into northern Nigeria. Délànọ̀'s venture into northern Nigeria begins with Ìlọrin – then often considered part of the north, rather than the Yoruba region – where he is surprised to find that he is 'still encompassed by familiar life. The language with little variations remained the same, though the busy life of Lagos and other important towns in the South Province has disappeared' (25). However, he notes, Ìlọrin is a largely Muslim city, where the people are 'coming and going in curious turbans and white gowns' (25), and he describes the mixing of Hausa ways of life with that of the Ìlọrin people, whom he views as distinct from the Yoruba people, but yet surprisingly similar to them in nature: 'The ordinary Ilorin man displays a good deal of serene pride, self-respect and fortitude and something of the surprising wit of the Hausa without the sharpness of his intellect. The methodical and decent living of the Yorubas is not as exceptional as I had thought' (27). Amongst the Hausa people of Kano, however, Délànọ̀ encounters a stranger world, which he views as belonging to the past: 'Nowhere in Nigeria does the past live before your eyes as it does in Kano', Délànọ̀ writes, adding that 'The wonderful inscriptions on the walls of houses all over the town are significant of a glory that has passed. The glory of Kano is the glory of the North' (49). Adopting missionary discourse, he calls for Christians to preach the gospel in northern Nigeria: 'A troop of men and women to the crusade on the other side of the Niger is urgently needed' (50).

In *Notes and Comments*, Délànọ̀ establishes hierarchies of civilisation within Nigeria: the southerners are more progressive than the northerners – recalling a dispute about the north and south of the country, he states that 'The prevailing view was that the North should be cut off from the South because with its weight the South cannot climb the ladder of progress' (51) – and within the northerners, the Ìlọrin people are the closest to Yoruba civilisation, followed by the past glories of the Hausa people, and then the 'naked tribes' and the Gwari people: 'The Gwari people are cannibals. Those in the hinterland are more backward than those at Zaria, and these latter than those in the Niger Province. They are all more backward than the Hausas' (54).

In fact, the Gwaris are not the only cannibals Délànọ̀ warns the reader about: he devotes several pages to discussing the dangers for travellers of the 'naked tribes' of the north in general:

> You who are going to the North of Nigeria having personal interest in knowing something about the people, be prepared to face many odds. Sometimes, even in this year of grace, you hold your life in your hands. There are those who look on you as a good meal. They are the naked tribes. You will be disgusted at looking at the nakedness of men and women, old and young, living in hills, caves and forests. (52)

The reason that the traveller is taking their life into their own hands rests in the people's propensity to eat vulnerable solo travellers:

> Do not stroll singly to watch the dances, marriages, burials and religious ceremonies. If you do, you will meet things to complain of. You will create appetite in them and you will see signs of it. Be prepared to be sociable and chatty, if you are many and with a trustworthy guide. A single traveller wandering about at random may soon find himself in trouble of being cooked or fried. (53)

Délànọ̀ wields the figure of the cannibal to express perceived civilisational difference in the way that we have already encountered in the earlier travel narratives discussed in this book. Yet he does not characterise the 'naked tribes' entirely unfavourably, noting that the traveller in this region will also encounter 'wonders and surprises': 'You will see how these nudists adhere to their ancestral principles and you will be astounded with the high morality existing among them', he explains, adding that as he progressed on his journey, his initial unfavourable impressions were somewhat dispelled: 'I had the gratification of finding that I was, despite other faults and circumstances, surrounded on all sides by people whose intelligence and patience are wonderful' (52–3). Délànọ̀'s surprise at the favourable qualities of the people echoes the benevolent paternalism of some Western missionary travellers in Africa in the nineteenth century, but also suggests an effort by Délànọ̀ both to distance himself from the people – they are still 'nudists' and cannibals, after all – and to find potential points of connection within a shared nation that he now acknowledges as stretching, if uneasily, beyond the Yoruba region.

## Sifting knowledge

Another consequence of the colonial era and the rise of Western-style education and literary culture was a shift in the way that knowledge was produced and shared. As J. D. Y. Peel has argued, in the late nineteenth and early twentieth centuries, the 'traditional esotericism of Yoruba knowledge, hoarded by the powerful as a key resource, gave way to a more open conception in the twentieth century, linked to conversionary religions', to the new forms of knowledge valorised by missionary education including *èkọ́* (education) and *iwé* (books, book-learning), and to *ọ̀làjú* (civilisation or enlightenment).[39] The forms and genres in which knowledge was disseminated also changed. Karin Barber has suggested that knowledge transmitted through oral forms in pre-colonial Yoruba society was segregated into particular genres such as *ìtàn* (historical narrative) and *oríkì* (praise poetry), which in turn were controlled and performed

---

[39] Peel, 'Olaju', pp. 139, 144–9.

only by certain groups in society, such as elderly men, women or *babaláwo*s. Colonial-era written texts, such as the town histories discussed in Chapter 1, began to break the divisions between these genres and the knowledge that was segregated within them, assembling knowledge associated with these genres within one text and defusing the secrecy associated with knowledge, which was now presented as accessible to any literate person.[40] Thus, as Insa Nolte writes, 'a re-ordering and re-interpretation of existing categories of knowledge in order to gain a new understanding of the world not only changed the content of historical debate but could also lead to the emergence of new forms of historical argument and representation', as new written histories 'brought together different aspects of historical knowledge which had previously been separated', and addressed wider audiences than had previously been imagined to be possible.[41] These audiences were potentially made up of anyone who was able to read: southwest Nigeria's new literate elite and its 'clerk' class.

Isaac Délànọ̀ was, in common with many of the Yoruba writers and intellectuals of the early twentieth century, concerned with the ways that knowledge could be produced and transmitted in this new era. The Yoruba travel writers of the 1920s used travel writing, and claims about the benefits of both travel and travel writing, to justify the value of the printed text. *The Soul of Nigeria* is also concerned with the ways that knowledge can be contained and transmitted through the written text, but is particularly concerned with the role of the 'clerk' or the writer in producing knowledge that is suitable for the new age. As we saw, Délànọ̀ claims that his knowledge was gained from travelling and '[o]n train, canoe and lorry I gathered my information from the rank and file of the people of Nigeria, much of which I had to sift very carefully to avoid repetition, uncertainty and irrelevancy' (7). Indeed, Délànọ̀'s mode of knowledge production throughout the book can be characterised as 'sifting', as Délànọ̀ positions himself as the arbitrator and mediator of knowledge. Through travel, he comes into contact with stories, ideas, 'customs' and oral histories, and he decides from these which can be considered valid knowledge. Travel comes to stand for the way that knowledge can be obtained through contact with orality and through personal experience.

In this way, Délànọ̀ positions himself in a similar manner to the cultural collectors that Karin Barber identifies amongst the Lagos elite in the 1920s. Barber suggests that when the educated elite of late nineteenth- and early twentieth-century Lagos researched and wrote down aspects of local culture in print, they saw their work as not simply documentation and preservation, but

---

[40] Barber, 'I. B. Akinyele', p. 33.
[41] Insa Nolte, 'Colonial Politics and Precolonial History: Everyday Knowledge, Genre, and Truth in a Yoruba Town', *History in Africa*, 40.1 (2013), pp. 125–64 (p. 128).

as sanitising culture, 'judiciously selecting and revising in order to constitute it as a firm foundation for future progress'. Print, Barber suggests, was 'central to this process, for it made revised versions of the traditions both definitive and openly accessible'. This 'incremental cultural editing' was considered a form of 'progress', for in this way knowledge can be selected, standardised and corrected.[42] Délànǫ presents himself as a mediator between the era of orality and that of the 'present civilization':

> The history of the Yoruba people is based on records passed on by word of mouth from generation to generation. For that reason it is difficult to compile, and many irrelevant matters continually recur. But from available information gathered from the natives, it is evident that there was a civilization before the advent of white men. (206)

Délànǫ does not dismiss orality as not belonging to 'civilisation' – indeed, here it provides evidence of 'civilisation' – but he presents it as demanding his intervention to sift out 'irrelevant matters'.

In travelling to obtain knowledge to collect and sift in this way, Délànǫ insists on the viability of information obtained as an outsider. Délànǫ presents himself as a product of the era of more open knowledge that Peel identifies, in which it is possible to present even truer knowledge because, as a traveller, he is able to generalise and obtain a broader perspective, and as an educated man, he is able to 'sift'. Délànǫ positions himself as seeing more than the 'natives'; he, the traveller, has a panoramic view of the whole region, echoing the bird's eye views of Abǫ̀òkúta and Ìbàdàn he includes in the photos, but also as a 'civilised' person, he has a panoramic, 'edited' view of history. He is able to survey and select knowledge, compared to the authentic yet static and piecemeal knowledge that he imagines embodied in the 'natives'.

However, as Délànǫ also shows, this is not a straightforward process; knowledge is not always open and available. Describing the *Egúngún* masquerade, Délànǫ writes: 'I am not divulging any religious secret when I say that an "Egungun" is a full-grown man, covered in a big assortment of clothes, sewn on him in a way that leaves no part of his body uncovered.'[43] Revealing that there is a man underneath the masquerade, rather than it being a direct manifestation of an ancestral spirit, is not a contravention of ritual secrecy, Délànǫ explains, because '[t]his is now an open secret' (164). The temporality of this sentence indicates Délànǫ's sense that this openness of ritual knowledge is a product of 'now', or 'civilisation'. But not all ritual knowledge is open in this way. By contrast, the *Orò* festival rituals and masquerade cannot be described

---

[42] Barber, 'I. B. Akinyele', pp. 32–3.
[43] An ancestral masquerade.

in detail, Délànọ̀ writes later in the book, for fear of 'the displeasure of "Oro" worshippers' (185).[44]

As well as reaching the limits of knowledge when he addresses ritual, Délànọ̀ is forced to acknowledge limits to the knowledge an outsider can obtain when he tries to research recent events that have a continued political significance. In attempting to learn about the Àdubí Rising of June–August 1918, in which the Ẹ̀gbá people unsuccessfully rose up against colonial taxation policy, Délànọ̀ is met with silence from the Ẹgbá people: 'Almost all the heroes connected with the Adubi Rising had died. The people were not over-willing to disclose what they knew, being in evident fear of authority, and not altogether satisfied with my identity and the purpose for which I told them I wanted the information' (96). Délànọ̀'s difficulty in trying to obtain knowledge is explicitly linked to his status as an outsider:

> At Abaren village I was warned never to talk about demonstrations or to question people about how the Osile met his death, what they did during the Adubi Rising, or their capability in any branch of medicine. In doing so I ran a great risk, as the people would not consider any investigation about themselves, their mode of life and other things that might be of interest to outsiders. (96)

The little information that he is able to obtain he describes as 'trifling stories', which 'were for the most part ninth or tenth hand, and so might have been distorted in the process' (96). Délànọ̀'s identity as both a 'clerk' and an outsider are here distancing him from knowledge, rather than affording him a broad perspective.

*The Soul of Nigeria* ends with a curious anecdote that can be read as establishing scepticism and the need to 'sift' all claims as Délànọ̀'s defining mode of investigation. Délànọ̀ describes how a confidence trickster attempts to convince Délànọ̀ to take part in a scam in which the fraudster claims he will multiply Délànọ̀'s money from £50 to £500 using a charm. Délànọ̀ asks for a demonstration before parting with his money, and the trickster agrees and succeeds in turning ten shillings in copper coins belonging to Délànọ̀ into fifty shillings in silver coins. But Délànọ̀ then tricks the trickster, convincing him to give him twenty of these shillings before returning next week for Délànọ̀'s £50. When the trickster returns, Délànọ̀ at first refuses to return the extra ten shillings, saying they have disappeared, and eventually returns them in copper coins, not the silver the trickster had given him. The closing sentence of the book is a moral extracted from this experience: 'I had bested him after all, in spite of his besting

---

[44] *Orò* is an *òrìṣà* worshipped with ceremonies distinguished by the use of a bull-roarer. Women are traditionally forbidden to watch the procession of *Orò* masqueraders or to know the secrets of *Orò*, and must stay indoors on the nights when the *Orò* masquerade is taking place.

me, and I strongly advise others who may read of my experience to give such people a very wide berth' (242). This odd, sudden ending to the book can be read as a warning to the reader to always 'sift' stories, to use one's own experience to make judgments and to trust Délànǫ's advice, which is based on 'my experience'.

In *The Soul of Nigeria*, Délànǫ posits a method of coming to knowledge that includes orality, personal experience and first-hand knowledge transmitted over generations, but combined with a 'sifting' that verifies the most valuable forms of such knowledge, while rejecting 'foolish superstition' (69) and 'irrelevant matters' (206), and allows openness of knowledge and the validity of outsider perspectives. Délànǫ's idealised traveller must, in effect, be someone like himself, who is able to stand both within and outside the world he travels in, as each particular moment demands. Délànǫ implicitly posits his own subjectivity in *The Soul of Nigeria* as a model of an 'African' form of civilisation. It is a civilisation that 'sifts', that selects the most authoritative and suitable versions of the stories, or models of life, that it is presented with. This methodology for producing knowledge was derided by Charles Kingsley Meek as 'mere gossip'. Meek prefers it when Délànǫ claims authority over only his own experience, not history or politics: 'Mr. Delano is most interesting, not when he is discussing the higher politics, but when he is recounting minor incidents that occurred during his travels'.[45] But Délànǫ sees the authority he gains from his travels, combined with his ability to sift, as allowing him to comment much more widely than on only his own experience, and he asks the reader to take this on trust.

## Délànǫ as the traveller at the crossroads

Describing his journey from Lagos to Yaba, Délànǫ addresses the reader, imagining us as a fellow traveller: 'You feel too that you are entering a new world as you pass a mixture of modern and antiquated houses in a condition of habitable decay' (14). This sentence can be read as a key to understanding the book. Through reading his book, Délànǫ invites the reader to join him on his journey into a 'new world', a mixture of 'modern and antiquated' in a condition of 'habitable decay'. Délànǫ must travel to the Yoruba region to encounter 'native ways', but the reader, too, is invited to enter into this 'new world' full of rupture and change.

What appears to be an autoethnographic text, writing about Nigeria for an imperial audience, can also be read as Délànǫ picturing himself at a crossroads, travelling back and forward in time and space, translating between 'civilisation' and 'native', between modes of knowledge creation, between modes of narrative, and between Yoruba, Nigeria and Africa in the dawn of Nigeria's

---

[45] Meek, '*The Soul of Nigeria* by Isaac O. Delano', pp. 119–20.

nationalist era, as he illustrates the ways that one might come at knowledge and choices about ways of life. 'Tradition explains the why and wherefore', he writes, 'and we naturally feel somewhat in a difficulty when we happen to cross its border and nullify darling beliefs which our fathers and grandfathers before us have carefully nursed and preserved' (65–6). *The Soul of Nigeria* is an investigation into this 'difficulty' in crossing borders and trying to establish a place for the 'darling beliefs' of generations before while also 'sifting' knowledge to make it suitable for the present age. It is through activating travel writing as a lens to read this text that we are able to access this layer of it: it is because he is a traveller who has seen for himself the places he writes about that Délànọ̀ is able to make his claims to knowledge, including both the authentic 'native' knowledge and new-style knowledge of the outsider, based on 'sifted' orality and first-hand experience.

Like *The Soul of Nigeria*, his later travel narrative *Notes and Comments from Nigeria* is concerned with Délànọ̀'s sense of standing at a crossroads, facing differences of civilisation between regions of Nigeria and, more significantly, ways of life in Nigeria. In a chapter called 'Old v. New', Délànọ̀ notes that 'At present Nigeria is passing through a transition. The old laws and customs are giving way to the new, and changes are taking place in all directions. Occasionally the blood of bravery and statesmanship that glows in the veins has caused a clash between the new and old systems of government' (45). Indeed, as Délànọ̀'s observation on systems of government suggests, *Notes and Comments* increasingly imagines Délànọ̀ – and contemporary Nigeria – standing at a political crossroads, as well as civilisational. The publisher's note that authors such as Délànọ̀ were left only 'as far as possible' to express their own views suggests that *Notes and Comments* was a text that, even more than *The Soul of Nigeria*, was positioned as being written in accordance with British views and prejudices, at the same time as being aimed at African readers. Indeed, Délànọ̀ offers some expressions of gratitude to the British colonial government for the 'modern conveniences and amenities which the present civilization has brought in its train' (63–4). But the text also clearly expresses nationalist views. It makes a diversion, in its final chapter, into a discussion of the Nigerian Youth Movement, the nationalist political organisation founded in 1933. *Notes and Comments* is dedicated to the Nigerian Youth Movement, and this final chapter sings the praises of the movement and is unapologetic about the nationalist views Délànọ̀ shares with this movement: 'The last day when it is possible to be both enemy and friend of the British Government has come; the day of self-interest must bow to the day of public interest', he argues, calling for self-government for Nigeria despite the challenges it presents, and characterising this as a time when a man's 'spirit rises in revolt against the Church and the Government merely because it is not his native own, even though the Government is better and loftier than his own' (62).

In his final chapter, Délànǫ describes his journey as a 'search for Nigeria', explaining that despite remembering the horrors of the past, the 'days of undeserved cruelty and public flogging' in northern Nigeria, the traveller may 'look up to the future with hope, as I have hope in the younger generation' (63). His travel book can thus be read as a 'search for Nigeria' in both the geographical and political sense, as he sees a country standing at a crossroads where it can choose between 'service to one's country or servility on the road which leads to public honour and free attendances at banquets at the Government House' (62). Despite Délànǫ's concerns about the differences between southern and northern Nigeria, as epitomised in the 'naked tribes' and the cannibals, the journey in *Notes and Comments* can thus be read as a political journey that takes up where *The Soul of Nigeria* left off, seeking a political vision for all of Nigeria as well as the vision of 'civilisation' that *The Soul of Nigeria* explored in the Yoruba region: 'my travels made me a proud Nigerian', he writes, 'proud of the struggle of our youths to-day; proud also of our history; proud of my people and glad that they too are awakening' (64).

Writing through the figure of travel became one of the ways writers could try to produce new forms of knowledge about their relationship with the Yoruba region and, later, with Nigeria, presenting themselves as translating and editing cultural knowledge, presenting new truths for a new era, but still based on old forms. Délànǫ pictures himself at a crossroads of enormous cultural, social, epistemological and, later, political change, attempting to direct readers down a road of development along 'African' lines, selecting the best of European 'civilisation' without becoming hybridised. Simultaneously, he also reveals the complexities of the current era, the multiple directions readers might take, the moments of indecision and contradiction: contradictions he embodies even within himself as his relation to the 'natives' shifts throughout the text.

Those travel writers such as Délànǫ who operate from such liminal positions can be read as an elite who gaze at the Yoruba region, or at Nigeria, with alienated eyes, looking down on fellow Lagosians from Carter Bridge, as Délànǫ himself puts it. However, *The Soul of Nigeria* also disrupts this reading by positing Délànǫ standing on the borders within, where there is always strangeness to be encountered, no matter how Yoruba or Nigerian the writer may be. This sense of the multiple potential meanings of 'we' Yoruba or 'we' Nigerians, and the differences contained within that collective 'we', stretching in unstable ways across time and space, is something we will encounter again in subsequent chapters of this book, amongst travel writers who attempt to establish a national 'Nigerian' subjectivity much more firmly in the wake of Nigeria's civil war, and also others who cross borders within Nigeria and establish multiple subject positions contained within 'we Nigerians', and who have, in some cases, been similarly criticised for doing so.

# Journeys of experience and transformation: the quest narrative in Yoruba and English fiction    4

An old man asks a scribe to write down his story, because 'ẹru nba mi ki nmá ba lọ ku ni ai-rotẹlẹ, ki itan nã si ku pẹlu mi' ('there is this fear that I may die unexpectedly and my story die with me').[1] The old man, whose name is Àkàrà-õgùn, has an extraordinary tale of travel to tell. Following the death of his father, Àkàrà-õgùn, 'ọkan ninu awọn ogboju ọdẹ aiye atijọ' (*OO* 2) ('one of the formidable hunters of a bygone age', *FTD* 9), sets out into the Forest of a Thousand Daemons. He arrives in the forest intending to hunt, but on encountering a fearsome spirit, he flees. He quickly returns to the forest, however, to try again. Thus begins a journey in which Àkàrà-õgùn encounters numerous spirits who dwell in the forest, and countless other challenges: 'Kò si ohun ti kò pe tan sinu igbo ti a nsọ yi – ibẹ ni ile gbogbo awọn ẹranko buburu aiye, ibẹ si ni ibugbe awọn abami ẹiyẹ' (*OO* 6) ('There is no breed of animal missing in this forest we speak of; it is the home of every vicious beast on earth, and the dwelling of every kind of feathered freak', *FTD* 14).

This tale of travel into the forest is from D. Ọ. Fágúnwà's novel *Ògbójú Ọdẹ Nínú Igbó Irúnmọlẹ̀*, the best known of renowned Yoruba writer Fágúnwà's five novels, translated into English by Wọlé Ṣóyínká as *The Forest of a Thousand Daemons*. As *Ògbójú Ọdẹ* continues, Àkàrà-õgùn tells the scribe of three such journeys he made. The first two journeys take him through the Forest of a Thousand Daemons, while on his third journey, he is sent via the forest to Òkè Lángbòdó (Mount Langbodo) on a quest to bring the king of his town a mysterious 'nkan' (*OO* 50) ('thing', *FTD* 72; original emphasis) currently in the possession of the king of Òkè Lángbòdó. After finally arriving and overcoming numerous perils, the travellers are sent home with gifts from the king. Not all the hunters make it home: 'Idi iparun ọpọlọpọ kò ju igberaga lọ' (*OO* 100) ('Many perished through simple conceit', *FTD* 138). But when the surviving hunters arrive back in their town, the king 'fi ọpọlọpọ ẹbun fun wa

---

[1] D. Ọ. Fágúnwà, *Ògbójú Ọdẹ Nínú Igbó Irúnmọlẹ̀* (Ibadan: Nelson Publishers, 2005 [1950]), p. 2; Wole Soyinka and D. O. Fagunwa, *The Forest of a Thousand Daemons* (Walton-on-Thames: Thomas Nelson and Sons, 1982 [1968]), p. 8. Subsequent references are to the same editions and will be given in parentheses in the text, along with the abbreviations *OO* and *FTD* respectively.

a si di olowo lati ọjọ nǎ wa' (*OO* 101) ('gave us many gifts and from that day of our return we became men of means', *FTD* 139).

Fágúnwà's fictional tales of hunters' travels, as fantastical as they are, are not necessarily as distinct as they may at first seem from the non-fiction travel writing that is the focus of the rest of this book. In her study of intercontinental francophone African travel writing, Aedín Ní Loingsigh argues for 'a re-appraisal of the division within the literature of travel between the categories of fiction and non-fiction by highlighting how each can infiltrate the other'; she argues that such a border-crossing between fiction and non-fiction can bridge the gulf between African and Western travel writing by recognising the importance of fiction as a mode of writing about travel in African contexts, and the substantial number of African fictional texts in which travel is the 'organizing principle'.[2] In the case of southwest Nigerian travel writing, we have seen already the overlap between I. B. Thomas's non-fiction travel narratives and his fictional serial *Sègilọlá*; although there are some differences of theme and no explicit emphasis on travel in *Sègilọlá*, the two texts cross over extensively, both formally and stylistically, in their use of the serialised narrative, the language of popular culture and their rhetorical features. This chapter explores even more closely this 'infiltration' of fiction and non-fictional forms of writing about travel.

Many twentieth and twenty-first century Nigerian novels join Fágúnwà's novels in placing a journey at the heart of their narrative; in fact, the journey away from home, often striking out from the village to the big city, is 'the single most common theme in [English-language] Nigerian novels', according to Wendy Griswold, cropping up, with variations, in novels as distinct as, for instance, Cyprian Ekwensi's *Jagua Nana* (1961), Zaynab Alkali's *The Virtuous Woman* (1987) and J. F. Ọdúnjọ's Yoruba-language novel *Kúyè* (1964). I discuss this recurring journey motif in Chapter 5, looking at novels and memoirs about Nigeria's National Youth Service Corps (NYSC) and their portrayal of young women who leave home to serve the nation.[3] Conflict, too, has prompted literary journeys in novels about or inspired by Nigeria's civil war of 1967–70 such as Ken Saro-Wiwa's *Sozaboy* (1985) and Chimamanda Ngozi Adichie's *Half of a Yellow Sun* (2006), and also about conflicts across West Africa, such as Helon Habila's *Measuring Time* (2007). Novelists have also written postcolonial adventure and exploration narratives, such as Habila's later novel *Oil on Water* (2010), in which journalists Rufus and Zaq journey up a river into the Niger Delta on a quest to find the kidnapped wife of an oil executive, and in doing so venture into a contemporary 'heart of darkness': a landscape physically and politically devastated by the oil industry. Moreover,

---

[2] Ní Loingsigh, *Postcolonial Eyes*, pp. 16–20.
[3] Griswold, *Bearing Witness*, p. 143.

many novels follow the fortunes and misfortunes of Nigerian travellers overseas, from Buchi Emecheta's *In the Ditch* (1972) and *Second-Class Citizen* (1974) to Ọládipọ̀ Yemitan's *Gbóbaníyì* (1972), Chimamanda Ngozi Adichie's *Americanah* (2013) and Chika Unigwe's *On Black Sisters' Street* (2009).

Out of this wealth of stories of travel in Nigerian fiction, this chapter focuses on narratives of the quest by D. Ọ. Fágúnwà, alongside transformations of the quest narrative in novels by Amos Tutùọlá, Ben Okri and J. Akin Ọmọ́yájowó. The quest is the form of journey that critic Paul Fussell identifies as also underlying the conventional non-fiction travel book. Fussell suggests that travel books generally operate with a 'displaced' version of the quest romance, in which, as in the quest romance, 'the modern traveller leaves the familiar and predictable to wander, episodically, into the unfamiliar or unknown, encountering strange adventures, and finally, after travails and ordeals, returns safely', but in which the quest has been displaced from its usual realm of fantasy or romance into the realist realm of non-fiction.[4] In fiction, meanwhile, some Nigerian novels have adopted the picaresque form of the quest; Tutùọlá's *The Palm-Wine Drinkard*, for instance, centres 'endless episodes of travel and adventure of the trickster figure' in a manner characteristic of the picaresque tale. Others are closer to the Bildungsroman, depicting the traveller's social and psychological development, so that their physical journey is accompanied by an interior 'journey toward self-awareness' and individual subjectivity.[5] Indeed, echoing the significance of the quest in many African epics, in which, Daniel Kunene argues, the journey represents a rite of passage for a flawed hero whose journey leads 'from experience to wisdom and new patterns of behaviour', Mildred Mortimer suggests that in postcolonial francophone African novels, journey narratives of this type typically result in either a triumphant or a chastised return. However, postcolonial novels also increasingly problematise the journey motif and particularly its notion of a 'return to the hearth', suggesting the difficulty of finding a metaphorical way back to the village in an unsettled postcolonial age.[6]

The significance of the quest in both non-fiction and fiction accounts of travel thus suggests a new way of reading the quest narrative that underpins Fágúnwà's novels, exploring the links between fiction and non-fiction forms of travel writing. Critics have read the quest narratives of D. Ọ. Fágúnwà as

---

[4] Fussell, *Abroad*, p. 208.

[5] Susan Z. Andrade, 'Representing Slums and Home: Chris Abani's Graceland', in *The Legacies of Modernism: Historicising Postwar and Contemporary Fiction*, ed. by David James (Cambridge: Cambridge University Press, 2011), pp. 225–42 (p. 237).

[6] Daniel Kunene, 'Journey in the African Epic', *Research in African Literatures*, 22.2 (1991), pp. 205–23 (p. 211); Mortimer, *Journeys*, pp. 1–6.

drawing inspiration from other literary texts, particularly Bunyan's *Pilgrim's Progress,* but also Homer's *Odyssey,* Swift's *Gulliver's Travels,* Spenser's *The Faerie Queene,* Aesop's *Fables* and Defoe's *Robinson Crusoe.* They have also located them as a 'strategic transformation', to use Ato Quayson's term, of Yoruba 'folktales' or oral genres, although Ayọ̀ Bámgbóṣé suggests that Fágúnwà draws less heavily on oral sources than he does on literary works such as the *Odyssey* and on Christian religious literature, and notes that he draws on oral narrative techniques (such as episodic narrative, coincidences, the fantastical, humour and didacticism) and particular folktales that are incorporated into the novels as episodes rather than adopting the quest story as a whole from oral narratives.[7] The particular form the journeys in Fágúnwà's novels take can therefore be understood as a mingling of elements from oral and written literature, both Yoruba and Western, transformed by Fágúnwà's own imagination into a 'vast tapestry of adventure', as Bámgbóṣé puts it.[8] The quest motif has also been considered a universal mythic trope along the lines that Fussell suggests – in particular, a form of Jungian scholar Joseph Campbell's notion of the cross-cultural 'monomyth' of the hero's journey – and an allegory for life and its challenges. Indeed, *Ògbójú Ọdẹ* ends with Àkàrà-ògùn entreating his listeners to 'fi itan igbesi aiye mi yi ṣe arikọgbọn ki aiye tiyin ba dara' (*OO* 101) ('use this story as a mine of wisdom that your lives may be good', *FTD* 139), before he disappears, leaving behind only a scrap of paper with the words 'Akara-ògun baba omulẹmofo' (*OO* 101) ('Akara-ògun, Father of Born Losers', *FTD* 139). The scribe similarly entreats readers to 'fi itan inu iwe yi ṣe arikọgbọn' ('put the story of this book to wise use'):

> Olukuluku yin ni o ni iṣoro lati ba pade ninu aiye, olukuluku ni o ni Oke Langbodo tirẹ̀ lati lọ, olukuluku ni o si ni idina tirẹ̀ niwaju, bi didun ti mbẹ ni inu aiye bẹ̀ ni kikoro mbẹ, bi oni dun ọla le koro, bi ọla tun koro ọtunla le dabi oyin: kọkọrọ aiye kò si lọwọ ẹnikan; bi ẹ ba ti nba irin ajo yin lọ ninu aiye, ti ẹ nti ori didun bọ si ori kikan, ẹ mã gba ohun gbogbo tẹrintẹrin ki ẹ mã ṣe bi ọkunrin ki ẹ si mã ranti pe, ẹniti o ba ran ara rẹ̀ lọwọ ni Ọlọrun Oke iran lọwọ. (*OO* 101–2)

Each of you meets with difficulties in the world, each of you has his Mount Langbodo to attain, each of you has obstacles in front of him, for as there is

---

[7] Isabel Hofmeyr, *The Portable Bunyan: A Transnational History of the Pilgrim's Progress* (Princeton: Princeton University Press, 2004), p. 194; Bernth Lindfors, 'Form, Theme, and Style in the Narratives of D. O. Fagunwa', *The International Fiction Review,* 6.1 (1979), pp. 11–16 (pp. 12–14); Ayọ Bamgboṣe, *The Novels of D. O. Fagunwa* (Benin City (Nigeria): Ethiope Publishing Corporation, 1974), pp. 16–28.

[8] Bamgboṣe, *D. O. Fagunwa,* p. 28.

sweet, so there is sour in this world; if today is good, tomorrow may be bitter, if tomorrow is bitter, the day after may be like honey. The key to this world is in the hands of no man, as you pass through your journey in the world, meeting with good luck and encountering the bitter, accept everything cheerfully, behave like men and remember that God on High helps only those who help themselves. (*FTD* 139–40)

The scribe appears to give us a key to reading the journey in this novel as an allegory of life and its obstacles.

However, what if, instead of taking *Ògbójú Ọdẹ*'s scribe's word for it that the allegorical reading is the best way to interpret the journeys in these novels, we were to take the example of Àkàrà-ògùn's mysterious note – its elusiveness seeming to suggest that further layers of interpretation of the novel, beyond those that have already been presented, are possible – and re-open the interpretive lenses through which we read the novel, so that the scribe's straightforward allegorical lens is not the last word on the novel's meaning? That is, alongside the significant literary influences from both European and Yoruba written and oral texts, are there other ways of understanding why the travel in Fágúnwà's novels takes the shape it does? As Ayọ̀ Bámgbóṣé suggests, Fágúnwà's novels were no doubt influenced by his rural childhood in Òkè-Igbó, whose 'forests and hills' inform the setting of Fágúnwà's novels.[9] The influences of Christianity and of education are also evident in his novels, with their incorporation of Christian imagery and stories and their didactic addresses to readers.

But travel also played a role in Fágúnwà's life, and the experience and culture of travel in southwest Nigeria in the first half of the twentieth century is also an important backdrop to his novels. In his reading of the novels, Ọlákúnlé George argues that Fágúnwà uses the quest motif to 'allegorize the subject's potential in modernity', situating the outer and inner journeys represented in the novels in a particular historical and epistemological epoch.[10] Adélékè Adéèkọ́ similarly shows how Fágúnwà's novels speak to what Adéèkọ́ characterises as an era of epistemic change and instability in mid-twentieth-century southwest Nigeria.[11] Following this argument, rather than taking at face value the mythical time of the forest that Fágúnwà's novels impose on the reader, and reading the novels' rhetoric of travel as if it represents 'tradition' or timeless truth, Fágúnwà's novels can be read as part of a broader discourse about travel in the 1930s to the 1960s, as Nigeria moved towards independence. His novels do not represent simply 'traditional' or 'mythic' ideas about the journey as an

---

[9] Bamgboṣe, *D. O. Fagunwa*, p. 4.
[10] Olakunle George, *Relocating Agency: Modernity and African Letters* (Albany: State University of New York Press, 2003), p. 125.
[11] Adéèkọ́, *Arts of Being Yorùbá*, pp. 48–74.

allegory for life and its challenges, but are also implicated in contemporary textual cultures and discourse about the meanings and potentials of travel.

*Ògbójú Ọdẹ Nínú Igbó Irúnmọlẹ̀* (1938) is the first of five novels that established D. Ọ. Fágúnwà as the most renowned Yoruba-language writer of the twentieth century. Although I. B. Thomas's realist novel *Sẹ̀gilọlá* was published nearly a decade earlier than *Ògbójú Ọdẹ*, it is nonetheless Fágúnwà's fantastical novels that are often considered to have inaugurated the Yoruba novel tradition, owing to their widespread popularity and the perception that they capture a distinctively Yoruba mode of storytelling. *Ògbójú Ọdẹ* was followed by the novels *Igbó Olódùmarè* (1949), *Ìrèké-Oníbùdó* (1949), *Ìrìnkèrindò Nínú Igbó Elégbèje* (1954) and *Àdììtú Olódùmarè* (1961). All five of Fágúnwà's novels follow a male adventurer who sets out on a journey, with an episodic plot driven by the spirits, people, and places the protagonist encounters, and who, in most of the novels, narrates his adventures to the scribe who is the author of the novel. However, the settings differ somewhat between the novels. In *Igbó Olódùmarè* and *Ìrìnkèrindò*, once again, a hunter sets out into a forest where he and his companions test their wits and strength, encountering fantastical places, spirits and creatures, both hostile and helpful. The hunter sometimes lingers in particular places in the forest for years before returning home and telling his story. *Ìrèké-Oníbùdó* follows the adventures not of a hunter, but of an orphan living in poverty who wanders from town to town and through the forest where, again, he encounters strange people and places. *Àdììtú Olódùmarè*, Fágúnwà's final novel, takes place in an ostensibly realist setting, with a protagonist who has also been driven out of home by poverty, who journeys between towns displaying features of modern urban life, such as cars, and who ventures into the forest for only part of the novel. In this chapter, I focus on Fágúnwà's three forest novels *Ògbójú Ọdẹ*, *Igbó Olódùmarè* and *Ìrìnkèrindò*, which, as Ayọ̀ Bámgbóṣé points out, appear to have been conceived as a trilogy and are more similar to each other than to the other two novels, although I return briefly to the significance of *Àdììtú Olódùmarè*'s distinct mode of narration and setting later in the chapter.[12]

As they venture into the forest, Fágúnwà's travellers cross a set of borders that have not been traversed by any of the other travellers we have encountered so far in this book: between the human and the metaphysical or spiritual realm, signified by the town and the forest. The borders between the two are crossed only by the traveller; at the beginning of his journey to Òkè Lángbòdó, the citizens of Àkàrà-õgùn's town 'sin wa de bode ki nwọn to fi ẹkun pada ki nwọn to lọ si ile' (*OO* 57) ('accompanied us [travellers] right to the border and returned home in tears', *FTD* 81), unable or unwilling to go any further than the border. As Àkàrà-õgùn returns home from his second journey, meanwhile,

---

[12] Bamgboṣe, *D. O. Fagunwa*, pp. 51–3.

the price for crossing the boundary back into the human world is that Àkàrà-ŏgùn must lose his spirit wife:

> Olufẹ mi, Olufẹ mi, Olufẹ mi ọwọn julọ, nkò mọ̀ pe bayi ni ipinya yio ṣe de si ãrin wa, oju mi nba ọ lọ nigbati iwo de ibi abule nì ti iwọ ri awọn enia rẹ. Emi bi iwin kò lè ba enia ṣe ajọpin nitori ero inu wọn ibi ni lojojumọ. (*OO* 45)

> My beloved, my beloved, my most dearly beloved one, I did not guess that parting would befall us thus. My eyes went with you when you reached that hut and met your own people. A spirit like the ghommid cannot join with human beings to live together, for evil are their thoughts every day of their lives. (*FTD* 66–7)[13]

Only the traveller is a border-crosser: perceiving each other as dangerous, other humans and ghommids do not cross this border, from town to forest or vice versa.

One way of reading the traveller's ability to cross into the world of the spirits is that it invokes a 'traditional' Yoruba world view, in which the spiritual world exists closely alongside the human world. Lérè Adéyẹmí suggests that early Yoruba novelists' focus on the spiritual and the fantastic emerged out of a cultural revisionist desire to recapture perceived 'Yoruba ontological and metaphysical beliefs'.[14] In Fágúnwà's novels, the traveller's ability to enter into the spiritual world can be read as reflecting and recreating such metaphysical beliefs about the nature of *aiyé* ('life' and 'the world', also spelt *ayé*) as home to both humans and spirit beings. These spirits may be benevolent or destructive, making *aiyé* 'a playground for contradictory powers and a perilous and complex place to live in'.[15] People other than travellers into the forest may come into contact with the spirits, since *aiyé* is understood to be all around us. But the forest or bush has often been represented as a particularly appropriate home for spiritual beings, as a zone of perpetual border-crossing between human and other. In many pre-colonial representations of the bush and the forest in West African orature, according to Vanessa Guignery, the bush was conceived as an 'Other' place, representing the unknown and the supernatural, while in colonial discourse it represented darkness and barbarism.[16] Simultaneously, though, in

---

[13] 'Ghommid' is Ṣóyínká's term for the spirits Àkàrà-ŏgùn encounters in the forest.

[14] Adéyẹmí, 'Magical Realism', p. 91.

[15] Afe Adogame, '*Aiye Loja, Orun Nile* – the Appropriation of Ritual Space-Time in the Cosmology of the Celestial Church of Christ', *Journal of Religion in Africa*, 30.1 (2000), 3–29 (p. 6); Olatunde Bayo Lawuyi, 'The world of the Yoruba taxi driver: an interpretive approach to vehicle slogans', *Africa* 58.1 (1988): 1–13 (p. 10).

[16] Vanessa Guignery, 'Landscapes Within, Landscapes Without: The Forest and Other Places in Ben Okri's *The Famished Road*', *Études britanniques contemporaines* 47 (2014), <http://ebc.revues.org/1974>; see also Ato Quayson, *Strategic*

Yoruba town histories, people are often depicted travelling through the bush to find the right site for a town, meaning that the bush represents potential, as well as wilderness – indeed, in many West African societies, the spirits of the bush have been represented as the originators of human culture, who teach humans the arts of life.[17] However, in such histories the bush or forest are also reminders that human settlements are a work in progress, since 'at any time the conquest of the bush can be reversed'.[18] The bush or forest is a reminder of the limits of humanity – and it is the very liminality of this border-zone that allows the traveller to become 'betwixt and between' human and other, and thus become something other than they were.[19]

Indeed, travel into the spiritual realm in Fágúnwà's novels enables an encounter with the world beyond everyday human experience: 'ẹniti o fi inu iyãra ṣe ibugbe ọgbọn iyara nikan ni yio ni mọ' ('anyone who made his living room the totality of his environment would acquire only the knowledge of the room'), states Bàbá-Onírùngbọn-Yẹ́úkẹ́, the 'Furry-Bearded-One', in *Igbó Olódùmarè*.[20] Such statements commending the *ọgbọn* or wisdom of the person who has left home need not necessarily be taken literally as recommending travel. In common with most proverbial statements in Yoruba, their meaning resides below the surface. In the instance above, the choice to stay at home in the figurative 'living room' can be read as referring to the more general dangers of ignorance, arrogance, and being small-minded enough not to know what one does not know. Nonetheless, the spatiality of the metaphor used in this proverb – the living room – reminds us that this is not solely an intellectual journey after knowledge that can be fulfilled by thought alone, but a physical journey into strangeness and experiential knowledge that can only be fulfilled by crossing the boundary of the metaphorical 'room' into the unknown.

The claustrophobia of the 'room' as the 'totality of his environment' contrasts with the broad, open experience, both spatial and epistemological, that Àkàrà- õgùn in *Ògbójú Ọdẹ* considers himself to have gained through travel:

*Transformations in Nigerian Writing: Orality & History in the Work of Rev. Samuel Johnson, Amos Tutuola, Wole Soyinka & Ben Okri* (Bloomington, IN: Indiana University Press, 1997), p. 46; Simon Gikandi, *Maps of Englishness: Writing Identity in the Culture of Colonialism* (New York: Columbia University Press, 1996), p. 169.

[17] Jack Goody, *The Myth of the Bagre* (Oxford: Clarendon Press, 1972), p. 19.
[18] Barber, *I Could Speak until Tomorrow*, p. 43.
[19] Victor Turner, 'Liminality and Communitas', *The Ritual Process: Structure and Anti-structure,* 94 (1969), p. 130.
[20] D. Ọ. Fágúnwà, *Igbó Olódùmarè* (Ibadan: Nelson Publishers, 2005 [1949]), p. 117; D. O. Fagunwa and Wole Soyinka, *In the Forest of Olodumare* (Ibadan: Nelson Publishers, 2010), p. 160. Subsequent references are to the same editions and will be given in parentheses in the text, along with the abbreviations *IO* and *ITFOO* respectively.

'mo ti ri okun mo ti ri ọsa ẹru omi kan kò tun bà mi mọ' ('I have beheld the ocean and have known the sea, water holds no further terror for me!'), he opens his account of his third journey, adding that: 'oju mi ri nkan sinu aiye!' (*OO* 48) ('My eyes have witnessed much in this world' *FTD* 70). In *Ìrìnkèrindò Nínú Igbó Elégbèje*, too, Fágúnwà describes how Inúlaiyéwà, one of the protagonist Ìrìnkèrindò's companions on the journey, 'jẹ ẹniti o mã nṣiṣẹ kakiri ẹhin odi oju rẹ̀ si ti ri nkan pupọ sẹhin, o ti gbe ọpọlọpọ ilu, o ti gbe ãrin onirũru enia' ('had travelled wide and had acquired the civilizations of various foreign countries; his eyes had witnessed great bafflements, he had dwelled in towns and amongst peoples of the strangest natures').[21] Thus by 'travell[ing] wide', Inúlaiyéwà's experience encompasses new social and physical worlds. Although travellers may also embody some less desirable characteristics – Àkàrà- õgùn's avaricious wives gradually leave him on account of 'iwa ọdẹ mi ati iwa jagidijagan ti mo fi nba awọn iwin ati ẹranko lò ninu igbo ọkọkan' (*OO* 49) ('my hunter's ways and my riotous temperament which came from long dealings with beasts and ghommids of the forest', *FTD* 70) – the overwhelming assertion of these novels is that the novelty and variety of the traveller's physical experience of the world effects their eventual transformation into what Tóyìn FáỌlá identifies as 'wise, strong, and competent men, able to narrate stories and teach society what they have learned', and so their journeys also become, as Ọlákúnlé George writes, 'inward journeys into material or spiritual stations of the self.'[22]

In common with many narratives of travel, Fágúnwà's novels particularly emphasise the dangers and discomforts his travellers encounter and the travellers' reactions to them, which range from outstanding courage to anti-heroic fear. *Ògbójú Ọdẹ*'s characteristic mode is one of hyperbole, not only in Àkàrà-õgùn's self-presentation as a hero but also in the melodrama, danger and near-tragedy Àkàrà-õgùn relates throughout his journey:

> Nigbati ọba sọ ọrọ yi ẹru ba mi gidigidi; nitori o pẹ ti mo mã ngbọ onirũru nkan nipa Oke Langbodo yi nkò si ti iri ki ẹnikẹni lọ sibẹ ki o bọ ri. Ki ẹnikẹni to lè de ilu nã pãpã oluwarẹ̀ yio nilati la Igbo Irunmalẹ̀ kọja, igbati oluwarẹ̀ ba si la a kọja tan ni o to ṣẹ̀ṣẹ̀ bẹrẹ irin. A kò lè ka ilu nã si ọkan ninu awọn ilu ti mbẹ ninu aiye, nitori gbangba ni awọn ara ibẹ mã ngbọ akukọ ti o ba nkọ ni isalu ọrun. (*OO* 50)

---

[21] D. Ọ. Fágúnwà, *Ìrìnkèrindò Nínú Igbó Elégbèje* (Ibadan: Nelson Publishers, 2005 [1954]), p. 20; Dapo Adeniyi, *Expedition to the Mount of Thought (The Third Saga)* (Ile-Ife: Obafemi Awolowo University Press, 1994), p. 30. Subsequent references are to the same editions and will be given in parentheses in the text, along with the abbreviations *INIE* and *ETMT* respectively.

[22] Toyin Falola, 'Yoruba Writers and the Construction of Heroes', *History in Africa*, 24 (1997), pp. 157–75 (pp. 160–61); George, *Relocating Agency*, p. 113.

When the king had spoken these words, I was greatly frightened. For a long time now, I had heard many tales of Mount Langbodo but had never yet encountered anyone who had made the journey and returned to tell the tale. Before anyone came into that city he would first have to brave the length of the Forest of Irunmale, and that is only the beginning of the journey. It can hardly be regarded as a place on earth, because the dwellers of Langbodo hear, in the most distinct notes, the crowing of cocks from the heavenly vault. (*FTD* 72)

Àkàrà-ògùn's journey, he tells his listeners, takes him to the extremities of the world, almost to heaven, and he is, implicitly, the most extraordinarily brave of travellers. As his travels continue, he confronts ever greater dangers until he and his fellow hunters conquer a spirit called Èrù (Fear) itself, as well as the terrifying Wèrè-Òrun, on whose approach 'idi wa di omi nitori ẹru, diẹ lo si ku ki nyangbẹ si ṣokoto mi' (*OO* 64) ('our buttocks turned to water from fear, and I nearly excreted in my trousers', *FTD* 91). As Fálọlá's comment that the hunters become 'wise, strong, and competent men' suggests, all of Fágúnwà's chief protagonists are male (although they sometimes travel with female companions they meet on the way), and as such their bravery contributes to a performance of heroism that seems particularly masculinised in the novels, perhaps drawing on idealisations of the hunter – a specifically male occupation – as courageous.

In emphasising the danger of their journeys, however, Fágúnwà's travellers are not only self-dramatising as heroes, but can also be understood as drawing on a wealth of understandings of the dangers of travel, likely including contemporary discourse about travel. By the late 1930s to the 1960s, when Fágúnwà was writing, travel within Nigeria had become more widely possible and desirable than previously, but the newspapers still frequently published reports and complaints about accidents, the bad state of transport infrastructure and the poor quality of driving; in 1958, for instance, the *Daily Service* published a reader's letter deploring the 'gruesome accidents' he had seen in Lagos. 'One would like to know that he is sure to come back to his next meal after a day's outing either on a bus, a car, or on a bicycle', the reader suggested.[23]

Moreover, Fágúnwà's evocation of the dangers of travel again emphasises the nature of travel as a border-crossing between the human and the spiritual world, as vividly evoked by Dàmọlá Òṣínúlù in his discussion of the spiritual world of public transport in Lagos:

To understand the prominence of written prayers on *molues* and other buses, it is necessary to enter the spiritual world within which the owners and drivers operate. It is a complex world layered with Christian and Islamic elements, but these elements operate within a spiritual world constructed by the drivers' and

---

[23] 'Keep Death Off Lagos Roads', *Daily Service*, 6 October 1958, p. 7.

owners' explicit and implicit Yoruba religious beliefs. In this construct, the road is understood to be a dangerous place where malignant forces abound. The high number of accidents on Nigerian roads provides a physical confirmation of the spiritual dangers of the road.[24]

The link between the pragmatic dangers of the road and the road's symbolism as a place of spiritual danger is as pertinent to Fágúnwà's novels as it is to the twenty-first century Lagos of which Ọ̀ṣínúlù writes. As it is also imagined in Wọlé Ṣóyínká's play *The Road* (1965) and Ben Okri's *The Famished Road* (1991), the road is, in both Ọ̀ṣínúlù's twenty-first century Lagos and in Fágúnwà's novels, a perilous place that connects the human and the spiritual, and in doing so can consume both literal travellers and travellers on the road of life more generally.[25]

Because of this inherent danger, to become a traveller in Fágúnwà's novels is imagined to require a certain kind of character and experience, as well as generating it. Selected to accompany Ìrìnkèrindò on his journey are people who embody experience of the world, knowledge, courage, spiritual skills and existing experience of travel. Earlier in the novel, Ìrìnkèrindò describes how his father had previously forbidden him from accompanying Àkàrà-õgùn on his journey to Òkè Lángbòdó, with his father justifying his decision in terms of the experience required to even set out on such a journey:

> mo fẹ ki oju iwọ pãpã tubọ là si i: nitori ẹniti o ngbe aba oko ọgbọn abà oko nikan ni yio ni; ẹniti ngbe ileto, ọgbọn ileto ni yio ni, ṣugbọn ẹniti o ba nlakaka lati de ibi pupọ ni ile aiye yi, oju oluwarẹ̀ yio la ju ti ọpọlọpọ lọ. (*INIE* 5)

> your eyes have not really gathered enough experience to equip you for such a project as Langbodo. This is because the one who lives in the farm-hut cannot really possess experiences extending beyond his farm-hut. The experience of the village dweller will be limited to his village. The man who strives to journey round places must encompass a wealth of experiences within himself. (*ETMT* 8)

Travel is imagined by characters in Fágúnwà's novels as one way to develop a particular form of personhood, realising qualities and experience that enable an individual not only to reach his or her full capacity, but also to become recognised as a socially valued person. Experience of the world is a kind of 'wealth' that enables a person to proceed to greater experience.

---

[24] Damola Osinulu, 'Painters, Blacksmiths and Wordsmiths: Building Molues in Lagos', *African Arts,* 41.3 (2008), pp. 44–53 (p. 51).
[25] Wole Soyinka, *The Road* (London: Oxford University Press, 1965); Ben Okri, *The Famished Road* (London: Jonathan Cape, 1991).

## Gaining experience of the world in twentieth-century Nigeria

This emphasis in Fágúnwà's novels on the value of travelling into the world beyond home echoes ideas that were circulating in contemporaneous Yoruba print and literary culture about the value of travel in shaping forms of person-hood and experience. Fágúnwà's involvement in colonial Nigeria's educational service and Christianity means that it is certainly possible that he had read African and European missionary and colonial travel writing about Nigeria. As a pioneer Yoruba-language writer, conceivably he was familiar with the work of fellow Yoruba intellectual Isaac Délànọ̀, including Délànọ̀'s book *The Soul of Nigeria*. Fágúnwà was certainly familiar with the earlier generation of Yoruba literary pioneers; he dedicated his novel *Ìrìnkèrindò* to, amongst others, A. K. Ajíṣafẹ́ and E. A. Akintán, both of whom we encountered in Chapter 2 as authors of travel narratives in 1920s' Yoruba newspapers, amongst their many other journalistic and intellectual endeavours.

But perhaps the most illuminating way to consider Fágúnwà's own under-standing of travel and travel writing is through reading his non-fiction travel narrative, *Irinajo*. In 1946–48, Fágúnwà travelled to the UK as a guest of the British Council, reflecting the post-war shift in British colonial policy to an emphasis on African 'development' and the promotion of literature and cul-ture, both Nigerian and British, particularly through the British Council, which opened a Nigeria office in 1943.[26] Fágúnwà was one amongst many Nigerian intellectuals invited to Britain in this era; in 1943, for instance, *Akede Eko* editor I. B. Thomas travelled to the UK as part of a press delegation, and he described his stay in Britain in a serialised travel narrative in *Akede Eko* in 1944. Fágúnwà, too, wrote a Yoruba-language account of his journey to the UK, titled simply *Irinajo* ('A Journey' or 'Travels'), and published in 1949 by Oxford University Press as part of a series entitled 'Iwe Oxford Fun Ode Oni' ('Oxford Books for Today'). The series contained Yoruba-language stories and writing by authors such as Isaac Délànọ̀, J. O. Oyèlẹ́ṣẹ and L. J. Lewis, and other stories by D. Ọ. Fágúnwà – locating Fágúnwà as one of several key Yoruba intellectuals of his generation, echoing the positioning of Isaac Délànọ̀'s *The Soul of Nigeria* by a British publisher, a decade earlier, as offering a Nige-rian intellectual's own viewpoint on Nigeria (see Chapter 3).

In common with Délànọ̀'s *The Soul of Nigeria*, Fágúnwà's narrative is posi-tioned as a travelogue, in articulation with conventional understandings of the genre in the West at the time; although Fágúnwà's text does not reference any other travelogues, it carefully situates itself as a non-fiction text that reflects

---

[26] Tiyambe Zeleza, 'The Political Economy of British Colonial Development and Welfare in Africa', *Transafrican Journal of History*, 14 (1985), pp. 139–61; John Harris, 'Libraries and Librarianship in Nigeria at Mid-Century', Occasional Paper No. 2 (Accra: University of Ghana Department of Library Studies, 1970).

on its author's own experience of travel, and describes sights and encounters along the way: 'itan pataki ni igbesi aiye mi ni, itan ti o jẹ ọ̀tọ̀ patapata gbã ni, itan ohun ti mo fi oju mi yi ri gãn ni, o jẹ itan igbati mo lọ si Ilu Oyinbo' ('it's an important story in my lifetime, it's a completely true story, it's the story of things I saw with my own eyes, it's the story of when I went to the UK').[27] Part One of *Irinajo* describes Fágúnwà's journey by ship from Lagos to Glasgow, followed by a train journey to London. Fágúnwà describes his preparations for his journey, his emotional goodbyes to his wife, his experiences on board the ship, his views of the West African coast and Europe from sea, a day of sight-seeing in Las Palmas and his arrival in Glasgow, along with his first glimpses of life in England and his journey by train to London. Part Two describes his stay in London and ends with the promise of a third part describing his travels elsewhere in the UK (although, to the best of my knowledge, this third part was never published).

Despite its focus on travel outside Nigeria, Fágúnwà's narrative is strikingly similar in some ways to I. B. Thomas's intra-Nigerian travel narratives published in the Lagos press twenty years earlier. In common with Thomas, Fágúnwà describes his view from the ship as, in his case, it traverses the Gold Coast, Liberia and Sierra Leone, and then on into Europe. Most of these places are viewed from a distance only: he remarks that 'O dun mi pe awọn ọlọkọ wa kò jẹki a sọkalẹ ni Freetown' (13) ('It pained me that our captain didn't allow us to disembark in Freetown'). Keeping in mind his intended readership of schoolchildren, when Fágúnwà is not able to offer to readers first-hand experience of those cities, he sometimes recalls history or other forms of knowledge instead; passing by Freetown, the narrative pauses to explain the significance of the city's name as a place of freedom for former slaves. Echoing Thomas, Fágúnwà emphasises the exceptionalism and novelty of his journey; he describes his journey by ship in detail – the food served, the stratifications between first- and second-class passengers, the emergency procedures, the signing of a passenger log book, the barber, the church services, the horrors of sea sickness – presumably aware that his readers may not have experienced similar scenes themselves. Both Fágúnwà and Thomas reflect on the value of travel, travel writing and reading travel narratives, and structure their narratives through proverbs, didacticism and moral instruction to their readers. Here, we can trace a shared sense of the potentials and conventions of travel writing being established in Yoruba literary culture.

*Irinajo* can also be read as an intertext for Fágúnwà's own novels, which Ọláyínká Àgbétúyì suggests are products of 'an imaginary longing to fulfil

---

27 D. Ọ. Fágúnwà, *Irinajo, Apa Kini* (London: Oxford University Press, 1949), p. 1. Translation is my own. Subsequent references will be given in parentheses in the text.

what a fertile imagination considers to be the educative lessons from such travel' – a longing that was realised through Fágúnwà's own travels to the UK.[28] *Irinajo* is in some ways very different from Fágúnwà's novels. Written ten years after he had published his first novel, when Fágúnwà was already a writer of some renown, *Irinajo* is not only written in a resolutely realist mode, but also concerns a different kind of travel: overseas, and directly implicated in Nigeria's colonial relationship with Britain, unlike Fágúnwà's forest novels in which colonial Nigeria is not explicitly mentioned as the context for the novels. Yet there are also indications that Fágúnwà envisages a continuity between his novels and his non-fiction writing: he uses a permutation of his habitual address to readers of his novels to address readers of *Irinajo*, too, explaining that as well as being for schoolchildren, *Irinajo* is also 'fun gbogbo ilẹ Yoruba ati fun ẹnikẹni ti o ba mọ Yoruba ika dãdã' (i) ('for all of Yorubaland and anyone who knows how to read Yoruba well') and indeed for anyone: 'Ẹnyin ọmọ araiye, lọkunrin, lobinrin, lọmọde, lagbalagba, ati pãpã ẹnyin ọmọ ile iwe' (1) ('You people of the world, men, women, children, elders and especially you schoolchildren'). This, along with the text's didactic, moralising impulse shared with his novels, points to the possibilities for reading *Irinajo* as a continuation of his fiction, despite its different form and realist setting.

An even more immediate comparison between Fágúnwà's own travels and the fictional travels of his hunters is in their shared notion of gaining *ọlàjú* – civilisation, enlightenment – through travel. Returning to Ìrìnkèrindò's father's discussion of the qualities of the traveller mentioned above, when the father says, 'ẹniti o ba nlakaka lati de ibi pupọ ni ile aiye yi, oju oluwarẹ̀ yio la ju ti ọpọlọpọ lọ' (*INIE* 5) ('the man who strives to journey round places must encompass a wealth of experiences within himself', *ETMT* 8), the metaphor Fágúnwà uses, which is not brought out fully in Dàpọ̀ Adéníyì's English translation, is of eyes being opened by experience ('oju oluwarẹ̀ yio la'), a phrase that also implies *ọlàjú* through invoking 'ojú' and 'là', two components of the word *ọlàjú*. Fágúnwà places a similar emphasis on the relationship between travel, experience and 'civilisation' or 'enlightenment' in his non-fiction travelogue. His desire to travel, he says, came from his sense that there was something more in the world that he wanted to learn that he couldn't learn at home: 'Baba mi sa ipa rẹ̀ de gongo ki o ba le fun mi ni ẹkọ ti o jina ṣau, o si kọ mi ni iwe ti enia le kọ ni ilẹ wa, ṣugbọn a kò ni owo ràbàtà ni ile wa to bi wipe ki a ran ọmọ ẹni lọ si Ilu Oyinbo lọ kọ iwe rara' (1) ('My father exerted himself to the utmost to give me a deep education, and he taught me everything that people

---

[28] Olayinka Agbetuyi, 'Representing the Foreign as Other: The Use of Allegory in Fagunwa's Novels', in *The Foundations of Nigeria: Essays in Honour of Toyin Falola,* ed. by Adebayo Oyebade (Trenton: Africa World Press, 2003), pp. 333–44 (p. 335).

can learn in our land, but we really didn't have lots of money in our household for him to send his children to the UK to study there'); the journey is thus a way to learn things beyond that which can be learnt 'in our land'.

According to Fágúnwà, Adélékè Adéẹ̀kọ́ suggests, '"ọ̀làjú" is not exclusively Yorùbá; other people have it too. But not all people have it in equal measure: the Europeans have it more than the Yorùbá, and the Yorùbá have always had it more than other Nigerians'; and indeed, Fágúnwà represents himself gaining ọ̀làjú through the new things he sees as he travels to, and within, Britain.[29] The British themselves are not entirely strange to Fágúnwà; he represents them as a known reality of colonial Nigerian life. However, familiar differences between the British and Africans become even more pronounced away from home, as Fágúnwà encounters Britons up close; thus, on board the ship he describes how 'iyatọ ti mo ri nibẹ ni eyi pe onjẹ wọn ko ni ata rara' (7) ('the difference that I encountered here was that their food didn't have pepper at all'). By encountering British *iyàtọ̀* or 'difference', Fágúnwà represents himself encountering implicitly undesirable strangeness, such as the under-peppered food, but also new forms of *ọgbọ́n* (wisdom) and *ọ̀làjú* (civilisation or enlightenment). Indeed, although Fágúnwà does occasionally wonder at the natural world during his journey, it is the manmade world of twentieth-century 'civilisation' that proves more of a draw during his trip, and to which he suggests Yoruba readers should aspire. Describing the many different kinds of people and houses he saw during his view of Britain from the ship, he writes: 'nigbati mo si gbe gbogbo nkan ti mo ri le ori iwọn mo ri i pe o yẹ ki a yin awọn enia nã, oju wọn là, ọgbọn mbẹ ni inu agbari wọn, ibiti nwọn de ninu oju lila wọn yi, ki Olodumare jẹki awa nã le de ibẹ lọjọ kan' (28) ('when I weighed up all the things I saw, I felt it was befitting that we should praise these people, they are civilised, there is wisdom in their heads, where they have got to in this civilisation of theirs, may God let us too get there one day').

Fágúnwà's novels, too, emphasise the 'difference' to be encountered through travel, here transposed from the twentieth-century human world to the spirit world of the forest. But, contrasting with the relatively familiar and sometimes admirable *iyàtọ̀* (difference) of the British in *Irinajo*, the spirit world in Fágúnwà's novels is initially represented as an exotic 'other' to the human world, reminiscent of the way that Africa becomes 'other' in much imperial Western travel writing. Yet Fágúnwà frequently represents uncanny traces of familiarity in even these strangest of spirits. Àkàrà-ògùn emphasises the visual strangeness of the beings he encounters, such as Àgbákò, the 'sixteen-eyed dewild':

---

[29] Adéẹ̀kọ́, *Arts of Being Yorùbá*, p. 70.

Nigbati mo ri i, ẹru ba mi, afi bi mo ba mã purọ; o de fila irin, o wọ ẹwu òjé, o si wo ṣokoto penpe kan bayi ti a fi awọ ṣe. Lati orunkun rẹ de ẹsẹ, kiki mariwo ọpẹ ni. Lati idodo rẹ si de ekiti idi, kiki onde ni – kò si ohun ti kò pe tan si ara awọn onde rẹ yi, ãye ejo mbẹ ninu wọn a mã yọ ahon rẹ bere bi Agbako ba ti nrin lọ. (*OO* 12)

When I set eyes on him, I was – unless I lie in this matter – smitten with terror. He wore a cap of iron, a coat of brass, and on his loins were leather shorts. His knees right down to his feet appeared to be palm leaves; from his navel to the bulge of his buttocks, metal network; and there was no creature on earth which had not found a home in this netting which even embraced a live snake among its links, darting out its tongue as Agbako trod the earth. (*FTD* 22)

Àgbákò is terrifyingly strange and unfamiliar: his legs are palm leaves, his lower body 'metal network' and he is writhing with creatures. And yet he also wears recognisable clothes and has a physiology similar to a human. Places, too, are marked by this conjunction of the strange and the seemingly familiar. Àkàrà-õgùn describes finding himself in a 'strange house' in the interior of the earth after fighting Àgbákò, where he encounters not total strangeness but a transgressive inversion of the usual form of human existence:

nwọn si fi imi ẹlẹbọtọ pa ilẹ rẹ ati ẹgbẹ ogiri pẹlu, ṣugbọn ibọn ni nwọn tò ti nwọn fi ṣe aja rẹ. Kò si ferese kò si si ilẹkun ninu ile yi bẹni ibẹ si mọlẹ kedere. Ibiti imọlẹ nã ti nwa kò ye mi. Nigbati mo de ibẹ ãrin inu ile nã gãn ni mo wà, bi mo si ti duro to mo nwo yika ni mo dede ri ti ogiri mẹrẹrin ile nã nbọ ni ọdọ mi, ti ile si tubọ nkere ti o si dabi ẹnipe awọn ogiri nã nfẹ fun mi pa si ãrin […] hilahilo ba mi gẹgẹ bi ọrọ Egbere. (*OO* 14)

cow dung was used in plastering the floor and the walls also, but the ceiling was lined entirely with guns. There was neither window nor door, yet the house was full of light; where this light came from remained a puzzle. I first discovered myself right in the centre of the room, and even as I stood inspecting my prison, I saw the four walls of the house coming towards me, so that the room became progressively smaller as if the walls planned to squeeze me to death […] disorientation became my lot like the monologue of a gnom. (*FTD* 26)

Àkàrà-õgùn describes 'disorientation', unfamiliarity and danger in a manner that is reminiscent of the adventure narratives of British explorers who encounter the 'radical difference' and estrangement, as Carl Thompson puts it, of lands inhabited by people who look human and yet do things very differently from the traveller's home society.[30] In this case, the house does not conform to the familiar form of a house; its lining of guns, its lack of windows and doors,

---

[30] Thompson, *Travel Writing*, p. 66.

and its walls that squeeze make it dangerously strange. The inhabitants of the terrible town of Ēmọ (Filth) similarly invert the normal rules of human presentation: 'ọpọlọpọ ni o wọ òdì aṣọ: omiran a kọ oju agbada si ẹhin, ẹlomiran ninu awọn obinrin a fi inu gele si ita – aṣọ gbogbo wọn ndan fun ẽri: o dabi àpò ọdẹ' (*OO* 19) ('many of them wore their clothes inside out; some wore their *agbada* back to front, some among the women wore their head-ties inside out; every garment shone with filth, it was more like the inside of a hunter's bag', *FTD* 32). Inside becomes outside, back becomes front; as Àkàrà-õgùn himself puts it, 'bẹ̀ni nkan wọn gbogbo lọ ti o ri jagbajagba rederede' (*OO* 19) ('even so did the affairs of these people run higgledy-piggledy, topsy-turvy', *FTD* 33).

Cannibalism also makes an appearance in both *Ìrìnkèrindò* and *Àdììtú Olódùmarè*; in the latter, the travellers enter what a notice on the road to the town describes as 'ILU AWỌN TI NJẸ ENIA' ('THE TOWN OF HUMAN EATERS'), as one of the many transgressions of human social norms that they encounter. In this town, the notice continues, 'ẸRAN ENIA NI NWỌN FI NJẸ IYÁN, ON NI NWỌN FI NJẸ ỌKÀ, ON NI NWỌN FI NJẸ ÈBÀ, ON NI NWỌN SI FI NJẸ ÈKO' (AO 82; original emphasis) ('THEY EAT THEIR POUNDED YAM WITH HUMAN FLESH, THEY EAT THEIR YAM FLOUR WITH HUMAN FLESH, ALSO THEIR EBA, FARINA MEAL AS WELL AS THEIR CORNMEAL', *MOG* 119; original emphasis); this town serves as a reminder of how far the protagonists have travelled outside normal human experience. The protagonists' strangeness renders them vulnerable to attack by unknown beings, but another danger of the strangeness they encounter is that they themselves may be transformed by it, in an echo of the imperial traveller's fear of being incorporated into or swallowed up – cannibalised – by the strange people and places they encounter.[31] Thus in the 'strange house' Àkàrà-õgùn falls into after his fight with Àgbákò, he is caught by strangers who transform him:

mo ba ara mi lori aga nla kan mo tobi pupọ iyẹ si bò mi lara. Bi mo ti tobi to nì, ki iṣe gbogbo ara mi lo tobi si i: apa mi kò yipada ẹsẹ mi kò gun si i bẹ̀ni kò si tobi si i, ṣugbọn ikùn mi tobi ni iwọn igba mejìlã ori mi si tobi iwọn igba mẹrindilogun. Ọrun mi kò tobi pupọ ṣugbọn o gùn rekọja. (*OO* 15)

I found myself on a large chair, my size was enormous and I was covered in feathers. I had grown in size, but my entire body was not uniformly increased; my arms had not changed, my legs had neither lengthened nor thickened, but my belly was twelve times distended and my head was sixteen times its normal size. My neck was not much thicker but was stretched beyond imagination. (*FTD* 27)

---

31 Watson, *Insatiable Appetites*, p. 170.

The traveller is potentially transformed into something 'beyond imagination' by his journey, just as he encounters a strangeness 'beyond imagination' that is inconceivable at home. Àkàrà-õgùn experiences the potential for the traveller to become something other than he was, but perhaps too far: no longer recognisably one of the people whom he had left behind. In addition, however, Fágúnwà is also using tropes that, as we have seen in other chapters of this book, have been used elsewhere to speak to contemporary southwest Nigerian fears about intra-Nigerian otherness. Karin Barber points out that in his novels, Fágúnwà writes with a constantly shifting sense of scale and readership, shifting between addressing and writing of Ègbá, Yoruba, Nigeria, Africa and even the whole world.[32] The trope of the cannibal may thus also be read as a fear of otherness intruding as the reader slips into some of these larger and stranger scales, beyond the known world.

However, while all of the places Àkàrà-õgùn encounters are strange, not all of them are disgusting or frightening to the traveller. On entering a cave on his second journey, 'onirũru ohun alumọnì aiye yi ni mo ba – awọn bi ilẹkẹ sẹgi, iyùn, lagidigba; ati awọn onirũru aṣọ bi àrán, sãnyan, alãri, àdìrẹ ati awọn kijipa ti o gbẹ hau ti nwọn si lù ni òlùpopo' (OO 26) ('I discovered all manner of precious things – segi, coral beads, waist beads and expensive cloths such as velvet, sanyan, red northern, dyed cloth and exquisitely seasoned kijipa which had been smoothly beaten', FTD 43); while in a nearby city, the traveller discovers ghommids who 'wọ aṣọ daradara: nwọn dara bi ẹiyẹ ologe' (OO 27) ('were attractively attired; they were like birds of plumage', FTD 43).[33] Echoing Fágúnwà discovering the wonders of the natural world at sea and of life in Britain, the traveller in Fágúnwà's novels discovers the treasures of the world as well as its horrors.

Indeed, the traveller recognises the material as well as the intellectual and social rewards of travel, as Àkàrà-õgùn explains: 'ohun ti mo mu bọ nigba ẹkeji ti mo lọ yi pọ tobẹ ti, nigbati mo ta wọn tan, emi ni o ni owo julọ jakejado ilu wa: owo mi ju ti ọba pãpã lọ' (OO 46) ('the things I brought back with me that second time were so numerous that, when I had sold them, I was the wealthiest man up or down the entire kingdom – I was richer even than the king', FTD 67). His third journey is one of conquest: the king 'bẹ ọ tọkantọkan pe ki iwọ ki o máṣai lọ fi oju gãnni Oke Langbodo nã fun mi ki o si gba nkan nã wa lati ọwọ ọba ibẹ' (OO 50) ('beg[s] of you from the very depths of my heart not to fail to snatch a brief glimpse of this same king and bring me this *thing* in his possession', FTD 72; original emphasis). In recognising both the risks and rewards of travelling, Fágúnwà's travellers echo the ideology of acquisition

---

[32] Barber, 'Time, Space and Writing', pp. 123–4.

[33] *Sẹgi*: a type of bead. *Sányán* and *kíjìpá*: types of cloth (silk and coarse cotton respectively).

behind many travels in West Africa in the nineteenth and early twentieth centuries, from those of European imperialists to the traders who crossed the Sahara accumulating wealth. But they also echo Fágúnwà's emphasis on his own travels as rewarding despite their hardships, although in *Irinajo* he more piously emphasises the rewards of knowledge and *ọ̀làjú*.

## The transmission of experience in Fágúnwà's novels

In *Irinajo*, Fágúnwà describes how it was not until he saw the ocean on this journey that he was able to fully believe what he had been told at school about its great extent: 'lõtọ ni mo ti gbọ ọrọ yi ri ki ng to lọ, ṣugbọn gbigba ti mo gba a ko jinlẹ pupọ ninu mi, ṣugbọn nigbati emi pãpã wa lọ fun odidi ọjọ mẹrindinlogun ti o jẹ pe ọkọ wa ko duro tọsantoru ti mo si ri i pe oju omi ni mo wa ọrọ nã tubọ wa ta gbongbo ninu mi, o fi idi mulẹ, o gba ibẹ kankan' (34) ('in truth I had heard about this kind of thing before I went, but I didn't really accept it deeply, but when I myself went for sixteen days on the sea, during which our ship did not stop from morning to night and I saw that I was still afloat on the ocean, this matter increasingly gained roots, it became established, it took over my heart'). Fágúnwà emphasises the value of travel as offering empirical experience of the world that transcends second-hand knowledge.

Fágúnwà's sense of the value of travel as offering empirical experience was circulating more broadly in mid-twentieth-century southwest Nigeria. In 1950, the Yoruba Translation Committee of Ìbàdàn published a pamphlet called 'Anfani Irin-Ajo' ('The Benefits of Travel'), seemingly a Yoruba translation of an Efik text by E. N. Amaku, a novelist and poet from Calabar. Though originally published outside the Yoruba region, its translation into Yoruba suggests that its ideas resonated for its Yoruba translators and their intended readers. In the Yoruba translation, Amaku points to the knowledge to be gained from travelling: 'arìnrìn-àjo a mã kọ lati mọ iwa awọn ẹlomiran nipa bibẹ wọn wò, ati nipa riri ìhùwàsí wọn ati ayika wọn' (5) ('the traveller will learn to know the character of others through visiting them, and experiencing their behaviour and their surroundings'). He adds that travelling thus enables one to judge the character of one's own town and people better, and he concludes by arguing for the importance of travelling as education:

Ki iṣe asọdun, ẹkọ́ ti a nkọ́ ninu irin-ajo ko ni ẹgbẹ, iriri oju ni arìnrìn-àjo fi nri ohun ti a nrohin fun ẹlomiran. Ẹkọ́ ti ẹniti nrin kiri bayi ba kọ, a mã fi ẹsẹ mulẹ ju ti ẹniti o joko si oju kan o. (6–7)

It's no exaggeration, the lessons that we learn on a journey have no comparison. The traveller sees for himself things that we tell other people about. The lessons learnt by someone who is travelling about like this will be more permanent than those of the person who sits in one place.

For Amaku, one of the important benefits of travel was *èkọ́* (lessons, moral instruction or education) gained by seeing a place with one's own eyes, which could then be taken home to better evaluate one's own people and their way of life. Writing in an age when *ọ̀làjú* meant this kind of knowledge of the world beyond one's home, Amaku suggests that the traveller undergoes a character transformation not necessarily in the moral sense, as Fágúnwà's hunters some-times do, but rather in becoming an embodiment of *èkọ́*, which can then be used to benefit those at home, by telling them about the world, bringing a new, broader perspective to one's home.

In common with Amaku, in *Irinajo* Fágúnwà emphasises the importance of telling others stories of travel. But he goes a step further and insists that this 'telling' should be in writing, so that the *èkọ́* one has gained do not disappear:

> Bi enia ba joko si ilu rẹ̀ ti ko mọ ibomiran ãbọ ẹkọ ni oluwarẹ o ni [...] ki iṣe gbogbo enia l'o le ri owo ati mã fi rin kiri, nitorinã l'o si fi jẹ ohun ẹtọ wipe ki ẹniti o ba lọ si ibomiran mã sọ ohun ti on ba ri nibẹ han ẹniti ko lọ. Pupọ ninu awọn itan pataki ti awọn baba nla wa ti mọ l'o ti sọnu patapata nitori nwọn ko kọ awọn itan wọnni silẹ, igbati nwọn si ku, itan nã ku pẹlu wọn. (35)

> If someone stays in their town and doesn't know other places, that person is only half educated [...] Not everyone can find the money to go travelling around, so it's important that someone who goes to other places describes the things that they see there to show to people who don't go. Many of the impor-tant stories that our ancestors knew have disappeared completely because they didn't write these stories down, and when they died, the stories died with them.

This concern with the relationship between travel, experience and 'stories' or writing can also be read as a commentary on the position of the written text in southwest Nigeria in the mid-twentieth century – a discussion that Fágúnwà's novels are also interested in, as they use travel to reflect on the connection between experience and narration. Many critics have noted the meta-fiction-al or self-reflexive commentary on orality and writing in Fágúnwà's narra-tives, voiced chiefly through the relationship between narrator and scribe.[34] *Ìrìnkèrindò* traces a three-fold relationship between experience, telling and writ-ing, or the eyes, voice and writing. As the novel opens, the hunter Ìrìnkèrindò – whose name literally means 'Wandering' – is wandering on a search for the scribe to whom he can tell his story of travelling. Thus although Ìrìnkèrindò's initial wanderings on his quest generate the plot, these wanderings do not end until their story can be turned into written narrative; he continues to wander in

---

[34] For example, Jane Wilkinson, 'Between Orality and Writing: The Forest of a Thou-sand Daemons as a Self-Reflexive Text', *Commonwealth: Essays and Studies,* 9.2 (1987), pp. 41–51; Adéẹ̀kọ́, *Arts of Being Yorùbá,* pp. 48–74.

search of the path from oral to written narrative. Ìrìnkèrindò further elaborates on this relationship between experience, orality and written narrative:

> baba mi to ṣe alaisi o ti wi fun mi pe ki nwa ọnakọna lati ri ọ ki nto kuro lori ilẹ aiye, ki nsọ nkan ti oju mi ti ri sẹhin fun ọ, nitori ki iwọ ba kede rẹ̀ fun awọn olugbe inu aiye, eleyini le mu anfani ba awọn ọmọ enia ki nwọn fi ọgbọn kun ọgbọn inu wọn. (*INIE* 2)

> It was my father who suggested it, long before his death, that I seek you every-where, so that I might relate all the things which my eyes have encompassed to you, that you in turn may pass them on to the sons of the world, and more wisdoms be added unto them. (*ETMT* 4)[35]

Ìrìnkèrindò suggests here that knowledge passes through a three-fold chain of transmission: experiences pass first-hand through Ìrìnkèrindò's eyes, and then through his voice, becoming spoken narrative, and finally through the writ-ten word, so that they can be read elsewhere, and 'more wisdoms be added unto them'. Thus telling and, especially, writing can allow greater wisdom (*ọgbọ́n*) to be added to an existing narrative of first-hand experience.

The audience for these tales seems to appreciate this wisdom: by the time *Ògbójú Ọdẹ*'s Àkàrà-ōgùn comes to recount his third and final journey, the crowd who have assembled to hear his stories exceeds one hundred and fifty people: 'gbogbo ilu ti rọ́ de, nwọn bo ile mi ṣikanṣikan' (*OO* 47) ('the entire populace had arrived; they covered my home like a swarm of locusts', *FTD* 68), the scribe remarks, using the novel's characteristic mode of hyperbole. And yet, not all experience is imagined to be captured within the telling of the tale. Later in *Ìrìnkèrindò*, the narrator describes how 'Nko le ka ohun ti oju mi ri tan ki nto de ohun nitori nko iti irin iru ìrìn bẹ̀ ri' (*INIE* 7) ('I cannot recount all the things which my eyes witnessed before I arrived at my destination, for a strange journey it proved to be, such that I had never before experienced', *ETMT* 11). Similarly, in *Ògbójú Ọdẹ*, Àkàrà-ōgùn teases the reader by an-nouncing that 'Ọpọlọpọ nkan ni oju mi ri ni ọja yi ṣugbọn nkò ni lè to gbogbo wọn tan nisisiyi ngo mã sọ ọ ni ọjọ miran' (*OO* 18) ('Many, many things did my eyes behold but I will not state them all now, I will recount them another day', *FTD* 32). The narrative pace of the novel speeds up as it moves towards its end, with Àkàrà-ōgùn repeatedly telling the listeners that he cannot possibly recount everything that happened in the Forest; his encounters in the Forest 'pọ ju ohun kikà lọ – didakẹ lo ya' ('were more numerous than lips can tell – the rest is silence'), and '[ọ]pọlọpọ idina ni a tun ba pade ṣugbọn nkò ri aye sọ wọn tan' (*OO* 66) ('[m]any hindrances did we encounter but there is not time to tell

---

[35] Adéníyì's translation here is unnecessarily gendered; this could be rendered 'in-habitants of the world' or 'people of the world'.

you everything', *FTD* 93–4). In this 'silence', Fágúnwà's narrators describe a gap between experience and text that urges readers not to take for granted that all wisdom can be passed on through the text – while, simultaneously, they also suggest that more wisdom can be added by virtue of the text being written down. Fágúnwà points to the textuality of the text: it is not a faithful, mimetic representation of experience, but a narration and interpretation.

AdéléKè Adéèkọ́ aptly suggests that the world in which Fágúnwà's novels is set is characterised as living through a moment of rupture, 'agitation', and epistemic uncertainty, as an older hunter anxiously seeks a young scribe to write down his story before he dies, and as the most seasoned professionals of the kingdom – the hunters and their companions – are repeatedly sent away from home to gain something from outside that that kingdom apparently needs very urgently. The sense of epistemic uncertainty Adéèkọ́ detects in the novels encompasses not only an apparent shift from orality to the written text, but a more widespread sense that new values, forms of power and modes of knowledge have risen in the colonial era; the world of the novels is 'a changing world that is not yet quite fully understood, but to whose inevitability the community has reconciled itself'.[36] The quest, I suggest, is deployed in Fágúnwà's novels as a metatextual motif, through which fictional narratives of travel explore the relationship between empirical experience and the wisdom to be gained from such experience, and between text, narrative and reader, in this era of epistemic change when these relationships could not be taken for granted. Mildred Mortimer suggests that the journey motif in contemporary African novels can be read as a form of *métissage* between African oral traditions and epics and European novels, through which African 'oral tradition' is 'transposed' to literature, and so the journey motif 'provides a way back to the village' for novelists.[37] Fágúnwà's journeys suggest a more complex relationship between orality and literacy. Although his protagonists' journeys may eventually take them quite literally back to the village, they also continue to require both written and oral narration to constitute 'experience' and 'wisdom'. The oral is not the 'way back'; it exists alongside the written, in a chain of transmission of knowledge.

The two modes of framing and narration that Fágúnwà employs across his five novels reinforce this textuality of the text and its distance from the 'reality' of experience. In most of his novels, the narrative is presented as an oral travel narrative – a 'travel telling' rather than 'travel writing' – transposed to written text by the scribe. The narratives are recounted by the protagonists as if they were non-fiction, first-person accounts of journeys (like Fágúnwà's own *Irinajo*). However, the fifth novel, *Àdììtú Olódùmarè*, dwells not so much on the journey itself as on the challenges its protagonist faces on the way; the

---

[36] Adéèkọ́, *Arts of Being Yorùbá*, pp. 54–5.
[37] Mortimer, *Journeys*, pp. 1–6.

journey brings the protagonist face-to-face with these challenges, but it is not the focus of the novel. Moreover, although still framed through a scribe's encounter with a traveller, the novel is told in the third person instead of the first person, privileging the scribe's voice over that of the traveller, as if Fágúnwà was starting to imagine modes of storytelling that emphasised writing over telling. Nonetheless, Fágúnwà does not seem to view the oral as superseded by the moment of twentieth-century ọ̀làjú. Rather, the movement between orality and literacy is figured as one of the many border-crossings valorised by Fágúnwà's novels, given fictional form in the shape of the traveller's quest, but which also extend to Fágúnwà's own border-crossings between fiction and non-fiction, and the shared emphasis, in both his novels and his non-fiction travel writing, on the value of the text in allowing a border-crossing between experience and narrative.

## Writing the quest after Fágúnwà

Ayọ̀ Bámgbóṣé credits Fágúnwà's novels with a 'profound influence' on the Yoruba novel – in fact, so profound that Bámgbóṣé, writing in 1978, was able to argue that '[u]ntil comparatively recently, almost all the Yoruba novels followed Fágúnwà's pattern of the story of the wandering hero (generally a hunter) and his experiences in a forest or some other locale peopled by supernatural beings'.[38] While Yoruba novels are now more diverse, both the border-crossing and the quest have nonetheless remained important motifs in southwest Nigerian fiction. They have proved supple forms, moving between the Yoruba and English languages, fiction and non-fiction, non-realist to realist fiction, and beyond southwest Nigeria. After Fágúnwà, subsequent fantastical novels such as J. Ògúnsínà Ògúndélé's *Ibú Olókun* (1956) and *Èjìgbèdè Lọ́nà Ìsálú Ọ̀run* (1956) and D. I. Fátànmí's *Kórimálẹ Nínú Igbó Adimúla* (1967), for instance, similarly involve quests – under the sea, between heaven and earth or in the forest.[39] In Chapter 6, we will encounter a travel writer, Kọ́lá Túbọ̀sún, who claims Fágúnwà's journeys as one of several inspirations for his own non-fiction travel writing.

Some of the most well-known transformations of the quest motif have, however, been the novels of Amos Tutùọlá and Ben Okri. In this final part of this chapter, I read the quest motifs in novels by these two canonical writers alongside a realist iteration of the quest motif in a less well-known Yoruba novel, J. Akin Ọmọ́yájowó's *Adégbẹ̀san*, to show how the quest motif has been transformed over the twentieth century and between realist and non-realist texts, and Yoruba and English writing. These novels, like Fágúnwà's,

---

[38] Bamgboṣe, *D. O. Fagunwa*, p. 5.
[39] Babalọla, 'Yoruba Literature', pp. 169–70; Ogunsina, *Yoruba Novel*, pp. 80–91.

thematise border-crossing journeys, with protagonists setting out into the world where they encounter difference and strangeness. They do so in quite different ways, however, depicting journeys between the human and spiritual world in some cases and in realist settings in others, and with the quest itself adopting a fairly linear form in some cases and in other cases becoming highly fragmented as the protagonist is cast out to wander involuntarily. Like Fágúnwà's novels, these novels use the quest not simply as a mythic trope and not only as a transformation of oral tales of travel, but also to speak, in different ways, to conditions of Nigeria in the age in which the novels are set; border-crossings in particular come to represent, variously, transgressions of colonial space, being thrust involuntarily into chaos, and the potentials for encounter and translation within the nation.

In Amos Tutùọlá's *The Palm-Wine Drinkard* (1952), a lazy 'drinkard' sets out on a quest in search of his dead palm wine tapster. This quest takes the drinkard to the Dead's Town, where he hopes he will be able to find his palm wine tapster and bring him home to re-establish the drinkard's supply of palm wine. Tutùọlá's eight subsequent novels similarly deployed versions of the quest motif, although with variations such as female protagonists, but in this chapter I focus on *The Palm-Wine Drinkard*, the most widely read of Tutùọlá's novels.[40] Although, along with Chinua Achebe, Fágúnwà and Tutùọlá are now two of the most well-known Nigerian writers of the late colonial and early independence era, and the latter two are considered by Abíọlá Irele to form the backbone of the Yoruba literary tradition along with Wọlé Ṣóyínká, Tutùọlá was initially much less revered than Fágúnwà.[41] African reviewers and critics in particular saw *The Palm-Wine Drinkard* as poorly written in its use of 'young English' rather than the polished literary English of writers such as Achebe and, as Simon Gikandi writes, as 'simply a translation of Yoruba ideas into English'. They also considered it disturbingly apolitical in the era's nationalist climate. Later, however, Tutùọlá gained recognition amongst critics for not only the wide range of literary influences, both Yoruba and European, that he brought to his novels, but also for the ways in which contemporary life did, after all, feature in his fantastical stories.[42]

Early criticism of his novels argued, as for Fágúnwà, that Tutùọlá had borrowed the quest motif from Yoruba oral forms, and also that it drew on

[40] Simon Gikandi, 'Tutuola, Amos', in *Encyclopedia of African Literature,* ed. by Simon Gikandi (London and New York: Routledge, 2005).

[41] Abiola Irele, 'Tradition and the Yoruba Writer: D. O. Fagunwa, Amos Tutuola and Wole Soyinka', *Odù: Journal of Yoruba and Related Studies,* 11 (1975), pp. 75–100.

[42] Gikandi, 'Tutuola'.

'universal' mythic patterns.[43] Ato Quayson has persuasively shown that this picture is in fact more complicated: while Tutùọlá was 'heavily dependent on the themes, motifs and tales of Yoruba storytelling traditions', his quest narratives did not draw on a single direct parallel in Yoruba oral traditions, but rather mingled together romance narratives focused on a hero's adventures, cautionary tales told to children, riddles, proverbs and narrative techniques such as episodic storytelling and formulaic endings, together with his own imagination and influences from Fágúnwà.[44] But, like Fágúnwà's novels, the drinkard's journey and its boundary-crossings can also be understood as speaking to and about conditions of modernity and travel in late colonial Nigeria. While Fágúnwà's travellers embody orthodox notions of the hunter-traveller as hero and seeker of wisdom, Tutùọlá's novels adopt a more ironic position towards the character of the traveller. As well as travelling on a search for his tapster, the drinkard, in common with Fágúnwà's hunters, makes a journey into strange places where he encounters out-of-the-ordinary aspects of the world, or *aiyé*, and also danger, surprise, the indescribable and the unknown on the way. However, his motivation is a mixture of self-interest and curiosity, not the vaunted heroism and adventure of many of Fágúnwà's hunters – and alongside taking his juju with him, he drinks forty kegs of palm wine before setting out on one of his journeys, as if satirising the more po-faced spiritual and practical preparations of Fágúnwà's hunters.

Nonetheless, as in Fágúnwà's novels, the drinkard crosses borders that are not ordinarily crossed: he frequently passes between road and bush, and also between the spirit and the human world, life and death, heaven and earth and, in Paul Edwards' reading of the novel, the 'opposed worlds' of the farm, characterised by harmony, and the wilderness, characterised by 'states of terror and distress'.[45] It seems as though it is only the drinkard, the unpredictable, unconventional layabout, who would choose to cross these borders repeatedly: he is, Edwards suggests, a born wanderer, unable or unwilling to stay on the farm even though it is a place of contentment and harmony, favouring the 'journey of the imagination' over the 'contented existence' of the farm.[46]

Where Fágúnwà's hunters' border-crossings lead them to new encounters with the world that transform them into experienced and wise men, Tutùọlá's

---

[43] Bernth Lindfors, 'Amos Tutuola's Television-Handed Ghostess', *ARIEL: A Review of International English Literature,* 2.1 (1971), pp. 68–77 (p. 75); Judy Anne White, 'Quest for Selfhood: The Female Hero in Amos Tutuola's The Brave African Huntress', *Contributions in Afroamerican and African Studies,* 187 (1998), pp. 131–42.

[44] Quayson, *Strategic Transformations*, pp. 45–6, p. 58.

[45] Paul Edwards, 'The Farm and the Wilderness in Tutuola's *The Palm-Wine Drinkard*', *Journal of Commonwealth Literature,* 9.1 (1974), pp. 57–65 (p. 58).

[46] Ibid. p. 60.

drinkard's transformation through his travels is more ironic. Edwards suggests that through his wanderings the drinkard is transformed 'from a layabout to a man of spiritual powers', since on returning home, he brings with him an egg that will produce anything he demands of it, and he manages to put a stop to the famine in his town.[47] But unlike Fágúnwà's heroes, he does not seem to undergo a heroic character transformation. The drinkard and his wife experience only relatively minor transformations during the course of their journey – 'And within one month my wife and I became good dancers. This was rather queer', the drinkard notes – as if mocking the heroic transformations expected of Fágúnwà's protagonists.[48] Although by the end of his journey the drinkard has developed from being concerned only with his own pleasure – drinking palm wine – to supporting communal pleasure as he uses his egg to supply the town with food and drink, he remains lazy, relying on the material gains of travel rather than his own character to bring good to the town: 'I had become the greatest man in my town and did no other work than to command the egg to produce food and drinks' (299). The egg eventually breaks, and produces only leather whips with which to flog the people of the town who broke the egg. While Fágúnwà's heroes are transformed into great men, the spoils of the drinkard's travels are destroyed by the carelessness that is seemingly part of human nature.

The drinkard is in many ways a typical picaresque protagonist, not only in that he does not come to a straightforward narrative of personal growth through his wanderings – as the protagonist of the Bildungsroman, by contrast, might be expected to do – but also in that he is humorously flawed, and an ironic anti-hero compared to Fágúnwà's more straightforwardly heroic hunters. The picaresque protagonist will not, Susan Z. Andrade writes, 'join the ranks of bourgeois conventionality but will remain outside the system of compromise that produces disciplined subjects'.[49] Indeed, a closer reading of the drinkard's border-crossings in *The Palm-Wine Drinkard* reveals that they constitute a means through which the drinkard resists becoming a 'disciplined subject' of the colonial era. The world of *The Palm-Wine Drinkard* is one in which the land is divided up between creatures who are 'forbidden to touch another creature's land or bush' (232), with the traveller, as in Fágúnwà's novels, seeming to be one of the few people who can pass through these borders. These borders between lands echo twentieth-century regimes of national boundaries and border controls and as such, Madhu Krishnan argues, they can be read as reflecting

---

[47] Ibid. p. 64.

[48] Amos Tutuola, *The Palm-Wine Drinkard; and, My Life in the Bush of Ghosts* (New York: Grove Press, 1994), p. 250. Subsequent references are to this edition and will be given in parentheses in the text.

[49] Andrade, 'Representing Slums and Home', p. 237.

colonial regimes of space and their attempts to control movement and impose boundaries. The drinkard's great talent, Krishnan suggests, is to undermine colonial demarcations of space by crossing borders.[50] The drinkard's seemingly drunken, perhaps somewhat mindless wanderings reveal the drinkard as in fact a transgressive figure in the face of colonial modernity, refusing to become a 'disciplined' subject of the era.

Yet the drinkard, too, places an emphasis on forward movement that seems aligned to the ethos of modernity. Although his journeys are meandering, his overall impetus is for forward movement, towards his goal: 'To go back was harder and to go further was the hardest, so at last we made up our mind and started to go forward' (245), he explains part way through his journey, and he is told later, by the Red-king, that in the old days, 'we were walking backwards and not forwards as nowadays' (255), while the inhabitants of the Deads' Town still walk backwards. Travelling forward, both literally and metaphorically, becomes a condition of both life and modernity, and the wanderer becomes one who makes potential progress under the regime of 'nowadays'. If there is a transformation wrought by the drinkard's border-crossings and his determination to move forward, in line with the age, it is not so much in the drinkard's character, but in the text itself. Though, as the drinkard tells it, 'all our trials, difficulties and many years' travel brought only an egg' (295), not the safe return of his tapster, his travels also, of course, result in the production of narrative: *The Palm-Wine Drinkard* itself. The drinkard has a story to tell, and so does Tutùọlá: a story that speaks to the contemporary age by enacting a ground-breaking border-crossing of the quest motif and storytelling modes from Yoruba language to English, and by imbuing the hero narrative with a cynicism and irony that echoes the drinkard's own ability to transgress borders and slip outside a 'disciplined' subjectivity to create an anti-hero for the late colonial age.

Both Fágúnwà's and Tutùọlá's novels may be read as addressing or drawing on the conditions of the Nigeria of their age, but the authors do not explicitly set their novels in contemporary Nigeria. Ben Okri's *The Famished Road*, published in 1991, similarly does not name its setting as Nigeria, though it is often read as being set in a creatively imagined version of Nigeria at the dawn of independence from Britain, while also claiming 'Africa' more broadly as its space of representation. The novel follows the *àbíkú* or 'born-to-die' child Azaro as the country around him is in turmoil, and he himself is under constant threat from his spirit companions and enemies who often threaten to return him, unwillingly, to the spirit world. Azaro's mother and father, meanwhile, attempt

---

[50] Madhu Krishnan, 'From Empire to Independence: Colonial Space in the Writing of Tutuola, Ekwensi, Beti, and Kane', *Comparative Literature Studies,* 54.2 (2017), pp. 329–57 (pp. 332–5).

to keep him in the human world, but are also afflicted by their own troubles, particularly their poverty and struggle to survive. Okri himself does not identify as Yoruba, but he adopts the Yoruba notion of the *àbíkú* in his novel in a way that reflects the national perspective that he adopts within the novel: he writes so as to avoid associating the setting or the narrative itself with any one ethnic group. Indeed, Okri's background itself reflects a national perspective that challenges the boundaries of ethnicity and regionalism in a way we will encounter increasingly in this book; he is of Urhobo and Igbo ancestry, was born in Minna, grew up in London and Lagos, and has since lived in the UK. I therefore discuss his novel in this chapter not to suggest it should necessarily be included within the rubric of southwest Nigerian writing, but to demonstrate the way the motif of the traveller crossing continually back and forth between the spirit world, like the figure of the *àbíkú*, itself crosses borders to a broader Nigerian literary culture beyond southwest Nigeria.

*The Famished Road*'s Azaro is a perpetual wanderer, prone to what Ọlátúbọ̀sún Ògúnsanwó calls 'compulsive wanderlust'.[51] Throughout the novel, Azaro finds himself – sometimes by choice and sometimes by force, and particularly in moments of struggle – wandering the many paths around his home, often taking him deep into unknown parts of the forest, where he gets lost. Sometimes, the novel suggests, this is an intellectual or spiritual wandering as well as a physical wandering, as Azaro enters the spiritual realm through his journeys of the mind and soul. Thus as in both Fágúnwà's and Tutùọlá's novels, the traveller in Okri's novel journeys back and forth between the human world and the spirit world but, as Ògúnsanwó points out, the space for this border-crossing has now changed: whereas in Tutùọlá's and Fágúnwà's novels, the spirits are usually encountered only in the forest, in Okri's novels, the spirits are now understood to be a constant presence in the human world, too, at least for those who can see them.[52]

However, rather than adopting the more conventional quest motif, as we saw in Fágúnwà's and Tutùọlá's novels, in *The Famished Road* the journey across borders has become fragmented. Azaro travels not on one path, with a destination in mind, but rather repeatedly finds himself being cast out, or arriving in a state of confusion or turmoil in the forest, on some kind of quest whose nature he does not always know. In Fágúnwà's and Tutùọlá's novels, as we have seen, travel is considered a way to encounter danger – and it is this that makes it, in part, such a valuable experience. But in *The Famished Road*, the road itself becomes dangerous. As the title of the novel makes clear, the

---

[51] Olatubosun Ogunsanwo, 'Intertextuality and Post-Colonial Literature in Ben Okri's *The Famished Road*', *Research in African Literatures*, 26.1 (1995), pp. 40–52 (p. 50).
[52] Ibid. p. 46.

road is 'famished', and in danger of consuming the traveller – drawing here on a symbolism of the hungry road that, as Ògúnsanwó reminds us, Wọlé Ṣóyínká also exploited in both his play *The Road* and his poem, 'Death in the Dawn', in which a mother prays, 'Child / May you never walk / When the road waits, famished', itself echoing the Yoruba prayer 'May you never travel when the road is hungry'.[53] Thus, where in some of the other texts we have encountered in this book, the fear of being consumed comes from the intra-Nigerian other, represented metaphorically in the form of the cannibal, here it is the road itself – travel, the path of life – that may eat up the traveller. The travel of the novel is thus chaotic, unlike the sense of progress – even if with obstacles, pauses and diversions – that pervades Fágúnwà's and Tutùọlá's novels.

*The Famished Road* is also concerned with a journey into the Nigerian nation. Though 'Nigeria' is not named as such in the text, the novel dramatises repeatedly the politics of the independence era – the period in which it is set – and foreshadows the losses that are to ensue in the postcolonial nation, such as deforestation and creation of urban slums, which become a repeated motif of the novel. Azaro, the *àbíkú*, becomes a figure representing the people of the nation, coming and going, subject to violence, continually thrust onto journeys of uncertainty by those more powerful than him. And here there is a boundary-crossing of the journey motif, too, as Okri, a non-Yoruba writer, takes up the Yoruba notion of the *àbíkú*, rendering it a Nigerian motif as well as a Yoruba motif, just as he takes the journey itself into the sphere of the nation. Karin Barber and Rita Nnodim have both shown how Fágúnwà's novels imagine themselves to be convening audiences simultaneously composed of individual Yoruba towns, all black people, even the whole world, and often many different senses of *orílè-èdè wa*, 'our nation'.[54] The novels operate with a series of 'nested' references; thus, Barber writes, 'the Yoruba are the Egba writ large, Nigeria is Yorubaland writ large, and Africa, perhaps, is Yorubaland writ even larger, [which] means that no new resources are deployed for imagining a composite, multi-ethnic, multilingual nation state such as Nigeria'.[55] By contrast, in *The Famished Road*, Okri writes of a still uncertain, unnamed but more closely Nigerian nation through the figure of the journey.

The journey into the nation also began to feature in realist novels dealing with the late colonial and early independence-era period. From the 1950s onwards, realist narratives gradually became another important route for the Yoruba novel, focusing on either the recent historical past, or on urban, 'modern'

---

[53] Ibid. pp. 48–9.
[54] Barber, 'Time, Space and Writing', pp. 123–4; Nnodim, 'Configuring Audiences', pp. 160–4.
[55] Barber, 'Time, Space and Writing', p. 124.

life.[56] J. Akin Ọmọ́yájowó's novel *Adégbẹ̀san* (1961), an early Yoruba thriller, is the tale of its eponymous protagonist's pursuit of his mother's murderer from his home town of Ayetoro, across central and northern Nigeria, all the way to Sokoto. *Adégbẹ̀san*, set in the 1950s and published shortly after Nigerian independence, can be read as a form of the quest novel, but unlike Fágúnwà's novels, *Adégbẹ̀san* emphasises not character transformation as the outcome of travel, but encounters with difference that engender translation, both literal and metaphorical, between parts of the nation. The boundaries the questing traveller crosses are no longer those between the spiritual and human worlds but those within the nation, as Adégbẹ̀san travels far beyond his home in southwest Nigeria to central and northern Nigeria in pursuit of his mother's killer. The novel revels in representing the strangeness and exoticism of northern Nigeria to its Yoruba readership, as if a kind of realist – if fictional – travel writing: the Sultan of Sokoto, for instance, wears 'agbádá rẹpẹtẹ kan ti a fi òwú sílíkí ṣiṣẹ aràmọdà si lara. O wé láwàni rururu, o si wọ bàtà sálúbàtà' ('a huge *agbádá*,[57] which was embroidered in silk in fabulous patterns. He wore a high-wound turban, and sandals').[58] In its dwelling on the foreign and the strange, *Adégbẹ̀san* is reminiscent of both Fágúnwà's descriptions of the fantastical towns his heroes travel through, and his interest in *ọ̀làjú* or civilisation in his non-fiction narrative *Irinajo*. Thus Ọmọ́yájowó describes the central Nigerian town of Bida:

> Nitori náà, a pinnu lati rin ilu naa yíká lati lè ri ìlàjú wọn. Ilu Bida tobi púpọ̀. Ile wọn yàtọ̀ si ti ilẹ wa. Erùpẹ tabi bíríkì ni wọn lò fun ile wọn. Ọ̀pọ̀ ninu awọn ile naa ni kọ̀ ní igun bi tiwa: gbogbo wọn ri kìrìbìtì-kìrìbìtì yika ni. Ọpọlọpọ ni ki i ṣe paanu ni a fi bò wọn, ti o si jẹ wi pe koríko tabi erùpẹ ni, sibẹsibẹ ilu wọn mọ́ tónítóní, o si lẹ́wà. Ile ọjà wọn pọ̀, ọpọ̀lọ́pọ́ ati orisirísi ohun ọ̀ṣọ́ ni a si ń tà nibẹ, Orísirísi iṣẹ́ ọnà, awọ, bàtà, ìlẹ̀kẹ̀ ati awọn nkan bẹ́ẹ̀-bẹ́ẹ̀ gbogbo ni ó kún inu oja naa. Aṣọ awọn ọkunrin wọn funfun o si tobi gbẹ̀rẹ̀gẹ̀dẹ̀-gbẹrẹgẹdẹ, ọpọlọpọ wọn ni o wé láwàni. Awọn gbajúmọ̀ ati awọn olówó wọn gun ẹṣin, awọn obinrin wọn fi ìlẹ̀kẹ̀ ṣe ọ̀ṣọ́ si ara wọn. (22–3)

Therefore, we decided to walk around the town to see its level of civilisation. Bida was very big. Their houses were different from those in our land. They used mud or bricks for their houses. Many of these houses were not angular like ours; all of them were curved all the way round. Many of them were not roofed with galvanised iron sheets, but with grass or mud, nonetheless their

[56] Ogunsina, *Yoruba Novel*, p. 110; Adéyẹmí, 'Magical Realism', p. 92.
[57] A long, flowing gown for men – *agbádá* is the Yoruba word, rather than the Hausa equivalent.
[58] J. Akin Ọmọyajowo, *Adégbẹ̀san*, 2nd edn (Lagos: Longman Nigeria, 1979 [1961]), p. 59. Translation is my own. Subsequent references are to this edition and will be given in parentheses in the text.

town was spotless and beautiful. Their market stalls were many and they sold various adornments there. All kinds of craftsmanship, leather, shoes, beads and other such things filled that market. The men's clothes were white, and they were big and broad, many of them wore turbans. The prominent and wealthy men rode horses, and the women wore beads to ornament themselves.

Ọmọ́yájowó's representation of Nigeria through this fictional travel writing is of separate and distinct people and places, a polyglot nation in which Yoruba speakers and Hausa speakers co-exist but are unable to understand one another straight away. On first meeting a Hausa man, Adégbẹ̀san is frightened, unable to understand him and struck by their differences:

O pe mi ni ede Gambari ṣugbọn ọrọ ti o sọ kò ye mi […] ọkunrin naa soríkọ́, o ronu fun iwọn iṣẹju kan, o mi ori, o fa oju ro, ẹru ba mi, mo si wòye pé ko fẹ ṣe iranlọwọ fun mi. (26)

He called to me in Hausa, but I didn't understand what he said […] the man paused and thought for a minute, he shook his head, he looked unhappy, I was scared, and I assumed that he didn't want to help me.

But despite this initial incomprehension, the novel in fact goes on to insist on the translatability of Nigeria; characters who do not share a language eventually find ways to communicate through sign language, while many minor characters are bilingual. English is used only occasionally, principally by representatives of the state; instead of using a national language, the characters translate between Yoruba and Hausa. The nation encountered through travel, in this novel, is thus also one of exotic difference encountered and made comprehensible through translation.

'Translational reason', António Ribeiro argues, is 'a cosmopolitan reason' – not only in the sense of one place knowing about the other, but in 'its ability to situate itself *on* the border, to occupy the spaces of articulation and to permanently negotiate the conditions of that articulation', to be a 'get-between' as well as a 'go-between'. Thus, Ribeiro envisages cosmopolitan translation configured 'in such a way as to provide for mutual intelligibility, without having to sacrifice difference in the interest of blind assimilation'.[59] At first glance *Adégbẹ̀san's* model of translation may not seem cosmopolitan in this sense, since it does not envisage the border between Yoruba and Hausa as a 'space of articulation', but simply as a place to be crossed back and forth, without resting in between. However, though it is set in the 1950s, *Adégbẹ̀san* was published in 1961, shortly after independence and at a time of public debate

---

[59] António S. Ribeiro, 'Translation as a Metaphor for Our Times: Postcolonialism, Borders and Identities', *Portuguese Studies,* 20 (2004), pp. 186–94 (pp. 187, 192); emphasis added.

about what the newly independent nation would mean for relations between northern and southern Nigeria. Translation – overtly, linguistic translation, but implicitly also cultural translation, which the text itself undertakes as it makes northern Nigeria intelligible to Yoruba readers – allows *Adégbèsan* to encounter the north without being changed by it, as if beginning to envisage a national space of mutual encounter that sits on the borders between Yoruba and Hausa, without either having to 'sacrifice difference', in Ribeiro's terms. The novel makes tentative steps towards imagining a nation that allows room for co-operation and translation through encounter, even if it falls short of the 'get-between' nature of the translator in Ribeiro's sense. Thus if, in Fágúnwà's novels, character is the means through which travel engenders change, the quest narrative of *Adégbèsan* suggests that translation, and thus language, can also be a means of transformation through travel. Through travel and encounter the nation can eventually be comprehended, while still kept at arm's length, imagined through a series of border-crossings and translations rather than as-similation into sameness.

The quest that underlies not only Fágúnwà's novels but also, with variations, the novels by Tutùọlá, Okri and Ọmọ́yájowó discussed in this chapter, has thus proven an enduring, and flexible, motif of travel. It allows these writers not only to draw on the quest as an archetypal literary trope of endeavour and transformation – or, as in the case of Okri, to disrupt that trope by depicting fragmented and chaotic wanderings instead – but also to address specific mo-ments of change, linked to historical, political and social crossroads at which the writers find themselves, from the epistemological change that George and Adéẹ̀kọ́ identify as central to Fágúnwà's writing, to the moments of postcolonial national formation and encounter that I have suggested underlie both Okri's and Ọmọ́yájowó's novels, in very different ways.

In all of these novels, the quest, even when highly fragmented, takes the traveller across borders, between one world and another – the home and the forest, the human and the spiritual realms, or Yoruba and Hausa Nigeria. For Fágúnwà, this border-crossing into a world in which one can gain experience of new and strange things engenders a transformation for the traveller, in both his novels and in his own non-fiction travel narrative, *Irinajo*. Writing of an era of uncertainty and rupture in which, as Adéẹ̀kọ́ suggests, it had become important to go out into the world to find something needed at home, Fágúnwà uses the quest, and the telling and writing of that quest, to dramatise some of the changes that this era brought about. He addresses similar concerns in *Irinajo*, exploring his own late colonial encounter with Britain and 'civilisation' through his travels, which he sought to convey to his readers through his travel narra-tive. The later quest novels discussed in this chapter also explore the question of what is to be gained from travelling, but their authors seem less confident than Fágúnwà that travel necessarily engenders transformation of character and enlightenment – instead, they picture partial transformations, traumatic wandering, or encounters with difference that can be mediated through translation without necessarily engendering personal transformation.

The next chapter of this book picks up the figure of border-crossing journeys into the nation again, but turns now to non-fiction travel narratives describing journeys into the nation in the years after Nigeria's independence and subsequent civil war. It explores how they envisage crossing borders into previously unknown parts of the nation to engender not only personal transformation – echoing Fágúnwà's more optimistic sense of the potentials of travel – but also national transformation, creating a new sense of Nigeria for both the traveller and the reader of travel writing.

# Surveying and serving Nigeria in national travel writing after the civil war

After the euphoria of independence from Britain in 1960, Nigeria found itself a nation formed out of what Tóyìn Fálǫlá and Ogechukwu Ezekwem characterise as 'a conglomeration of various ethnic nationalities whose loyalties lay with their various ethnic groups', dating back to the British colonial amalgamation of Nigeria in 1914 out of a vastly heterogeneous region.[1] One of the most significant consequences of the fractures within this newly independent nation, and the rise of ethno-regional political movements that sought to convince Nigerians to abandon the colonial borders imposed on them by the British in favour of greater political autonomy for regional groupings, was the civil war of 1967–70, during which the Igbo region of southeast Nigeria sought to secede as the independent nation of Biafra. Enormous numbers of casualties resulted, along with calamitous civilian suffering on the Biafran side. The Nigerian federal government was eventually victorious. However, the fissures in the nation that emerged during this period (and continue to resonate to this day) made it clear that Nigeria's nationhood could not be taken for granted.

In the wake of the Nigeria–Biafra war, fiction and memoirs about the war have emerged as an important forum for discussion of questions of ethnicity, nationalism and neo-colonialism linked to the war, as well as a mode of expression of its hardships and suffering.[2] But the civil war has also continued to reverberate more indirectly in Nigerian literary culture, through texts that consider the longer-term project of nation-building in the decades after the civil war. Nation-building had now become an urgent task for those who sought to keep this new nation together, and required finding a way to reconcile the many ethno-nations within Nigeria to what Wálé Adébánwí characterises as the 'Nigerian grand nation'.[3] The creation of textual narratives of nation has played a significant role in such nation-building. Adébánwí shows how the Nigerian press has been central in producing 'competing and clashing narratives on the idea and ideal of the "Nigerian nation"'.[4] Writers of fiction, too, have sought

---

[1] Toyin Falola and Ogechukwu Ezekwem, *Writing the Nigeria–Biafra War* (Woodbridge: James Currey/Boydell & Brewer, 2016), p. 6.

[2] Ibid. pp. 9–10.

[3] Adebanwi, *Nation as Grand Narrative*, p. 5.

[4] Ibid. p. 12.

to narrate the nation; Kọ́lé Ọmọ́tọ́sọ̀ argues that before the Civil War, novelists often represented 'a Nigerian national consciousness but through a single ethnic national framework', but after the Civil War, the multi-ethnic nation in its entirety began more frequently to be addressed.[5]

Travel writers, too, have produced narratives of the 'Nigerian grand nation' in postcolonial Nigeria, using the figure of the traveller into the nation as one who encounters Nigeria's diverse peoples and ways of life, and who can therefore explain to fellow Nigerians what their nation is. In this chapter, focusing on travel narratives by surveyor Babátúndé Shàdẹ̀kọ̀ and by participants in Nigeria's National Youth Service Corps (NYSC), I examine the way that travel writers have woven together narration of nation and self, while surveying and serving the nation. These texts are not narratives of the civil war itself, but can be read as a product of the longer-term consequences of the war and the search for national unity that ensued: Shàdẹ̀kọ̀ writes explicitly in search of national unity in the immediate post-war years, while NYSC was established in 1973, shortly after the end of the civil war, also as a means of fostering national unity. The texts about NYSC I discuss in this chapter, written in later decades, demonstrate the continued salience of the nation-building project as they reflect on intra-national encounters and Nigerians' knowledge of each other through their authors' travels, but they also demonstrate some of the challenges of producing nationhood as they wield figures such as the cannibal and the 'pregnant Corper' that, I argue, are used to express doubts about the nation. In these texts, travel writing is seen a way of uniting the fractured postcolonial nation through narrative, and representing it through the 'multi-ethnic framework' that Ọmọ́tọ́sọ̀ suggests is also characteristic of post-civil war novels, while also exploring its differences. At the same time, in these texts, the production of Nigerian nationhood is intimately connected to production of selfhood. In Shàdẹ̀kọ̀'s travelogue, the author envisages both travel and reading travel writing as a way of creating 'detribalised' Nigerians. The NYSC narratives by Dámilọ́lá Ajénifújà and Chibuzor Mirian Azubuike that I focus on in this chapter, meanwhile, contain elements of memoir and self-development texts as well as travel writing, and they explore the way both travellers and readers of travel writing, particularly women, can be shaped by their experience of travel.

## 'How to be a detribalized Nigerian': Babátúndé Shàdẹ̀kọ̀'s travel memoir

In a foreword to Babátúndé Shàdẹ̀kọ̀'s *The Magic Land of Nigeria* (1980), Chief Simeon O. Adébọ̀ (the former head of the civil service of the western

---

[5] Omotoso, 'The Nigerian Federation in the Nigerian Novel', pp. 146–7.

region of Nigeria and a representative of Nigeria to the UN) offers some faint praise for the book:

> In my school-days, travelogues were even more the vogue, for both writers and readers, than they are today. But then, as now, not all travelogues were popular. Not all deserved to be. For one thing, a travelogue can, more so perhaps than most other kinds of books, very easily become boring. But this one retains the reader's interest most of the time.[6]

This not-so-boring travelogue, *The Magic Land of Nigeria*, is an account of Shàdẹ̀kọ̀'s travels across 'all the nooks and corners of Nigeria while working as a Federal Government Surveyor' between 1969 and 1975 (xiii). Babátúndé Shàdẹ̀kọ̀ was educated at the elite King's College in Lagos, the University of Ibadan and the University of New Brunswick in Canada, before beginning his career as a surveyor. *The Magic Land of Nigeria*, published by Nationwide Survey Services in Lagos, traces the author's travels around Nigeria by road and rail during his career as a surveyor, during and directly after the civil war. Shàdẹ̀kọ̀ writes in colourful detail of his experiences across the nation, focusing particularly on northern Nigeria, where his work as a surveyor was concentrated, but also describing cities such as Lagos, Ọ̀yọ́ and Ifẹ̀ in the southwest and Onitsha and Enugu in the southeast. Although full of digressions into Shàdẹ̀kọ̀'s opinions, observations and intellectual interests, including reflections on the civil war, the book's main chapters focus primarily on Shàdẹ̀kọ̀'s experiences of the places to which he travelled. His chapter titles – 'From Lolloping Lagos to Culture-Conscious Kaduna', 'The Giggling Gaiety of Gwandu "City"' – reflect not only Shàdẹ̀kọ̀'s fondness for alliteration, but also his book's suggestion that it is able to give readers an insight into the unique character of each place to which Shàdẹ̀kọ̀ travelled. The book ends with a short essay on 'Some Prospects for a New Nigerian Nation' and with the Nigerian national anthem and national pledge, framing the travelogue section of the book within this context of Nigeria's nationhood.

Indeed, working as a surveyor in the 1970s, establishing new inter-state boundaries within Nigeria through the science of surveying rather than through war and violence, Shàdẹ̀kọ̀ writes, 'I had the feeling of a nation-builder' (175). Shàdẹ̀kọ̀ also envisages himself creating a new, national subject through his travel and travel writing: what he calls the 'detribalized' Nigerian, an implicitly modern and rational subject who has overcome their former loyalties and prejudices tied to ethnicity. *Magic Land* was, Shàdẹ̀kọ̀ writes, 'inspired by

---

[6] Babatunde A. Shadeko, *The Magic Land of Nigeria: A Surveyor's Scintillating and Thoughtprovoking Account of His Wanderings in Nigeria* (Lagos: Nationwide Survey Services, 1980), p. x. Subsequent references are to this edition and will be given in parentheses in the text.

my quest for and sincere belief in the unity and stability of Nigeria', and he hopes reading it will enable Nigerians to 'appreciate each other's virtues and foibles in the spirit of unity and fraternity' (xiii). Thus Part One of Shàdẹ̀kọ̀'s travelogue is titled 'How to be a Detribalized Nigerian', followed by Part Two, 'Probes into our Common Bonds and Origins', and Part Three, 'The Challenges of Unity in Diversity', and his book advocates a move from 'tribalism' to patriotism. Shàdẹ̀kọ̀ attempts to frame the nation as a unified but heterogeneous space, in which every Nigerian is entitled to be everywhere – and about which anyone can read. Indeed, the book is dedicated to showing how through travel, Shàdẹ̀kọ̀ was able to become what he calls a 'detribalized Nigerian'. The term 'detribalised' bears a different resonance in Shàdẹ̀kọ̀'s book from its usage in the early twentieth century, when the colonial establishment was concerned about 'detribalisation' as an indicator of the supposed alienation of newly educated Africans; Nigeria's first governor, Frederick Lugard, sought to 'civilise' Africans without 'detribalising' them, rendering them 'modern' but still 'authentic', 'native' African colonial subjects.[7] In *Magic Land*, by contrast, Shàdẹ̀kọ̀ uses the term 'detribalisation' to refer approvingly to the adoption of a national identity centred on Nigeria rather than on ethnic identities, which he configures as 'tribal'; he commends 'detribalisation' to his fellow Nigerian readers for the sake of national unity, and expresses his hope that by familiarising themselves with Nigeria through his memoir, they too will become 'detribalised'. Shàdẹ̀kọ̀'s 'detribalised' Nigerian is a modern, national and educated reading subject, with the modern 'nation' standing as the antithesis of what he portrays as the outdated and potentially dangerous ideology of the 'tribe'.

Shàdẹ̀kọ̀'s choice of the non-fiction travelogue as his genre for writing about Nigeria is therefore related to his creation of the 'detribalized' Nigerian; the non-fiction travelogue enables him to convey his own knowledge of Nigeria, gained through experience, to the reader who will, by reading the travelogue, become better informed about the 'common bonds' between Nigerians. *Magic Land* is clearly framed as a text in the conventional Western travelogue tradition, as Adébọ̀'s invocation of the travelogue in his foreword to the book affirms. Neither Adébọ̀ nor Shàdẹ̀kọ̀ describe the travelogues that were in vogue during Adébọ̀'s school days (which were presumably in the 1920s and 1930s, since Adébọ̀ was born in 1913), although the book's occasional references to classical and renaissance Europe – from Cassiodorus to Francis Bacon – suggest that Shàdẹ̀kọ̀ was likely to have been familiar with Western travel writing traditions, too. There is nothing in the book to suggest that Shàdẹ̀kọ̀ had encountered any of the Nigerian-authored travel narratives discussed in this book (although it is not impossible that he had); rather, Shàdẹ̀kọ̀'s text can more

---

[7] Newell, 'J. G. Mullen', p. 389; George, *African Literature*, p. 87.

straightforwardly be read as a postcolonial continuation and reconfiguration of the British imperial travel writing tradition for new, Nigerian nationalist purposes. This sense of continuation of the genre can be located particularly in the figure of the explorer surveying the land through which he travels, which is central to Shàdèkò's text as it was to many travel narratives of empire. Indeed, narratives of African travel by professional surveyors form a sub-genre of the travel writing genre, reflecting the move from exploration to bureaucratisation in the late colonial era; British colonial officer David Anderson's *Surveyor's Trek* (1940), for instance, describes Anderson's work as a government surveyor in Nigeria in the 1930s, beginning with his departure from the UK and following him across Nigeria as he maps the colony. *Magic Land* can thus be read as an independence-era reframing of the surveyor narrative, surveying the nation both literally and metaphorically from the perspective of its new independence-era elite rather than that of its colonial officials, while still drawing on the genre and rhetoric of its predecessors.

Simultaneously, *Magic Land* can be read within Nigeria's tradition of elite memoir and autobiography. Stephanie Newell traces the mainstream beginnings of the print autobiography in West Africa to the 1920s, when instances of 'writing the self' began to emerge not only in newspapers, as we have seen, but also in journals, missionary archives and biographies of men of high standing, 'offering exemplary lives for the edification of readers'.[8] Numerous locally published autobiographies and biographies in both Yoruba and English have been published since then, especially since developments in printing technology have fostered the growth of self-publishing and small publishing firms. These autobiographies and biographies tell the life stories of a wide range of Nigerians, from entrepreneurs to politicians, civil servants, soldiers, religious leaders, *ọba*s (traditional rulers) and intellectuals. Such texts, even if not framed principally as travelogues, frequently involve significant episodes of travel, often describing the writer's educational and professional experiences. They often connect travel with the formation of character and achievement, and they emphasise the relationship between travelling and being 'civilised' and progressive. Shàdèkò's *Magic Land*, too, can be read within this tradition as a nostalgic account of Shàdèkò's 'wanderings', and it is framed around the figure of the traveller who gains knowledge and experience through both literal journeys and the journey of life.

Shàdèkò's claim to the knowledge of Nigeria and appreciation of its diversity that has enabled his own 'detribalisation' comes from the extent of his

---

[8] Newell, 'J. G. Mullen', p. 396. Beyond print, autobiography also has precolonial origins in Nigeria, in not only the well-known accounts of ex-slaves but also oral genres: Ademola O. Dasylva and Remy Oriaku, 'Trends in the Nigerian Auto/Biography', *History Compass,* 8.4 (2010), pp. 303–19 (p. 304).

travels through the nation for his work. While the non-fiction travel narratives we have encountered so far in this book have generally focused on towns, institutions and people rather than landscapes and rural scenes, Shàdẹ̀kọ̀'s surveying also takes him to villages and the bush, and he often describes the process of charting the land between the roads and towns. Yet despite Shàdẹ̀kọ̀'s focus in the course of his work as a surveyor on the physical landscape, in *Magic Land*, he is interested primarily in peopled rather than natural landscapes:

> At Bida we carried out a 'visual survey' of the ways of life of the people of the town within the few minutes at our disposal. We saw the people at work in their various trades. At the market, I drew the attention of my colleague to the modes of dress of the men and the women which were similar to those of some other people and parts of the country. I also pointed out the methods of salutations and social courtesies and curtseys. (111)

Shàdẹ̀kọ̀'s 'visual survey' – echoing the colonial explorer's 'sweeping visual mastery of a scene' – is the unspoken method underlying his travels, his work and his text.[9] The aim of Shàdẹ̀kọ̀'s book is 'to give a panoramic but essentially personal account or appraisal of the life and culture of the various ethnic groups in Nigeria whom the author had encountered and with whom he had shared his troubles as well as his joys in the course of his work as a government surveyor' (vii). *Magic Land* envisages itself conjoining Shàdẹ̀kọ̀'s personal viewpoint with his panoramic view as a seasoned national traveller, to interpret his 'visual survey'.

In common with the Yoruba newspaper travel writers of the 1920s we encountered in Chapter 2, Shàdẹ̀kọ̀ describes his street-level view of the places he visits, 'the local markets and places of amusement or entertainment' (xii). On arriving at Misau, he visits the market, the Emir's palace, the courts, the Arabic school, and 'a number of other places of historical or administrative interest' (16). He makes some similar observations about patterns shared by northern Nigerian towns to those made by E. A. Akintán during his visits to Yoruba towns in the 1920s:

> During my brief visits, I noticed a pattern emerge which was quite typical of the northern administrative system at the time. The Emir's palace was the centre of authority at the local government level and all other institutions and paraphernalia were built around his person and residence. In fact, in more cases than one, the Emir's palace was always ringed about with the Area Court, the District Council offices, the Dispensary, the Sub-treasury, the local prison and so on. This administrative pattern was also re-enacted at the lower district and

---

[9] Spurr, *The Rhetoric of Empire*, p. 17.

village levels where the district and village heads form the pivot of authority. (16–17)

Shàdẹ̀kọ̀ is able to conclude from his observations that this is 'the basic pattern of traditional architecture in the home, particularly outside the city or town environment' (17). He portrays himself looking for patterns, making maps, here taking the entire northern region as the unit for his pseudo-ethnographic study.

Shàdẹ̀kọ̀'s understanding of the ways knowledge is gained through travel also echoes the empiricist orientation of the Yoruba newspaper travel writers in the 1920s and of Isaac Délànọ̀. Shàdẹ̀kọ̀'s book is a compilation, he claims, of the knowledge 'which wittingly or unwittingly I acquired in the course of my work':

> I deeply felt that it would be worthwhile passing this personal but perishable knowledge of the country and its magic vistas, panoramas and people to fellow Nigerians in the hope that they would share my exciting experience. (xiii)

This experiential knowledge is accompanied, however, by a conviction in his ability to marshal history to supplement his narrative. In Chapter One alone, Shàdẹ̀kọ̀ accompanies descriptions of his travels with discussions of linguistic politics in northern Nigeria, the geography, colonial and social history of Kaduna and the history of colonial language policy. He stresses the limits of prior knowledge; on arriving at his post in Kaduna, he admits that 'some of the names of the places mentioned were known to me while some others were not quite familiar'. But he is certain that travel will, in turn, provide the knowledge he lacks: 'I was however assured that the place-names would soon become common knowledge as I began to travel about that part of the country' (9). Surveying, Shàdẹ̀kọ̀ suggests, is similarly a process of improving existing knowledge about places; so he describes making a second sweep of an area of northern Nigeria to improve an existing map with 'more information about names of villages, directional flows of rivers and such things that would enhance the accuracy and utility of the map' (70). He stresses the importance of accuracy as a surveyor, recalling that 'I was intent on getting the names of the neighbouring villages right, correct the spellings, and so on' (94). His descriptions of the process of surveying, the technicalities of making sure the measurements are accurate, of double checking and triangulating, echo Shàdẹ̀kọ̀'s belief in his process of documentation as a travel writer.

Shàdẹ̀kọ̀ characterises surveyors as the inheritors of the exploration discourse in independent Nigeria. He romanticises the surveyor as 'pathfinder', not only of physical space but of knowledge:

> For his work begins where the roads end. The main and minor paths are his routes. When he has left behind all contacts with means of communication and transportation, the surveyor is usually alone with the elements. As pathfinder

on the frontiers of knowledge, he heads for the wooded virgin and untrodden land to complete, if he can, the unfinished task of a 'Discovery of Africa'. (89)

Shàdèkò sees his work as a continuation of the 'unfinished task' of colonial exploration, not a subversion of it. However, Shàdèkò's 'Discovery of Africa' – the colonial framing he borrows – becomes, also, a postcolonial 'Discovery of Nigeria'; not only does Shàdèkò use his travels to reflect on national unity, but he also uses his knowledge of one area of Nigeria to compare it to another. Echoing the romanticisation of northern Nigeria that we encountered amongst the English-language newspaper travel writers of the 1920s in Chapter 3, Shàdèkò remembers northern Nigeria as exotic and grand. However, unlike his predecessors, Shàdèkò finds that southwest Nigeria compares unfavourably:

> Having been to the North and seen the gorgeous and imposing palaces of some of the Emirs, I could not but reflect upon the old and dilapidated nature of some of the palaces in the then Western State. They mirrored the fact that the institution of Obaship itself was out of repair and had fallen into decline. (130)

By the end of the text and his travels, Shàdèkò proclaims that 'I had read the vast Nigerian landscapes from cover to cover' and that '[i]n the course of my tramping over the moors and through the mountains of this country I have been able to identify the "true Nigerian" aspects of our history and culture' (177). Shàdèkò's journeying through the landscape is transformed into an interpretive 'reading' of that national landscape.

Echoing his discovery of 'true Nigerian' history and culture, through his panoramic view of Nigeria, Shàdèkò also develops a sense of what a 'detribalized Nigerian' might look like, and it is often a cosmopolitan Nigerian traveller. Shàdèkò is particularly interested in cosmopolitanism across three axes: between Yoruba- and Hausa-speaking Nigeria; between Nigeria and the Arabic-speaking world; and pan-Atlantic black consciousness. His sense of northern Nigerian cosmopolitanism is of an additive mingling energised by what Brian Larkin calls the 'heterogeneity of everyday life' for northern Nigerians, who 'respond to a number of different centres, whether politically to the Nigerian state, religiously to the Middle East and North Africa, economically to the West, or culturally to the cinematic dominance of India'.[10] Upon visiting the Scribe of Dikwa, for instance, Shàdèkò describes how the Scribe:

> brought out his tape-recorder and began treating us to some good Indian, Sudanese and other types of music. Among the Nigerian tunes he played were those by the Katsina-born Alhaji Shata, the popular minstrel, Danmaraya Jos and the Yoruba-born I. K. Dairo, M.B.E. The latter, an undeniably southern

---

[10] Brian Larkin, 'Indian Films and Nigerian Lovers: Media and the Creation of Parallel Modernities', *Africa,* 67.3 (1997), pp. 406–40 (p. 434).

musician of incontrovertible virtuosity, had added a typically northern flavour to his rolling beats. (46)

Returning to this sense of a mingling of cultural influences from within and beyond Nigeria, as he describes the durbar festival in Maiduguri, he notes that the horsemen were 'attired in spectacular and exquisite robes of Turkish and Arabian hues', but also that they were 'resplendent in their damasks and the very best of locally woven or dyed materials' (34) – epitomising the text's utopian vision of cosmopolitanism as an addition of foreign elements to the local. Shàdèkò's judgment of the Maiduguri durbar emphasises Nigeria's links to the world: 'The durbar scene had taken on a dimension that was unique and exotic, overpowering and tantalizing, and rooted in the cultural traditions of the people. It was like an irresistible pageant from one of the scenes in the film of Samarkand in Asia Minor' (34). This simile suggests that Shàdèkò perceives northern Nigeria to be so exotic that it can be best understood through reference to outside – the 'film of Samarkand in Asia Minor' – rather than a comparison rooted in southern Nigeria.

A somewhat utopian pan-African and transatlantic cosmopolitanism also emerges out of Shàdèkò's travels, again through the presence of such elements within Nigeria. For instance, on meeting an African-American traveller, a convert to Islam, on his way home from Saudi Arabia, their conversation ranges across the Black Atlantic, and concludes with an idealistic affirmation of black consciousness: 'We warmed up as we spoke about the common body of affection all [sic] black peoples the world over. And we concluded that in this inescapable spiritual affinity lies our strength and salvation' (36). Shàdèkò's vision of intra-national cosmopolitanism, however, is more complex, underlining a tension between local specificities and the need to be a 'detribalized Nigerian'. Shàdèkò's 'detribalized Nigerian' is aligned in some regards with Kwame Anthony Appiah's 'rooted' cosmopolitanism, which claims to value the particularities of place – in this case, Nigeria – while concurrently asserting the possibility of (potentially global) humanist 'conversation'.[11] However, Shàdèkò is clear that while localness is to be valued, it is at the level of the nation that the cosmopolitan is to be found, not within other forms of localness. He remarks, for instance, that 'Life in Maiduguri was typical of life in perhaps any other town in the country. Apart from the local tribal, linguistic and vestural peculiarities of the inhabitants, I found the town fairly cosmopolitan' (31). Being 'typical of life' anywhere else in the country is cosmopolitan, but 'peculiarities' are not. Shàdèkò is working here with a model of national encounter centred on translation rather than transformation. He envisages this

---

[11] Kwame Anthony Appiah, *The Ethics of Identity* (Princeton: Princeton University Press, 2005), pp. 213–72.

linguistic and cultural translation as creating a middle space that is Nigerian and cosmopolitan, and translates 'local peculiarities' into the national, but also allows those 'local peculiarities' to continue untouched around the national.

In fact, Shàdèkò's idealised cosmopolitan traveller is not necessarily always an elite traveller. Shàdèkò describes how during his travels he encountered a group of cattle drivers talking by a fireside. His account of their conversation sees in it a cosmopolitanism generated through contact with the 'outside world', even if just the next town: 'Some of the men who had gone out to the 'outside world' could speak Hausa and could talk excitedly of other places' (58). Shàdèkò's text and his mission to bring about 'detribalization' of Nigeria are both predicated upon being able to 'talk excitedly of other places' just as these cattle drivers do. However, his use of inverted commas for these cattle drivers' 'outside world' suggests that there are hierarchies of cosmopolitan knowledge, and that theirs is different from his own. Indeed, Shàdèkò's own cosmopolitanism is undeniably class-bound, based on an entitlement to 'feel at home' anywhere in Nigeria. His text describes stratified relations between the gentleman surveyors and their workers, and the curiosity of locals as the surveyors arrive, echoing the class-bound novelty of the travelling clerks of Délànò's *The Soul of Nigeria*. Moreover, *Magic Land* maps out elite connections stretching across the country at the same time as he maps the physical networks of the rivers; in common with I. B. Thomas and E. A. Akintán in the 1920s, Shàdèkò encounters by chance friends, schoolmates and former colleagues from Lagos as far away as Sokoto and Banki, where the text's emphasis is otherwise on the strangeness of these places. Meeting an old school friend, Shàdèkò remarks that 'as KCOB's (King's College Old Boys) we are Nigerians first and foremost and must feel at home any place in the country doing our duty to God and to the Fatherland, making friends wherever we could, and extending our hand of brotherhood to all' (63).

Though Shàdèkò does not spell it out, his book suggests a 'duty' to the nation owing to his elite education and status. Indeed, alongside its explicit claim to the travelogue tradition, this framing through class means that *Magic Land* can in fact also be read as a postcolonial continuation of the elite Lagosian intellectual travel narrative tradition espoused by the travel writers of the Yoruba newspapers of the 1920s and 1930s, and later travel narratives based on personal experience such as Délànò's *The Soul of Nigeria*. In common with Délànò before him, taking a view of Lagos from Carter Bridge, Shàdèkò imagines himself operating with a surveyor's overview of the nation: a class perspective that suggests he, like Délànò, has access to knowledge of the nation that those he surveys do not. Conjoining this class perspective with the methods and genre of the colonial surveyor-explorer, Shàdèkò imagines himself exploring and creating a nation, standing at a crossroads between 'tribalised' and 'detribalised' or ethnic and national perspectives, and pointing to a way forward. The travelogue form, with its characteristic rhetoric inherited from its imperial past, enables him to survey as well as serve the nation, but this surveying is imagined to be put to new use in the independent nation, seeking to create a 'nation' out of 'tribes', in the wake of the civil war.

## Writing the self and the nation in narratives of Nigeria's National Youth Service Corps

While Shàdèkò relishes his gentlemanly cosmopolitanism, another travel narrative written out of duty to the Nigerian nation and in the long legacy of the civil war recalls the author's travels with much less enthusiasm:

> We eventually got to their house, where I was introduced to a middle-aged woman. They all spoke in Efik, I did not understand them. So I became more afraid, thinking that they were planning to eat me. The woman asked me to sit down and said in English 'Poor girl, I learnt you were crying inside the bus thinking we would eat you in Calabar. We are not going to eat you. Now change your dress and have your bath.' I refused to take my bath. I told her I would go and do so in the camp. However, after much persuasion, I agreed. Before I could finish my bath, they had prepared food, which I ate reluctantly. The soup was quite delicious.[12]

This tale of fears of cannibalism in Calabar, in southeast Nigeria, is from *They Will Eat Me in Calabar* (2000), a short memoir-cum-Christian inspirational pamphlet by Dámilọ́lá Ajénifújà, published by Ìbàdàn-based Christian publisher Freedom Press, which describes the author's year as a member of Nigeria's National Youth Service Corps (NYSC). The NYSC was established in 1973, as part of the Nigerian state's attempt to rebuild the nation after the civil war of 1967–70. The scheme is compulsory for Nigerian university and polytechnic graduates under thirty years of age when graduating, who must serve for a year outside their home state or the one where they attended university. The NYSC year begins as the new Corps member receives their call-up letter and learns of their deployment location – a matter over which they officially have no choice, although there are rumours that there are ways to influence the posting. Corpers, as they are popularly known, first attend a three-week orientation camp, renowned for its military-style training and parades, but also for its vibrant social life. Corps members then proceed to their places of primary assignment where they work for the rest of the year, often in teaching or local government but also sometimes in private employment, as well

---

[12] Damilola Ajenifuja, *They Will Eat Me in Calabar ... the Story of a Youth Corper* (Ibadan: Freedom Press, 2000), pp. 12–13. Subsequent references are to this edition and will be given in parentheses in the text.

as being expected to undertake a small community development project. The ideal behind the scheme was not only to provide a workforce and reduce youth unemployment, but also to foster national consciousness and tolerance through encounters between Nigerians from across the nation, and improved knowledge of parts of the country other than one's own.[13]

Only the relatively small percentage of Nigerians who are graduates participate in NYSC, but nonetheless the scheme has a distinctive popular culture within Nigeria: Corpers have a highly recognisable uniform, making them a visible presence on the streets of Nigeria, and their own slang and songs. In addition, a literature about NYSC has been growing steadily. This literature spans novels, poetry, self-help books, blogs, films, memoirs and manuals for new Corps members, and ranges from witty and irreverent takes on the Corper experience detailing Corps members' sexual misadventures and efforts to avoid work, to earnest handbooks urging Corps members to take on the challenge of national unity. Most of these texts are self-published via small printing presses and circulate primarily within Nigeria, or are published online. Some of these texts are a form of autobiography or memoir that document the author's experience of the year and, often, their personal growth, as we shall see in the texts discussed in this chapter. Others, particularly novels, seem aimed at schoolchildren, as prospective future Corps members, as well as perhaps intended for nostalgic consumption by other former Corps members.

In this chapter I focus on two NYSC narratives: Ajénifújà's *They Will Eat Me in Calabar*, and Chibuzor Mirian Azubuike's *The Girl Who Found Water* (2014).[14] Their authors are both women who grew up in southwest Nigeria and who travelled to other parts of the nation for their NYSC year: Ajénifújà to Calabar in southeast Nigeria, and Azubuike to Bauchi, in northern Nigeria. Their accounts are travel writing in the broadest sense, invoking multiple genres: they offer non-fiction, first-person accounts of their authors' journeys and their impressions of the people and places they encounter, but the two texts can also be read, between them, as memoir, spiritual autobiography – Ajénifújà in particular characterises her NYSC year as a year of spiritual growth as a Christian – and self-development or inspirational texts that encourage the reader to learn from the lessons their authors learnt during their NYSC year.

My focus on Ajénifújà's and Azubuike's NYSC narratives allows me to explore, for the first time in this book, the particular resonances of travel for

---

[13] Otwin Marenin, 'Implementing Deployment Policies in the National Youth Service Corps of Nigeria: Goals and Constraints', *Comparative Political Studies*, 22.4 (1990), pp. 397–436 (p. 399).

[14] Chibuzor Mirian Azubuike, *The Girl Who Found Water: Memoirs of a Corps Member* (Lagos: Easy Voucher, 2014). Subsequent references are to this edition and will be given in parentheses in the text.

southwest Nigerian women. All of the travel narratives discussed in previous chapters have focused on men's experiences of travel, both fictional and non-fictional. But, echoing the increased publication of fiction by women writers in the decades after independence, travel writing by women has also increasingly emerged over these decades (as will be apparent in the remaining chapters of this book, which all discuss travel writing by women as well as men). Along-side Ajénifújà's and Azubuike's texts, several other writers, including male authors, have published memoirs of their NYSC year; Joe Agbro Jr's *Served* (2012), for example, narrates its author's journey from Lagos to a rural region of Ebonyi state in southeast Nigeria for his service year, describing in humorous detail the author's experience of the NYSC orientation camp, his placement as a teacher, the fellow Corps members he encountered, and his fondness for the community that hosted him for the year.[15] While in this chapter I briefly discuss some of these other memoirs, as well as novels about NYSC, my focus on Ajénifújà's and Azubuike's memoirs in this chapter allows my discussion to centre on women's experiences of travel, particularly in the light of the repeated deployment of the trope of dangerous female sexuality in many NYSC texts by both male and female authors.

Both Ajénifújà's and Azubuike's texts open with dramatic descriptions of their fear of travelling to parts of Nigeria where they had never previously been. Ajénifújà describes her trepidation as she faced up to a long journey to southeast Nigeria, adding that '[t]o worsen things, whenever I told people that I was posted to Calabar, they would discourage me by saying that the people are cannibals' (10). Travelling alone to southeast Nigeria, Ajénifújà describes how she 'sat in a corner inside the bus sobbing', and explained her worries to her fellow passengers:

I told them that:

(i)     Calabar is too far (I heard it was a twenty-four hour journey)

(ii)    I would miss my family for three weeks

(iii)   they will eat me in Calabar

They encouraged me and assured me that nobody would eat me, that after three weeks I would go back to meet my family in peace and that before the next day we would be in Calabar. (11–12)

The figure of the cannibal (which likely draws on widespread Nigerian popular cultural fears and rumours about other parts of Nigeria) can be read as standing for Ajénifújà's fear of being away from home in a strange place,

---

[15] Joe Agbro Jr, *Served ... Memoirs of a Youth Corps Member* (Lagos: Grasshill Books, 2012).

the dangers of leaving the smaller world of family and home, crossing a border into unknown parts of Nigeria and emerging into the nation where she risks being consumed, both literally and metaphorically, by the other. Yet Ajénifújà's fears are relieved by the friendly reassurance she encounters on her journey to Calabar, and the feared cannibals fade into the background as the narrative instead focuses on Ajénifújà's friendships with locals and fellow Corpers, on Ajénifújà's NYSC life and her new knowledge of Calabar, and on the lessons her NYSC year taught her regarding her Christian faith.

While Ajénifújà's particular fear of cannibalism might be shown to be un-founded, it is however not altogether without reason that some Corps members fear the NYSC year. Corps members have been assigned to work as election officials in contexts where political violence is not uncommon, and they continue to be posted to regions of Nigeria that suffer from instability and violence. In 2011, for instance, thirteen Corps members were killed in a bomb blast in Suleja, and ten Corps members were killed during elections. It is with this history of violence in mind that Chibuzor Mirian Azubuike writes in her self-published NYSC memoir *The Girl Who Found Water* of her all-consuming fear at being posted to Bauchi, far away from her metropolitan life in Lagos: 'This was a state where just two months ago, it was in the news that ten corps members were killed during post-election violence' (23–4). The opening chapters of the book are dominated by descriptions of Azubuike's fear and sadness on learning of her posting, and are drenched with her tears: '"Jesus! No, no, no! Not me, it is a lie!" I began to cry', she writes: 'My heart wanted to burst out of my mouth. I felt like the castle of my dreams had been crushed. I never imagined that I would be posted to such a place; I was not prepared for this. My depression began that day' (21). She repeatedly describes her own and others' despair and worry, laden with tears and fear:

> My eyes were heavy; the tears kept flowing like water from a fountain – I had no control over them anymore. (23)

> *I will not go to Bauchi; I will never go to Bauchi.* My heart was burning; what I usually felt as a heartbeat now felt like a punching bag, so heavy that if I tried to stand I would stagger, like those frail retirees that faint after standing on the queue for hours to collect their pension. (24; original emphasis)

> [W]henever I told anyone I had been posted to Bauchi, they would begin exclaiming as if the world had come to an end. (26)

> Phone calls from people sympathizing over my posting to Bauchi made tears roll down my cheeks. (37)

Like Ajénifújà, however, Azubuike shows, through her memoir, how she overcame her fear and disappointment at being posted by Bauchi through her experience of the city during her NYSC year. She explains how her improved acquaintance with Bauchi and her personal determination enabled her to stay there for the year, even after encountering the violence she had feared in the form of a dynamite attack on the church compound in which she was staying. The memoir concludes with an account of Azubuike's successful establishment of a community development project installing new water boreholes in a poor rural community near Bauchi, and with a didactic ending that stresses the importance of overcoming fear through personal experience and endurance:

> I had seen my posting to Bauchi as terrible news. But it turned out to be one of the best experiences of my life. It saddens me now that I and many other well-meaning Nigerians are no longer inclined to go to northern Nigeria because of the ravages of Boko-Haram. And that is indeed a tragedy. The NYSC scheme has been the only institution that acquaints Nigerians with various parts of the country – parts of Nigeria which they would never have known even existed. (128)

Azubuike presents the outcome of overcoming fear as not only 'one of the best experiences of my life' but also improved knowledge of Nigeria.

This improved knowledge of Nigeria through travel is, in line with many of the travel narratives we have encountered in this book, imagined to be passed on to readers in both of these NYSC texts. In a foreword to *The Girl Who Found Water*, Mallam Dr Isa Yuguda, Governor of Bauchi State, writes of how Azubuike also uses her book as an opportunity to improve fellow Nigerians' knowledge of Bauchi, as she writes to 'expose the unsubstantiated stories of how unpleasant the region could be for corps members' (7), in the light of Nigerians' 'ignorance or little knowledge of the history, culture and traditions of other Nigerians' (8); Azubuike 'made us see that because we have little or no knowledge about our country, we rely on half-truths and sometimes lies from other people' (10). *They Will Eat Me in Calabar*, too, offers its readers knowledge: about the distinctive language and customs of NYSC, phrases of Efik and Ejagham along with their English translations, and local customs and ceremonies in Cross River State. Both texts yield knowledge about Nigeria for their readers – not only factual information about elsewhere in Nigeria, but also the exposure of their own fears of other parts of the nation as unnecessary.

Beyond fears of cannibalism or violence, some NYSC narratives describe Corpers' disappointment at being posted to rural locations – disappointment that is, again, often shown as being overcome through experience and better knowledge of Nigeria. On arriving in a village outside Ikom, in Cross River State, Dámilólá Ajénifújà writes in *They Will Eat Me in Calabar* that, 'I was discouraged because I was posted to a village. All the houses there were made of bamboo, except the Local Government Secretariat' (25). Ajénifújà initially refuses to accept her assignment, telling her local government chairman that 'there was no infrastructure and [I] also said since it is a village, mosquitoes would bite me' (26). But just as her worries regarding cannibalism are assuaged through experience, so, too, Ajénifújà gradually grows to enjoy her village experience.

As well as fears of danger in other parts of Nigeria, Azubuike describes her own and other Corps members' concerns about differences of class, infrastructure and education, echoing the perception of civilisational differences between parts of Nigeria that we have encountered in previous chapters; Azubuike has heard that Bauchi is 'bedevilled by illiteracy' (30), and a fellow Corps member, an architect, laments that 'my career is not here' on noticing the city's lack of two-storey buildings (51). However, another Corps member who grew up in Bauchi explains that the Corps members are seeing a contrast between urban and rural Nigeria, not northern and southern Nigeria:

> Guys, stop laughing. When you are traveling to your villages, do you see any upstairs there? No, it is mostly huts and houses made of mud. It is the same with Bauchi. Come on, Bauchi is just a state like other states. I can bet you will enjoy serving in Bauchi. Just have an open mind. I know why you are all talking this way: it is because of the post-election violence. Bauchi is a peaceful place and everything has returned to normal. My friend, the architect, when you go to Bauchi town you will find storey buildings – some of them even built by your brothers from the east. (52)

The speaker re-orients her fellow Corps members' perceptions of differences of modernity between northern and southern Nigeria towards the differences between rural and urban Nigeria instead. Later in the memoir, Azubuike cements this perception of differences of class, language and education between the Corpers, most of whom are used to city life, and the rural communities they encounter during their NYSC year, as she visits a rural region of Bauchi state and remarks with wonder at the strangeness of the experience:

> Soon we were on the other side of the hills. Although I was still in my country, I felt like I was in a strange land, like a tourist. Everything was so different. We were in a small settlement with houses made of mud, and stopped to buy water to quench our thirst. The children in the village were so excited to see us. Although they could not speak English and we could not speak Hausa, we somehow understood each other. The young girls fascinated me – their hands and legs were beautifully decorated with what seemed like tattoos but in artistic floral designs. The littlest girls – aged two or so – were dressed like their mothers: their entire bodies covered, revealing only their face, hands and feet. The older girls – aged seven or so – wore local make-up to enhance their eyes and lips. My mother never allowed me wear [sic] make-up at that age, but these kids were adorable. Their smiles were so generous; they made you

want to give them all you had in your pocket. They looked so innocent. I did not know if someone told them we were coming, because to me it seemed as though they had anticipated our arrival. They played drums for us to dance to, and they danced along with us. (79–80)

In this passage the Corpers are represented as English speakers – implicitly Nigerians, speaking a national language – while the village-dwellers are Hausa speakers. In a 'strange land, like a tourist', Azubuike finds herself 'on the other side of the hills' within her own country, as if crossing a border into a Hausa, non-English-speaking world where bodies and language are marked in terms of difference, young girls are 'adorable', 'generous' and 'innocent', drumming and dancing for the English-speaking visitors. Echoing the border-crossing into strange lands that we encountered in Fágúnwà's novels, Azubuike has crossed from the English-speaking, university-educated Nigerian sociality of NYSC to a seemingly Hausa world of sensual impressions, and of children doing things Azubuike would never have been allowed to do. The visual language of NYSC itself stresses this distance between the Corps members and the communities in which they live; *The Girl Who Found Water* includes newspaper clippings showing Azubuike in her NYSC uniform, surrounded by the people of Bigi Tudunwada, with Azubuike's uniform marking her out as a figure of the state and of educated youth, a Nigerian, contrasting with the villagers. As Azubuike leaves the village, she reinforces the boundary; the children, she writes, 'ac-companied us halfway', until they reached the limit of their world. She adds, 'The village gave me an idea of what life must have been like in pre-colonial times' (80). The distinction between national and ethnic identities, and the imagined differences of temporality and 'denial of coevalness', as Johannes Fabian terms it, echoes Shàdèkò's emphasis on the nation and the Nigerian as the modern formation.[16]

This perception of difference between the Corps members and the villagers of Bauchi district is increasingly figured as one of 'development'. On first visit-ing the village of Bigi Tudunwada, where she eventually built a water borehole, Azubuike writes of how she encountered a severe lack of drinking water for the village's population of six thousand people: 'I immediately made up my mind to do something. I wrote to the NYSC secretariat seeking permission to take this up as a community development project' (99). Azubuike locates her sense of the difference of these 'vulnerable people' (102) not in the divide be-tween north and south, but in lack of 'development' and infrastructure. Yet as *The Girl Who Found Water* concludes, Azubuike suggests how the worlds of Hausa and 'development' may converge, through an exchange: she gives the

---

[16] Johannes Fabian, *Time and the Other: How Anthropology Makes Its Object*, 3rd edn (New York: Columbia University Press, 2014 [1983]), p. 31.

villagers a borehole, school uniforms and writing materials, and in return the village women 'dressed me in a local outfit they had made for me. I wondered how they got my measurements. They put a calabash on my head like those who sell *fura de nunu*, and placed a hoe on my shoulders. All of these items had my name engraved on them' (126).[17] This scene of exchange epitomises Azubuike's idealistic desire to overcome difference through mutuality: 'This country is ours: the north, south and every cranny of it. No part should be left to itself. What affects the north, affects the south', she writes, adding that 'We must save Nigeria together' (128). *The Girl Who Found Water* does not affirm that the north and the south are the same; rather, it suggests that 'development' of the nation depends on mutuality and sharing of resources. Azubuike does not seek to create the 'detribalized Nigerian' that Shàdèkò idealises in *The Magic Land of Nigeria*; rather, she perceives hierarchies of 'development' and inequalities between both north and south, urban and rural, developed and underdeveloped regions, ameliorated by personal service to that nation.

Azubuike's emphasis on exchange is echoed by her enjoyment of interpersonal encounters during her NYSC year. In common with Shàdèkò, Azubuike envisages national travel as resulting in both 'mingling' and 'patriotism': describing her enjoyment of the NYSC camp in Bauchi, she writes that 'I felt like a patriot, ready to give up my life for my country. Yes, I was a patriot: I came all the way from home to the distant north, a place where I knew no one and had never been. If not for NYSC, would I have ever gone to the north? I mingled and became friends with total strangers. I wish we wouldn't stop' (77–8). *The Girl Who Found Water* maintains some scepticism about the Nigerian state and its ability to protect its Corpers; Azubuike relates how the director of the State Security Service concedes to Corps members that 'you are your own security. Just be alert and report any suspicious act' (65), and some Corps members accordingly feel that their questions about state protection are 'not fully answered' (66). Nonetheless, intra-Nigerian encounter seems to provide Azubuike with a framework for the nation, in spite of the state's failures.

In Ajénifújà's memoir, too, interpersonal sociality is presented as a means of overcoming fear of difference. Ajénifújà describes a close relationship with her 'foster mother' in Calabar, whom she visits every month during her service year; the nation is represented through intimate, kin-like sociality that emerges through personal encounters. Some fictional texts about NYSC similarly trace interpersonal encounters that come to stand for the broader national encounter. *Service of the Fatherland* (1985), an English-language novel by Rèmí Bámiṣaiyé, occupies a national vantage point as it follows Yoruba, Igbo and Hausa characters during their NYSC year (fictionalised as 'Service of the

---

[17] *Fura de nunu*: a milk drink served with millet or corn flour.

Fatherland'). It depicts NYSC as a forum for mixing across ethnic divides, with characteristic cultural and historical differences sketched into the characters' histories.[18] Káyǒdé Anímáṣaun's young adult novel *A Gift for the Corper* (2008) narrates a growing platonic friendship between a young Igbo girl, Nneoma, and a Yoruba Corper, Taiwo, in Ndoro, near Umuahia.[19] *A Gift for the Corper* tries to occupy a national middle space, imagining the experiences of both Taiwo and Nneoma; the reader is implicitly a Nigerian who could exist on either side of the exchange (although was presumably more likely, as a reader, to imagine themselves as the educated Taiwo than the naïve Nneoma), and the nation's linguistic diversity as well as its shared language is embraced as Taiwo and Nneoma exchange Igbo, Yoruba, English and Pidgin English words.

Azubuike's increasing engagement with Hausa Nigeria can similarly be traced through her memoir's shifting presentation of language and translation. On first arriving in Bauchi, Azubuike describes the Corps members' inability to communicate, and her surprise that her emotions are intelligible to the Hausa locals:

> We said goodbye to the friendly driver who, even though we could not communicate because he did not speak English, made funny gestures. His son, who was with him, spoke in Hausa to Bola and told us not to be afraid. Bola translated his words into English and we were shocked at how a young boy could know that we were all scared. I told Bola to ask him how he could tell, and he responded that it was through our behaviour. (53)

But Azubuike's expectation of non-communication slowly recedes: the Corps members learn some Hausa during a lecture at their NYSC camp, although they alter the Hausa phrases to produce a different meaning in Igbo: 'Some of the Corps members mischievously repeated – *sanu ukwu* (*ukwu* means a woman's waist or hip in Igbo language). [The Hausa lecturer] continued, – *Daya* is one, *biyu* is two, *ukwu* is three…. *Ukwu again*, I said to myself. These boys would have a lot to laugh about. The Hausa lecturer did not know why we were laughing as he did not speak Igbo' (69). Language becomes a vehicle of translation, but also of mistranslation – both crossing and maintaining boundaries. Yet after spending longer in Bauchi, language enables sociality for Azubuike: 'I had noticed that whether at work or in the market, most people were happy when strangers made the effort to speak Hausa. I always started conversations in the language to pave my way' (114–15). Azubuike's difference is maintained – she does not speak fluent Hausa – but language is now used for translation rather than mistranslation.

---

[18] Remi Bamisaiye, *Service of the Fatherland* (Lagos: Macmillan Nigeria, 1985).
[19] Kayode Animasaun, *A Gift for the Corper* (Ibadan: Kraft Books, 2008).

Ajénifújà's *They Will Eat Me in Calabar* places less emphasis on language, and instead offers Christianity as alternative vehicle for intra-Nigerian unity and sociality. Ajénifújà describes the NYSC Christian fellowships and lodging houses without any reference to ethnicity, and she explains how the Nigerian Christian Corpers Fellowship (NCCF) engages in 'evangelism and outreach, especially to the unreached parts of various states of Nigeria. Youth corpers are encouraged in the NCCF to serve the Lord while serving their nation' (33), recalling long hours spent in church and engaged in 'rural rugged evangelism' in a village outside Ikom (35). The spread of the idea of the united nation, through the NYSC year, is intertwined with the spread of Christianity. Ajénifújà's conception of a national Christianity may not necessarily apply equally in northern Nigeria, where there are larger communities of Muslims, but nonetheless Christianity is imagined in her memoir as a community of faith that can be shared across southern Nigeria, overcoming differences of ethnicity and language.

### Texts of self-development
Alongside these NYSC narratives' depictions of their authors and fellow Corpers coming to greater knowledge of the nation through NYSC, they also depict themselves undergoing forms of self-development during their NYSC year. In *They Will Eat Me in Calabar*, this personal development takes the form of Ajénifújà's depiction of how she overcame sexual temptation during her NYSC year through her Christian faith. Indeed, if Corps members are vulnerable to the dangers of the nation, as embodied in the spectre of the cannibal in Ajénifújà's narrative, there is also another danger that haunts these narratives: that of sexuality, particularly female sexuality. Ajénifújà's concern with the danger of sexuality begins as she arrives in the NYSC orientation camp where 'immorality was rampant':

> I couldn't understand how people would meet in one day and the next thing is sex. It got to a point that the camp commandant declared the parade ground as 'holy ground' and that anybody caught in such an act would be severely punished. (23)

Ajénifújà, through the figure of the camp commandant, positions sexuality against Christianity, seeking to make NYSC space a spiritual space rather than a sexual space. She dedicates much of the second half of the book to this clash of ways of being. NYSC is represented as a year of awakening to her sexuality: 'I just discovered that I suddenly became attractive to everyone, both young and old, as if I had just landed in the place. Every one wanted to be my spouse' (52). But this is a sexuality that she retrospectively recounts as a torment and a trial to her Christian faith: 'I thank God for my friends and fellowship members in school who, throughout, sent letters and admonished me time after time to take heed lest I fall' (52). As one man visits her at home with the intention of sleeping with her, 'the devil was at work', she writes, and she describes her encounters with another man as a period of intense 'lust' (53), resulting in him 'begging me to commit fornication with him' (54). The fear of the unknown, as symbolised in the imaginary cannibal, has been transformed into the fear of giving into temptation as a young, unmarried woman, away from home – rather than fearing being eaten, she now fears being devoured sexually, or maybe even fears her own sexual appetite.

It is striking how frequently the trope of sexuality having dangerous or un-wanted consequences for women occurs in NYSC texts. Numerous NYSC texts similarly describe young people's emergence into the world being disrupted by sexuality in the form of casual sexual relations with unwanted consequences, moments of sexual temptation, unwanted pregnancy, and even sexual assault and rape.[20] While some of these texts condemn men who engage in unmarried sexual relations during the national service year, and depict undesirable conse-quences for doing so, many operate with a conservative moralising message that views overt female sexuality as particularly dangerous, and places the blame for either these encounters or the unwanted consequences, or both, mainly on women. In particular, the trope of unwanted pregnancy as a consequence of sexual relations outside marriage recurs in several NYSC texts, particularly novels, perhaps offering their authors a freedom to depict particularly disastrous consequences for sexual encounters in a way that memoirs may not. 'Débò Awé's Yoruba-language novel *Kópà* (1990), for instance, begins as a story about a group of NYSC members in Ìlọrin. But it increasingly focuses on the story of Bọ́lá, who initially attempts to resist her attraction to fellow Corps member Màíkí and his attempts to seduce her, but eventually has a sexual relationship with him. She falls pregnant and Màíkí flees, leaving Bọ́lá alone to face her unwanted pregnancy. Tèmítáyọ̀ A. Ọtún's short novel *The Pregnant Corper* (n.d.), opens with its female protagonist, Ifeoma, hoping readers will not judge her for her story, before describing how she became pregnant following a drunken sexual encounter during her NYSC orientation camp.

This gendered motif is not one that dominates conventional travel writing (although travel narratives by women travellers, especially, sometimes high-light the particular dangers of sexual assault and rape that women may face when travelling), but the figure of the pregnant or sexually promiscuous female Corps member can be read as a variant on tropes of the sexually active 'modern girl' and her downfall, such as the 'good-time girl' – the young, educated, un-married woman of the city who flaunts her sexuality and accumulates wealth,

---

[20] See, for instance: Henry Batubo, *The NYSC Experience* (self-published, 2015); Ibukun Olagbemiro, *A Corper's Diary* (Abeokuta: IDOL Media Services, 2015); Bamisaiye, *Service of the Fatherland*.

particularly through relationships with sugar daddies or through prostitution – who has gripped the imaginations of many Nigerian popular novelists and their readerships, especially since the early 1980s.[21] In line with the general orientation amongst popular literary texts towards teaching the reader and generating debate on moral issues, Stephanie Newell suggests that the 'good-time girl' is usually wielded as one of a range of 'ethical figures which the reader will recognise and judge using existing repertoires of knowledge'.[22] Although the meanings attached to this figure vary across decades and between literary traditions, the good-time girl has often been read as an expression of the perceived dislocations of modernity and of shifting gender relations in postcolonial Nigeria, with the story of the 'sexually self-determining woman' who has 'removed herself from the household sphere' and her 'misuse of her sexuality' becoming a flashpoint for the author's condemnation of materialism in society more broadly.[23] The good-time girl is accordingly nearly always a woman of the city, either because she represents the city itself, or because she represents modernity and uprooting from an imagined 'traditional' past or village life.[24] Such journeys from village to city enable the text to hold out an alternative to the good-time girl's urban sexuality by showing the city and the village as parallel 'worlds in collision [...] contending for the protagonist's soul'.[25]

In NYSC texts, however, the journey the female Corps member makes is not always between the village as home and the city as place of sexual temptation or encounter: Ajénifújà's time of temptation comes during her stay in the small town of Ikom. The accumulation of wealth also seems less central to the authors' condemnation of these women than to the figure of the good-time girl in popular fiction more widely. Nonetheless, they similarly depict 'worlds in collision' mediated through the figure of the unmarried 'sexually self-determining woman', who is punished for her sexuality. Here, however, these 'worlds in collision' are not the village versus the city, but home versus the nation. In foregrounding the figure of the pregnant Corper who has, like the good-time girl of the city, 'removed herself from the household sphere' by travelling away from home, NYSC texts not only teach moral lessons about the dangers of untamed female sexuality, but also seem to dramatise a broader anxiety about the shift from the home to the national space, and thus about the meaning and dangers of the nation itself. The figure of the pregnant Corper,

---

[21] Newell, 'Introduction', pp. 6–7; Onookome Okome, 'Nollywood, Lagos, and the Good-Time Woman', *Research in African Literatures* 43.4 (2012), pp. 166–86 (p. 167).

[22] Newell, 'Introduction', p. 5.

[23] Ibid. pp. 6–7.

[24] Barber, *Print Culture*, p. 21.

[25] Griswold, *Bearing Witness*, p. 166.

drawing on the existing resonances of the well-known figure of the good-time girl, thus seems to sit alongside the figure of the cannibal as a symbol of the dangers of the nation, with the danger shifting between fear of being devoured and fear of being too sexually devouring.

Some novelists have, however, set aside this condemnation of female sexual autonomy through the figure of the good-time girl, and have recast the city as a place of escape from oppressive gender roles and expectations of wifehood and motherhood – from the possibilities of self-determination in the city envisaged in Flora Nwapa's *One is Enough* (1981), for instance, to Sefi Atta's and Chimamanda Ngozi Adichie's depictions of the complexities of women's sexuality and sexual pleasure on its own terms. More conservative NYSC texts, however, have so far not tended to emphasise women's sexual freedom away from home in this way. They do sometimes valorise cross-ethnic marriage resulting from NYSC encounters as a patriotic contribution to national unity, or simply as evidence of lack of ethnic prejudice amongst Nigerians.[26] Additionally, some texts depict sexual relations as a fun and somewhat inevitable aspect of the NYSC year; however, these are often texts by male authors depicting male sexual pleasure, as in Henry Batubo's novel *The NYSC Experience* (2015), for example, which is subtitled 'a romantic novel' and traces the romantic and sexual encounters of its protagonist, James, during his NYSC year (with the author dedicating the novel 'to the ladies that inspired it').[27]

Ajénifújà's *They Will Eat Me in Calabar* does not depict the author actually experiencing the disastrous consequences of sexual temptation that she initially feared. The reason, however, is not that the text emphasises the pleasures of sexuality or female self-determination. Instead, the text increasingly focuses on showing how the author was able to resist temptation and turn towards God. While this may simply reflect the turn of events during the author's service year, it can also be interpreted as related to the additional generic orientations of the text; in addition to being read as a travel narrative, *They Will Eat Me in Calabar* can be read as a self-development text that teaches the reader how to develop him- or herself through reading about the author's own self-development during her NYSC year. In common with many popular literary texts, this memoir seeks to educate its readers, but unlike the negative examples of female sexuality in popular novels, Ajénifújà's memoir moves from depicting temptation to offering readers direct messages of self-improvement. It can also be read as a form of spiritual autobiography that posits Christianity as the key to Ajénifújà's self-development during her service year, and thus to her avoidance of the dangers of sexuality. Ajénifújà retrospectively reframes her physical, emotional and spiritual journey during her NYSC year as having been

---

[26] See, for instance, Olagbemiro, *A Corper's Diary*.
[27] Batubo, *The NYSC Experience*.

guided by God: 'During my final examination in The Polytechnic, Ibadan, the Lord instructed me to fast and pray for three days about my National Youth Service Corps posting so that His will would be done. And I obeyed' (9). On her arrival in Calabar, she recalls, 'the Lord told me that He was taking me to Ikom for blessings and temptations' (39).

Ajénifújà writes that initially 'I did not understand, but I prayed that God should see me through' (39). The NYSC year gradually reveals both to Ajénifújà and to the reader what Ajénifújà initially did not understand: the mercy of God and the dangers of 'fornication' and 'backsliding':

> Though I have heard of how Christian sisters (who would be so zealous while on campus) backslide during the service year, I did not believe it until I almost fell a victim. I heard of a sister who said, 'so now service year has ended! I've lost my faith, I've wasted my life!' because she fell into fornication during the service year, then the Lord spoke to me 'do you know it was not by your power or by might but it had been by my Spirit'; and that 'not unto him that willeth but unto him that the Lord sheweth mercy'. I could say I received the mercy of God during my NYSC when temptation would have swept me away. (60–1)

This explanatory nature of the narrative is underscored in the book's final chapters, which are directly addressed to the reader, using scripture to expand on some of the themes described in previous chapters and extracting moral lessons from the many trials, temptations and dangers that Ajénifújà encountered on her journey. The reader is imagined to learn both from Ajénifújà's experience and from her reinterpretation of her experience through the Bible. Writing of her initial fear of cannibalism, for instance, Ajénifújà writes:

> Many people discouraged me on hearing about my posting to Cross River State. They said that the people there are cannibals. We need to understand that God works in mysterious ways, we don't have to be discouraged. The Bible says of Joshua and Caleb who were among the twelve that Moses sent to spy the land of Canaan, the two a gave [sic] good report of the land. Numbers 13:30, *'Then Caleb silenced the people before Moses and said, we should go up and take possession of the land, for we can certainly do it'*. (69; original emphasis)

The cannibal becomes a symbol of lack of knowledge – not only of Nigeria and the people of Cross River State, but also of God's protection and his 'mysterious ways'. If Ajénifújà 'did not understand' initially, she presents herself as coming to knowledge of God's will through her service year. Similarly, the reader of the memoir may at first not understand the Christian significance of Ajénifújà's travel narrative, but it becomes clear in the last chapters. Just as Ajénifújà offers her readers guides to the Efik language, Ikom customs and

NYSC traditions, she also gives the reader a guide as to how to read and interpret the text through the Bible.

In a move that Stephanie Newell suggests is characteristic of contemporary West African Christian self-help literature, Ajénifújà gestures to a perceived link between her own authority and that of the Bible.[28] '[H]ere is the message of truth for you', she writes, referring implicitly to both her own text and her reinterpretation of her text through the Bible as the 'truth' (66). After all, she claims, God is the real author of her book: 'I am still trusting God to write another book on what is happening after "They Will Eat Me in Calabar"' (76). Christianity is an authorising and explanatory framework for Ajénifújà's trial and overcoming, and for *They Will Eat Me in Calabar* itself. The text shifts between being a travel memoir, a guide to NYSC and Cross River State, a Christian self-development text, and an evangelical tract, as it concludes by inviting the reader to be born again. Without the travel narrative, the text would lack the authority of the narrative of temptation away from home, and without the Christian instruction, it would lack the authority of the Bible as an interpretive lens for both the travel narrative and the account of sexual temptation.

Azubuike, too, emphasises the significance of travel for progress and self-development in *The Girl Who Found Water*, but with less discussion of Christianity and instead a greater emphasis on the significance of personal efforts and determination. During an account of a fierce debate amongst a group of Corps members as to the causes of Nigeria's problems, Azubuike advocates personal action instead of discussion:

> I wish there would be less passionate talk and more passionate doings. [...] I resolved that it would not be enough to just argue, but I must do something, no matter how small. I had not wanted to be here in Bauchi, but Nigeria is my country and I will go wherever I needed to go to serve my country. (94)

Throughout the book Azubuike presents personal effort as a way of overcoming difficulty and fear, and improving Nigeria. On a long endurance trek at the NYSC orientation camp, she is persuaded to continue by Ezuma, a fellow Corps member, who says 'Mirian, did you believe that you could climb the rope and even walk on those tiny rods during yesterday's Man-O-War training? But you made an attempt, right? And you succeeded! Why not make an attempt now, too?' (78). Ezuma, Azubuike notes, is akin to a 'motivational speaker' – and indeed, this language of self-development is apt, for if *The Girl Who Found Water* is in part about national development and progress, it is also a text that sees travel as a mode of self-development. While not explicitly instructing

---

[28] Stephanie Newell, 'Devotion and Domesticity: The Reconfiguration of Gender in Popular Christian Pamphlets from Ghana and Nigeria', *Journal of Religion in Africa*, 35.3 (2005), pp. 296–323 (pp. 302–5).

the reader as Ajénifújà's memoir does, *The Girl Who Found Water*'s narrative of overcoming through personal effort, and its charting of the transformation of its author's character through travel and NYSC, can be read as a self-help guide or inspirational text both for NYSC and for becoming a young Nigerian. The language Azubuike uses to describe her own shift in subjectivity – 'the woman I was becoming', 'develop myself' (19) – combines a sense of travel as personally transformative and subject-forming with the vocabulary of the self-development industry. Azubuike sometimes represents her self-development in material terms, as she imagines success in the form of a good job and buying a car. But it is also expressed in terms of gradually learning to make decisions, not listening to others over herself and God, embracing the full range of 'wonderful experiences' (74) that NYSC offers her, and using experience to make good choices about her future profession. While Christianity is one part of Azubuike's NYSC-formed subjectivity, it does not dominate her narrative as in Ajénifújà's book, but rather forms part of her transformation from childhood to maturity.

The climax of the book is the opening of the borehole and, again, this project of national development is imagined in terms of Azubuike's personal development: she describes how she is 'very happy that my dream of leaving my footprints in the sands of time was finally becoming a reality' (106), and how '[t]here was joy in my heart, knowing that I made [my father] proud' (123–4). The affective focus shifts from the overwhelming tears and fear that dominate the opening chapters to more mature descriptions of joy and recognition of the happiness of others. Azubuike's memoir charts a development of subjectivity from child-like affect to maturity, and from challenges to overcoming through personal effort, which it melds together with the development of a national consciousness or subjectivity. Azubuike is 'The Girl Who Found Water', centring her own subjectivity in this trope of exploration not out of self-aggrandisement, but because the book's project is to show the link between personal and national self-development: it shows how Azubuike becomes 'The Girl Who Found Water', and implies that so, too, may readers become the kind of person who contributes to the nation.

These NYSC texts of national and personal becoming envisage travel as a mode of writing both the self and the nation, linked by figuring the NYSC experience as a rite of passage bursting with dangers, temptations and challenges. These post-civil war travel narratives, in common with Shàdèkò's *Magic Land*, envisage the production of Nigerian national space to be bound up in the production of selfhood. Nigerian youths' encounters with Nigeria through travel for NYSC are characterised by twinned fears of the cannibal and of (female) sexual temptation. By overcoming fear, ordeals and temptations on their journeys, the travellers are imagined as coming to both new knowledge of the nation and new subjectivities. These are accounts of national becoming, but rather than writing narratives of nation, they are told through the creation of cosmopolitan, knowledgeable national subjects who know one another; they are more concerned with Nigerians than Nigeria. These texts are sometimes ambivalent about this nation encountered through travel and personal progress: they depict patriotism and personal encounters, but also a failing or distant state, and a need for personal efforts to 'develop' Nigeria. Nonetheless, as in Shàdèkò's *Magic Land*, travelling and reading the travel text are imagined to help foster the national subject, the 'patriotic' Nigerian who overcomes differences. These NYSC texts can thus be understood generating a form of the 'emerging class consciousness' that Karin Barber detects in many African popular cultural forms: they create and reinforce a particular idea of the patriotic, educated, knowledgeable Nigerian youth.[29]

However, the writers' avowals of patriotism and national unity do not mean that they do not represent differences within Nigeria. While they often aspire to expose the similarities or equivalences between Nigerians of different ethnicities, they often do so by exposing even greater differences between urban and rural Nigeria, and between Corps members and the communities in which they serve. They bring about an 'emerging class consciousness' in another sense: in their valorisation of the educated sensibilities of the Corps members, often clearly differentiated from the communities in which they serve. Shàdèkò, too, uses his memoir *The Magic Land of Nigeria* to draw out Nigerians' differences as well as the common threads of unity that bind them together; while he aims to create a 'detribalised Nigerian' in the aftermath of the civil war, he does not seek to erase 'local peculiarities' in doing so, and he pictures himself as a cosmopolitan, gentleman traveller, able to 'survey' and interpret the landscape in a way that he imagines few of those he meets on his travels are able to do.

In the next chapter, we will see how travel writers in the years after the new millennium, adopting new forms such as the travel blog, have continued to valorise the nation as a space for travel, and have sought to render Nigeria a nation that Nigerians and foreigners alike enjoy travelling in – they do so through an emphasis on tourism and travel for its own sake, rather than the national service emphasised in the texts discussed in this chapter.

---

[29] Karin Barber, 'Popular Arts in Africa', *African Studies Review,* 30.3 (1987), pp. 1–78 (p. 58).

# 'Nigeria is my playground':     6
## travel for travel's sake in twenty-first century Nigeria

Contemporary Nigeria is not typically thought of as a mainstream tourist destination. Even Nigerian travel writer Pèlú Awófèsò, who avidly promotes the country's potential for travellers, conceded in an interview with me in 2010 that he feared that 'nobody will go anywhere in Nigeria specifically on vacation'.[1] Nonetheless, as we saw in Chapter 1, the idea of travel for its own sake has had a limited but not insignificant resonance in southwest Nigeria throughout the twentieth century: in the notion of personal development and ọ̀làjú associated with travel in many travel narratives, or in the newspapers' promotion of travel as an improving, 'civilised' and relaxing leisure activity. In the post-independence era, there has been a growing interest in domestic tourism as both an aspirational leisure activity and a source of economic growth for the state, reflected in the publication of official tourist guides to Nigeria and the foundation of state tourism institutions such as the Nigeria Tourism Association (now the Nigeria Tourism Development Corporation) in 1962, the National Institute for Hospitality and Tourism in 1988, and the Federal Ministry of Culture and Tourism in 1999.

The press, too, has continued to promote tourism both within and beyond Nigeria. Today, many of Nigeria's newspapers host dedicated travel sections; these typically focus on domestic and international tourism news, information and PR pieces, although they occasionally publish short, first-person narratives describing journalists' or readers' own travels. Tourism journalism has undergone a professionalisation, including the foundation of the Association of Nigerian Journalists on Entertainment and Tourism and the Guild of Tourism Journalists, the latter of which is headed by Wálé Ojó-Lánre, a veteran of Nigerian tourism journalism. Some journalists have become known particularly for their extensive reporting on travel and tourism and for their occasional publication of narrative accounts of their own travels, such as Maurice Archibong, who wrote the 'Travels' column in the *Daily Sun* newspaper from 2003. Travel photojournalist and tourism professional John Olú Fáòṣèké has also

---

[1] Awófèsò, interviewed by Rebecca Jones, 16 December 2010, via email.

published several works on tourism prospects in Nigeria and Africa, as well as a guidebook, *Travellers' Guide to Nigeria* (1997).[2]

Perceiving a gap in the state provision of travel infrastructure and marketing, private travel and tourism advocates have also sprung up to encourage Nigerians to travel within Nigeria. In 2014, for instance, Nigerian travel writer Pèlú Awófèsò and a group of fellow writers, photographers and bloggers established a domestic tourism project called 'Travel Next Door':

> This year, Nigeria marks its centenary anniversary (1914–2014). And so we believe the occasion offers a genuine opportunity for Nigerians at home (and those visiting home) to travel around the country, from January through December: this they can do by first crossing the border to the village/town/city next to where they live for a start, locations they have never been to before.
>
> Our plan and desire is to inspire ONE MILLION Nigerians to travel locally; the whole idea is to use travel as a tool to learn something new about a new place, to travel for leisure for a few days and to make new friends whose friendship will endure for many years after the centenary celebration.[3]

Initiatives such as Travel Next Door encourage Nigerians to view Nigeria through the 'tourist gaze', and similarly to understand themselves in a new way, as potential Nigerian tourists or travellers. Simultaneously, sharing with Nigerian writers more broadly a sense of the possibilities the internet offers as an accessible space for publishing in the first two decades of the twenty-first century, a number of Nigerian writers have taken to travel blogging, alongside other forms of online publishing and internet-based self-publishing.[4] Often, like Travel Next Door, they envisage Nigeria as a tourist destination when blogging about their travels, or represent themselves enjoying travel for its own sake. Travel Next Door's sense of both lack and opportunity – Nigerians do not travel at home enough, but they have a 'genuine opportunity' to do so – the project's notion of travel as 'a tool to learn something new', its use of social media and the online space, its reference to Nigeria and Nigerians, and its perception that it is doing something new, are characteristic of a generation

---

[2] *The ABC of Travel and Tourism*, ed. by John Olu Faoseke (Lagos: Keystone Tourism Promotion Publications, 2000); John Olu Faoseke, *Travel and Tourism: The Road Ahead in Africa* (Lagos: Keystone Tourism Promotion Publications, 2001); John Olu Faoseke, *Travellers' Guide to Nigeria* (Ikeja: Africa Pilgrims' Books, 1997).

[3] Travel Next Door, *About* (2014) <https://www.facebook.com/travelnextdoor/info> [accessed 16 February 2014]; original emphasis.

[4] Shola Adenekan, 'Transnationalism and the Agenda of African Literature in a Digital Age', *Matatu – Journal for African Culture and Society,* 45 (2014), pp. 133–51 (pp. 134–6).

of southwest Nigerian travel writers who have sought to explore both the country's tourism potential, and the opportunities for travel writing and blogging, in the early twenty-first century. This chapter examines the work of this generation of southwest Nigerian travel writers writing with a focus on tourism and travel for its own sake, and making use of the opportunities the internet offers for publishing travel writing, around the year 2014, Nigeria's centenary. The writers I discuss in this chapter include Pèlú Awófẹ̀sọ̀, one of the most prolific travel writers of this era, who has published books of travel writing alongside newspaper journalism, blogging and other forms of online publishing, and travel bloggers Kọ́lá Túbọ̀sún, Lápé Ṣóẹ̀tán and Fọlárìn Kọ́láwọlé. These writers are not Nigeria's first or only travel bloggers, but they were amongst the most prominent of southwest Nigeria's travel bloggers in 2014 (although see the Epilogue for a brief account of how Nigeria's travel blogging and tourism scene has evolved since 2014). As well as reading their travel writing, I draw on interviews I conducted with the writers, which I present as an aspect of the genre's intellectual history and as a form of commentary and discourse about travel writing that parallels other travel writers' textual discussions of the benefits and significance of travel writing, such as I. B. Thomas's and D. Ọ. Fágúnwà's commentaries on travel and travel writing as education.

Travel Next Door's founder Pèlú Awófẹ̀sọ̀ is a Lagos-based journalist, travel writer, editor and publisher. After taking a UK-based correspondence course in creative writing, Awófẹ̀sọ̀ began his career in 2002 as a print journalist, reporting on domestic tourism for both Nigerian newspapers and overseas-based publications such as *Africa Today*. However, his interest in travel writing quickly took him beyond the tourism-focused news that characterises many of the newspapers' travel sections. Awófẹ̀sọ̀ turned to writing first-person accounts of his own experiences of travel, alongside information for tourists, which he published in online and print newspapers and magazines, and on various travel websites, including his own website, *Waka-About*. He also self-published – via his own publishing house, Homestead Publications – three books based on his travels in Nigeria: a guidebook to Jos called *A Place Called Peace* (2003), followed by *Nigerian Festivals* (2005), a short book featuring travel narratives about festivals as well as factual information for aspiring tourists, and *Tour of Duty* (2010), an anthology of first-person travel narratives describing Awófẹ̀sọ̀'s journeys to 'all four corners' of Nigeria. In 2016, Awófẹ̀sọ̀ published his edited collection *Route 234* (2016), an anthology of travel writing by Nigerian arts and culture journalists that focuses on accounts of international travel, and in 2017, *White Lagos*, a guide to Lagos's Èyọ̀ masquerade festival.

*Tour of Duty*, subtitled 'journeys around Nigeria and sketches of everyday life', conjoins Awófẹ̀sọ̀'s interest in domestic tourism with first-person, reflective travel writing, unlike *A Place Called Peace* and *Nigerian Festivals*, which are written more within the guidebook genre. Its short narratives encompass

**Figure 2** Pèlú Awófèsò's *Tour of Duty* (2010); photograph from Pèlú Awófèsò's collection, reproduced with permission

**Figure 3** *Route 234* (2016) edited by Pèlú Awófèsò; photograph from Pèlú Awófèsò's collection, reproduced with permission

nineteen of Nigeria's thirty-six states and are deliberately national in their purview, following Awófẹ̀sọ̀ on journeys to the north, south, east and west of the nation, taking in cities such as Abuja, Calabar, Benin, Jos, Lagos and Kaduna as well as smaller towns and rural areas in Akwa Ibom, Nasarawa and Ọ̀sun state. The travelogue is bookended by two short essays: the Author's Note describes the beginnings of Awófẹ̀sọ̀'s tour of duty:

> There was no elaborate planning involved and I did not have all the money in the world. But having resolved in my mind that this was what I wanted to do at that stage in my life, I simply stuffed some T-shirts, toiletries, a laptop and a couple of other bare essentials (torch, a small hardback notebook) in a backpack and I hit the road.

Awófẹ̀sọ̀ also cites a desire to improve the image of Nigeria as a tourist destination: 'Nigeria at the time did not rate highly on the global list of most preferred holiday destinations, and it hurt me so bad'.[5] The book ends with an essay on 'Making Nigeria attractive again', in which Awófẹ̀sọ̀ reflects on the need both to change Nigeria and to change perceptions of Nigeria. While Nigerians themselves are pessimistic about Nigeria, he says, foreign visitors often see the country's potential, and he implies that his travel writing can help Nigerians to be reminded of that potential, too. 'The tour has shown me that there is a lot we can still be proud of', he says, locating the positive aspects of Nigeria in '[t]he everyday Nigerians that I have come across' who 'ooze with the human nature called goodness'.[6]

These essays, with their focus on the attractive side of Nigeria and its tourism potential, serve as a commentary on the travel narratives themselves, some of which describe visits to places framed as tourist attractions – museums, festivals, durbars, palaces – while others focus on everyday life in the towns Awófẹ̀sọ̀ visits, through his encounters with religious worshippers, hunters, sand sellers, palm wine tappers and indigo dyers. The narratives are short pieces written in the first person, usually between five hundred and two thousand words long, echoing the typical length of a newspaper article or blog post. Their style, too, is reminiscent of the relatively concise nature of print journalism and blog posts: Awófẹ̀sọ̀ focuses on storytelling, often describing an encounter he had during his journeys or a particular place he has visited, aiming to pique the reader's interest through an account of his personal experience rather than provide a comprehensive account of the place to which he has travelled. Reflecting his background in tourism journalism and his interest in the domestic tourism industry, Awófẹ̀sọ̀ often includes quotes from tourism

---

[5] Pelu Awofeso, *Tour of Duty* (Lagos: Homestead Publications, 2010), p. xv.
[6] Ibid. p. 176.

industry professionals alongside the voices of people he meets on his travels, and includes historical and cultural information for the benefit of the reader.

Awófẹ̀sọ̀ initially sought to publish his travel writing via conventional publishing houses, but was constrained by a lack of publishers, distributors and bookshops; when I first spoke to him in 2010 and 2011, Awófẹ̀sọ̀ felt 'there is no publishing house that's interested in travel journalism or travel books', since those that had survived the economic crisis of the 1980s were focused on publishing educational books and textbooks.[7] Since the turn of the millennium, publishing houses such as Cassava Republic and Farafina have done much to revive the Nigerian publishing industry (and in the Epilogue I discuss Emmanuel Iduma's recent travel book *A Stranger's Pose* (2018), published by Cassava Republic). Nonetheless, as Shọlá Adénẹ́kàn explains, the conventional publishing industry in Nigeria is not always accessible for new writers, who complain that: 'even established local publishing houses often ask writers to finance the publication of their own work, and will, further, ask them to sign a contract that will give the publishing house a substantial percentage of book sales'.[8] Awófẹ̀sọ̀ felt, too, that 'it's still difficult getting people to read those books' published by Nigerian publishers, owing to the books' cost and limited circulation.[9] Western publishers also fail to offer an accessible route to publication for Nigerian travel writers such as Awófẹ̀sọ̀, perhaps owing to what Adénẹ́kàn identifies as 'the politics of postcolonial literary production which expects African writers to write in a certain way and publish books pitched at certain markets'.[10]

Awófẹ̀sọ̀ turned to self-publishing in order to put physical copies of his books into circulation. As he put it to me, 'Many people have their impressions about vanity publishing or self-publishing [...] In Nigeria people don't care, because that's the only way they can get their books out'.[11] Awófẹ̀sọ̀ set up his own travel writing publishing company, Homestead Publications, planning to publish books by other travel writers as well as his own work. Nonetheless, the costs of publication remained problematically high, and Awófẹ̀sọ̀ saw the potential of digital on-demand self-publishing in allowing him to bypass these costs:

---

[7] Awófẹ̀sọ̀, interviewed by Rebecca Jones, 22 April 2011, Ìbàdàn, Nigeria; Muta Tiamiyu, 'Prospects of Nigerian Book Publishing in the Electronic Age', in *Issues in Book Publishing in Nigeria: Essays in Honour of Aigboje Higo at 70,* ed. by Festus Agboola Adesanoye and Ayo Ojeniyi (Ibadan: Heinemann Educational Books Nigeria, 2005), pp. 143–57 (pp. 143–4).

[8] Adenekan, 'Transnationalism', p. 137.

[9] Awófẹ̀sọ̀, interviewed by Jones, 22 April 2011, Ìbàdàn, Nigeria.

[10] Adenekan, 'Transnationalism', p. 139; see also Madhu Krishnan, *Contemporary African Literature in English: Global Locations, Postcolonial Identifications* (Basingstoke: Palgrave Macmillan, 2014), pp. 1–17.

[11] Awófẹ̀sọ̀, interviewed by Jones, 22 April 2011, Ìbàdàn, Nigeria.

When I finished writing this one [*Tour of Duty*], I asked the graphics company to give me a quote for a thousand copies. At that time we were going to run all the photos in colour, and it was N635,000. And I didn't have that. But then I stumbled upon [travel self-publishing website] GuideGecko through Twitter. The beautiful thing is that it's print on demand, I don't need to pay for the print shop. I'll upload it on GuideGecko; anybody who wants to buy it can get an online copy.[12]

Awófẹ̀sọ̀ subsequently published further editions of his books as Amazon Kindle e-books, alongside more limited runs of hard copies. But while digital and on-demand publishing can result in lower costs for the writer, Awófẹ̀sọ̀ realised that his book *Tour of Duty* was still 'so very expensive that I don't think many people will be able to buy it'.[13] This high cost for the reader meant that he felt he had a mainly international, rather than Nigerian, readership, and his book *Nigerian Festivals* reflects that readership, including an introduction to Nigeria and descriptions of international visitors enjoying the country. This emphasis on the international visitor suggests, too, Awófẹ̀sọ̀'s sense of the importance of Nigeria's self-objectification as a tourist destination for both foreign and domestic visitors, contrary to earlier southwest Nigerian travel writing, in which foreign visitors to Nigeria barely featured except as colonial officials.

However, Awófẹ̀sọ̀ also sought to reach a Nigerian audience, and the internet helped him to do so. He first ventured into online publishing after finding that he was not receiving the reader feedback he had hoped for from newspaper journalism:

Any writer who hasn't caught the online bug needs to do so fast – that appears to be the future of writing/publishing. A writer needs a huge readership to make the necessary impact on society; the internet provides that better than print publications.[14]

Indeed, as Awófẹ̀sọ̀ suggests, online writing – in the form of blogging, dedicated writing websites, online literary journals, newspapers and magazines – and the relative ease of self-publishing both physical books and e-books via the internet, potentially allow writers a greater readership than that afforded by traditional print media and physical books, helping overcome challenges of both cost and distribution associated with physical books in Nigeria.

Awófẹ̀sọ̀ therefore established a travel website called *Waka-About* on which he published his own and other writers' travel narratives. Like other Nigerian online writers, he also used social media platforms such as Facebook and Twitter to foster a community of readers and gain feedback on his work: 'for

[12] Ibid.
[13] Ibid.
[14] Awófẹ̀sọ̀, interviewed by Jones, 16 December 2010, via email.

Facebook', Awófẹ̀sọ̀ said, 'my immediate targets are Nigerians and I must say the followership and feedback I have there is so inspiring to the point that anywhere I travel to on assignment I make sure I report the events on a daily basis on my wall on Facebook, with words and images'.[15] The immediacy of interaction that is possible between online writer and reader enables an intimacy with readers that is harder to generate in print media, but is reminiscent of the Lagos newspaper travel narratives of the 1920s, with their relatively small, intimate readerships (see Chapter 2). Echoing the way that the writers of those travel narratives addressed and thanked their readers, in some of Awófẹ̀sọ̀'s Facebook posts, he names and thanks friends who helped him on his travels. A small but engaged audience of mostly Nigerian readers responds to his Facebook posts; typically around five to twenty readers per post comment on the content of his posts and encourage him to continue his work: 'PELU KEEP UP THE GOOD and GREAT WORK!!!'; 'Pelu, one Nigeria, well done'; 'Just love your work Pelu, so much to learn out there ... history/cultures ... loving it ... we wil [sic] wait to read them ... keep on keeping on'.[16] In addition, readers sometimes add their own information about the places to which Awófẹ̀sọ̀ has travelled, or suggest new places for him to visit. Awófẹ̀sọ̀ does not follow up on all of his readers' suggestions. Nonetheless, the interactivity enabled by travel writing via social media means that his readership not only receives and comments on his writing but is also, to some extent, incorporated into the production of the work and the creation of knowledge about the places to which Awófẹ̀sọ̀ travels.

Awófẹ̀sọ̀ is one of several southwest Nigerian travel writers who have turned to the digital space and self-publishing. The online space has provided a flexible and low-cost platform for a new generation of writers to publish work in genres, such as travel writing, that may previously have been difficult to publish via conventional publishing houses, or simply to experiment with a range of genres while finding their voices as writers. Fọlárìn Kọ́láwọlé, a travel writer, tourism developer and photographer, began publishing travel narratives on his website, *NàìjáTreks*, in 2010.[17] By 2015, when the website's blog was last updated, it hosted over two hundred blog posts describing Kọ́láwọlé's and other guest writers' travels around Nigeria, accompanied by photographs and Kọ́láwọlé's own poetry. The travel narratives focus often on sites of natural beauty such as waterfalls, hills, lakes and forests, but also feature towns and cities across Nigeria, principally the southeast and the southwest of the country. Alongside his writing, Kọ́láwọlé's NàìjáTreks Foundation have organised conservation projects and travel writing workshops for schoolchildren.

---

[15] Ibid. Adenekan, 'Transnationalism', p. 149.
[16] Pelu Awofeso, *Pelu Awofeso* (2013) <https://www.facebook.com/pelu.awofeso> [accessed 16 February 2014].
[17] At <http://naijatreks.com/> [accessed 2 April 2019].

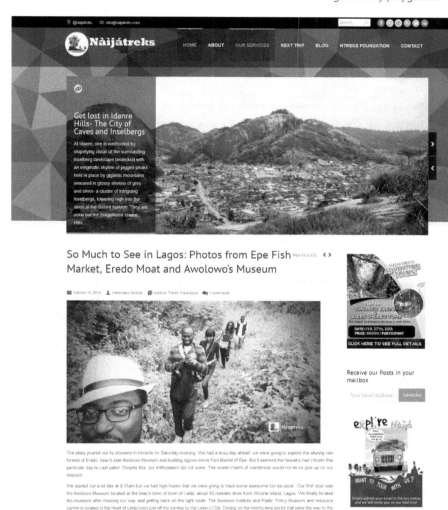

**Figure 4** NàìjáTreks website, reproduced with the permission of Fọláyìn Kọláwọlé

While Kọláwọlé's writing focused on travel, the flexibility of blogging has also enabled other writers to experiment with travel writing as part of a broader repertoire of genres on their blogs. Kọlá Túbọ̀sún is a Yoruba linguist and a blogger with a particular interest in travel writing. While in the US teaching Yoruba on a Fulbright scholarship in 2009, Túbọ̀sún started a blog about his travels called KTravula: a play on his initials and the word 'traveller'. Returning to Nigeria in 2010, Túbọ̀sún maintained his blog and, his interest in travel writing having been piqued by his writing about the US, began to write travel narratives about journeys around Nigeria. Túbọ̀sún continues to publish his own and others' travel writing on his blog alongside pieces on his many other interests, such as the Yoruba language, Nigerian history, heritage, literature and current affairs, and language learning and technology. His interest in travel writing has now moved beyond his blog; in 2018, he published *Edwardsville by Heart*, a poetry collection inspired by his travels in the US. Túbọ̀sún's other major project at the time of writing is a searchable, crowd-sourced online dictionary of Yoruba names. His travel writing and other work thus continue the project of cultural, historical and linguistic documentation that has been an aspect of southwest Nigerian travel writing and literary culture more broadly since its very beginnings: from the travel narratives of the early twentieth-century Lagos newspapers to Isaac Délànọ̀'s travelogue *The Soul of Nigeria*, similarly part of Délànọ̀'s broader repertoire of work on Yoruba language, history, culture and literature.

Lagos-based blogger and writer Lápé Ṣóẹ̀tán's interest in travel writing was also sparked by the potentials of blogging as a platform. Ṣóẹ̀tán began her blogging career in 2011, writing short blog posts about her travels both within and outside Nigeria. Her blog has since evolved into first a 'lifestyle' blog that focused mostly on Lagos life – restaurants, fashion, places to go – and then into a blog about romantic relationships and marriage. After realising that her blog readers particularly enjoyed her writing about relationships and romance, Ṣóẹ̀tán self-published several short e-books offering advice about life as a single woman, dating and marriage in Lagos, the best known being *How to be a Single Woman in Your 30s in Lagos* (2015), and has since established herself as a relationship coach for women. As such, Ṣóẹ̀tán writes into a longer lineage of both fiction and non-fiction literary texts that help readers navigate the challenges of life as a woman in urban Nigeria, from self-help literature – a booming literary field in contemporary Nigeria – to novels such as Sefi Atta's *Everything Good Will Come* (2004) and newspaper columns such as 'Life with Treena Kwenta', published in the *Vanguard* newspaper in the 1980s and 1990s.[18] Ṣóẹ̀tán's travel writing, too, although not always explicitly addressing issues of gender and relationships, can be seen as part of her broader repertoire focused on female self-realisation and enjoyment of the world as a woman: 'I just really want women to find happiness', Ṣóẹ̀tán explains, 'and I want to

---

[18] Rebecca Jones, 'How to Be a Writer in Your 30s in Lagos: Self-Help Literature and the Creation of Authority in Africa', in *Routledge Handbook of African Literature*, ed. by Moradewun Adejunmobi and Carli Coetzee (New York: Routledge, 2019); Jane Bryce, 'A Life on the Women's Page: *Treena Kwenta's Diary*', in *Writing African Women: Gender, Popular Culture and Literature in West Africa*, ed. by Stephanie Newell (London: Zed Books, 1997), pp. 47–66.

help them find that, whether it's through travelling, or through building their confidence no matter their marital status'.[19]

In line with the entrepreneurial, do-it-yourself approach to writing and marketing one's work that the online publishing space both encourages and necessitates, some travel writers of this generation have also sought to raise the profile of travel writing more broadly, to create new opportunities for travel writers, and to generate excitement about the genre in Nigeria's literary scene. Awófẹ̀sọ̀ and Túbọ̀sún, for instance, have both published pieces by a number of other Nigerian travel writers on their websites, and Awófẹ̀sọ̀'s anthology *Route 234* features the work of fifteen fellow Nigerian arts and culture journalists. Túbọ̀sún writes that he is particularly interested in publishing travel writing by other writers on his blog because of 'the lack of many avenues online to read travel accounts (by Africans) that are engaging and entertaining but not aimed solely for commercial attention'.[20] Meanwhile, Social Media Week Lagos – a week-long conference established in 2012, a franchise of the global Social Media Week conference, dedicated to discussing online innovation in Nigeria and beyond – has frequently included panels on travel blogging, featuring Pẹ̀lú Awófẹ̀sọ̀ and Lápé Ṣóẹ̀tán amongst others, suggesting that the genre is becoming institutionalised in Lagos's literary and media circles.

In their use of online and self-publishing, and their sense of the need to develop and promote travel writing as a genre, this generation of travel writers shares some features with the 'author-cum-publisher-cum-printer-cum-bookseller pioneer' that novelist Vincent Chukwuemeka Ike identifies as characteristic of a previous generation of popular literary publishing in West Africa.[21] These writers use the online space to experiment with the kinds of travel and travel writing that interest their readers, and to promote their work. In this, and in their use of the serialised regular blogging format, their approach to writing and publishing is also reminiscent of the Lagos newspaper travel writers of the 1920s, who similarly used their newspapers to experiment with genre and style, and to respond quickly to readers' interests, as we saw in Chapter 2. In common with those newspapers writers, many of this generation of travel writers find themselves constantly experimenting with genre and style in an attempt to attract new readers and distinguish themselves from other writers. But where the newspapers may at least have offered a familiar, if often small, readership,

[19] Lápé Ṣóẹ̀tán, interviewed by Rebecca Jones, 28 April 2016, Lagos, Nigeria.
[20] Kọ́lá Túbọ̀sún, *About Ktravula.Com* (2009) <http://www.ktravula.com/about> [accessed 14 September 2016].
[21] Vincent Chukwuemeka Ike, 'A Critique of the Problems of the Book Industry in Nigeria', in *Culture and the Book Industry in Nigeria,* ed. by Sule Bello and Abdullahi Augi (Lagos: National Council for Arts and Culture, 1993), pp. 129–47 (p. 137), cited in Newell, 'Introduction', p. 3.

these writers instead face the challenge of capturing the interest of a potentially limitless and global audience, but also one that is highly fragmented and easily distracted, as new blogs constantly emerge, and readers can both summon up and close websites at just the click of a mouse button.

## Nigerians telling Nigerian stories through travel

In spite of the opportunities the internet offers for travel writers, however, and their work in creating space for Nigerian travel writing, many of the travel writers I discuss in this chapter perceived Nigerian travel writing to be in a state of lack. Túbọ̀sún reminds us that even blogging, which is seemingly open to anyone with access to the internet, is still dominated by Western accounts of African travels: 'one might [more] easily find blogs written by foreigners about travel around the continent than one might of blogs by Africans of travel experiences in their own continent.'[22] Lápé Ṣóẹ̀tán described how when she first started blogging, she was not aware of any fellow Nigerian travel bloggers: 'First of all, I didn't even know any Nigerian travel writers. The ones I found like Pẹ̀lú Awófẹ̀sọ̀ and Fọlárìn [Kọ́láwọlé], I discovered them after Social Media Week [Lagos] asked me to come [in 2014]. I didn't even know them. The travel writers I knew were European or American'.[23]

Awófẹ̀sọ̀, too, shares Túbọ̀sún's perception of a lack of African voices describing 'travel experiences in their own continent'; he traced his interest in travel writing to an encounter with colonial travel writing about Nigeria while he was reading in a library in Jos, where he had been posted for his National Youth Service Corps service year, and where he realised that there was space for Nigerians to take up travel writing where colonial writers had left off:

> Many foreigners have travelled extensively in Nigeria and they have documented so many things. Especially after they left I don't think many people were doing that any more. I think those sort of encounters seeded me to want to follow in their footsteps, to also want to travel extensively in Nigeria and also document what I've seen.[24]

Awófẹ̀sọ̀'s comment that not 'many people were doing that any more' points to his sense of the loneliness of the contemporary Nigerian travel writer. He described to me in 2010 how 'I am all by myself', explaining that 'no other

---

[22] Kọ́lá Túbọ̀sún, *Travel as Life: A Review of Route 234* (2016) <http://www.ktra-vula.com/2016/09/travel-as-life-a-review-of-route-234> [accessed 16 September 2016].

[23] Ṣóẹ̀tán, interviewed by Jones, 28 April 2016, Lagos, Nigeria.

[24] Awófẹ̀sọ̀, interviewed by Jones, 22 April 2011, Ìbàdàn, Nigeria.

Nigerian journalist of my generation has written any travel book I know of'.[25] 'Nigeria is my playground', he elaborated further in a 2011 interview, gesturing to his confident sense of entitlement to write about Nigeria. But at the same time, he added: 'I'm the only one just playing all over Nigeria. People are not playing with me; they are not enjoying the country with me.'[26] Awófẹ̀sọ̀'s focus on 'Nigeria' as his playground is characteristic of the southwest Nigerian travel writers I discuss in this chapter, who typically describe themselves as Nigerians and the scope of their travels as Nigerian or even as 'African', as Túbọ̀sún does, rather than identifying with southwest Nigeria or the Yoruba region in particular. Nonetheless, this is not to say that they do not encounter and represent differences between themselves and fellow Nigerians as they travel; as we shall see below, such encounters often remind them of their particularity as Lagosians or southern Nigerians, even as they may lay claim to 'Nigeria' as their space for travel.

Awófẹ̀sọ̀'s comment that he initially envisaged his work as travelling 'in the footsteps' of the colonial tradition of African travel writing is echoed by his sense that there is no homegrown travel writing tradition into which he writes; like Lápé Ṣóẹ̀tán, he considers himself to be writing 'within an already established heritage of travel writing as popularised by Western writers'.[27] Nonetheless, Awófẹ̀sọ̀ identifies a difference in the type of travel writing he was producing compared to that of Western travel writers about Africa; he sees himself countering 'lopsided information', in that '[w]e don't have thoughts by Africans about places, but we have more than enough thoughts by foreigners about Africa'.[28] In a blog post inspired by *Route 234*, Awófẹ̀sọ̀'s anthology of Nigerian international travel writing, Túbọ̀sún similarly asks 'why is it that unless in rare cases Africans are not known globally to document our adventures in writing?' Echoing Awófẹ̀sọ̀, Túbọ̀sún laments that 'I haven't read many books about travelling around Nigeria written by Nigerians' compared to the narratives written about Nigeria, and Africa in general, by foreign writers. Túbọ̀sún concludes that *Route 234* represents 'an intervention in a space where much more effort of this nature is needed'.[29]

However, while these writers perceived Nigeria to lack a homegrown travel writing tradition in the narrower sense of the genre, as non-fiction, first-person accounts of travel, some writers nonetheless located themselves within a Nigerian travel writing lineage in a wider sense that includes fiction. When I asked Túbọ̀sún what he had read that had inspired him to write about his travels, he

[25] Awófẹ̀sọ̀, interviewed by Jones, 16 December 2010, via email.
[26] Awófẹ̀sọ̀, interviewed by Jones, 22 April 2011, Ìbàdàn, Nigeria.
[27] Awófẹ̀sọ̀, interviewed by Jones, 16 December 2010, via email.
[28] Awófẹ̀sọ̀, interviewed by Jones, 22 April 2011, Ìbàdàn, Nigeria.
[29] Túbọ̀sún, *Travel as Life: A Review of Route 234*.

cited both Jack Kerouac's *On the Road* (1957) and D. Ọ. Fágúnwà's novels, which he says, 'always had the theme of movement'.[30] His blog was originally subtitled 'A Nigerian Ghoul in an American Forest', echoing Fágúnwà's spirits and forests and the image that is so central to Fágúnwà's novels of a traveller gaining experience of the world far from home in a strange place. The NàìjáTreks website also features a piece by Fọlárìn Kọ́láwọlé in which Kọ́láwọlé travels to the 'real-life' Igbó Olódùmarè, a forest outside Òkè-Igbó that has been packaged for visitors as the forest in which one of Fágúnwà's novels is set. Kọ́láwọlé justifies the journey by explaining that Fágúnwà 'wrote of things that makes one wonder, things that sparks [sic] the fire of wanderlust at the reader's heart.' Kọ́láwọlé expands on the link between reading about the 'mysterious' and travelling to see it:

> Some people believe that the forest is filled with all the mysterious things that had been said about it (especially in the awardwinning [sic] novel), while some believe they're all lies. Nevertheless, a visit to the Forest of a thousand demons keeps you craving for more adventure, therefore we say 'seeing is believing'.[31]

Travel in Igbó Olódùmarè is playfully imagined as a way of turning fiction into fact through seeing and therefore discovering the truth about the forest for oneself, echoing the shift from fiction to non-fiction that Kọ́láwọlé envisages himself making as he places himself in Fágúnwà's lineage.

These fictional predecessors aside, these travel writers' sense of a lack of a local tradition of non-fiction travel writing may simply reflect the fact that earlier Nigerian travel writing is often difficult to access, since it is not widely available in bookshops in Nigeria or beyond. Additionally, when these writers characterise Nigeria as not yet suffused with fellow travellers and travel writers, or as what Awófẹ̀sọ̀ calls 'virgin territory, waiting to be explored by adventurous fun seekers', they are making the ground-clearing gesture characteristic of many forms of travel writing, in which 'travellers want to supersede their predecessors and take along texts by these rivals as research tools, but then return to write a fuller, more detailed account that often sets up the predecessor's as the inaccurate version'.[32] The predecessors whom this generation of writers both connect themselves with and differentiate themselves from are

---

[30] Kọ́lá Túbọ̀ṣún, interviewed by Rebecca Jones, 26 March 2016, via Skype.
[31] Folarin Kolawole, *Exploring the Wilds of Igbo-Olodumare: The Forest of a Thousand Demons* (2011) <http://naijatreks.com/2011/06/exploring-the-wilds-of-igbo-olodumare-the-forest-of-a-thousand-demons> [accessed 20 September 2016].
[32] Pelu Awofeso, *Nigerian Festivals: The Famous and Not So Famous*, 2nd edn (Lagos: Homestead Publications, 2013 [2005]), Amazon Kindle e-book, location 224; Carli Coetzee, 'Sihle Khumalo, Cape to Cairo, and Questions of Intertextuality: How to Write About Africa, How to Read About Africa', *Research in African Literatures*, 44.2 (2013), pp. 62–75 (pp. 72–3).

not Nigerian travel writers such as I. B. Thomas, Isaac Délànọ̀ or Babátúndé Shàdẹ̀kọ̀, but Western travel writers. These writers' work could thus be characterised as autoethnographic, in Mary Louise Pratt's sense of writing back to the West's accounts of Africa while inserting one's work into that tradition, or as a product of the 'extroverted' nature of some contemporary African writing, as Eileen Julien identifies in her notion of the 'extroverted African novel' that positions itself in relation to Western audiences and discourses.[33]

In writing against the perceived narratives of the West and their 'lopsided information', these writers are also writing into a larger discourse in the production, circulation and reception of postcolonial African writing, which insists that 'thoughts by Africans about places', as Awófẹ̀sọ̀ puts it, should be central to the stories told about Africa. A panel organised by the Black Travel Bloggers society at Lagos Social Media Week 2013, which featured Pẹ̀lú Awófẹ̀sọ̀ and Fọlárìn Kọ́láwọle as well as US-based travel blogger Janice Temple, aimed to discuss 'how in the new normal of Web 2.0 we can tell our own story to create a different narrative of Nigeria, and Africa in general, than the one in mainstream media; and how creating this new narrative on social media can encourage travel to the region'.[34] The notion of 'telling our own stories' – also the slogan of Lagos-based Kachifo Publishers – has resonated loudly in postcolonial African literary culture for several decades, as African writers and publishers position themselves as wresting discursive power from the West. Like their more visible fiction-writing counterparts, Nigerian travel writers, too, are seeking to tell the world their stories.

## National and self-improvement through travel writing

This desire to 'tell our own stories' through travel writing is aimed at changing conversations within Nigeria about the desirability of Nigeria as a travel destination, and seeking to improve Nigeria by producing better knowledge of the country amongst Nigerians, as much as it is about telling new stories about Nigeria to the rest of the world. Awófẹ̀sọ̀ contends that his focus gradually shifted from a concern with foreign perceptions of Nigeria to also wanting to change internal narratives about the country:

> [T]here was actually a time that I purposely was taking pictures of a large crowd of white people [...] I did that for so many years. And then I felt, OK, no, I don't want to please anybody anymore. I don't want to please any white

[33] Julien, 'The Extroverted African Novel'.
[34] Folarin Kolawole, *Social Media Week Is Here and Black Travel Bloggers Are Storming Lagos Live #Visitnaija* (2013) <http://naijatreks.com/2013/02/btbvisitlagos/> [accessed 28 September 2016].

man; I don't want to please any white woman. I will just basically write what I want to write, the best way I can. If a visitor comes across it, fine. If a Nigerian or African comes across it, fine. But I won't be writing mainly to appease the foreign visitor. [...] I also write so that Nigerians can appreciate their own country. Because we talk down on Nigeria a lot. And that is because we are very angry with the government. The government has not really done a lot for the country. So many people are pissed off. I'm also going through all of that stress, but we all can't continue to write negatively about Nigeria.[35]

The Nigeria that Awófẹ̀sọ̀ wants other Nigerians to know is a place that it is possible to enjoy travelling in and reading about. 'I encounter difficulties when I travel', Awófẹ̀sọ̀ says, '[but] I would never mention all of those unhappy aspects of my journeys in my articles; they would spoil the fun in the reading'.[36] Awófẹ̀sọ̀ recounts how he was challenged by a fellow journalist who felt that Awófẹ̀sọ̀'s optimistic portrayal of Nigeria was irresponsible: 'Believe me, Nigeria is so bad, things are so bad, you just can't close your eyes to those things. You are a journalist, journalism is also about telling the truth. You can't close your eyes to all the rubbish you see on the road'.[37] The journalist's condemnation of Awófẹ̀sọ̀'s 'closed eyes' is similar to the criticism of tourism as blindness that Judith Adler identifies, drawing on Louis Turner's and John Ash's discussion of the inequality between tourists and their hosts, in which 'leisure travel is condemned as a hedonistic practice involving blind indifference to surrounding misery'.[38] But for Awófẹ̀sọ̀, the 'rubbish you see on the road', the 'surrounding misery', is the story that is already being told, both within and beyond Nigeria: the equivalent of the voyeuristic 'poverty porn' that has been criticised as the stereotypical subject of some African literary fiction.

Awófẹ̀sọ̀ emphasises his sense that he is re-representing Nigeria, telling a story that is not otherwise being told, as he distances his work from that of other Nigerian tourism journalists, suggesting that although there are 'writers who write about tourism [...] I don't know any writer doing travel writing the ideal way'.[39] Awófẹ̀sọ̀'s notion of the 'ideal way' makes an epistemological distinction between first and second hand knowledge:

So many of the newspapers now have a travel section or tourism section, but they don't fill it up with the right things. Nothing about travelling or about real

---

[35] Awófẹ̀sọ̀, interviewed by Jones, 22 April 2011, Ìbàdàn, Nigeria.
[36] Awófẹ̀sọ̀, interviewed by Jones, 16 December 2010, via email.
[37] Awófẹ̀sọ̀, interviewed by Jones, 22 April 2011, Ìbàdàn, Nigeria.
[38] Judith Adler, 'Travel as Performed Art', *American Journal of Sociology*, 94.6 (1989), pp. 1366–91 (p. 1384); Louis Turner and John Ash, *The Golden Hordes: International Tourism and the Pleasure Periphery* (London: Constable, 1975).
[39] Awófẹ̀sọ̀, interviewed by Jones, 22 April 2011, Ìbàdàn, Nigeria.

experiences [...] It's about people who have actually gone to the field to do those stories. It's not about somebody sitting down somewhere, reshaping a press release, and then looking for information in the internet and just slapping it there.[40]

Awófèṣọ̀ suggests that personal experience of travel, 'people who have actually gone to the field', is essential in creating travel writing in 'the ideal way'. But as well as travelling the right way in order to produce the right kind of knowledge of Nigeria, Awófèṣọ̀ emphasises the need to create the right kind of narrative: '[the] oral form is not suitable for the world of today. It has to be written, it has to be printed, it has to be somewhere where people can access it'.[41] The enduring narrative is further imagined as a contrast not just to orality, but also to transient forms of written knowledge, such as that of the contemporary newspaper:

> There are so many things going on [in Nigeria] that we need to document. But the sad thing in Nigeria is that writers are not so keen on non-fiction, documenting everyday life. The journalists themselves are only about news gathering and news reporting. They are just about the now, what is going on to-day, what is going on tomorrow. They don't think long-range [...] I came into writing and to journalism knowing I wasn't just going to be writing for today; I wanted to be writing for tomorrow. So that has always been my approach to writing: documenting, documenting, documenting.[42]

Awófèṣọ̀'s characterisation of early twenty-first century print culture as ephemeral runs contrary to perceptions of the role of the Nigerian press in earlier years; the newspapers of 1920s and 1930s Lagos, for instance, saw themselves as creating an important archive of knowledge about Nigeria for posterity.[43] Awófèṣọ̀ implicitly characterises himself as having a similar mission to the early twentieth-century Lagos press in documenting the world around him and 'everyday life' for posterity, but suggests that in his view the press itself no longer plays this role in creating long-term, more durable knowledge. In common with earlier travel writers Isaac Délànọ̀ and Babátúndé Shàdèkọ̀, Awófèṣọ̀ sees himself producing an archive of everyday life in its 'multiplic-ity', describing the work of palm wine tappers, fishermen and sand sellers, and differences of landscape, architecture and food, and like Shàdèkọ̀, doing so across a clearly and deliberately national space.

[40] Ibid.
[41] Ibid.
[42] Ibid.
[43] Barber, 'I. B. Akinyele', p. 37.

In seeing his work as 'documenting, documenting, documenting', Awófèṣò set up in his travel narratives the conventional expectation of the primacy of the traveller's personal experience as a source of knowledge. Indeed, Awófèṣò represents his knowledge as being gained through observation of new places, through dialogue, and typically through a street-level interaction with the places he visits, both literally and metaphorically. Describing the Èyò festival in Lagos, he writes of the sights and sounds of the streets, of how 'heavy-duty speakers boom with every kind of music – traditional (adults) and western (youths). Both sides of every street, by now chocked with expectant peoples, throb with tireless traders and meticulous merchandising.'[44] Alongside this emphasis on personal experience and observation, Awófèṣò's narratives also include knowledge that he has gained from reading (usually tourist information and historical texts), from official sources and from other people: in the introduction to *Tour of Duty*, he thanks 'every Nigerian I have met on my journeys', adding that, '[m]ore than anything else, they have enriched my knowledge of their own parts of the country like nothing (and no one) else could'.[45]

Some of Awófèṣò's narratives themselves reflect on the process of creating and interpreting history to supplement personal experience. Visiting the palace of the *Aláké* (ruler) of Abéòkúta in his narrative 'Holy Throne', Awófèṣò is taken on a tour of the palace. He is surprised by the lack of interpretation and narrative attached to the historical remnants he sees there:

> I tell him that it would pep up the palace experience, if someone fetches the identities and histories of the images. Standing there and listening to the story could be a one-hour thrill in itself. Derenle nods as if agreeing with my point but something tells me he doesn't take my suggestion seriously.[46]

Awófèṣò is suggesting here that his guide does not take 'seriously' the need for an interpretive process, beyond observation alone, in constructing knowledge for the visitor. Awófèṣò's suggestion seems to be that there should be a dialogic relationship between personal experience and historical information as ways of knowing. Nonetheless, Awófèṣò's overall emphasis is on empirical experience. In the Author's Note in *Tour of Duty*, Awófèṣò writes that he set out to 'document everyday Nigeria *as I saw it*', adding that in doing so his tour '*will attempt to reveal the real spirit and the real essence of the Nigerian*'.[47]

---

[44] Pelu Awofeso, *The Eyo Festival* (n.d.) <http://www.travelintelligence.com/travel-writing/2919/africa-and-middle-east/nigeria/lagos-region/lagos/the-eyo-festival.html> [accessed 6 May 2010].

[45] Awofeso, *Tour of Duty*, p. xiv.

[46] Pelu Awofeso, *Holy Throne* (2007) <http://www.travelintelligence.com/travel-writing/writers/Pelu-Awofeso/page-1> [accessed 6 May 2010].

[47] Awofeso, *Tour of Duty*, p. xvi; added emphasis; Ibid. p. xvii; original emphasis.

He asserts faith in the power of empirical experience to perceive and allow him to document the 'real' Nigeria.

Awófẹ̀sọ̀'s preoccupation with re-representing Nigeria is connected to his understanding of travel writing as a method of promoting national unity-in-diversity by improving readers' knowledge of Nigeria. Awófẹ̀sọ̀'s travels for *Tour of Duty* traversed 'all four corners' of Nigeria, and Awófẹ̀sọ̀ proclaims that 'Nigeria is my playground', with his national subjectivity entitling him to travel within Nigeria: 'I always have it in the back of my mind that I am a Nigerian. I am free to travel the length and breadth of the country, like a Nigerian should'.[48] He considers himself to be writing for the survival of Nigeria as a nation, 'with the hope that Nigerians would see the value of the multiplicity of our different cultures and fight for its continued unity'.[49] Awófẹ̀sọ̀'s perception of the value of writing and reading in shaping knowledge of the nation is shared by Fọlárìn Kọ́láwọlé of NàìjáTreks, who described his objective as: using 'the tool of knowledge to rekindle the pride and love for our culture and our country in the heart of all'.[50] These writers suggest that a purported lack of 'unity' or 'pride' are a problem of lack of knowledge, that there is something Nigerians presently don't know about one another, but that they can learn through reading travel writing about one another. This assumption that by knowing more about each other – becoming more cosmopolitan Nigerians – they will become unified, is similar to Babátúndé Shàdẹ̀kọ̀'s notion that a Nigerian reader of travel writing may become 'detribalised' by knowing more about other Nigerians. In common with Shàdẹ̀kọ̀, these travel writers are attempting to produce a sense of Nigerian nationhood based on knowledge of one another, without rejecting what Awófẹ̀sọ̀ describes as Nigeria's 'multiplicity'.

If Awófẹ̀sọ̀ and Kọ́láwọlé imagine themselves improving readers by shaping them into more knowledgeable Nigerians, they also see themselves creating Nigerians who understand the value of both travel and travel writing. Awófẹ̀sọ̀ explained to me in 2010 that travel writing is a genre that 'Nigerians are yet to appreciate', implicitly comparing Nigerian readerships to those of the West.[51] Kọ́lá Túbọ̀sún similarly explained a perception in Nigeria that 'travel for leisure and travel writing is a Western chore, done by the privileged few, and those conditioned to it by their profession in journalism'.[52] He points out that he had not recognised the value of knowing Nigeria through travel until he travelled in the US:

[48] Awófẹ̀sọ̀, interviewed by Jones, 22 April 2011, Ìbàdàn, Nigeria.
[49] Awófẹ̀sọ̀, interviewed by Jones, 16 December 2010, via email.
[50] Folarin Kolawole, *About* (n.d.) <http://naijatreks.com/about/> [accessed 6 December 2013].
[51] Awófẹ̀sọ̀, interviewed by Jones, 16 December 2010, via email.
[52] Túbọ̀sún, interviewed by Jones, 26 March 2016, via Skype.

when I got back [to Nigeria from the US] it occurred to me that I had lived all my life in this country and I had never been many places around it. And that sense of being ashamed that it was easier to travel around in another person's country than in my own, brought that on me [...] I realised that the reason why I hadn't travelled around the country was not because it wasn't there, but because I hadn't taken it upon myself.[53]

Echoing Awófẹ̀sọ̀, Túbọ̀sún suggests that Nigeria is full of potential for travellers, but is not fully recognised by Nigerians as a place that one might travel in. He gained this new sense of Nigeria's potential by leaving Nigeria and returning; his perspective echoes that of the diaspora travel writers we shall encounter in Chapter 7, whose distance from Nigeria both compels and enables them to seek new routes around the country.

Awófẹ̀sọ̀ also imagines new routes around Nigeria for his Nigerian readers. He explains that through his travel writing, he wanted to tell both his Nigerian and his international readers that 'Look, you can have fun in Nigeria. Forget everything else you hear. Nobody is saying that Nigerians don't have stress [...but] I was so bent on capturing some of these images and then releasing them with a good narrative, so that when people see them it gives them a good, different view of Nigeria'.[54] If Nigeria is Awófẹ̀sọ̀'s 'playground', it is partly because Awófẹ̀sọ̀ envisages his travel writing presenting a 'good, different view of Nigeria' as a place people can imagine themselves 'playing' in. Awófẹ̀sọ̀ see himself not only teaching Nigerians how to 'play' or travel, but also re-representing Nigeria to itself as a playground – a leisured place where people have fun – so that Nigerians and visitors alike are willing to 'play' in it.

While some anglophone Western travel writers try to distance themselves from tourism, Awófẹ̀sọ̀ encourages his readers to participate in domestic tourism, and he describes the growth of the Nigerian tourism industry as an important motivation for his writing:[55]

When I do a travel article, that helps to draw people to a particular part of the country, it's bringing some sort of economic benefit to that part of the country. Because when tourists go to Calabar, for instance, lodge there, if they go for excursions or trips around, in that sense I have delivered added value to the environment, and on a larger scale to Nigeria as a country.[56]

In creating a particular kind of traveller, these writers are imagining a particular kind of subjectivity, invested in modernity through an implicit break with more

---

[53] Ibid.
[54] Awófẹ̀sọ̀, interviewed by Jones, 22 April 2011, Ìbàdàn, Nigeria.
[55] Holland and Huggan, *Tourists with Typewriters*, pp. 2–4.
[56] Awófẹ̀sọ̀, interviewed by Jones, 22 April 2011, Ìbàdàn, Nigeria.

conventional, established ways of travelling in southwest Nigeria: they create an ideal of 'the Nigerian tourist', someone with money to spare who appreciates the value of travel for leisure, enjoyment and edification.

Fọlárìn Kọ́láwọlé, too, sought to create new Nigerian travellers. In 2011, Kọ́láwọlé launched an annual travel writing competition for schoolchildren. The children were asked to write a short piece of writing about a visit to a Nigerian location, with most of them writing about their hometown or somewhere nearby. Through this, Kọ́láwọlé explained, he hoped to 'arouse the intellectual consciousness of young Nigerians towards the tourism potentials in their environment'[57] – in other words, to make them see both their local area and the Nigerian nation in a new light, as somewhere with potential for leisure, travel and tourism. Equally, the competition sought to establish travel writing as a literary genre of merit amongst a new generation of potential writers. The new crop of travel and tourism initiatives such as Travel Next Door and Kọ́láwọlé's travel writing competition are therefore a more explicit embodiment of the work they see their texts also to be doing, not just addressing but actually making cosmopolitan Nigerian subjects, readers and travellers.

This perception of travel writers as creating new types of Nigerians and new ways of seeing Nigeria is developed even more explicitly by Lagos-based blogger and writer Lápé Ṣóètán, who describes how she hopes her writing about her own travels will entice others to travel as she has done. It is no coincidence that some of Ṣóètán's travel narratives are entitled 'How to ...' ('How to make friends when travelling solo'), that they jostle for space on her blog amid articles featuring advice on fashion, beauty and romance, and that her e-books are self-help books giving Lagosian women advice on relationships. Drawing on the language of the self-help industry, Ṣóètán's blog explicitly imagines itself to be creating travellers out of its readers, not only by inspiring readers to travel but also through its self-help discourse of tips and advice about travelling: 'If you want to be the most-requested travel companion you know, here are some tips to help you', Ṣóètán writes in one blog post.[58] Elsewhere she encourages readers to travel for the sake of creating new possibilities for themselves, through the typical self-help narrative of 'success':

> If you go to a place where you don't know anybody and you go alone and actively try to enjoy yourself, you'll be amazed at how proud of yourself you'll be when you get back home. You find out that you've done something many

---

[57] Folarin Kolawole, *Naijatreks Young Writers' Contest* (2014) <http://naijatreks. com/naijatreks-young-writers-contest> [accessed 1 November 2014].

[58] Lape Soetan, *Would You Travel with You? How to Be the Best Travel Companion* (2012) <http://www.lapesoetan.com/would-you-travel-with-you-how-to-be-the-best-travel-companion/> [accessed 26 September 2018]. For more on Lápé Ṣóètán's self-help writing, see Jones, 'How to Be a Writer in Your 30s in Lagos'.

people in the world want to do but don't have the courage to and you find that you actually liked stepping out of your comfort zone. If you made a success of that, what else could you be successful at if you tried?[59]

Ṣóètán now works as a life coach with a focus on relationships, embodying the work that she perceives her travel writing to be doing, too: using her own experiences to encourage other women to improve themselves. Kọ́láwọlé's NàìjáTreks blog makes the links between travel writing and the 'work' of national and personal improvement similarly explicit as it juxtaposes travel narratives with 'inspirational quotes' from Dale Carnegie and other international self-help writers, and readers' comments often express their appreciation of the blog's focus on the positive: 'Nigeria is truly bleesed [sic] and you have shown us so much that we forget whiles [sic] struggling for Visa' writes one commenter. Another praises Kọ́láwọlé's 'good work', noting that 'it helps those outside Nigeria to get another view of our beloved nation'.[60] Reading travel writing is seen by readers of NàìjáTreks not so much as a way of changing Nigeria, but as a way of changing the reader, both inside and outside Nigeria.

Though Lápé Ṣóètán and Fọlárìn Kọ́láwọle connect the self-improvement offered through travel and travel writing closely to self-help literature, the notion of travel and reading about travel as self-improvement has a long history in southwest Nigerian travel writing.[61] As we saw in Chapter 2, some of the writers of the Yoruba newspaper travel narratives of the 1920s imagined their readers would be educated by reading their travel writing. Moreover, this concern with learning through reading is shared more broadly by West African popular literature, which has typically been understood by both writers and readers as having something to teach its readers.[62] In the case of travel writing, texts are imagined not just to teach their readers about the texts' subject matter itself, but also to act on readers, making them into better, more curious or knowledgeable Nigerians through the act of reading about Nigeria. Whether in developing Nigeria's tourism sector, documenting Nigeria's heritage and ecology, enabling women to realise their potential as travellers, or simply creating more knowledgeable, unified and proud Nigerians and readers, southwest Nigerian travel writing retains the impulse for social activism that has

---

[59] Lape Soetan, *6 Great Reasons to Travel Alone* (2014) <http://www.lapesoetan. com/6-great-reasons-to-travel-alone/> [accessed 26 September 2018].

[60] Folarin Kolawole, *About* (n.d.) <http://naijatreks.com/about/> [accessed 28 February 2019].

[61] Coetzee, 'Sihle Khumalo', pp. 69–70 makes a similar connection between self-help literature and the work of South African travel writer Sihle Khumalo.

[62] Newell, 'Introduction', p. 1.

commonly been recognised as the 'organising principle' behind Nigerian (or indeed, African) writing.[63]

## The politics of travel – encountering difference within Nigeria

Although Awófẹ̀sọ̀ says his travel writing is designed to present a more appealing side of Nigeria and his overall message is one of embracing national unity-in-diversity, his travel narratives themselves admit a greater ambivalence, imagining both ease and unease as he travels in Nigeria's heterogeneity, and in doing so, reflects the politics of difference within Nigeria that many of these writers encounter as they venture into the nation. In order to enable cosmopolitan knowledge of Nigeria's multiplicity, Awófẹ̀sọ̀'s narratives represent simultaneously heterogeneity and unity, or difference and the means for transcending or communicating through difference. Thus Awófẹ̀sọ̀ describes how he is aware of his difference, as a southern Nigerian, from the northern Nigerians he encounters on his travels, but is able to live with the difference:

> When I go to the north they may know I'm not a northerner. When I go there in my t-shirt and jeans they know that this guy is from the south. So they will immediately place me, they automatically know I'm a stranger, there's no need to argue about that.[64]

While here knowledge of difference within Nigeria is re-imagined as enabling a national cosmopolitanism about which 'there's no need to argue', elsewhere Awófẹ̀sọ̀'s narratives frequently refer to a more uneasy heterogeneity, whether on the grounds of religion – before going to Jos, he was worried that 'I would be an easy target being a solo Christian travelling in a largely Muslim territory'[65] – or language, as he describes in an article entitled 'A Visit to Kano':

> That aside, how do I chat (like: 'Can you please point me in the direction of a phone booth?') when the average pedestrian I may approach speaks plain 'heavy' Hausa and can make out nothing of the Yoruba that I speak? 'Broken English may help', I console myself trying to wave that line of thinking off my mind.[66]

Again, here, however, Awófẹ̀sọ̀ raises a potential source of difficulty related to Nigeria's heterogeneity – its linguistic diversity – before quickly offering a

[63] Niyi Osundare, *Thread in the Loom: Essays on African Literature and Culture* (Trenton, NJ: Africa World Press, 2002), p. 24.

[64] Awófẹ̀sọ̀, interviewed by Jones, 22 April 2011, Ìbàdàn, Nigeria.

[65] Awófẹ̀sọ̀, interviewed by Jones, 16 December 2010, via email.

[66] Pelu Awofeso, *A Visit to Kano* (n.d.) <http://www.travelintelligence.com/travel-writing/writers/Pelu-Awofeso/page-1> [accessed 6 May 2010].

way to overcome that problem, here through 'Broken English' or Pidgin English offering a means of communication across Nigeria's internal linguistic borders. The implicit suggestion to the reader is that by reading about such moments of linguistic translation they, the reader, will also be able to engage in a form of intercultural translation, realising that other Nigerians are comprehensible and nothing to be afraid of.

A travel narrative from Awófèṣò's book *Tour of Duty* entitled 'Height of Devotion' epitomises the way that Awófèṣò's narratives admit both ease and unease with Nigeria's heterogeneity, even as their overt aim is usually to illuminate the commonalities between Nigerians. The narrative describes Awófèṣò's visit to Sóbí Hill in Ìlọrin, which is used by both Muslims and Christians as a prayer ground. Awófèṣò uses the hill to illustrate the unity between the practitioners of these two religions; he describes them in terms of their equivalence, their shared appeal to a creator God, and their ability to create space for one another: 'Christians and Muslims come here to talk to the Creator', he says. They both engage in prayer. Both 'look up to heaven unobstructed by church or mosque roofing', and there is 'space enough for thousands of people to congregate and conduct their fellowships; there are no loud hailers here, and so there is no issue of one congregation disturbing the other'.[67] He reports an absence of conflict on the hill: '[t]his must be one of the few spots in the country where Muslims and Christians relate at close quarters and have no ill feelings towards one another'.[68] As is common throughout his travel narratives, Awófèṣò strategically acknowledges the spectre of a conflict-ridden Nigeria – but does so in order to subvert it by representing instead Nigeria's unity-in-diversity. He also depicts himself as unproblematically part of this Nigerian unity-in-diversity by adopting a neutral stance on religion. Awófèṣò at first represents himself as merely an observer, walking quietly through the Christians and Muslims praying. But, mid-way through the narrative, Awófèṣò says 'a silent prayer of my own'.[69] He does not acknowledge whether he is Christian or Muslim; instead, he adopts a neutral – but not secular – religious position based on 'prayer' rather than a particular faith, enabling him to represent himself as part of this Nigerian-ness, the unity of prayer, rather than having to take a side. Yet conflict prowls ever more insistently around the edges of this narrative. Awófèṣò describes how his companion points out the presence of the military and the police in a nearby barracks: '[i]f there is any crisis, they would be alerted and they would be here in no time'.[70] We now realise that this vision of peaceful

[67] Awofeso, *Tour of Duty*, p. 40.
[68] Ibid. p. 42.
[69] Ibid. p. 42.
[70] Ibid. p. 41.

religious equivalence is possible only because of the state apparatus, and threat of discipline, that lurks just out of frame.

Although ethnic, religious and linguistic differences tend to be the most prominent intra-Nigerian differences that writers represent themselves encountering during their travel, these travel writers' representations of themselves and their travels are also shaped by gender. The male travel writers I discuss in this chapter rarely acknowledge the masculine nature of their experience as travellers. Lápé Ṣóètán, however, explained how she began writing because of her sense of a particular lack of Nigerian women travellers:

> I wished that there was somebody out there that I could look at. I wanted almost like a role model in travelling, I wanted to see a Nigerian woman going to these far-flung places, and learn about these places and see her pictures and see what she was doing, and I didn't see anything like that so I wanted to create that.[71]

Ṣóètán, who says she has frequently been asked by friends and readers how she, a woman, could travel alone, described her connection with the Scottish missionary Mary Slessor who lived in Calabar:

> It was quite an adventure, Calabar alone, actually, I went to many places, I went to the house that Mary Slessor used to live in, which I thought was an adventure in itself. Because she was this Scottish lady, I'm not sure she was quite 30, and she came to this place in Africa not speaking the language, not knowing anybody and, I couldn't believe it, it's not something I could do. But at the same time, I felt some kind of connection, because I felt like I was this girl alone, going somewhere strange, not speaking the language really, everybody thinking you are crazy, you are doing it because you like it.[72]

Ṣóètán acknowledged that Slessor was travelling as a missionary, while 'me, I was looking for fun!' Nonetheless, she added, 'I really saw the similarity in this young person, going somewhere that she didn't know, and not being afraid, or being afraid and doing it anyway.'[73] For Ṣóètán, being a young woman travelling alone to a strange place and 'not being afraid' was enough to evoke a connection with Slessor, despite the differences between them. Ṣóètán thus seeks to create the beginnings of a lineage of Nigerian women travellers to inspire future travellers, while also establishing a connection to other Western women travellers in Nigeria.

Ṣóètán's travel narratives also produce and reflect gendered subjectivities in a rhetoric centred on anxiety, fear and ways of overcoming them. Ṣóètán's

---

[71] Ṣóètán, interviewed by Jones, 28 April 2016, Lagos, Nigeria.
[72] Ibid.
[73] Ibid.

travel writing often follows the formula of raising fears in order to overcome them that we also see in Awófẹ̀sọ̀'s work, but here applied to personal fear of travel rather than fear of national difference. Her texts aim to create confident travellers who can model themselves on Ṣóẹ̀tán's own confident overcoming of her fear. For instance, one of Ṣóẹ̀tán's blog posts discusses the dangers and attractions of travelling alone, and she begins by explaining her rationale for the piece: 'I travel alone so often that I quite like it now. The very first time I did it, I was nervous of course but today, it's a piece of cake. I want you to try travelling solo too so here are a few reasons why you should'.[74]

Her adoption of this rhetorical strategy of raising fears to show how they can be overcome means that Ṣóẹ̀tán's narratives are a mingling of anxiety and confidence. For instance, alongside her confident assertions about the pleasures of travel, she offers her readers 'a word of caution' about the strong waves at Lagos beaches, and she discusses how 'travelling, especially by air, is fraught with anxiety'. She explicitly diagnoses failure to travel as fear of travel:

> It's okay to not want to travel. People are different and though it's difficult for me to understand, there are people who don't like new places. However, if you say you like to travel then immediately come up with a list of excuses about why you can't, it doesn't sound to me like you like to travel. It sounds like you are afraid to travel.[75]

Some of Ṣóẹ̀tán's anxieties relate specifically to travelling as a woman. She advises (implicitly female) readers on how to respond if 'the person next to you is harassing you, for example, trying to rub your arm, thigh or just making you uncomfortable, it is okay for you to move to another seat if there is one available', and describes how she herself had to do so when she found herself sitting next to a drunk man on a plane.[76] In another blog post, she advises (again, implicitly female) readers on the sexual politics of dress in Lagos, explaining that, 'I have a friend who wore a really short dress and took a bus to a certain part of Lagos. She said when she got to the bus-stop, people actually gathered and followed her hurling insults at her until she got to where she was going. So, be sensible.'[77] Ṣóẹ̀tán's reader is implicitly also the kind of Nigerian woman who might wear a 'really short dress', a modern subject whose confident display

---

[74] Soetan, *6 Great Reasons to Travel Alone.*

[75] Lape Soetan, *Why Don't People Travel More? (Hint: It's Not the Reason You Think)* (2013) <http://www.lapesoetan.com/why-are-people-afraid-to-travel-hint-its-not-the-reason-you-think/> [accessed 26 September 2018].

[76] Lape Soetan, *Travel Etiquette or How to Get What You Want When You Travel* (2012) <https://www.lapesoetan.com/travel-etiquette-or-how-to-get-what-you-want-when-you-travel/> [accessed 26 September 2018].

[77] Lape Soetan, *How to Holiday in Lagos* (2012) <http://www.lapesoetan.com/how-to-holiday-in-lagos/> [accessed 26 September 2018].

of sexuality might incense more seemingly traditional sensibilities – echoing both the urban 'good-time girl' of popular fiction and the free woman of the city in some writing by women writers, whom we encountered in Chapter 5.

However, Ṣóètán's strategy of raising fears in order to be able to dismiss them with confidence sometimes breaks down. In a blog post discussing a visit to Balogun Market in Lagos, Ṣóètán describes how she had developed a fear of going there, owing to bad experiences there as a child:

> The market was always packed with people pushing and shoving. Although my mother generally held my hand in the market, sometimes our hands would be forced apart by the people rushing about and I would squirm through the throng desperately to catch sight of my mother. I feared that my mother wouldn't be able to find me and I would have to stay in the market and live there forever.

Facing the market again as an adult, she had hoped to apply her usual strategy of overcoming fear through experience: 'My heart sank at the thought of going there but I've been working hard on thinking positively about everything so I told myself that after all these years (it must be at least 20 years since I went to that market last), Balogun would have changed'. Unfortunately, 'It turns out that either positive thinking doesn't work or I haven't gotten the hang of it yet because my experience of Balogun market was the worst ever'. Ṣóètán describes how 'the whole experience of trying to park in an already-full parking lot, scrambling through the market, haggling with traders and being sexually harassed was so tiring that I wouldn't advice [sic] anyone to go there unless they absolutely had to'.[78]

The overall tone of Ṣóètán's narratives is excited, confident, and cognisant of the joys of travel and of Lagos life. To read these narratives as articulating trauma would therefore go against the grain of this tone; nonetheless, underneath their exuberance, the narratives articulate fear and anxiety, attempt to overcome it through verbalising it, and advocate re-exposure to the feared object, as if a narrative can be a way of working through the anxiety that may be associated with being a female Nigerian traveller. They also, perhaps, articulate the anxiety provoked by a state that does not provide the infrastructure and institutions necessary to make travel and leisure less fear-inducing, echoing the ambivalence of some of the NYSC narratives we encountered in Chapter 5 towards travelling in an under-protective state. While discussing the dangers of swimming on Lagos beaches, Ṣóètán warns readers that 'I've never seen a lifeguard at one before and people regularly drown. Stay safe. I never

---

[78] Lape Soetan, *Things to Do in Lagos: Balogun Market* (2015) <http://www.lapesoetan.com/things-to-do-in-lagos-balogun-market/> [accessed 26 September 2018].

advice [sic] swimming at the beach in Lagos.'[79] Ṣóẹ̀tán gestures towards how the provision of infrastructure might make leisure safer for Nigerians. But she does not suggest that one should not visit the beach. Rather, she suggests some adjustments that visitors might make to make the experience safer: in this case, still visiting the beach, but not swimming. Thus, as throughout her narratives, she articulates the difficulties and anxieties of travel, but does so in order to suggest ways to move beyond that anxiety.

This sense of danger surrounding travel also responds to generational differences. Reflecting on a disorganised and, in retrospect, potentially dangerous group outing to Èrìn Ìjẹ̀sà waterfalls as a student, Ṣóẹ̀tán writes, 'I wouldn't tell my mother about the trip for a long time'.[80] In common with many travel writers, Ṣóẹ̀tán emphasises danger to heighten the drama of her narrative. But simultaneously, this intergenerational secrecy, as light-hearted as it may be, echoes Ṣóẹ̀tán's implication that by travelling adventurously, often as a solo woman, she is doing something sometimes seen as socially unacceptable and even dangerous. Furthermore, Ṣóẹ̀tán suggests in another blog post that her mother 'never goes on the internet', so will not read about Ṣóẹ̀tán's travels.[81] Through her humorous account of the dangers of her travels and the creation of a narrative of intergenerational secrecy around travelling, Ṣóẹ̀tán again positions herself as a pioneer, opening up spaces for travel and writing for young woman, embodying a new adventurousness that breaks away from the old.

This sense of the traveller doing something unusual is also linked to perceptions of class and access to what these writers might call modernity, or what was typically termed 'civilisation' in early twentieth-century travel narratives. As well as differences directly linked to ethnicity and religion, Pẹ̀lú Awófẹ̀sọ̀'s narratives envisage wealth and being a Lagosian – in effect, class – as one of the markers of difference between traveller and travellee within Nigeria. In his article 'Horses' Day', he describes taking a motorbike taxi in northern Nigeria:

> The rider, I realised, had sort of surcharged me for the distance at 100 Naira. I should have expected it anyway; I looked every inch a Lagos boy (we are thought to be richer than most, in much the same way that the average African imagines the European traveller), a newcomer, so why not?[82]

---

[79] Lape Soetan, *Things to Do in Lagos: Elegushi Beach* (2012) <http://www.lape-soetan.com/beaches-of-lagos-elegushi-beach/> [accessed 26 September 2018].

[80] Lape Soetan, *Travelling When You Know No-One* (2011) <https://www.lapesoetan.com/travelling-when-you-know-no-one/> [accessed 26 September 2018].

[81] Lape Soetan, *1st Year Blog-Oversary* (2012) <http://www.lapesoetan.com/1st-year-blog-oversary/> [accessed 26 September 2018].

[82] Pelu Awofeso, *Horses' Day* (n.d.) <http://www.travelintelligence.com/travel-writing/writers/Pelu-Awofeso/page-1> [accessed 6 May 2010].

Awófèsọ̀ positions the Lagosian traveller, in his confrontation with northern Nigeria, alongside the European traveller, appearing to re-inscribe the hierarchy between traveller and travellee that was characteristic of some European colonial travel writing – as if Lagosians, with their presumed wealth and 'modernity', can now slot into the position in this hierarchy that Europeans once occupied. As we have seen in previous chapters, this is a position that Lagosian travel writers have perceived themselves adopting for almost a century, standing at the crossroads between European and African ways and representing each to the other.

Indeed, Awófèsọ̀'s narratives sometimes reflect directly on such differences between Lagos and the rest of Nigeria, although his terms are 'modern' or 'developed' and 'traditional' rather than 'civilised' and implicitly 'uncivilised', as was common in earlier travel writing. In 'A Visit to Kano', Awófèsọ̀ juxtaposes his imagined vision of the north with everyday life in Lagos, a 'supposedly more developed metropolis', writing, ironically, of his original expectations of 'strangeness', his dreams of a 'vast landscape of mud-and-straw houses and long herds of cattle shepherded by a cane-wielding lanky lad' and a rumour that the Emir of Kano knows everything that happens in the town without 'modern communication aid'.[83] In a narrative called 'To Jos and Back Again', Awófèsọ̀ reflects on his aspirations for an escape through travel into a romantic rural lifestyle: 'I want to live in a typical village, crush a chewing stick between my teeth, bathe with local soap for a change. If I am lucky, I should sip freshly tapped palm wine from little calabashes. That will be paradise.'[84] But as far as Awófèsọ̀'s narratives choose to tell us, he never finds this rural idyll. The romanticised village remains a Lagosian's dream.

As has been the case since the 1920s, these Lagosian travel writers use Lagos as their frame of reference against which to compare the rest of the country. Ṣóètán's travel writing and her blogging more generally is focused on her life as a Lagosian, and the implicit difference in her travel blogs is between Lagos and the rest of Nigeria. When I asked Ṣóètán why she thought so many Nigerian travel writers had grown up in Lagos, she suggested:

> if you grow up in Lagos or you come to Lagos when you are young, it means that – this might sound clichéd, but it means that you tend to be more open-minded, or more adventurous, than other people, or more forward-thinking […] Because for example, if you lived and grew up, let's say, outside Lagos or something, you're going to want to come to Lagos because Lagos is the city. But if you grew up in Lagos you will always still like Lagos, I think, you will

---

[83] Awofeso, *A Visit to Kano*.
[84] Pelu Awofeso, *To Jos and Back Again* (n.d.) <http://www.travelintelligence.com/travel-writing/writers/Pelu-Awofeso/page-1 > [accessed 6 May 2010].

always appreciate it because Lagos is the most modern part of Nigeria, you know, but you will also want to see how the other people live, how is it so different, why does everybody even come to Lagos anyway?[85]

Ṣóètán's sense of Lagos's exceptionalism, and the consequent curiosity of Lagosians about other parts of Nigeria, is reminiscent of the way some of the writers in the Lagos press in the early twentieth century used travel writing to seek reconnection with the Yoruba hinterland, a region from which they considered themselves distinct, but with which they also sought to affirm a common Yoruba origin. Ṣóètán, too, reproduces the notion that Lagos is the 'most modern part of Nigeria', but here seeks a connection through travel not with the Yoruba region specifically, but with the Nigerian nation more broadly, from which she perceives Lagos as somewhat removed. Thus Awófèṣò's and Ṣóètán's travel writing sometimes develops hierarchies of 'modernity' and contrasts between regions of the nation that echo the classifications of 'civilisation' found in European imperial travel writing – but also those of earlier travel writing by southwest Nigerian writers.

In these twenty-first century Nigerian travel narratives, the traveller, again, is pictured as a mediating figure, translating one part of the nation to another so that Nigerians might know each other and understand each other better, and therefore become more unified as a nation. While these writers tend to identify themselves as 'Nigerians', their narratives also reveal, in the case of Awófèṣò and Ṣóètán in particular, a sense of themselves as Lagosians that distinguishes them from fellow Nigerians, and links them to earlier forms of Lagosian travel writing. These travel writers see themselves standing at a crossroads within the nation and able to look in both directions, both to 'modern' Lagosians and other urban elites, and to the Nigerian 'other' elsewhere in the nation. Awófèṣò and Ṣóètán represent themselves as simultaneously Nigerians, at home in their Nigerian 'playground' as they travel, and as looking at others not like them, in an exotic, non-Lagosian Nigeria.

This dual sense of Nigeria as both one's own and as somewhere exotic is fundamental to the rise of tourism-focused travelling and travel for its own sake discussed in this chapter. Such travel, and the travel writing associated with it, depends on the sense of encounter with both difference and points of mutuality or similarity to foster the improved knowledge of Nigeria, and thus the more knowledgeable, patriotic Nigerian that many of the travel writers discussed in this chapter envisage themselves helping to create. Using the internet to experiment with ways of telling new Nigerian stories and re-representing Nigeria to itself and to the outside world, such travel writing thus both positions itself within the Western lineages elaborated by some of the writers discussed in this

---

[85] Ṣóètán, interviewed by Jones, 28 April 2016, Lagos, Nigeria.

chapter and addresses Nigerian conversations about Nigeria, while also some-times offering a postcolonial countertravel narrative about Nigeria that seeks to correct Western perceptions of the country. In the chapter that follows, we shall see how this dual perspective, of being both at home and from elsewhere, is developed even further in narratives of return to Nigeria by writers living in Nigeria's diaspora in the West.

# From the 'dark return' to the 'open' nation: diaspora travel narratives of return to Nigeria

So far, this book has focused on travel writing by southwest Nigerians living within Nigeria. However, with the rapid growth of the Nigerian diaspora in the twentieth century, and of the mobility of those descended from Nigerians around the world, a new form of Nigerian travel writing has emerged as emigrant Nigerians and their descendants have begun to write about their return to Nigeria from overseas. The best known examples of writing the diaspora return to Nigeria are to be found in fiction, such as Helen Oyèyẹmí's *The Icarus Girl* (2005) or Sefi Atta's *A Bit of Difference* (2012). However, perhaps reflecting the popularity of creative non-fiction in twenty-first century African and African diaspora writing more broadly, established writers of fiction and poetry in Nigeria's diaspora have also published non-fiction narratives describing their travels to Nigeria: for instance, Nigerian-American novelist Uzodinma Iweala's *Our Kind of People* (2012) sees the author travelling around Nigeria to document the effects of HIV/AIDS, while Scottish-Nigerian poet Jackie Kay travels to Nigeria in search of her birth father in her memoir *Red Dust Road* (2010).[1]

The narrative of return to Africa is not a new phenomenon. Return narratives, Anna-Leena Toivanen writes, have an extensive history in Afrodiasporic literatures, featuring heavily in the writings of the Harlem Renaissance and Négritude, and African-American writing about returns to Africa has interrogated and re-imagined the complexities of slavery, memory and belonging in the light of the history of the Black Atlantic.[2] Within Nigerian literary

---

[1] For examples of creative non-fiction, and travel writing in particular, in contemporary African literature more broadly, see Ellah Wakatama Allfrey, *Safe House: Explorations in Creative Nonfiction* (London: Cassava Republic Press, 2016); Alain Mabanckou, *Lumières De Pointe-Noire* (Paris: Le Seuil, 2013); Véronique Tadjo, *L'ombre D'imana: Voyages Jusqu'au Bout Du Rwanda* (Arles: Actes sud, 2000); Binyavanga Wainaina, *One Day I Will Write About This Place: A Memoir* (Minneapolis: Graywolf Press, 2011).

[2] Anna-Leena Toivanen, 'Uneasy "Homecoming" in Alain Mabanckou's *Lumières De Pointe-Noire*', *Studies in Travel Writing*, 21.3 (2017), pp. 327–45 (pp. 329–30); on African-American return narratives, see, for example, Farah J. Griffin and Cheryl J. Fish, *A Stranger in the Village: Two Centuries of African-American*

history more specifically, we saw in Chapter 1 how diaspora perspectives have informed southwest Nigeria's travel writing from its earliest days – from the travel accounts of the 'black whiteman' Samuel Àjàyí Crowther that Ọlákúnlé George reads as an instance of the formation of an African diasporic subjectivity, to the creole culture of early twentieth-century Lagos and its *Sàró* elite, home to the Yoruba newspaper travel narratives of the 1920s and 1930s.[3] Furthermore, as Nigerians increasingly travelled overseas in the twentieth century, particularly for education, those who returned to Nigeria began to write of the dual perspective their travels afforded them. Dillibe Onyeama's *The Return: Homecoming of a Negro from Eton* (1978), for instance, offers an account of its author's journey home to Nigeria in 1977 – to Lagos and to his family's home in Eke, near Enugu in southeast Nigeria – after nearly twenty years of living in Britain, including his school days at Eton. Onyeama's dual perspective is reflected in his recognition that he is perceived as 'a "black-white man"', as many people at home called me', and his ambivalent relation to contemporary Nigeria, of which he is extremely critical and yet to which he also feels drawn: '*nothing* works in that country' he writes, '[y]et for some reason that I can offer no other explanation than that it is my true home, there is nowhere else in the world I would rather live than in Nigeria'.[4]

Against this longer background of diaspora return narratives and diaspora perspectives in travel writing, this chapter reads three Nigerian diaspora return travel narratives – two non-fiction and one fiction – published in the late twentieth century and early twenty-first century: Adéwálé Májà-Pearce's travelogue *In My Father's Country* (1987), Téjú Cole's novel *Every Day is for the Thief* (2007) and Noo Saro-Wiwa's travelogue *Looking for Transwonderland* (2012). In reading two writers of Yoruba heritage alongside Saro-Wiwa, whose roots lie in the Ogoni region of southeast Nigeria, I show how these diaspora travel narratives challenge the lens of 'southwest Nigerian' writing that has so far structured this book, suggesting the possibilities for reading them through the lens of 'Nigerian diaspora writing', but also recognise the charge by some reviewers that such narratives are better understood as having been written 'through western eyes'.

---

*Travel Writing* (Boston: Beacon Press, 1999); Alasdair Pettinger, *Always Elsewhere: Travels of the Black Atlantic* (London: Weidenfeld & Nicolson, 1998). On African diaspora and 'migritude' narratives more generally, see, for example, Pius Adesanmi, 'Redefining Paris: Trans-Modernity and Francophone African Migritude Fiction', *MFS Modern Fiction Studies*, 51.4 (2005), pp. 958–75; Cooper, *A New Generation of African Writers*.

[3] George, *African Literature*, pp. 62–105.

[4] Dillibe Onyeama, *The Return: Homecoming of a Negro from Eton* (Isleworth: Satellite Books, 1978), p. 111. Original emphasis.

There are striking similarities between these three texts of diaspora return, despite the twenty-five years between Májà-Pearce's and Saro-Wiwa's texts: all three were written by authors or feature a protagonist who was born in or grew up at least partly in Nigeria, and who has now returned to the country after years away overseas. These narratives pair their authors' return journeys to Nigeria with a further journey following their arrival in Nigeria: a national tour in the case of Saro-Wiwa's and Maja-Pearce's narratives, and a journey of wandering around Lagos in Cole's text. They all position the narratives as travel writing: Májà-Pearce's and Saro-Wiwa's texts adopt the conventional 'travel book' form, while Cole's text, although fictional, reads as if a travelogue, narrated in the first person and following the narrator's arrival in Lagos and his journeys around the city. Most strikingly, all three texts have at their heart a lost father, through whom the author or narrator's often ambivalent feelings about their fatherland, Nigeria, are refracted. These texts, I argue in this chapter, use travel and travel writing to investigate alternative ways for the returnee author or narrator to relate to Nigeria in the absence of that father.

## Ambivalent returns

Dillibe Onyeama's ambivalence about Nigeria in his book *The Return*, his 'love–hate relationship with that country', is characteristic of postcolonial return narratives.[5] Focusing on global francophone postcolonial narratives of return, Srilata Ravi suggests that mid-twentieth-century return narratives were often 'resistant and combative', positioning 'home' as a 'space of political freedom and cultural liberty' in comparison with the challenges their writers encountered as they tried to make a place for themselves overseas.[6] In contrast to this demarcation between home and overseas, more recent postcolonial return narratives, including anglophone narratives, are often notable for their focus on questions of personal identity and on the ambivalence, contradictions and guilt of the return, as travellers come face-to-face with their home societies, their estrangement from them and what Ravi identifies as 'their own fragmented subjectivities'.[7] Thus, according to Helen Cousins and Pauline Dodgson-Katiyo, '[i]deas of strangeness, "exceptional sensibility and susceptibility", distress and disgust permeate narratives in which return is a theme'. 'There may be laughter', Cousins and Dodgson-Katiyo add, 'but it is a nervous

---

[5] Ibid. p. 47.
[6] Srilata Ravi, 'Home and the "Failed" City in Postcolonial Narratives of "Dark Return"', *Postcolonial Studies,* 17.3 (2014), pp. 296–306 (p. 297).
[7] Toivanen, 'Uneasy "Homecoming"', pp. 329–30; Ravi, 'Home and the "Failed" City', pp. 297, 304.

laughter, sometimes verging on the macabre'.[8] Toivanen similarly identifies 'unease' as a key feature of a postcolonial return narrative by Alain Mabanckou, centring on the writer's difficulty in negotiating dichotomies of native/tourist, belonging/unbelonging and nostalgia/loss.[9] A novel such as Helen Oyèyẹmí's *The Icarus Girl*, which narrates its child protagonist's uneasy 'return' to Nigeria from the UK, epitomises this strangeness, nervous laughter and unease, as its protagonist, Jessamy, faces the increasingly sinister and destructive acts of her imaginary twin, TillyTilly. As *The Icarus Girl*'s motif of the twin or split self, the 'half-and-half child' that the mixed race Jessamy feels herself to be, and its interest in the boundary between the fantastic and the realist suggests, such narratives of return often invoke a boundary-crossing, located not just in the physical borders the journey crosses, but also in the traveller's self.

A similar unease about the return, and about the relationship between the returnee and the country of return, may also be found within the societies to which writers return. Cousins and Dodgson-Katiyo point out that the 'been-to' (the recent returnee from overseas) is a common figure in African fiction, often depicted as struggling with both the material expectations placed on them and with their new, often unfavourable, perspective on their home society.[10] Dillibe Onyeama's *The Return* embodies this sense of disappointment located in the figure of the 'been-to' through Onyeama's depiction of his own highly critical reaction to Nigeria, and his perception that 'been-tos' 'are usually regarded with a high degree of envy', adding that 'in recent years this emotion has been accompanied with resentment when it became evident that the "Been to"s (sic) expected their less-privileged countrymen to owe them a living for now being in a position to impart the white man's secrets of greatness'.[11] The return to Nigeria is represented as difficult for both 'been-tos' and those at home to navigate.

The history of the Yoruba term *tòkunbò*, meaning something that has returned from overseas, also reflects an increasingly ambivalent perspective on the idea of things that come from overseas, as the narrator of Téjú Cole's *Every Day is for the Thief* reflects:

> Tokunbo: this is the term for the second-hand imported consumer goods that flood the Nigerian market. It means 'over the seas'. This word is also a Yoruba first name, give to those who were born in foreign countries before being

[8] Helen Cousins and Pauline Dodgson-Katiyo, 'Editorial: Leaving Home/Returning Home: Migration and Contemporary African Literature', in *African Literature Today: Vol. 34 Diaspora and Returns in Fiction,* ed. by Helen Cousins and Pauline Dodgson-Katiyo (Woodbridge: James Currey, 2016), pp. 1–11 (p. 2).
[9] Toivanen, 'Uneasy "Homecoming"', p. 329.
[10] Cousins and Dodgson-Katiyo, 'Leaving Home/Returning Home', p. 3.
[11] Onyeama, *The Return*, p. 50.

brought back home – people like me. That is the primary use of the word but the other sense, the adjectival one, has become common. *Tokunbo* cars, *tokunbo* clothes, *tokunbo* electronics. A word that was once a mark of worldliness now has a mildly pejorative air about it. (83)

As Cole writes, the term *tòkunbọ̀* was originally used primarily for children of Yoruba parents born overseas and was initially viewed as a highly prestigious name. Towards the late twentieth century, however, the term was increasingly used for second-hand goods from the West, imported both legally and illegally.[12] Nonetheless, in both cases, according to Oka Obono and Koblowe Obono, *tòkunbọ̀* has become a metaphor of the potentiality of international travel and extroversion: both people and goods from overseas 'imply movement and stand as status signifiers'.[13]

However, the term *tòkunbọ̀* is also a reminder of Nigeria's global peripherality, since *tòkunbọ̀* goods are usually used goods, and are sometimes in poor condition. Although, according to Ayọ̀kúnlé Ọmọ́bọ̀wálé, many Nigerians enthusiastically embrace *tòkunbọ̀* goods and see them as a symbol of Nigeria's global aspirations, the term also signifies Nigeria's precarious economic situation and its citizens' lack of access to global products in their prime.[14] Furthermore, the traveller from overseas is not always idealised in the way the positive associations of Tòkunbọ̀ as a personal name suggest; there are also irreverent slang Nigerian terms for returnees, such as 'I Just Got Back' or IJGB, implying someone who frequently makes reference to their overseas experience. As we saw in Chapter 1, while the perspectives of 'black whitemen' such as Crowther were repudiated by some in Nigeria's nationalist era, another international traveller, Àjàlá the traveller, was linked to Nigeria's energetic global aspirations in the optimistic independence era of the 1950s to 1970s. The term *tòkunbọ̀* thus encapsulates a continued ambivalence about Nigeria's relationship with the world and the significance of mobility in mediating that relationship, pointing to the country's aspiration but also its inequalities and frustrations. It is this ambivalence about Nigeria's unequal relationship with the world and, relatedly, about the return of Nigerians from overseas that I explore in this chapter, as I consider not only the travel narratives' own representations of diasporic returns to Nigeria, but also criticisms of the ways that

---

[12] Ayokunle Olumuyiwa Omobowale, *The Tokunbo Phenomenon and the Second-Hand Economy in Nigeria* (Bern: Peter Lang AG, International Academic Publishers, 2013), p. 3.

[13] Oka Obono and Koblowe Obono, 'Ajala Travel: Mobility and Connections as Forms of Social Capital in Nigerian Society', in *The Social Life of Connectivity in Africa*, ed. by Mirjam de Bruijn and Rijk van Dijk (New York: Palgrave Macmillan, 2012), pp. 227–41 (p. 233).

[14] Omobowale, *The Tokunbo Phenomenon*, pp. 70–1.

some such diaspora travel narratives – themselves *tòkunbò* narratives, in the sense of returning to Nigeria from overseas – are perceived to relate to Nigeria 'through western eyes'.

## Adéwálé Májà-Pearce's journey shaped by a lost father and fatherland

Adéwálé Májà-Pearce's *In My Father's Country*, published by British publisher Heinemann in 1987, describes the author's return to Nigeria in its years of military rule, many years after Májà-Pearce, aged sixteen, left his childhood home of Lagos for the UK. Májà-Pearce has also published literary criticism, fiction, cultural commentary and a memoir, *The House My Father Built* (2014), which describes his attempt to manage his late father's house in Lagos. Although Májà-Pearce grew up in Lagos and has now lived there for some time, when he wrote *In My Father's Country* he had spent many years in the UK, and the book is written with a highly self-conscious insider–outsider diasporic gaze upon Nigeria, represented in the text as a product not only of Májà-Pearce's years in the UK, but also of his dual heritage as the child of an English mother and Nigerian father. *In My Father's Country* is a non-fiction travelogue, but in common with many travelogues, it also encompasses other genres: it is partly memoir, partly commentary on Nigeria and its relations with the West in the 1980s, and partly an analysis of Nigerian literature and politics, combined with brief historical accounts of the towns and cities Májà-Pearce visits on his journey and snippets from Májà-Pearce's own family history. Echoing many post-independence and post-civil war Nigerian travel narratives, the book is determinedly national in its scope. While Májà-Pearce begins in Lagos and in the Yoruba region, home to his father's family, his tour quickly expands to regions where he has no family ties: 'north as far as Kano by way of Ibadan, Ilorin and Kaduna and back down through Jos, Lokoja and Benin', and then east, 'as far as Calabar before turning north again and heading for Maiduguri via Wukari and Yola and back down again through Enugu and Onitsha'.[15] Like most of the post-independence travel narratives discussed in this book, *In My Father's Country* thus takes 'Nigeria' as its field of travel, although it also recognises Lagos as the region of the country with which Májà-Pearce is most familiar and, to a much lesser extent, identifies some family ties with the Yoruba region. Although the book's origins, Májà-Pearce writes, lie in the offer of a contract from his publisher for a travel book about Nigeria, it becomes clear as the narrative progresses that this is also a journey of reconciliation with both

---

[15] Adewale Maja-Pearce, *In My Father's Country: A Nigerian Journey* (London: Heinemann, 1987), p. 10. Subsequent references are to this edition and will be given in parentheses in the text.

Nigeria and with the memory of Májà-Pearce's father, with whom Májà-Pearce depicts himself as having had a troubled relationship.

Májà-Pearce represents his return to Nigeria as plagued with difficulty from the start. The book begins with an account of Májà-Pearce's anxious departure from the UK and arrival in Nigeria, beset by last-minute changes to his travel plans and a fraught journey. '"Hassle, hassle, hassle; too much hassle"', are the book's opening words, as Májà-Pearce describes a fellow passenger's characterisation of life in Nigeria. The passenger, Májà-Pearce continues, describes how, '[s]he herself couldn't think of living in Nigeria. Life there was too difficult' (1). This hassle and difficulty is echoed by Májà-Pearce's own worries about his return to Nigeria, as he becomes anxious that he is bringing too much Nigerian currency into the country. By the time he arrives in Lagos, he is 'in a state of nervous exhaustion. My hand was shaking as I filled out the disembarkation card' (3). Májà-Pearce's anxious arrival fits with his depiction throughout the book of Nigeria as a troubled nation – unsurprisingly, considering his return took place in the country's era of military rule and economic downturn. Of Lagos, Májà-Pearce writes that '[o]ne sometimes wonders whether the rewards of living in such a dangerous city can be worth the constant worry that your turn may be next' (6). Danger accompanies him throughout his journey, from the relatively commonplace dangers of a journey by road – 'The wind rushed in through the open window and took my breath away. I was terrified. If we had a blow-out at this speed we were dead for sure' (41) – to his encounter with a military coup in Lagos. Anxiety underpins his narrative – 'I wasn't hungry. I hadn't slept in twenty-four hours and my nerves were ragged. I chain-smoked instead', he writes in the early stages of his journey (9) – and he declares that he is increasingly suffering from depression as his journey progresses.

Májà-Pearce's narrative can therefore be considered within the tradition of what Srilata Ravi characterises as postcolonial narratives of 'dark return', a diasporic variation on the notion of 'dark tourism' to sites of atrocities or disasters, or to places characterised by extreme poverty, crisis or violence that have become 'sites of grief and perpetual trauma'.[16] Moreover, as the travelogue progresses it becomes apparent that this physical 'dark return' to a dangerous, anxiety-provoking Nigeria is paired with an interior 'dark return' to the land of Májà-Pearce's father, as his difficult relationship with his father inflects and mirrors his troubled relationship with Nigeria. In her discussion of Noo Saro-Wiwa's *Looking for Transwonderland*, to which I return later in this chapter, Cristina Cruz-Gutiérrez argues that we can read Saro-Wiwa's journey through the figure of what Sam Knowles calls the ambivalent figure of the 'prodigal-foreigner' whose return, to a place where they are neither at

[16] Ravi, 'Home and the "Failed" City', p. 296.

home nor a foreigner, constitutes a 'reconciliation between returnee and father-figure' after a period of absence that may have been perceived as a rejection of the father-figure.[17] The guilt that is often characteristic of the return narrative is therefore also shaped by the generational guilt and ambivalence of sons and daughters who have chosen to leave both father and fatherland behind but now seek a reunion.

*In My Father's Country* may seem at first to represent little such ambivalence about Májà-Pearce's father; rather, it clearly sets out Májà-Pearce's hostility to his father: 'It had been because of him that I had first left [Nigeria] when I was sixteen', he writes (1). In describing his memories of his father, he emphasises his distance from Nigeria and his discomfort and alienation, the 'hours of boredom sitting in some distant relative's uncomfortable living room sipping soft drinks until we were sick', and his inability to speak Yoruba, 'my father's language', 'like a dark, shameful secret which cast doubt on my "Africanness"' (14). Májà-Pearce's link with Nigeria had, he assumed, 'been finally broken with my father's death' (12). Yet it is also 'only his death which had made my return possible' (1). His father's death appears to both break his connection to Nigeria and, in doing so, give him the freedom to make his physical and emotional journey around the country.

Májà-Pearce's alienation from both his father and his fatherland is refracted particularly powerfully through questions of race. Unlike most of the travel writers we have encountered in this book, who frequently confront ethnicity, language and class, but not race, while travelling within Nigeria, race is at the forefront of Májà-Pearce's negotiation with the country. As a mixed-race man, he frequently points to his light skin as a symbol of other Nigerians' perception of him as an outsider, and describes how he is often cast by both Nigerians and British in terms of binaries: he must be either white or black, English or Nigerian, African or Western. Májà-Pearce describes his teenage confusion as he attempted to reconcile this imposition of racial and national binaries: 'By rejecting my Englishness, I was colluding in a subtle form of racism. I couldn't be English, I was assuring them, since I was clearly not white. And yet, by the same token, I wasn't Nigerian either, since I was clearly not black' (15). Reflecting on his difficulties as a teenager in embracing this seemingly ambivalent racial subjectivity, he writes that, 'I didn't want to admit that I was considered different in my father's country' (15). Thus where earlier travel writers tended

---

[17] Cristina Cruz-Gutiérrez, '(Re) Imagining and (Re) Visiting Homelands in Looking for Transwonderland: Travels in Nigeria by Noo Saro-Wiwa', *Atlantis. Journal of the Spanish Association for Anglo-American Studies,* 38.2 (2016), pp. 141–60 (pp. 147–8); Sam Knowles, *Travel Writing and the Transnational Author* (Basingstoke, Hampshire: Palgrave Macmillan, 2014), p. 41.

to refer to difference within Nigeria through the lens of 'civilisation' and ethnicity, here Májà-Pearce instead locates difference in race.

Májà-Pearce's travelogue itself reproduces some of these binaries as it casts Nigeria unambiguously as Májà-Pearce's 'father's country'; Májà-Pearce's English mother is described almost exclusively in terms of her absence.[18] Májà-Pearce relates how, despite many years of marriage to a Nigerian man and being a parent to Nigerian children, his mother was frequently treated by Nigerians as an outsider without family; she 'didn't have her people. They lived elsewhere. She didn't even speak the language. She was a nobody' (29). He re-inscribes this notion of the stranger-mother as he describes the children of his friend Johnny, who also had an English mother: 'To look at the children you would never guess that they had a white grandmother. In another generation or two she will be recalled as an exotic curiosity, if she is remembered at all' (30). Májà-Pearce writes, he says, with 'a lot of respect' for the sacrifice he considers these women to have made in leaving England for Nigeria (29). But nonetheless he repeats their effacement as he leaves his mother scarcely 'remembered at all' in his own travelogue, reinforcing the notion that Nigeria is his 'father's country'.

This emphasis on binaries of race, culture and nationality is echoed by a doubling within the text itself, as Májà-Pearce's troubled intercultural father–son relationship is echoed by another such father–son relationship Májà-Pearce encounters on his journey: between Michael, an English lecturer from Leeds who had moved to Zaria, and his son, Ivan, who had been brought up mainly in Zaria. The father, Májà-Pearce writes, 'had embraced Africa', and had adopted what Májà-Pearce sees as a Nigerian lifestyle. However, 'everything has a price, and the price was his son'.

> Michael may have been fortunate enough to have found a home, but Ivan all too painfully lacked an identity. And identity is what it was all about. Ivan's accent alone betrayed him. With his father or me he spoke in a perfectly normal middle-class British accent; with Terry or with Jimoh he spoke in a perfectly normal Nigerian accent. When confronted with both worlds simultaneously he would often switch accents in mid-sentence. He was neither British nor Nigerian. He was an uneasy hybrid of both (85–6).

Májà-Pearce characterises Ivan as an 'uneasy hybrid' who echoes Májà-Pearce's own initial discomfort with racial and cultural hybridity, and he imagines him, in common with Májà-Pearce, to be paying the 'price' for this cultural mixing.

However, Májà-Pearce's journey is also imagined as an attempt to overcome such binaries of race, nationality and culture:

[18] Májà-Pearce's later book, *How Many Miles to Babylon? An Essay* (1990), centres more directly on his connection to his mother's country, the UK.

If I was a hybrid of two powerful cultures, my colour was only the outward symbol of a deeper confusion of identity. It was at least partly in an attempt to come to terms with this confusion – I couldn't say quite what I had in mind – that I was undertaking this journey. I didn't expect to come up with any answers. This is only one man's account of a journey through a country to which he is forever tied by blood. (15–16)

Through his journey, Májà-Pearce attempts to move from 'difference' and 'confusion' to finding a place for this 'hybrid of two powerful cultures', through the ties of family and ancestry, with race standing as a metonym for other kinds of hybridity, particularly cultural hybridity. The travelogue's desire to open up essentialist binaries is echoed by Májà-Pearce's impatience with what he describes as the 'romanticism' of maintaining Nigeria's 'small languages' and its 'multiplicity of tribes, each with its own language and customs, and each insanely suspicious of the others. To move from one village to the next, often a matter of a few kilometres, is to move from one closed world to another' (102–3). Instead of this 'closed world' characterised by ethnic boundaries, Májà-Pearce aligns himself with 'a wider and much more powerful geographic entity known as Nigeria' (103). His conception is primarily of Nigerians and of the nation, imagined as a space of openness to one another, rather than of the 'closed world' of ethnicity. While this may be viewed as an elite perspective on Nigeria, available to those with the ability to leave the 'closed world' of the village behind, it nonetheless speaks to his desire for the cultural hybridity that would make Májà-Pearce's own subjectivity as a Nigerian possible.

Yet as the journey and the book come to an end, Májà-Pearce seems to suffer with the weight of this hybridity and the struggle to reconcile the binaries that have plagued him. Writing of a period of inertia on his journey, Májà-Pearce reflects that '[i]t was only after I returned to England that I was able to identify this period as the beginning of a depression' (126). A visit to his former childhood home reminds Májà-Pearce of the breakdown of his parents' marriage, 'which was itself the symbol of the larger problem of the conflict of cultures: as the product of that marriage I *was* the conflict' (126; original emphasis). His attempt to resolve the conflict becomes something 'for which there is no resolution':

I owed allegiance to both – both parents, both cultures – and it was impossible to act without betraying one or other of them. It began with the question of where I lived. Nobody can live in two countries at the same time. I had chosen to live in England – I even had an English wife – but where did this leave Nigeria?' (126)

Picturing himself at a crossroads between England and Nigeria, this sense of doubt, conflict and the impossibility of resolving this question without 'betraying one or other of them' continues to haunt Májà-Pearce throughout the remainder of his journey:

> In the course of that last week my depression worsened. I suppose it had something to do with the journey coming to an end; but it also had something to do with my exhaustion. Now that the journey was over I was forced to face the fact that the precise nature of my relationship to the country was as ambiguous as when I had started out. In a sense nothing had really been resolved; but in another sense I was beginning to realize that nothing could be resolved. (171)

The result of Májà-Pearce's journey is represented here as recognition of the simultaneous need and impossibility of being 'both', and as characterised by depression, not an embrace of the nation and a restoration of his relationship with his father. Nonetheless, the journey does eventually succeed in reorienting Májà-Pearce's internal relationship with Nigeria, as ambivalence itself, an embrace of his position at the crossroads and the multiple routes it offers him, becomes as a new way of relating to the country:

> It was only later, during the course of writing this book, that I began to see the ambiguity as a source of strength. On the one hand I was destined to make a journey away from my father's country, a journey begun by my grandfather with his conversion to Christianity and continued by my father with his marriage to an Englishwoman; on the other hand – and this was equally true – I was also destined to make the journey back again, to rediscover something about myself that had been lost in that move. In other words I was tied to the country forever. I knew I would continue to return as often as I could. Perhaps my father had himself known this. His last act on earth was to leave me a small property in Lagos. (171–2)

Májà-Pearce's journey induces depression, but writing about it enables him to frame it as part of a larger journey, both away from and back to Nigeria and away from and back into his father's home – with the latter becoming the subject of his later memoir, *The House My Father Built*. Indeed, despite his hostility to his father, Májà-Pearce's return journey is still at least partly shaped by the memory of his father, who becomes the key to some of his encounters on his journey. A meeting with the husband of a client of a Májà-Pearce's lawyer friend Akin in Ìbàdàn, for instance, is facilitated by the memory of Májà-Pearce's father: 'I asked him whether he had known my father. As with his wife, I had noticed that my name hadn't registered when we had been introduced. At once his interest was aroused, which is what I had intended' (21). Májà-Pearce's memories of his father may often be inflected by disorientation, boredom, alienation and suspicion, but his father also links him to both a past and a sociality in the present. Thus, despite his hostility to his father,

Májà-Pearce as 'prodigal-foreigner' does enact a gradual ambivalent reconciliation with both his father and his fatherland through his journey.

Simultaneously, though, Májà-Pearce also uses his journey to find a new way of relating to Nigeria through literature. While some of the other travel narratives discussed in this book are intensely peopled, Májà-Pearce's travel narrative is instead characterised by its intertextuality. In a way that is reminiscent of I. B. Thomas's emphasis on his newspaper contacts on his journeys around Nigeria in the 1920s (see Chapter 2), Májà-Pearce's literary connections and his work as a writer shape his own journey around Nigeria as he visits writers, lecturers and publishers. Literary culture also offers an intellectual structure for both the journey and the book. Májà-Pearce's bag, he tells us some way into his journey, is 'heavy with the books I had bought since I had left Lagos' (105) and the text, too, is heavy with the weight of intertexts used to map Májà-Pearce's way through Nigeria, offering an alternative intellectual route to understanding Nigeria to that presented by his relationship with his father. He quotes and discusses newspaper articles, Nigerian novels, the journals and books of other travel writers such as Hugh Clapperton and Ryszard Kapuściński, a letter from Lord John Russell, Colonial Secretary in 1839, an extract from *A Diary of a Surgeon with the Benin Punitive Expedition*, V. S. Naipaul, and autobiographies of Ọbáfẹ́mi Awólọ́wọ̀ and Nnamdi Azikiwe. He also, less directly, mediates his journey itself with the texts of his travel writing predecessors: his expectations of the River Niger, for instance, and his subsequent disappointment at finding it 'a filthy, sluggish river with a sprinkling of canoes' are framed by the impressions he has gained from the great colonial explorers, 'Mungo Park, Denham, Clapperton, the Lander Brothers' (94).

Májà-Pearce's feelings of both hope and disappointment for the country are mediated through his vacillation between hope and disappointment in his encounters with Nigeria's literature as he travels: he considers '[t]he growth of indigenous publishing in Nigeria' as 'one of the most hopeful signs for the emergence of a truly indigenous literature' (21–2). Yet while the University of Ibadan's roll call of illustrious literary alumni raises Májà-Pearce's hopes for Nigerian literary culture, the university itself is a disappointment: 'The place looked a wreck. There were broken windows in the lecture halls, dirty marks on the walls and puddles of stagnant water in many of the buildings' (25) and its library fails to hold any copies of the magazine Májà-Pearce is looking for. Discussing a novel written by his childhood friend, Johnny, Májà-Pearce comments unfavourably on the use of English in Nigerian literary writing: 'it is the language that betrays the writer: he simply doesn't handle it with the ease and familiarity of the native English speaker', bemoaning the way that 'for him [the Nigerian writer] the centre of the real literary world is London, not Lagos; the real audience is British, not Nigerian' (31). Nonetheless, Májà-Pearce also endorses certain popular novels, such as E. Okolo's *No Easier Road*, as '[l]acking pretension' compared to 'the novels of the Western-educated, angst-ridden writers more familiar to the European reader' (141). He celebrates a bookshop in Aba with a 'good literature section', including mass market 'cheap English-language paperbacks from Nigerian publishing houses' (139). He lauds the novels of Festus Iyayi and Ben Okri for their contribution to Nigeria's intellectual culture, and endorses the poet and playwright Uche, whom he meets in Calabar, for writing in Igbo for a local audience. Májà-Pearce uses literature to reflect on his hopes and disappointments in relation to Nigerian intellectual culture, the role of the intellectual in Nigerian society, and the literary and intellectual relationship between Africa and the West.

As *In My Father's Country* ends, Májà-Pearce rejects other strategies for finding a place in Nigeria, instead idealising literature as offering an alternative route of travel through Nigeria, a means to relate to the country beyond wealth and personal connections, and a way out of the heavy weight of his father's legacy:

> It would all have been much easier if I had been a different person, if I had wanted to be a lawyer or a doctor or a university lecturer. I would have fitted in better with bourgeois Lagos society, where all the talk was about money: who was making it and who wasn't. I appeared to be making it – I was here, after all – but I knew it wasn't strictly accurate. I was a writer, but not the kind of writer it seemed to me Akin would understand. I was interested in money – who isn't? – but not primarily so. Literature meant more to me than the ability to eat in expensive restaurants. (172)

In search of this new route around Nigeria, *In My Father's Country* adopts what may seem a straightforwardly linear journey narrative, a form of the quest narrative imagined in many texts to offer self-discovery and knowledge. This is not a stylistically or formally innovative text, and it does not significantly embrace linguistic or formal hybridity to echo the racial and cultural hybridity that Májà-Pearce explores within the text. Its form is, moreover, that of the seemingly non-fiction travelogue. Yet of course, the travelogue is a form that has historically been beset by doubt and ambiguity regarding its veracity; hence, as Steve Clark observes, 'the ready and habitual equation of traveller and liar'.[19] Májà-Pearce appears to recognise this ambiguity in his choice of epigraph to the book, an excerpt from the poem 'Truth' by Stewart Brown:

> Today I write this fiction for my father,
> who was right. Truth is
> the only thing worth searching for,

---

[19] Clark, 'Introduction', p. 1.

though histories be proved untrue
and travelogues distortions.

Májà-Pearce's book offers both history and travelogue – so it, too, risks 'untru[th]' and 'distortions'. Indeed, its representation of Májà-Pearce's am-bivalent relationship with his father and his father's country offers plenty of scope for ambiguity and accusations of untruth or distortion. Yet the book is nonetheless written for Májà-Pearce's father (to whom the book is dedicated), after a search for truth – and the truth, at the end of the journey, appears to be located precisely in his ambivalence about both his father and his father's coun-try. The possibility of the travelogue form is to allow for these ambivalences and ambiguities, and thus find what Májà-Pearce considers a more meaningful 'truth'.

## Tẹjú Cole's Lagos as a city of texts

Tẹjú Cole's novel *Every Day is for the Thief* (2007) also explores grief, am-bivalence, lost fathers and lost fatherlands, in this case through the experiences of a Nigerian-American returnee to Nigeria after fifteen years in the US. Cole is a Nigerian-American writer, art critic, essayist and photographer who is best known for his novel *Open City* (2011), the story of a Nigerian-American psychiatrist's wanderings around New York and Brussels. *Every Day is for the Thief* was Cole's first novel, published by Nigeria's Cassava Republic Press in 2007, and since 2014 also available in a US/Europe edition by Random House. Published twenty years after Májà-Pearce's *In My Father's Country*, *Every Day is for the Thief* charts its narrator's return to Lagos after fifteen years away, in more optimistic but still crisis-ridden years for Nigeria after the country's transition to democratic rule in 1999. In short, lyrical chapters written as if part of a reflective travel diary, each chapter describing a different story or way of encountering the city, the book traces, in non-linear form, the story of the nar-rator's return to Lagos and his attempts to come to terms with both his own history and his new outsider–insider perspective on the city.

*Every Day* might at first be taken by its reader as the non-fiction travelogue it resembles. The book began life partially as a blog written by Cole during his own return to Nigeria in 2006, and it retains something of the form of a travel blog in its short, non-linear chapters interspersed with photographs. The narrator is nameless, and has some biographical similarities to Cole himself, while the city itself is the Lagos Cole knows: 'I have sought to capture a con-temporary moment in the life of the city in which I grew up', Cole writes in his Author's Note. However, Cole also describes *Every Day* as a 'novel' and a 'fic-tional story', although one whose 'impetus comes from real-life events', and as Katherine Hallemeier notes, Cole's narrator bears an even greater biographical similarity to Julius, the protagonist of Cole's second novel *Open City*, than he does to Cole himself.[20]

Despite its fictionality, *Every Day* has much in common with Májà-Pearce's non-fiction travelogue in its shock at the 'dark return', its ambivalence towards Nigeria, the absence of a father, and its search for new ways of relating to Nigeria. In common with *In My Father's Country*, *Every Day* begins with a difficult arrival. 'Going home should be a thing of joy', says a man seated near the narrator in the Nigerian consulate in New York (11), and Cole's narrator does allow small moments of joy in his return – 'And I, too, experience the ecstasy of arrival, the irrational sense that all will now be well. Fifteen years is a long time to be away from home' (14) – but these are outweighed by the challenges of arrival. At the Nigerian consulate he is confronted with a demand for a bribe – his version of Májà-Pearce's 'hassle'. 'It is what I have dreaded', he writes, even before he has left New York (12). The airport in Lagos 'looks sullen' and '[w]ith its shoddy white paint and endless rows of small windows, the main building resembles a low-rent tenement' (14). On the drive from the airport, '[p]olicemen routinely stop drivers of commercial vehicles at this spot to demand a bribe' (18). The narrator gears himself up for the dark return to a still-troubled city, despite Nigeria's return to democracy in the years since Májà-Pearce wrote of his own dark return.

The narrator's father, however, is rendered as a negative space, absent from the narrative, rather than an ambivalent presence as in Májà-Pearce's narrative; neither the narrator's mother nor his father make an immediate appearance in the text, and the death of the narrator's father is addressed explicitly only several chapters into the novel, as the narrator reflects on his fading memory of his father: 'Father's memory has already become so insubstantial, fixed to a few events only [...] Sometimes I try to make a mental image of his face at that table on that night, and I fail. I still have photographs, but I no longer know what my father looked like' (43). Only later is the story of this spectral father explained; he died from tuberculosis, and the narrator subsequently left Nigeria for the US 'under a cloud', as his father's death 'opened up the final cavern between me and my mother' (95). The narrator's mother, meanwhile, becomes as absent as his father – and this is a discovery the narrator makes by returning, through travel, to a place where his mother is not: 'In this journey of return, the greatest surprise is how inessential her memory is to me, how inessential I have made it, even in revisiting sites that we knew together, or in

---

[20] Teju Cole, *Every Day Is for the Thief* (Abuja: Cassava Republic Press, 2007). Subsequent references are to this edition and will be given in parentheses in the text. Katherine Hallemeier, 'Literary Cosmopolitanisms in Teju Cole's *Every Day Is for the Thief* and *Open City*', *ariel: A Review of International English Literature,* 44.2 (2014), pp. 239–50 (p. 240).

seeing many people who knew us both' (96). The narrator links this absence of his mother not just to his own break with his mother, but to his 'pale' (later identified as 'Caucasian' (112)) mother's nature as an outsider, with echoes of Májà-Pearce's English mother:

> People know better than to ask about her. That is what it is to be a stranger: when you leave, there is no void. Mother was a stranger here. She left no void after eighteen years, as if she had never been here. I am fatherless, and like a man without a mother, even if it is her face and her pale colour that looks back at me from every photograph and reflective surface. I roam all over Lagos, and even once, I travel along the road that links Unilag with Yaba Bus stop. But I cannot bring myself to revisit the site of my father's grave at Atan Cemetery. (96–7)

If his mother is absent through being 'a stranger', his father is absent through the difficulty of revisiting his memory, a difficulty that the text itself reproduces as it circles around his father's memory, and as the narrator's journey never quite makes it to the father's grave that lies insistently, yet in absence, at the heart of the text.

The novel slips between 'Lagos' and 'Nigeria' as its frame of reference, as the narrator seems to frame his journey home in terms of both his specific history in the city and what he perceives Lagos to tells him about contemporary Nigeria more broadly. Yet unlike Májà-Pearce, Cole's narrator does not attempt a national tour of reconciliation with Nigeria; with the exception of a visit to Abuja, he does not leave Lagos. His journey to Lagos can be read, nonetheless, as a similar search for a new way of relating to the city, in the absence of a father and with only a stranger-mother. His wanderings in Lagos are infused with the flâneur's ethic, making the streets, the danfo and the marketplace his idiom for discovering the city. He explains his preference for these ways of knowing Lagos as stemming from a desire to merge with the city's crowds:

> One goes to the market to participate in the world. As with all things that concern the world, being in the market requires caution. Always, the market – as the essence of the city – is alive with possibility, and with danger. Strangers encounter each other in the world's infinite variety; vigilance is needed. Everyone is there not merely to buy or sell, but because it is a duty. If you sit in your house, if you refuse to go to market, how would you know of the existence of others? How would you know of your own existence? (48)

To know others is to know oneself, for the narrator – this is his ethic of the city, a place of perpetual encounter. The narrator understands both the market and the danfo as places where he can 'know' the city and its others, through encounters with them as part of the crowd. Yet he also comes to recognise that he cannot merge with the crowd exactly as he would wish; his family remind him of the class ties that bind him (even if he seeks to reject them), as they plead with him to travel by car instead of by danfo. In the marketplace, he is reminded of both his light skin and his years away from Lagos:

> When I start speaking Yoruba, the man I've been haggling with over some carved masks laughs nervously. 'Ah oga', he says, 'I didn't know you knew the language, I took you for an oyinbo, or an Ibo man!' I'm irritated. What subtle flaws of dress or body language have, again, given me away? This kind of thing didn't happen when I lived here, when I used to pass through this very market on my way to my exam preparation lessons. (48)

The narrator wishes to merge with the city, and yet is simultaneously reminded of that which attempts to keep him apart from it, holding him in a liminal position.

Further reflecting an ambivalence in the narrator's relationship with Nigeria, when the novel does venture – if only through storytelling – beyond Lagos to the rest of Nigeria, it draws on the idiom of cannibalism that, as we have seen, is potent in numerous southwest Nigerian travel narratives. Discussing the Ogoni people of the Niger Delta region, the narrator's uncle says, '*Awon ko l'o m'an je'yan ni*? Aren't they the ones who eat people?' (103). His uncle tells the story of a colleague called Constance, an albino woman who was posted to the Ogoni region for her NYSC year:

> Well, during the orientation week, and this was in a fairly remote region, near the tribals and such, there was a racket at the gates every night. This went on for three nights, people singing and howling and rattling the gates late into the night. Until the Youth Service people said, you know, just what is going on out there? So they asked around, and it turns out that there's a belief in this village *pe afin o b'osi rara, won fe fa sita, won fe pa je*. Ah! They wanted the albino brought out to them so they could cook and eat her. (104)

In other southwest Nigerian travel narratives that use the cannibal motif, as we have seen in previous chapters, cannibalism is often presented as a real fear of the intra-Nigerian other but also, sometimes, as something that can be overcome by better knowledge of Nigerian others, and which thus represents one's own ignorance. Here, the narrator initially resists the cannibalism trope in this latter manner, humorously turning it back on the uncle: 'Oh come on uncle, come on. Why are you Nigerians so fond of rumours? We – and what I mean is you – are so tribalistic sometimes. And anyway, don't our Yoruba people also have some kingship-related and very non-vegetarian ritual?' (103). But as the story continues, the cannibal motif is even more light-heartedly presented, infused with laughter: '[m]y aunt chuckles', the narrator tells us, and to finish the joke, his uncle adds, '[s]o be careful around that Ben. You just never know when the guy might be hungry.' It is '[s]uch a terrible story', the narrator editorialises, 'but we are all in stitches the rest of the way home' (104). The motif becomes self-consciously ambiguous; are we to believe that the uncle really accepts any of it, or is it a 'rumour', a good 'story' or, with even more ironic distance, a joke?

Creating the 'unease' that Anna-Leena Toivanen suggests is characteristic of return narratives, cannibalism becomes, perhaps for the first time amongst the texts discussed in this book, entextualised: I draw here on the notion of entextualisation as the process by which, as Karin Barber writes, 'instances of discourse, by being rendered detachable from their immediate context of emission, are made available for repetition or recreation in other contexts'.[21] While Barber refers principally to the creation of texts, both oral and written, through direct repetition of verbal elements, I use the term slightly more loosely here to gesture to the way the story of the cannibal is reframed as a detachable and repeatable *story* or text about Nigerian others, understood as a 'rumour', and as an uneasy joke – rather than simply an anecdote from personal experience presented as an at least possible truth, as we have seen in previous chapters. Fusing the image of death that Srilata Ravi identifies as characteristic of the 'dark return' with the 'nervous [...] macabre' laughter that Helen Cousins and Pauline Dodgson-Katiyo detect in ambivalent return narratives, Cole turns this story back on the speaker and on the reader, who does not know whether to join the narrator in mocking the 'tribalistic' nature of the cannibalism narrative, or to laugh with him and his family at the self-consciously ironic joke.[22] The narrator, too, adopts an ironically ambivalent relation to this narrative, simultaneously claiming it and adopting the diaspora Nigerian's privilege of distance when he proclaims the 'tribalistic' impulse behind the cannibalism narrative to belong to '[w]e – and what I mean is you'.

This moment of ambivalent encounter with the rest of Nigeria is much less prominent in the novel, however, than the many moments in which Cole's narrator seeks out, reflects and perpetuates Lagos's cosmopolitan links with the rest of the world. One of those orientations to the world is through the Black Atlantic and slavery, as the narrator reflects on 'the secret twinship this city has with another, thousands of miles away': 'the thought', he writes, 'is of the chain of corpses stretching across the Atlantic Ocean to connect Lagos with New Orleans' (89–90). But Lagos's cosmopolitan links also stretch out across the rest of the world, through comparisons to places and peoples as disparate as a Moroccan souk (49) and Melanesian cargo cults (107), and through reference to the world in Nigeria: a Thai restaurant in Abuja (108), Chinatown in

---

[21] Toivanen, 'Uneasy "Homecoming"'; Barber, *The Anthropology of Texts, Persons and Publics*, p. 22.

[22] Ravi, 'Home and the "Failed" City', p. 301; Cousins and Dodgson-Katiyo, 'Leaving Home/Returning Home', p. 2.

Lagos (111–12), and '[p]eople from all corners of the world [who] have come to take advantage of the newly open economy. Indians, Lebanese, Germans, Americans, Brits' (112). Indeed, Lagos, the narrator suggests, is a newly 'open' city, prefiguring the title of Cole's second novel, *Open City*:

> When I was little, the sight of people like my mother was remarkable, always subject to stares from adults and cries of *oyinbo* from little children. Other Caucasians were few and far between, clustered in Ikoyi and on the campus of the University of Lagos. That has changed now. There is a lot of money to be made in Nigeria, and the world in all its colours is here to make it. The self-described 'giant of Africa,' closed for so long because of its reputation as a difficult place, is now open. There is now all this activity, as pent-up energy is released, and people are driven by a sense that business is possible. (112)

Thus if the narrator's return to Lagos is a 'dark return', it is also a return in which he continually seeks other ways of understanding Lagos, seeing the light as well as the dark, and looking for the 'open' city wherever he can find it.

This desire for 'openness' to the world is nowhere more clearly illustrated than in the novel's wide range of intertexts. In common with Májà-Pearce, Cole's narrator idealises literature and the arts as offering an alternative route around his return journey; but where Májà-Pearce's intertexts tighten his connection to Nigeria, *Every Day*'s intertexts offer the narrator a way to connect Lagos to the rest of the world, creating routes both into and out of Nigeria. Flitting through the novel's pages as the narrator connects his experience of Lagos to his own intellectual interests, or encountered on the streets of the city, the intertexts mentioned or quoted in the novel span some of the greats of European, American and world literature, popular literary texts, and Nigerian writers and musicians. Unquoted but perhaps one of the most significant intertexts of all, as many reviewers have noted, are the novels of W. G. Sebald, whose narratives of wandering and evocative vignettes, accompanied by photographs, resonate throughout *Every Day.*

The effect of this generous 'literary cosmopolitanism', as Katherine Hallemeier aptly characterises it, is not only to highlight the city's openness to the world, and its ability to be read as part of and through the world, in common with other major metropoles, but also to place the narrator's intimate memories and experience in a broader context of textuality.[23] Cole's narrator uses literary texts to navigate his way around, and recreate, his own memories of the city and his childhood. Describing his aunt's house, he writes:

> Part of this story has been told before: the broad doorway, the acrobats. These are incidents from a book I love. Incidents, to be exact, from a dream in that

---

[23] Hallemeier, 'Literary Cosmopolitanisms'.

book. But is it any less real to me now for having once happened to someone else elsewhere? For having been recorded in print in the dream, twenty five years ago, of a great writer returning to his ancestors' Sri Lanka? This is my story now, not his. I am in my aunt's house, but I make it a substitute for that other house of vanished histories, my demolished childhood home. (24)

The reference here, as Adam Mars-Jones points out, is to Michael Ondaatje's *Running in the Family* (1983), Ondaatje's fictionalised memoir of his own re-turn to his family in Sri Lanka.[24] *Every Day*'s narrator uses Ondaatje's memoir to demonstrate the textuality of his own text of return: he reminds us that *Every Day* is a 'story', even as the story is also 'real' for the narrator. His aunt's house similarly stands for his 'demolished childhood home', merging the two, echoing the way he merges Ondaatje's story and his own. The narrator journeys through text, with both his memory and the text of that memory mediated through other texts, while his invocation of Ondaatje places Cole's novel as potentially oc-cupying the same postcolonial and world literary canon as Ondaatje's memoir, evoking global anglophone experiences of return to postcolonial nations.

Texts also contribute to the narrator's navigation of the city and its intellec-tual culture, providing a route not so much for the narrator's wanderings around Lagos, but for his attempts to make sense of the Lagos he sees around him as he wanders. It is through a text that the narrator attempts to make a connection within the city's crowds as he encounters Ondaatje again, this time in a setting he regards as highly 'incongruous', as he comes across a woman reading an Ondaatje novel on a danfo (36). The narrator's intense sense of kinship with this fellow Ondaatje reader, as if two people together on a desert island, drives him to long for a conversation with her, 'my secret sharer, about whom, because I know this one thing, I know many things' (37). And yet, she disappears into the crowd, before he 'can say to her, with the wild look common to all those who are crazed by over-identification, "We must talk. We have much to say to each other. Let me explain."'. Instead, '[s]he disembarks, at Obalende, with her book, and quickly vanishes into the bookless crowd. Just like that, she is gone. Gone, but seared into my mind still. That woman, like an image made with the lens wide open' (38). The narrator is left only with the longing for the kinship and commonality that the book made possible – again, in the language of being 'open', with the camera lens letting light in.

This motif of hope followed by disappointment and a sense of a loss of what could be permeates the narrator's encounters with texts and 'high' culture in Lagos – a reversal of Pẹ̀lú Awófèsò's rhetorical strategy of raising worries or fears as he travels in order to overcome them. In common with Májà-Pearce's

---

[24] Adam Mars-Jones, 'A Family of Acrobats', *London Review of Books*, 36.13 (2014), pp. 21–3.

disappointment at the poor state of some of Nigeria's cultural institutions, Cole's narrator is disappointed by the National Museum's failure to live up to his expectations as a preserver of culture, and by 'dusty and damaged' books in the renowned CSS bookshop, and its emphasis on textbooks, Christian and 'inspirational' books (93), with only a 'small' shelf of general fiction: '[W]here are the Nigeria-based Nigerian writers?' he asks, '[w]here is the selection of international literary fiction?' (93). A jazz shop holds out the promise of culture but it, too, turns out to be a mirage, its CDs pirated copies. 'What I am looking for', the narrator laments, 'what Tranströmer described as a moving spot of sun, is somewhere in the city. But it is not easy to find, not here where one has to forget about yesterday' (94).

It is in the privately funded Muson Centre, a music conservatoire, that Cole's narrator eventually finds his 'moving spot of sun' in which to place his hopes for Nigeria's cultural renaissance. The book and music shop Jazzhole, too, revives the narrator's spirits, as he finds it 'an inspired and congenial setting': 'Here, I think to myself, is finally that moving spot of sun I have so hungrily sought' (100). The work of writers, photographers, musicians and cultural innovators similarly leaves him hopeful:

> There is really only one word for what I feel about these new contributions to the Lagosian scene: gratitude. They are emerging, these creatives, in spite of everything. And they are essential because they are the signs of hope in a place that, like all other places on the limited earth, needs hope. (101)

This turn to particular forms of 'high' art and literature as 'signs of hope' seems a stark rejection of Lagos's older and more locally rooted art forms: its drumming, sculpture, masquerades, tailoring, and oral and performance arts. The elitism of this approach to art could be seen to underline the narrator's alienation from Nigeria, and even Nigeria's alienation from itself, in its failure to create its own institutions to preserve its cultural patrimony and its valorisation of the arts of the West instead – a *tòkunbò* sensibility in the arts as well as consumer goods. Yet the narrator's valorisation of 'high' Western art forms and their Nigerian manifestations can also be read as part of a search for an artistic cosmopolitanism, echoing the cosmopolitanism that Babátúndé Shàdèkò seeks in his travels around Nigeria: an additive mingling of the best the world has to offer. The narrator's ideal is for the Nigerian people 'to have something that is theirs, something to be proud of, and that such institutions have a host of supporters':

> And it is vital, at the same time, to have a meaningful forum for interacting with the world. Molière's work can appear on stage in Lagos, as Soyinka's appear in London, so that what people in one part of the world think of as uniquely theirs takes its rightful place as a part of universal culture. (72)

The narrator's search is for something that is 'uniquely' Nigerian but that can also participate in 'universal culture'. The narrator's route into Nigeria, through texts and the arts, is also his – and fellow Nigerians' – route out of Nigeria.

However, the final chapter of *Every Day* quotes no other texts. This meditative chapter follows the narrator into a street of coffin makers, and is suffused with a quiet that contrasts with the din that characterises the city as we have come to know it in previous chapters. Perhaps, in this encounter with the coffin makers, the narrator glimpses another way to relate to the artistic life of the city, and to write the city. In this chapter, the narrator is lost, arriving in the street accidentally, and yet his being lost is meaningful:

> I am in a labyrinth. A labyrinth, not a maze: I hadn't really thought about the difference before, but it has become clear. A labyrinth's winding paths lead, finally, to the meaningful centre. A maze, in contrast, is full of cul-de-sacs, dead ends, false signals; a maze is the trickster god's domain. When I enter a little sun-suffused street in the heart of the district, I sense an intentionality to my being there. It feels like a return, like a centre, though it is not a place I have ever been before. (125–6)

In this 'return' to a 'meaningful centre' the narrator finds:

> A wholeness, rather, a comforting sense that there is an order to things, a solid assurance of deep-structured order, so strongly felt that when I come to the end of the street and see, off to my right, the path out of the labyrinth and into the city's normal bustle, I do not really want to move on. But I know, at the same time, that it is not possible for me to stay. (127)

The narrator must, in the end, continue to navigate the city through other texts because he cannot access this 'meaningful centre' for long – he must find an alternative route to 'wholeness' and an 'order to things'. The travel writer temporarily merges with the city, as he has longed to do throughout his journey, but he must also eventually adopt his own way of navigating.

The narrator's navigation of this 'meaningful centre' also offers a new way of reading his encounter with the Ondaatje reader on the danfo. The narrator imagines himself asking: 'What, lady, do you make of Ondaatje's labyrinthine sentences, his sensuous prose? How does his intense visuality strike you? Is it hard to concentrate on such poetry in Lagos traffic, with the noise of the crowd, as the tout's body odour wafts over you?' (37). Cole prefigures the labyrinth his narrator encounters at the end of the novel – but here, a textual labyrinth is contrasted with the noise and the smell of reality, whereas at the end of the novel, it is the city itself that becomes the labyrinth. This movement back and forth between text and city, between stories and their narration, offers a way to read *Every Day* as a meditation on the travelogue form itself. Lagos is imagined to be so full of texts that texts not only inform Cole's narrator's journey through the city, but are also represented as characteristic of the city itself. 'The city's air is dense with story', the narrator reflects:

> The narratives fly at me from all directions. Everyone who walks into the house, or every stranger I engage in conversation has a fascinating yarn to deliver. The details I find so alluring in Gabriel Garcia-Marquez here await their recording angel. All I have to do is prod gently, and people open up. And that literary texture, of lives full of unpredictable narrative, is what appeals. (53)

The city is a story awaiting a writer and its entextualisation – here, I use the term entextualisation metaphorically, to refer to making not discourse but the city itself into a text, detachable from its context and able to be 'reproduced and thus transmitted over time and space'.[25] '[T]here's the thought', the narrator says, 'that I could find a way back into the Nigerian reality and create something out of it' – as if, here, he is defining the possibilities of travel writing itself (53). The story of the cannibals is only one of the many Nigerian stories that permits entextualisation, as the writer-narrator sees it – but only if the conditions are right: 'the environment is anything but tranquil', he explains, and hence there is 'a disconnect between the wealth of stories available here and the rarity of creative refuge [...] Writing is difficult, reading out of the question' (56). There is a space between reality and the text that he cannot close without the conditions that would make entextualisation possible – and yet, it is that same reality that is so entrancing to the writer. Finally, the narrator decides to 'turn the volume up, listen to both the music and the noise. Nothing gives, either way. No victor emerges in the combat between art and messy reality' (58). Both text and 'messy reality' compete for the narrator's attention, and the possibility of creating a text of his own is left open and unresolved – even as *Every Day* itself becomes that text.

Writers of 'dark return' narratives may struggle with problems of representation, Srilata Ravi suggests, as they attempt to describe the city that they once called home but that tends to 'remain forever elusive'; the cities to which they return are characterised by their 'unrepresentability', as writers blur the boundaries 'between the real and the imagined, between autobiography and fiction, between their "tourist-selves" and their "writing-selves"', the 'failure' becoming one of representation rather than of the city itself.[26] In his Author's Note, Cole embraces this 'failure' of representation as he disclaims the possibility of literary imagination surpassing reality: 'What could possibly be said about this most complex of cities that could compete with the reality?' As the novel ends, the narrator celebrates '[l]osing my geographical bearings' as '[l]ittle streets wind in upon each other like a basketful of eels' (125). Similarly,

---

[25] Barber, *The Anthropology of Texts, Persons and Publics*, p. 22.
[26] Ravi, 'Home and the "Failed" City', pp. 297–8.

Cole's novel pushes the reader to let go of their desire for the certainty of the real, in pursuit of the 'meaningful centre' of the labyrinth rather than the real. As the narrator walks on, lost, he tells us that though he longs to photograph the streets, he is afraid to 'bind to film what is intended only for the memory, what is meant only for a sidelong glance followed by forgetting' (127). And so what Ikhide Ikheloa, in his review of *Every Day*, calls the 'enduring mystery of Lagos' prevails, 'trumps even the best story teller'.[27] Thus while many of the travel narratives we have encountered in this book make an explicit claim to document the real, *Every Day* weaves in and out of the 'real', but eventually aims, as Cole writes in his Author's Note, for the 'true', in 'the deepest sense of the word'; indeed, as Jeffrey Zuckerman notes, what the narrator perceives as Nigeria's lack of historical memory and the failure of its national institutions is counterbalanced by the novel's own intense determination to document the 'truth' about Lagos.[28] *Every Day* admits gaps and the possibility that writing cannot capture 'reality', but suggests it can nonetheless capture the 'true' – hence it is a fictionalised travelogue, its fictionality perhaps the only possible mode of travel writing for a text that is so highly aware of its own entextualisation of the city in which its narrator travels.

## Noo Saro-Wiwa's search for new routes around Nigeria

To include Noo Saro-Wiwa's *Looking for Transwonderland* – published in the UK by Granta and written by an author whose roots are in the Ogoni region in southeast Nigeria – within this book seemingly undermines the book's own organisational logic, which centres on texts with a clear link to southwest Nigeria. However, I discuss *Looking for Transwonderland* here not only because of its status as a particularly high-profile Nigerian travel narrative, but also because the points of comparison with the other two texts featured in this chapter are compelling. *Looking for Transwonderland* is another diaspora return travelogue that attempts to come to terms with both father and fatherland. Noo Saro-Wiwa is a British-Nigerian journalist and travel writer, and the daughter of the Ogoni activist Ken Saro-Wiwa who was executed by Sani Abacha's military government in 1995. Saro-Wiwa grew up in the UK but spent her childhood summers in Nigeria. After the execution of her father, however, Saro-Wiwa could not face returning to Nigeria: 'My father's murder severed my personal links with Nigeria', Saro-Wiwa explains: 'Though safe to travel, I was not obliged by my

[27] Ikhide R. Ikheloa, *Every Day Is for the Thief* (2008) <https://www.inigerian.com/every-day-is-for-the-thief/> [accessed 2 February 2019].

[28] Jeffrey Zuckerman, *Teju Cole's* Every Day Is for the Thief (2014) <http://www.musicandliterature.org/reviews/2014/3/31/teju-coles-every-day-is-for-the-thief> [accessed 2 February 2019].

mother to go there any more, nor did I have the desire'.[29] Saro-Wiwa worked as a travel writer for major travel publishers such as Rough Guides and Lonely Planet. Eventually, she decided to re-engage with Nigeria, encouraged by her brother's successful return to the country. The result was her travelogue, *Looking for Transwonderland*.

Saro-Wiwa's journey around Nigeria in *Looking for Transwonderland* is, like Májà-Pearce's, deliberately national in scope, taking 'Nigeria' as its frame of reference while also acknowledging the author's origins in a specific region of the country. Thus although it pauses to reflect on Saro-Wiwa's ambivalent relationship with her parents' village in Ogoniland and its language, it also takes in numerous cities and towns across Nigeria, particularly the north. *Looking for Transwonderland* is also structured by the search for the metaphorical as well as literal Transwonderland theme park of the title, which comes to stand for the prospect of conventional tourism in Nigeria. Each chapter is structured around both a destination and a theme and, perhaps reflecting Saro-Wiwa's professional background as a journalist and guidebook author, it offers a greater sense of storytelling about place than Májà-Pearce's more idiosyncratic take on Nigeria, while still constituting a highly personal story of return to Nigeria. The book is also a reflection on Saro-Wiwa's own relationship with Nigeria in the light of her father's death, and an analysis of Nigerian history, culture and politics, unafraid to explore what Saro-Wiwa sees as the country's failings.

Echoing both Cole and Májà-Pearce's texts, *Looking for Transwonderland* begins with a narrative of 'dark return', perhaps even more explicitly; Saro-Wiwa clearly lays out her pain at her father's execution and her subsequent avoidance of Nigeria, whose leaders had caused that pain. It is only by 'disassociating [Nigeria] from the painful memories lurking in my mind's dark matter' that Saro-Wiwa feels able to make her return to Nigeria, and to do this, she decides, 'I needed to travel freely around the country, as part-returnee and part-tourist with the innocence of the outsider, untarnished by personal associations' (9). The position of outsider-tourist allows Saro-Wiwa to reassume a lost innocence. Saro-Wiwa's tone of humour, wit and admiration for individual Nigerians also acts as a narrative counter-balance to the 'darkness' of her return. Nonetheless, her book shares with Cole and Májà-Pearce's texts a scene of troubled arrival in Nigeria: enduring the rowdiness of Nigerian passengers at Gatwick airport, Saro-Wiwa reflects that '[b]eing Nigerian can be the most embarrassing of burdens' (2). She links her contemporary embarrassment to years of anxiety about returning to Nigeria: recalling an occasion during her childhood in which she and her fellow passengers endured a long delay for

---

[29] Noo Saro-Wiwa, *Looking for Transwonderland: Travels in Nigeria* (London: Granta, 2013), p. 7. Subsequent references are to this edition and will be given in parentheses in the text.

a flight to Nigeria, Saro-Wiwa reflects that 'I remember the shouting, chaos and feelings of national shame with visceral clarity. From that day onwards, travelling from England to Nigeria became a source of anxiety for me, a journey I repeated only under duress' (3). Her return to Nigeria for *Looking for Transwonderland* repeats this anxiety of return: as the captain of the aeroplane announces their departure, '[t]hose words triggered old spasms of apprehension. The plane took off and I ascended, moving away from England's lights and into the black canvas of night, trying not to write my unease all over it' (9). Indeed, *Looking for Transwonderland* can be read as an attempt to 'write' something other than the 'unease' of the diaspora traveller's 'dark return' to Nigeria, even as it repeats some of the tropes of such a return.

The most striking likeness between Saro-Wiwa's, Cole's and Májà-Pearce's travelogues, however, is their lost fathers, and the use of the journey to try to come to terms with that loss and with the author's own relationship with Nigeria. However, while Májà-Pearce's father registers mainly as a 'suspect' presence, and Cole's narrator's father as an ambiguous absence, Saro-Wiwa's father is the most unambiguously mourned. Though Saro-Wiwa allows some ambivalence about her father to creep into the narrative through the voices of others who held less favourable opinions of him, and through her own memories of him as a father rather than as a political figure, she also quickly counters such opinions. A memoir by Saro-Wiwa's brother Ken Wiwa, *In the Shadow of a Saint* (2000), by contrast, depicts Wiwa's relationship with his father Ken Saro-Wiwa as more complex and troubled, even as it seeks to restore his father's legacy. In *Looking for Transwonderland*, instead, ambivalence is a feature of Noo Saro-Wiwa's relationship with her fatherland, rather than her father. The country is represented primarily as the place that stole her father from her: 'Nigeria was an unpiloted juggernaut of pain', Saro-Wiwa writes of the years after her father's death: 'and it became the repository for all my fears and disappointments; a place where nightmares did come true' (7–8). But it is also 'a potential "home"' (9), and Saro-Wiwa makes an insistent claim to Nigeria and Nigerian-ness, which she refers to throughout the text using the pronouns 'our' and 'we'.

Although *Looking for Transwonderland* gestures to numerous intertexts, it does not demonstrate the same almost compulsive need as Cole's and Májà-Pearce's travelogues to use literary texts as an alternative route around the country. Yet it, too, seeks alternative routes around Nigeria, and a new way of relating to the country beyond the father's legacy. At first, this search for an alternative route takes the form of tourism, as Saro-Wiwa visits not only the Transwonderland theme park but also other potential tourist sites such as Yankari National Park Game Reserve, the Stone Age mountain kingdom of Sukur, and Ọsun Grove in Ọṣogbo. However, as the book ends, Saro-Wiwa instead turns to everyday life and to culture, in the broadest sense, as offering the most promising route around Nigeria. What makes Nigeria special, the book suggests, is '[t]he weddings, the humour, the music – often too visceral to convey in our tourism brochures' (215), 'the jagga jagga of Nigerian life' (245) and Nigeria's 'indigenous heritage, the dances, the music, the baobab trees and the drill monkeys', not 'the mirage of a Transwonderland-style holiday' (304).

This is not to say that texts do not have a place in Saro-Wiwa's book; guidebooks such as *Lonely Planet* make an occasional appearance, reflecting Saro-Wiwa's background as a guidebook writer and her interest in tourism. Even more so, however, it is Nollywood movies that accompany Saro-Wiwa's journey around Nigeria, rather than the novels to which both Májà-Pearce and Cole turn. Having seen just 'a handful of Nollywood movies' at the start of her journey (76), as Saro-Wiwa travels through Nigeria she becomes an aficionado, nights alone in her hotel rooms often accompanied by a Nollywood movie. In common with both Cole and Májà-Pearce, Saro-Wiwa's travel narrative itself embodies the need to turn to both a journey and to stories and texts, in the broadest sense, to create a new means of belonging, if still ambivalently, to Nigeria.

The ease with which we can compare Saro-Wiwa's text to Májà-Pearce and Cole's texts, despite their differences, suggests they may all be read through a lens that we might call Nigerian diaspora travel writing. Reviewer Ikhide Ikheloa suggests as much when he proclaims that 'Saro-Wiwa is Teju Cole prowling Lagos in pumps and a wicked wit […] reading her book reminded me of Cole's book. There is the same consistent approach and attitude to the hapless subject – Nigeria'. Ikheloa's comparison affirms a shared trajectory between Cole's and Saro-Wiwa's texts, even if, as we will see below, Ikheloa's point of comparison – both writers' take on Nigeria as 'hapless' – is one that he also criticises.[30] Echoing Cole's and Májà-Pearce's emphasis on the (idealised) 'open' city and the 'open' nation that embraces 'hybridity' and cosmopolitanism and extends beyond boundaries of ethnicity and culture, these texts can thus potentially be read within a shared framework of 'Nigerian diaspora travel writing', reaching beyond the regional southwest Nigerian framework that has informed other chapters of this book, to Nigeria as a nation and to its diaspora.

However, not all readers are comfortable with the inclusion of such writing as 'Nigerian' writing, without first making some distinctions between diaspora and locally based Nigerian writing. Frustration with Saro-Wiwa's difference of perspective leads Ikheloa to proclaim *Looking for Transwonderland* to be possibly 'the last straw, that marker that separates Diaspora writing from what I call truly indigenous on-the-ground writing'. Saro-Wiwa 'seems determined to be miserable', Ikheloa remarks, adding that while Saro-Wiwa is a 'good

---

[30] Ikhide Ikheloa, *Noo Saro-Wiwa: Peering into Nigeria Ever So Darkly* (2012) <https://xokigbo.com/2012/06/27/noo-saro-wiwa-peering-into-nigeria-ever-so-darkly/> [accessed 15 September 2018].

travel writer' and her account is 'entertaining and engaging', she writes 'from a Western point of view [...] despite her strong roots in Nigeria, certainly, I see her as someone looking into Nigeria from the Diaspora'. His critique centres on Saro-Wiwa's analysis of Nigeria's failings, in which he sees her 'look[ing] at Africa using Western civilization as an asymptote' and, in the travelogue's 'seeming self-loathing and condescension', as 'another objectification of Black Africa as (the other) exotica'. 'Memo to the Nigerian Diaspora writer', Ikheloa concludes, reflecting on his own position in the Nigerian US diaspora, 'We should probably all leave Nigeria alone, we no longer live there.'[31]

In her discussion of the 'extroverted African novel', Eileen Julien argues that '[w]hat African readers and readers beyond Africa think of typically as the African novel is, I submit, a particular type of narrative characterised by its intertextuality with hegemonic or global discourses and its appeal across borders'. This, Julien contends, is the 'extroverted African novel': that which is turned outward, speaking 'to a nation's "others" and elites in terms (which is to say, about issues and in a language and style) they have come to expect.' Such novels, Julien suggests, engage with Western discourses, and 'have tended to explain Africa to the world': 'their primary feature may be their intertextuality with hegemonic or international texts of all sorts, ethnographic, historical, fictional, and travelogues, even as they may reconfigure indigenous discursive materials.'[32] Ikheloa seems to characterise Saro-Wiwa's travelogue as similarly an 'extroverted' African travelogue that speaks to the West in terms the West has 'come to expect'. While the book's explicit intertexts may be Nollywood movies, its more implicit intertexts are Western travelogues, ethnographies and historical writing about Nigeria, which shape both the travelogue's form and its readers' perception that it seeks to 'explain Africa to the world'.

Adéwálé Májà-Pearce's own review of Saro-Wiwa's book is more understanding of Saro-Wiwa's pessimistic analysis of Nigeria, but his critique centres on Saro-Wiwa's own position as a diaspora writer, which he feels is not sufficiently acknowledged within the narrative. 'The constant intrusion of the personal pronoun [our]', Májà-Pearce writes, 'sits uneasily within the narrative':

> It suggests an intimacy that is at odds with her predicament as a foreigner who happens to have been born to Nigerian parents. This is a pity. Had she acknowledged that she was seeing Nigeria largely through western eyes she might have opened up connections between where she is and where she has come from that would have thrown light on both.[33]

[31] Ibid.
[32] Julien, 'The Extroverted African Novel', pp. 681, 83, 95.
[33] Adewale Maja-Pearce, *Looking for Transwonderland: Travels in Nigeria by Noo Saro-Wiwa* (2012) <https://www.theguardian.com/books/2012/jan/06/looking-transwonderland-saro-wiwa-review> [accessed 15 September 2018].

Májà-Pearce suggests that this lack of acknowledgement of Saro-Wiwa's 'western eyes' limits her analysis. Májà-Pearce appears to be looking, to use the language of *In My Father's Country*, for a more 'hybrid' analysis: one that is able to combine Nigerian and Western perspectives. Without acknowledging this double or 'hybrid' gaze, his critique suggests, Saro-Wiwa is unable to make the transnational comparisons that would deepen her analysis. Májà-Pearce's review of *Looking for Transwonderland* can be read as a continuation of his book *In My Father's Country*'s own concern with being 'both', continuing to straddle boundaries and open up new ways of being Nigerian. Yet by labelling Saro-Wiwa a 'foreigner', while suggesting that she characterises herself as a Nigerian, Májà-Pearce seems to deny Saro-Wiwa the possibility of being 'both' in the way that he suggests would have benefited her analysis, and in the way he comes to characterise himself in his own travel narrative.

Indeed, in sustaining a divide between 'diaspora' and 'indigenous' writing, Ikheloa's critique of Saro-Wiwa's book may underestimate the complexity of the interaction between Nigeria and the rest of the world, and the extent to which ideas from 'outside' have shaped Nigeria's sense of itself, including in its travel writing, associated in some cases with diaspora and creole perspectives since the nineteenth century. The contemporary Nigeria-based travel writers discussed in Chapter 6, moreover, frequently insert themselves into what they see as global travel writing cultures and lineages, rather than imagining themselves contributing to a distinct 'indigenous on-the-ground' form of travel writing, although still recognising the difference between their own perspectives and those of their Western predecessors. Moreover, we have seen throughout this book that there have been unflattering gazes exerted upon the 'other' *within* Nigeria, using Lagosian or Yoruba 'civilisation' as the point of comparison, as well as Western 'civilisation'; Cole's and Saro-Wiwa's diaspora gaze on Nigeria is not necessarily different in this regard, although it may differ in degree and in terms of the power differentials between Nigeria and the West.

The diaspora travel narratives discussed in this chapter are connected to earlier forms of Nigerian travel writing in other ways, too. The Yoruba newspaper travel narratives of the 1920s discussed in Chapter 2 were overwhelmingly full of people and incorporative in their sociality, with the writers' personal connections offering new routes for travel spreading out from Lagos. The diaspora travel narratives of the late twentieth century and early twenty-first century discussed in this chapter also operate with new maps to guide their journeys, setting them free from the legacies of family and lost fathers, but they hold a different preoccupation: rather than people, they are suffused with literature and other art forms, and tourism in the case of Saro-Wiwa's text, as the basis of the new routes their authors take. Simultaneously, though, their use of literary culture and art forms as a way to foster and chart their changing relationships with Nigeria reminds us of the way the Yoruba newspaper travel writers of the early twentieth century used travel narratives to both reflect and encourage along the spread of the nascent Yoruba print culture of the age. In both cases, travel and literary culture are intimately bound up with one another.

As well as straddling the boundaries between Nigerian and overseas through the ambivalently perceived figure of the *tòkunbò̩*, the returnee from overseas, these texts of diaspora return cross other boundaries: between binaries of race and culture, between fiction and non-fiction, and between southwest Nigeria and the rest of Nigeria. Even though Májà-Pearce's and Saro-Wiwa's travel narratives are more closely aligned to the conventional Western travelogue than some of the other texts discussed in this book, in their search for lost fathers and fatherlands, their apparently conventional travel narratives of post-colonial return also aspire, along with Cole's travel novel, to border-crossing, ambivalence and 'openness' as a way of understanding Nigeria. The Epilogue takes up this way of reading travel writing, as it considers the categories and borders both undermined and reified by the travellers and their texts discussed throughout this book.

# Epilogue: Southwest Nigerian travel writing and literary culture at the crossroads

Excitement seems to be gathering amongst contemporary Nigeria's writers about the potentials of travel writing. Noo Saro-Wiwa may have led the way in encouraging the mainstream visibility of Nigerian travel writers in the West, but since 2014, where the main part of this book's discussion ends, the genre has also been adopted by some of contemporary Nigeria's most promising writers, as well as some who are already more prominent. Invisible Borders, a trans-African collective of writers and photographers, has embarked on a regular series of road trips across the African continent, which I discuss in more detail below; poet and playwright Níyì Òṣúndáre has recently published a book of travel poetry, *If Only the Road Could Talk* (2017), inspired by his journeys in Africa, Asia and Europe; travel writer Lọlá Akínmádé Åkerström's *Due North* (2017) relates, through photography and travel narratives, the author's travels across Africa, Asia, Europe and the Americas; writer and art critic Emmanuel Iduma, one of the founders of the literary magazine *Saraba* and a writer with Invisible Borders, has just published *A Stranger's Pose* (2018), a much-anticipated book of African travel writing and photography; Kọ́lá Túbọ̀sún, too, has just published *Edwardsville by Heart* (2018), a poetry collection about his travels in the US; and in 2016, emerging poet and travel writer Tọ́pẹ́ Salaudeen-Adégọ̀ke established an online travel writing journal, *Fortunate Traveller*, which has solicited travel writing from poets Níran Òkéwọlé, Tádé Ìpàdéọlá, Fẹ́mi Oyèbọ̀dé and Jùmọ̀kẹ́ Verissimo, amongst others.[1] This turn by literary writers to occasional travel writing continues the tradition that we have seen stretching back to I. B. Thomas, E. A. Akintán, Isaac Délànọ̀ and D. Ọ. Fágúnwà, all accomplished writers who published travel writing alongside their better-known novels. But the contemporary moment also seems to be a time when the possibilities for travel writing by Nigerian writers are stretching wide open. Were this book to be written ten years from now, when this new generation of travel writers has fully established itself, its later chapters

---

[1] I am a co-founder of the journal *Fortunate Traveller*, with some responsibility for editorial work and the overall strategy of the journal, but the idea behind the journal was Salaudeen-Adégòkè's and most of the work is done by him.

would likely be bursting with new, experimental work by both emerging and established writers.

Across the African continent, African travellers and writers have been similarly reclaiming travel writing and travel itself as practices involving Africans and African gazes. In 2010, the Chinua Achebe Center for African Writers and Arts at Bard College and South African literary magazine *Chimurenga* established 'Pilgrimages', an ambitious travel writing project that sent fourteen African writers to thirteen African cities and one Brazilian city during the football World Cup hosted in South Africa that year. The intention was that each of the writers should produce 'non-fiction books' about their travels, which would 'prompt a shift in the focus of African reportage'.[2] Some of the travel narratives that resulted were published in the *African Cities Reader*, a literary journal published by Chimurenga Magazine and the University of Cape Town's African Centre for Cities. The three volumes of the *African Cities Reader* that have to date been published were themselves an ambitious attempt to offer new perspectives on African cities, and included a number of travel narratives by African writers (including, from Nigeria, Chris Abani, Akin Adéṣòkàn, Emeka Ogboh, Téjú Cole and Jùmọ̀ké Verissimo). In the decade since the Pilgrimages project began, writers from across the African continent such as Kofi Akpabli, Maskarm Haile and Sihle Khumalo have published travel narratives in book form, and African travel writers have discussed their work in dedicated panels at literary festivals such as the Pa Gya! Festival in Accra and the Aké Festival in Lagos in 2018.[3]

Alongside the growth of interest in travel writing as part of Nigeria's booming literary culture, the rapid spread of access to the internet and social media has also led to the emergence of new forms of both travel and travel narrative centred on tourism. Chapter 6 left the story of Nigeria's online travel writing scene in 2014, when writers such as Pèlú Awófèṣò, Fọlárìn Kọláwọle, Lápé Ṣóẹ̀tán and Kọlá Túbọsún were popularising travel blogging as a form of travel writing. Since then, a new wave of Nigerian travellers has rapidly launched itself into the online space, combining accounts of their own and others' travels

[2] 'Pilgrimages', in *African Cities Reader: Mobilities and Fixtures,* ed. by Ntone Edjabe and Edgar Pieterse (Vlaeberg: Chimurenga and the African Centre for Cities, 2011), p. 42.

[3] Kofi Akpabli, *A Sense of Savannah: Tales of a Friendly Walk Through Northern Ghana* (Accra: TREC, 2011); Kofi Akpabli, *Tickling the Ghanaian: Encounters with Contemporary Culture* (Accra: TREC, 2011); Maskarm Haile, *Abyssinian Nomad: An African Woman's Journey of Love, Loss, & Adventure from Cape to Cairo* (n.p., 2018); Sihle Khumalo, *Dark Continent, My Black Arse* (Cape Town: Umuzi, 2007); Sihle Khumalo, *Heart of Africa: Centre of My Gravity* (Cape Town: Umuzi, 2009); Sihle Khumalo, *Almost Sleeping my Way to Timbuktu: West Africa on a Shoestring by Public Transport with no French* (Cape Town: Umuzi, 2013).

in Nigeria and around the world with advice on how to travel, photography and writing across social media platforms such as Instagram, Facebook and Twitter. Few of these travellers are solely or even principally writers; some combine travel blogging with photography, while others run tourism businesses, offering tours and package trips to primarily Nigerian travellers who want to travel both within Nigeria and beyond. For these bloggers and tourism entrepreneurs, travel blogging, along with their use of social media platforms such as the photograph-sharing platform Instagram, feeds into their tour operations as they share both written accounts of their trips and lively and adventurous visual images of the travellers who take part in their trips around Nigeria. In doing so, these travellers continue to combine some of the features that I argued in Chapter 6 are characteristic of recent southwest Nigerian travel writing: the performance of being a traveller, and the notion of leisure travel as improving, modern and indicative of a middle-class habitus, or a form of 'conspicuous cosmopolitanism', to borrow Krystal Strong and Shaun Ossei-Owusu's formulation.[4] They continue to encourage other Nigerians to travel through their own example, but what is new about their travel blogging and photography is their confidence that other Nigerians will want to travel, as the success of many of these new tour operators demonstrates.

It remains to be seen whether Nigerian travel writers will adopt the distinction between travel and tourism that has become characteristic of Western travel writing. Tọ́pẹ́ Salaudeen-Adégòkè, editor of the travel journal *Fortunate Traveller* and himself a travel writer, expresses discomfort with travel writer Pèlú Awófèsò's emphasis on tourism (see Chapter 6): 'I don't see him as a traveller but a tourist [...] Pèlú Awófèsò is a sightseer, he is more interested in beautiful places, monuments, museums, palaces that promote tourism when he travels'.[5] Instead, Salaudeen-Adégòkè emphasises the alignment between travel writing and literary fiction when he explains his belief that Nigerian travel writing, along with other forms of creative non-fiction, is due the kind of visibility that Nigerian fiction currently enjoys:

> I anticipate African writers will shift focus from fiction and engage non-fiction in the future when awards and prizes are institutionalised for the genre. When we have awards like, say, the Thomas Cook Travel Book Award, it will stimulate interest in the genre and young writers will find it attractive and established writers will come into itinerary narratives.[6]

[4] Krystal Strong and Shaun Ossei-Owusu, 'Naija Boy Remix: Afroexploitation and the New Media Creative -Economies of Cosmopolitan African Youth', *Journal of African Cultural Studies* 26.2 (2014), pp. 189–205.

[5] Tọ́pẹ́ Salaudeen-Adégòkè, interviewed by Rebecca Jones, 24 June 2016, via email.

[6] Ibid. The recent acclaim for *Safe House* (2016), an anthology of African creative non-fiction edited by Ellah Wakatama Allfrey that includes several pieces of travel

However, although Salaudeen-Adégòkè and Awófẹ̀sọ̀'s ideas of the right kind of travel and traveller may differ, they share a sense of the importance of travel and travel writing in creating more knowledgeable Nigerians; Salaudeen-Adégòkè, echoing Awófẹ̀sọ̀, suggests that Nigerians should 'travel their own country and observe for themselves the peculiarities of their country so as to learn to live in unity'. The purpose of travel writing, for him, is 'to pleasurably cure ignorance'.[7] Like Awófẹ̀sọ̀, Salaudeen-Adégòkè pictures travel narratives translating the sensory experience of travel for the reader who has not travelled herself:

> I write so people can enjoy and discover the pleasure of travel so that my readers get to know the people I meet that grace what they perceive as dots on the map, and see them, hear them and smell them. I want to personify places so any reader could easily have clear idea of those places. And maybe exclaim, 'Oh! This is my town!', 'I have been to that village before!', 'I never knew that part of the city!'[8]

In an essay on the 'portfolio of influences' behind his recent travel book, *A Stranger's Pose*, Emmanuel Iduma, too, complicates distinctions between tourism-focused travel writing and literary travel writing; he acknowledges Awófẹ̀sọ̀'s 'tour-guide lingo' and 'adulatory prose', but reads Awófẹ̀sọ̀'s writing, along with Noo Saro-Wiwa's, as 'aptly postcolonial, a way to transcend and go beyond the legacies of colonialism', putting them in the same bracket as what Iduma describes as Wọlé Ṣóyínká's 'similar trans-national trip around 1960, the year of Nigeria's Independence', recalled in Ṣóyínká's memoir, *You Must Set Forth At Dawn* (2006): 'He traveled around the country in a Land Rover, with a tape-recorder and a camera, sponsored by the Rockefeller Foundation, who expected him to write a book on drama. The book was never written, but the experience, one could argue, informed his 1965 play *The Road*'.[9] Alongside Ṣóyínká, Iduma invokes as his Nigerian literary forebears the fiction of Amos Tutùọlá and Tádé Ìpàdéọlá's poetry collection *The Sahara Testaments* (2013), gesturing to the broad sense of travel writing as a genre extending beyond non-fiction that has underpinned this book.

In addition, both Iduma and Salaudeen-Adégòkè suggest that they hold the same ambivalent relation to Western travel writing about Africa as that which

---

writing, suggests that Salaudeen-Adégòkè's aspirations for African creative non-fiction are not unfounded.

[7] Ibid.

[8] Ibid.

[9] Emmanuel Iduma, *How to Be an African Travel Writer in Africa?* (2018) <https://lithub.com/how-to-be-an-african-travel-writer-in-africa/> [accessed 23 February 2019].

has characterised much of the travel writing we have encountered in his book, especially in more recent decades. Salaudeen-Adégòkè describes how he was inspired initially by medieval English adventure literature and by contemporary Western travel literature, particularly Paul Theroux. However, he also considers himself to be writing against what he calls 'the outlandish paganish exposé' of nineteenth-century missionary travel writing about Nigeria; he cites North American Baptist missionary W. H. Clarke's *Travels and Explorations in Yorubaland 1854–1848* as an example, referring, perhaps, to Clarke's descriptions of the Yoruba people as 'enshrouded in almost impenetrable darkness and in one sense need the light of heaven as much of as those who have sunken deeper into the pit of ruin'.[10] This form of missionary travel writing, with its hierarchies of religion and 'civilisation', is the kind of Western travel writing that he writes against, producing what he sees as a more even-handed account of Nigeria, even as he also admires the work of other Western travel writers. Iduma, too, recognizes the complexities of the legacy of Western travel writing about Africa: acknowledging that he admires Polish travel writer Ryszard Kapuściński's 'flights of lyricism', he adds that 'I do not believe that only Africans should write stories about life in Africa, just as it is facetious to imagine Europe written about only by Europeans'. 'It seems to me', he concludes, that 'those who do not claim an African country as their place of origin enrich African writing, but only as far as they do not assume that a distance in worldview can be bridged by a single, or series of visits.' Yet simultaneously, conscious of the heavy weight of 'derogatory narratives' about Africa, he characterises his own travel writing as a work of 'repair', 'a way to participate in a genre that historically speaks for – rather than with, or even to – me'.[11]

One of the ways that Iduma has found a way into the genre to enact this 'repair' has been through experimenting with form. Iduma's African travelogue *A Stranger's Pose* combines writing with photography (chiefly by other photographers); this movement back and forth between the visual and the verbal underscores the fragmented form that characterises the whole text, involving movements back and forth between voices, places and perspectives, while the insertion of images by other photographers into the narrative emphasises the role of other gazes and viewpoints in shaping Iduma's own travels and narrative. Other travel writers are similarly exploring the potential for combining the verbal and the visual. Swedish-Nigerian travel writer and photographer Lọlá Akínmádé Åkerström, whose work focuses mostly on destinations outside Nigeria, but who has also published travel writing and photography about her hometown of Lagos, combines writing and photographs throughout her work,

[10] Clarke, *Travels & Explorations in Yorubaland (1854–1858)*, pp. 276–7; Salaudeen-Adégòkè, interviewed by Jones, 24 June 2016, via email.
[11] Iduma, *How to Be an African Travel Writer in Africa?*

in book form, online and in print publications. Téjú Cole's *Every Day is For the Thief* (see Chapter 7), meanwhile, blends writing with photographic vignettes from around Lagos, most of them not commented on in the text, but left as if a mark of the presence of the traveller's gaze as well as his verbal imagination.

The visual image is also becoming increasingly important in travel writing and blogging more focused on tourism, fuelled in part by the accessibility of photography in the era of the smartphone and the ease of publishing images online. Travel blogger Lápé Ṣóẹ̀tán describes how 'I'm always aware of the importance of taking pictures [...] When I go to a place, I'm constantly think-ing, oh will this look good in a picture, so I take several'.[12] By creating visual and textual images of fellow Nigerians travelling and enjoying Nigeria, travel writers and internet-based tour operators alike often aim to create mirror im-ages that will produce more Nigerian travellers by encouraging viewers to see themselves, too, as prospective travellers – just as writers such as Pèlú Awófèṣò aim to do with their writing.

One of the most significant and ambitious African travel writing projects to have emerged in the last decade, and one that epitomises this fascination with the conjunction of the visual and the verbal in contemporary travel narratives, is the Invisible Borders Trans-African Photographers Organisation. The organi-sation was established in 2009 and visual artist and writer Emeka Okereke is now its artistic director. Since 2009, Invisible Borders has regularly invited a group of African photographers, filmmakers and writers to make a long journey, mainly by road, from Lagos to another city, usually in Africa: destinations have included Bamako, Addis Ababa, Lubumbashi, Sarajevo and Maputo. Although based in Lagos, Invisible Borders describes itself as a trans-African organisa-tion; it invites artists from across Africa to participate. The artists document their road trips in photography, writing and film, and their work is published as blog posts on the Invisible Borders website and, recently, smartphone app as they travel; selected photographs and written pieces have also been displayed in exhibitions and published in chapbooks.

In 2016 and 2017, the road trip participants were exclusively Nigerian writ-ers and photographers; rather than travelling across the African continent, their journeys were trans-Nigerian, and these editions of the project were titled 'Borders Within'. The 'Borders Within' trans-Nigerian road trip of 2016 aimed to 'map diversity across regions, states and ethnic formations in post-colonial Nigeria', and its artists 'interrogated both the elusive and apparent borders within the country years after the amalgamation of its Northern and South-ern Protectorates'. Its writers, photographers and administrators – Innocent Ekejiuba, Yínká Elújọba, Yagazie Emezi, Emmanuel Iduma, Ellen Kondowe,

---

[12] Ṣóẹ̀tán, interviewed by Jones, 28 April 2016, Lagos, Nigeria.

Zaynab Odunsi, Emeka Okereke, Uche Okonkwo and Eloghosa Osunde – travelled for six weeks across Nigeria, making, as Okereke writes, 'about 15 stops in cities scattered across all the regions of the country'.[13] For the 2017 iteration of the project, the participants – this time, James Bekenawei, Innocent Ekejiuba, Yínká Elújọba, Kẹmi Fálọ́dún, Nengi Nelson, Kechi Nomu, Kenechukwu Nwatu, Emeka Okereke and Amara Nicole Okolo – traced a different route across Nigeria; they travelled north from Lagos, through Ìbàdàn and Ìlọrin to the northern cities of Minna, Sokoto, Bauchi and Zaria, and then back through Jos and Lafia to the southern cities of Afikpo and Yenagoa, before returning to Lagos via Àkúrẹ́. During this second road trip, the artists sought to 'draw a map that is at once historical and contemporary while elucidating the ambiguities of what it means to be Nigerian', and produce 'impressionistic, yet critical readings of contemporary Nigeria'. Once again, the project emphasised the way that travel enabled its artists to encounter Nigeria's 'borders within', asking questions such as: 'Who am I in relation to the artificial map? How am I [a] product of what I have been inevitably named? How do I interact across the several visible and invisible borders I confront as a Nigerian?'[14] Framing their project insistently around Nigeria, the 'Borders Within' writers', in common with many of the post-independence travel writers we have encountered in this book, emphasise their Nigerian-ness rather than ethnic or regional affiliations; as such, the lens of 'southwest Nigerian' travel writing invoked by this book becomes redundant, as the 'Borders Within' project insists on being Nigerian. At the same time, the project makes space for individual writers to reflect on their own histories and identities, including regional and ethnic identities, as they travel; therefore, while 'Borders Within' and the writing it produces may be Nigerian, it is a form of Nigerian-ness that also makes space for other affiliations alongside and within it, including those held by individual writers.

   While travelling, each of the artists published short pieces of writing on the 'Borders Within' website, accompanied by at least one photograph by one of the travelling photographers. The form of the pieces varies from artist to artist, but most pieces are short, around five hundred words in length, and describe a moment or encounter from a stop on the road trip, or the artist's reflections on the process of travel and writing or photography. The writing that has resulted from both trans-Nigerian road trips is inherently polyphonic, offering the varied perspectives of the multiple writers on each trip, so it is difficult to generalise about its writers' mode of travel writing. Nonetheless, taken as a

---

[13] Emeka Okereke, *Welcome and Join Us On 'The Borders Within: Trans-Nigerian Road Trip'* (2016) <http://www.borders-within.com/hello-world/> [accessed 29 December 2018].

[14] Borders Within, *About Borders within II* (n.d.) <http://www.borders-within.com/about-borders-within-ii/> [accessed 29 December 2018].

body of work, 'Borders Within' is so self-reflexive about the practice of both travel and travel writing (and photography) that it comes the closest of all the texts discussed in this book to constituting its own theorisation of travel and travel writing. Themes its writers come back to repeatedly include the nature of Nigeria's diversity, the differences and commonalities between Nigerians and preconceptions of each other, the challenges and possibilities of language and translation, gaps and misunderstandings between traveller and travellee, the role of the gaze and visuality in travel and travel writing, the creation of archives and the relationship between history, documentation and witnessing.

Above all, the project's writings circle insistently around the notion of border-crossings, both literal and metaphorical. The 'Invisible Borders' referenced in the organisation's name refer to its founders' sense that the African continent is characterised by 'invisible' borders and frontiers between peoples, as well as the literal borders between nations, and it envisages itself, through travel and art, 'contributing to the patching of numerous gaps and misconceptions posed by frontiers within the fifty-four countries of Africa through art and photography', as well as overcoming borders through trans-African exchange between its artists and audiences.[15] The organisation adopts a similar sense of the power of borders within Nigeria for its 'Borders Within' editions. 'How do I interact across the several visible and invisible borders I confront as a Nigerian?', asks the statement of approach for the 2017 road trip, and this edition of the road trip centres on Nigeria's heterogeneity and its internal borders between peoples, particularly borders of ethnicity and language. Travel, in the writings of the 'Borders Within' artists, is often seen as a way of crossing borders – not just to overcome them, but also to experience and interrogate them through an emphasis on the individual traveller's subjectivity. For instance, writer and photographer James Bekenawei, who participated in the 2017 road trip, writes that he intends to 'explore the Nigerian-ness of things. The subtle similarities and corresponding differences that cuts across different regions. How that Nigerianness is expressed on the road and how it changes across different places.'[16] The road is understood as a border-zone, and the traveller crosses borders through his or her continual movement, able to see both differences and similarities as he or she confronts such borders.

---

[15] Invisible Borders, *Manifesto* (n.d.) <http://invisible-borders.com/manifesto/> [accessed 1 January 2019].

[16] James Bekenawei, *Artist Statement – 'On This Journey, I Intend to Explore the Nigerianness of Things… How That Nigerianness Is Expressed on the Road and How It Changes across Different Places'* (2017) <http://www.borders-within.com/artist-statement-on-this-journey-i-intend-to-explore-the-nigerianness-of-things-how-that-nigerianness-is-expressed-on-the-road-and-how-it-changes-across-different-places/> [accessed 29 December 2018].

Some of the project's writers demonstrate a particular intellectual and ethical commitment to border-crossing through travel. In a piece called 'Three Notes on Movement', writer Yínká Elújọba writes of the borders on maps as 'leaning on a contemptible premise: that an entity must exist on a single side of a dividing line' – but, he adds, 'nothing undermines a border like movement – to move is to shift the full-stop in a conversation'. The traveller, in their movement, is one who can undermine the 'contemptible premise' that divides one thing from another, and who can expose and thereby weaken a border. For Elújọba, however, '[m]ovement is the characteristic of every living thing'; the traveller embodies a more general border-crossing potential of humanity.[17] In a companion piece, his 'Final Notes on Movement', Elújọba concludes that through travel, 'I push away this map before me, this construct that fails so elegantly to define who I am. I embrace instead, the map my mind has made: of people, of places, of lines I have carried my body through, of hours filled with targeted and undulating questioning.'[18] Echoing Invisible Borders' overall emphasis on being a *trans*-African organisation, Elújọba reminds us of the importance of 'trans', or 'movement across' in the work of the traveller her- or himself, and the creative potential of this movement in bringing about new ways of seeing Nigeria or the world more broadly – a potential that Elújọba suggests lies within 'every living thing' through the power of movement.

Despite Elújọba's desire to 'undermine' Nigeria's internal borders, the 'Borders Within' writers seem to envisage themselves not so much creating a united or 'detribalised' Nigeria, as some of the other writers we have encountered in this book have done, but as producing a 'critical reading' of Nigeria through its borders, or its internal differences and divisions. Nonetheless, in a piece called 'How Much is a Picture Worth?', James Bekenawei suggests a desire to produce a different narrative of Nigeria, characterising his work as a form of what Patrick Holland and Graham Huggan term 'countertravel writing'.[19] 'Every day as we transit between cities', he writes:

> I redefine what it means to own our narrative, to tell our story differently and correctly. I remind myself to always remember what pisses me off about the Western Media. About how they photograph things relating to Africa, about how they capture Nigeria, and about photographs by Nigerian documentary photographers I consider demeaning. I remind myself that I ought to do things differently, I have to do things differently, I must do things differently.

---

[17] Yinka Elujoba, *Three Notes on Movement* (2016) <http://www.borders-within.com/three-notes-on-movement/> [accessed 29 December 2018].

[18] Yinka Elujoba, *Final Notes on Movement* (2016) <http://www.borders-within.com/final-notes-on-movement/> [accessed 29 December 2018].

[19] Holland and Huggan, *Tourists with Typewriters*, p. 21.

A similar desire to 'tell our story differently and correctly' leads many of the 'Borders Within' artists to consider self-reflexively the ethics of the traveller's gaze in their work. Recognising their position as not only outsider-observers in many of the places to which they travel, but also as Nigerians privileged by the appearance of wealth, education or mobility in comparison to many of those they encounter on their journeys, the writers often reflect on the power and limitations of their gaze and positionality, as does Bekenawei:

> I remind myself that I am not a voyeur. I am not here just to take pictures. To intrude people's privacy, force myself into their personal space and insert a preconceived narrative on them. I re-echo Emeka Okereke's sentiment that I do not have the right to tell other people's stories. I am not a savior appearing with a halo disguise as a camera to shine the light on their dark world. They have always been telling their stories and because these stories haven't been heard by others outside their space doesn't make them less valid.[20]

This emphasis on not intruding on others through the traveller's gaze is echoed in several other pieces, in which the writers describe their response to other Nigerians rejecting their presence. In 'Notes on Seeing', Kẹ́mi Fálọ́dún describes how her attempt at dialogue was rejected by a woman selling corn in Ìlọrin: 'I don't want to talk to you, she says. Go meet other people. Why do you even want to speak to me? Go.' 'It's a privilege to be allowed into other people's spaces', Fálọ́dún reflects, 'not my right. Not my right.'[21] In a piece on Warri, writer and photographer Eloghosa Osunde describes how, as she sought to take a photograph of a teenage boy, she was approached by a woman who said: 'You want to capture his poverty, our poverty.' Osunde describes how she sought neither to retreat from the implications of the accusation, nor to underestimate the value of dignified portraits of her subjects:

> I'm learning that you can preserve a person's dignity, pull them out from the claws of shame, by telling their story correctly. And you can corrode their identity by emphasizing the wrong things. I know that even though I hadn't been wrong at all in that context, I could have been in another.[22]

As this response suggests, rather than allowing rejection to overwhelm their narratives, or despairing at the possibility of dignified and accurate representation of others, the writers work out several strategies for repositioning

---

[20] James Bekenawei, *How Much a Picture Worth?* (2017) <http://www.borders-within.com/how-much-a-picture-worth/> [accessed 1 January 2019].

[21] Kemi Falodun, *Notes on Seeing* (2017) <http://www.borders-within.com/notes-on-seeing/> [accessed 29 December 2018].

[22] Eloghosa Osunde, *Warri: A Two-Part Portrait* (2016) <http://www.borders-within.com/warri-a-two-part-portrait-2/> [accessed 1 January 2019].

themselves as travel writers alert to the ethics of their enterprise. Emmanuel Iduma writes that '[m]y prompt has always been the notion of an intimate stranger: a person who's in a place for a short period, but hopes to relate with those encountered with empathy and attention'.[23] Meanwhile, adopting the figure of exchange that pervades the work of several of the project's writers, Kẹ́mi Fálọ́dún turns the traveller's gaze back onto the traveller:

> In occupying spaces in other people's lives, how much is too much? When do we talk from the entrance, raising our voices, and at what point do we come in? In the past few weeks, we – my co-travellers and I – have let ourselves into unfamiliar spaces, exposing ourselves to be observed. Who are you people? What do you do? Where are you from? Why do you want to speak to me?[24]

The 'Borders Within' artists also experiment with form to reflect the challenges of representing people and places they encounter. Seen as a collective body of work, the travel narratives produced by the project's writers are a collection of polyphonic fragments, as each writer produces not a linear, encompassing narrative of their journey, but rather a series of blog posts giving their impressions and reflections on particular moments of the trip, often according to a theme the writer has chosen. This sense of fragmentation extends formally to the pieces themselves; alongside photo essays and pieces written in a conventional linear style, relating anecdotes or reflecting on encounters from the writers' journeys, several pieces by Yínká Elújọba, James Bekenawei, Innocent Ekejiuba, Nengi Nelson and Eloghosa Osunde are written in variations on a fragmented style, juxtaposing short, related impressions or reflections. In doing so, these writers acknowledge the necessarily incomplete or partial nature of narratives they produce from their fleeting impressions of the places to which they travel.

Simultaneously, in working with many different fragments of text, the writers celebrate the value of polyphonic writing from multiple perspectives and telling numerous different stories, reflecting the organisation's sense that Nigeria is home to 'multiple histories' that must be illuminated 'through a mishmash of voices: ethnicities, religions, and visions of modernity'.[25] Iduma explains his own sense of how the multiplicity he encountered during his travels, and the difficulty of retrieving linear narrative from the memory of his journeys demanded a fragmented, non-linear form, a version of this 'mishmash':

---

[23] Emmanuel Iduma, *A Statement of Intent* (2016) <http://www.borders-within.com/statement-of-intent/> [accessed 29 December 2018].

[24] Kemi Falodun, *Notes on Seeing* (2017) <http://www.borders-within.com/notes-on-seeing/> [accessed 2 April 2019].

[25] Borders Within, *About Borders Within* (n.d.) <http://www.borders-within.com/sample-page/> [accessed 2 April 2019].

As a culmination: I knew I would write something extended at the end of the trips, but traditional travel writing formats didn't appeal to me. My memories, I perceived, had taken uncertain detours, as a result of passing time. So I set out to complete a manuscript structured as fragments; a collection of stories imagined, remembered, and collected (forthcoming as *A Stranger's Pose*). I wrote about the lives that entered mine: co-travelers, photographers, wayfarers, strangers, and residents.[26]

A piece by Yínká Elújọba offers another example of formal experimentation; quoting the writer's own assertion that 'movement is the character of every living thing', the piece is written as a paragraph-long sentence, ending with the question, 'how your body would constitute itself if all of the world was simply one long continuous road?'. The form echoes the 'long and narrow' road that the writer describes as the piece opens, allowing words and phrases to run into each other as if in movement.[27] Movement becomes form, as the 'Borders Within' writers look for ways to transform the process of travel into the text itself.

The emphasis on border-crossing in the 'Borders Within' road trips points to the broader significance of travel writing as a border-crossing form in the contemporary age. Theories of world literature and postcoloniality have emphasised the centrality of movement across borders, particularly international borders, in the production, circulation and reception of literary texts. This movement is often understood as a contemporary phenomenon in the age of postcoloniality, globalisation, digital culture and, in Africa and its diaspora, the Afropolitan – 'so that', as Helen Cousins and Pauline Dodgson-Katiyo write, 'being away from home is normalized, and even the need to be geographically connected to a home place is no longer necessary'.[28]

Yet mobility has long been central to the production of literary texts. As Eileen Julien argues, the novel is a global 'creole' product, made possible out of 'the context of movement across borders' and 'born from the contact of peoples and cultures'.[29] Similarly, interchange across not just international borders but also borders *within* Nigeria – physical, literary, intellectual, social and cultural – has also underpinned the production, circulation and reception of travel writing in southwest Nigeria. Border-crossing, and the ability to stand at the crossroads between different parts of Nigeria and different ways

---

[26] Emmanuel Iduma, *A Statement of Intent* (2016) <http://www.borders-within.com/statement-of-intent/> [accessed 2 April 2019].

[27] Yinka Elujoba, *A Thinking, Moving Body* (2017) <http://www.borders-within.com/a-thinking-moving-body/> [accessed 29 December 2018].

[28] Cousins and Dodgson-Katiyo, 'Leaving Home/Returning Home', 5.

[29] Julien, 'The Extroverted African Novel', 675.

of being Nigerian, are imagined as the particular power of the traveller in many of the texts examined in this book. The recognition of their ambivalent position as both at home and a stranger that we see in some diaspora return travel narratives is not alien to travel writing by southwest Nigerians who live within Nigeria, who often find themselves, although from a different perspective, in the position of being at once at home and a stranger within Nigeria, reflecting on powerful differences in ways of life within Nigeria: not only between Nigerians of different ethnic groups, religions and languages, but also between 'civilisation' and 'our ways', between past, present and future, between 'clerk' and 'native', and between Lagos and the Yoruba region. In some cases, the traveller depicts themselves slipping between regional or ethnic and national affiliations, between being Western and Nigerian, between 'civilised' and 'native' ways of life, even if, at the same time, they may seek to concretise other categories. Their texts also frequently slip between genres, sometimes between languages, and even, as we have seen in some cases, between pronouns used to denote both self and Nigerian others. They reveal and sometimes revel in underlying instabilities in all of these categories, even as they also seek to create or reinforce communal formations such as particular towns and cities, the Yoruba people or Nigeria, and the sense of cultural difference and superiority often ascribed to Lagos. The traveller is thus frequently invoked as a liminal figure, imagined as one who stands at a crossroads and can move back and forth in time, ideas, cultures, ways of being and space, translating parts of Nigeria, or Nigerians, to each other.

Even within the Yoruba-speaking region, writers find themselves translating: literally, from one dialect to another, as both Crowther and Délànọ̀ claimed they struggled to do, or between Yoruba and English, but also in the form of cultural translation between 'native' and 'civilised' ways in the early twentieth century, or between perceived rural and urban differences in more recent years. Travellers have sometimes adopted the position of intra-Nigerian translator, aiming to make Nigerians from one part of the nation speak to and understand those from another, and therefore know each other better, although that translation has often been partial, one-sided and mediated by the translator's own biases – as in the case of I. B. Thomas's limited translations of southeast Nigerian languages, in the incomprehension many writers register as they encounter other Nigerian languages, or the mischievous mistranslations that Chibuzor Mirian Azubuike remarks upon in her NYSC narrative. Travel writers have also imagined themselves translating culture in its broadest sense, making parts of Nigeria intelligible for their readers so that they become more knowledgeable Nigerians, less afraid of one another and less prone to misunderstanding each other – as cannibals, for instance. But this utopian sense that through knowing each other better, Nigerian differences can be overcome is also sometimes one-sided; writers such as Délànọ̀, Awófẹ̀sọ̀ and Azubuike have tended to depict themselves as the cosmopolitan subject doing the translating, while it is less clear that those whose ways of life they are translating also participate in this encounter as fellow cosmopolitan subjects.

Some writers' ability to stand at the crossroads in this way can be read as a product of their diaspora or creole subjectivity and writing, as in the case of Samuel Àjàyí Crowther, or in the Lagos newspaper travel writers of the 1920s and 1930s. Adéwálé Májà-Pearce, meanwhile, posits this back and forth between two or more ways of being as a form of hybridity, as he uses travel to interrogate his own position in relation to his English and Yoruba heritage. For these writers, this crossroads position can therefore induce anxiety, confusion and doubt, but it can also be productive and creative. Indeed, for many travel writers, travel enables transformation as well as translation, creating new ways of being – whether as more knowledgeable Nigerians, or simply better, more experienced versions of the self. Fágúnwà's questing travellers cross borders between the human and the spiritual realm and in doing so, are imagined to become better, richer versions of themselves – although Tutùolá and Okri, in different ways, question the inevitability of the idealised transformation of self through travel. The border-crosser powerfully undermines some forms of order and reinforces others, and yet does so in a way that is creative and constitutive of self and of place. Travel thus constitutes one of the metaphors through which southwest Nigerian writers have written of ways of knowing self and other in Nigeria.

Although this book has focused on southwest Nigerian writing about Nigeria as its lens, both 'southwest Nigeria' and 'Nigeria', as well as the implicit 'Yoruba' contained within 'southwest Nigeria', are all unstable categories, imagined, reflected and sustained through travel writing, as well as through other forms of literary and cultural products. Travel writers encounter Nigeria's heterogeneity: difference within the Yoruba-speaking region; the constitutive heterogeneity of Yoruba towns, imagined to have been created through waves of travellers of diverse origins; the perceived exoticism of southeast or northern Nigeria; and the complexities of translation, both linguistic and cultural, across the nation. In some earlier twentieth-century travel writing, regional or ethnic identities appear a more salient category than 'Nigeria': travel writers seem more comfortable calling themselves Lagosian or Yoruba than Nigerian, and distance themselves both from northern Nigeria and from other southern Nigerians whom they perceive to be less 'civilised', in an age when overlapping and competing cultural nationalist, regional and nationalist politics were all beginning to take shape. But 'Yoruba' is also an unstable category – created and reinforced through difference, and through the 'cultural work' of the region's intellectuals, including its travel writers, and often claimed unevenly, as Lagosian writers such as Délànọ̀ both make claims to being Yoruba and distinguish themselves from the 'hinterland' or 'natives'. After Nigerian independence and the civil war, we see amongst some writers a pressure to make ethnicity give way to a Nigerian national identity – that is, to create a sense of a Nigerian nation that coincides with the (fragile) existence of the state. Travel writing appears to some writers a useful medium for doing this, as writers imagine that it is better knowledge of Nigerian others – of their shared humanity or Nigerian-ness, and their lack of difference from readers – that is lacking in fostering a sense of Nigerian nationhood. The southwest Nigerian travel writers discussed in this book increasingly refer to themselves as 'Nigerian', and picture themselves travelling within 'Nigeria', even as they also maintain a sense of their difference from fellow Nigerians, as Lagosians, for instance. The power of travel and travel writing for some of these writers is that it allows them to slip both physically and culturally between categories such as Lagosian, Yoruba, Nigerian, and African, investigating their overlaps while sometimes aligning themselves with one or another. Travel and travel writing are a means through which these writers both celebrate and flatten difference; difference becomes part of what it means to be a postcolonial Nigerian, rather than a marker of 'tribe' or ethnicity, as some of these writers imagine it has been previously. At the same time while, on the surface, travel writers often celebrate their own ability to produce better knowledge of others within Nigeria or the ability of travel to transform the traveller, we have seen how their texts themselves can often be read (sometimes against the grain) as admitting or revealing greater doubts or anxieties about travel, about the intra-Nigerian encounters they represent or about the dangers of the nation.

The influence of outside, and of travellers from outside, also contributes to making Nigerian and other collective identities. J. Lorand Matory argues that as a political and cultural identity, 'Yoruba-ness' was created by 'the creole society of the [West African] Coast', particularly the *Sàró* and Afro-Latin returnees from Brazil, and through their interchange and dialogue with the Afro-Brazilian diaspora and its intellectuals.[30] Through travel writing, too, Yoruba-ness – and also Nigerian-ness – is created in contact with the rest of the world, from Samuel Àjàyí Crowther's perspective as a 'black whiteman', to the value placed on *ọ̀làjú*, often taken to mean an orientation towards externality, and the ambivalent prestige of the *tòkunbọ̀*, returning to Yorubaland or Nigeria from overseas – including the diaspora return narrative itself, which helps tell new stories about Nigeria. We can thus read some travel narratives through an idealisation of what Májà-Pearce and Cole figure as 'openness', or a form of cosmopolitanism that emphasises the role of 'elsewhere' in creating narratives of home.

---

[30] Matory, *Black Atlantic Religion*, p. 51.

When some of these writers ask us to think beyond ethnicity in understanding Nigeria, they implicitly suggest that we must *read* beyond ethnicity, too. It is certainly possible, in the light of the narrative of Nigerian nation produced by some of these writers, to read them beyond the lens of 'southwest Nigeria'. It may be that for some contemporary Nigerian writers who see themselves writing into this national conversation, conducted mainly in English, 'Nigeria' is a more appropriate frame of reference than 'southwest Nigeria' or any other regional appellation – and ties of class, perspective and aspiration, along with the use of the English language, might be more binding than the differences of ethnicity that appear to separate these writers. This is certainly the perspective that a self-proclaimed 'detribalised' writer such as Shàdẹ̀kọ́ would wish us to take – and yet, of course, his perspective is in itself a class perspective, available to a highly educated elite writer who can survey Nigeria from the perspective of a traveller, and potentially less available to some of his fellow Nigerians whom he depicts in his travel writing. As Pẹ̀lú Awófẹ̀sọ̀ reminds us, he remains a 'Lagos boy' when he travels, despite his ambitious attempts to unify Nigeria (while still celebrating the differences that make it worth travelling in). And Awófẹ̀sọ̀'s attempts to create a Nigerian 'playground' suggest an understanding of travel as a leisure activity – reminding us that the utopian, knowledgeable Nigerian traveller is often one with the time and money to spare to get to know Nigeria better.

Language also plays a role in ways of reading travel writing. This book has discussed travel narratives in both Yoruba and English, with an increasing focus on English-language travel writing in the postcolonial age. While this should not be taken as suggesting that Yoruba-language travel writing no longer has a place in postcolonial Nigerian writing, when undertaking research for this book, it was certainly more challenging to locate instances of more recent Yoruba-language travel writing. To some extent this is, again, a question of genre: as we saw in the case of both quest novels such as Fágúnwà's and novels about NYSC, which include 'Débọ̀ Awẹ́'s Yoruba novel *Kọ́pà*, fiction has proved particularly fertile ground for Yoruba travel writing. Yoruba historical writing and oral genres, as discussed in Chapter 1, have also been a home for travel narratives. But it is also the case that in an age when English-language writing is particularly prized for its potential to reach to larger audiences and to insert its writers into prestigious and potentially rewarding national and international literary circuits – and when travel writers themselves are often seeking to create national narratives, speaking to Nigerians as a whole – English has dominated the postcolonial travel accounts discussed in this book. Nonetheless, my expectation is that continued research will document further instances of Yoruba-language travel writing in postcolonial Nigeria, and moreover put these into dialogue with travel writing in other Nigerian languages, such as Igbo and Hausa.

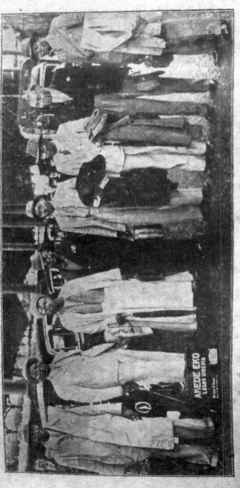

**Figure 5** 'Awọn Ẹgbẹ Oniwe-Irohin Ero L'Ọna Ilu Oyinbo' ('The Association of Newspaper Editors Travelling in the UK'), *Akede Eko*, 1 January 1944, p. 1; sourced from the National Archives, Ìbàdàn, Nigeria, reproduced with permission

We may also read the intra-Nigerian travel narratives discussed in this book in light of Nigerian travel writing about the rest of the world. As we have seen, D. Q. Fágúnwà's account of his travels to the UK in *Irinajo* closely intersected with his hunters' travels into the forest, particularly in their shared preoccupation with gaining *ọ̀làjú* through travel and exposure to the world beyond home in the mid-twentieth century. The Yoruba- and English-language newspapers that hosted travel narratives in the early twentieth century also published accounts of journeys overseas, especially as opportunities for international travel emerged increasingly in the 1940s and 1950s. I. B. Thomas, for instance, travelled along with several other West African newspaper editors, including Nnamdi Azikiwe to the UK on a press delegation in 1943, and throughout 1944 he published a serialised travel narrative describing his journey in his newspaper *Akede Eko*.

As well as examining how travel writers themselves have crossed national borders, readings of such travel writing might also cross national borders. The turn to models of travelling, writing and publishing characterised as pan-African or trans-African in the work of major African literary innovators and publishers such as Invisible Borders and Chimurenga suggests the significance of such models of reading beyond the nation. Within West Africa, Stephanie Newell identifies transnational francophone and anglophone 'zones of culture' stretching across the West African coast; recognising the interconnected print and literary cultures within the region opens up possibilities for reading travel writing across that transnational West African zone.[31] The Gold Coast press of the early twentieth century, for instance, hosted travel narratives by J. G. Mullen and the pseudonymous 'Rambler' in 1919.[32] Beyond the newspapers, J. Benibegnor Blay, one of Ghana's earliest authors of popular fiction, published travel books alongside novels, memoirs, history, poetry and essays.[33] The frequent presence of travel writing alongside such authors' more canonical works demonstrates that a reading of travel writing is important to the full history of West African print and literary culture more broadly, and suggests that travel writing can be read as part of the interlinked literary 'zones of culture' that stretch across the West African coast.

Travel writing certainly has potential as a liberatory genre that can be used to express African subjectivity and ways of seeing and understanding the world.

---

[31] Stephanie Newell, *West African Literatures: Ways of Reading* (Oxford: Oxford University Press, 2006), pp. 20–2.

[32] Newell, *The Power to Name*, pp. 8–9.

[33] Ime Ikiddeh, 'The Character of Popular Fiction in Ghana', in *Readings in African Popular Fiction*, ed. by Stephanie Newell (London: International African Institute, 2002), pp. 76–80 (p. 77).

Just as postcolonial African writers have adopted historical fiction as a way to write their own past, and science fiction as a way to write their futures, travel writing offers them a way to write place, wresting the genre away from its colonial history. The visibility and promotion of African travellers and travel writers can be read as a political statement about the presence of Africans as travellers and tourists in the contemporary world. This may especially be the case if travel writing itself can be decolonised or liberated from its imperial roots, perhaps through formal experimentation or through the deconstruction of the traveller's gaze and the prioritisation of African perspectives.

However, we should not be too hasty in proclaiming the utopian potential of travel writing to undermine borders and to open up Nigerian space. As Lápé Ṣóè̩tán reminds us, hostile visa regimes make some borders impossible to cross for many Nigerian travellers. Even where Nigerian travellers hold the required visas, they may face a more subtle, racialised reminder that they are not always perceived as the archetypal traveller. Janet Remmington points out that in her book *Due North* (2017), a collection of her international travel narratives and photography, Sweden-based Nigerian travel writer Lọlá Akínmádé Åkerström describes how her 'motives for travel were deeply questioned' by numerous immigration officers she encountered on her global travels: 'Why was I traveling? There had to be a more sinister reason beyond the need to explore and enrich my life through experiencing other cultures.' Travelling through Eastern Europe, she was frequently singled out amid a bus full of EU and US passport holders, and had to explain to immigration officers 'this unbelievable concept of a Nigerian traveling for the sole purpose of enjoyment'.[34] As Christabelle Peters put it, reflecting on the relative lack of scholarship on Africans travelling for the sake of travel itself, 'African travelers, it would seem, must still justify their movements across the planet (whether the motives be professional, economic or political). Passports may have replaced passbooks for a number of us; but we must still answer the question, "Why are you here?"'[35]

Thus while celebrating African travel writing's border-crossing potential, we must also recognise that what Janet Remmington calls 'the pervasive politicization and racialization of travel' in Africa and by Africans persists, making border-crossing sometimes more of an abstract concept than one that is practically possible for all prospective travellers – and travel an arena in which

---

[34] Lola Akinmade Åkerström, *Due North: A Collection of Travel Observations, Reflections, and Snapshots across Colors, Cultures, and Continents* (Stockholm: Geotraveler Media Sweden, 2017), pp. 17–19.

[35] Christabelle Peters, *The Myth of the African Travel Writer* (2016) <https://africasacountry.com/2016/04/the-myth-of-the-african-travel-writer/> [accessed 29 December 2018].

Africans may still be rendered different in the perception of others.[36] We also cannot ignore the material differences in access to publishing by African travel writers compared to Western travel writers, including writers of the African diaspora in the West. As we have seen, many of the travel narratives discussed in this book were self-published in various different forms, with the notable exception of those by diaspora-based writers that were published by major Western publishing houses, and those by Crowther, Délànọ̀ and Fágúnwà, which were published or sponsored by missionary and colonial-era publishing houses. For today's Nigeria-based travel writers, there is still relatively little recognition for their work in the publishing industry, whether in Nigeria or beyond, although the work of dynamic new publishers such as Cassava Republic may mean that this is beginning to change.

Borders also remain *within* travel narratives. The 'decontextualised generalizations and problematic assessments of cultural difference' that Aedín Ní Loingsigh detects in francophone African intercontinental travel writing have also been features of some southwest Nigerian travel writing.[37] The ideals of a 'detribalised', 'united' or 'open' Nigeria expressed by some travel writers are accompanied by stereotypes of class, ethnicity and urban–rural difference. Such travel writing sometimes reproduces differences of class, as writers revel in the freedom to travel to places they can leave: as the village or the rural hinterland becomes commodified as an object of travel, the return to the village, briefly, affirms one's own urbanity and modernity. It has also produced and reproduced gender ideologies, as in the trope of the 'pregnant Corper', even as travel also provides a space for women such as Lápé Ṣóẹ̀tán to assert freedom and seek self-determination.

Moreover, some southwest Nigerian travel narratives are characterised by the exoticism and otherness with which we are more familiar in Western travel writing, as in the strikingly frequent portrayal of fellow Nigerians of other ethnolinguistic groups as 'uncivilised', prone to eating disgusting food and walking naked, and or even cannibalistic. However, rather than simply dismissing the trope of the exoticised intra-Nigerian other, particularly the cannibal, as a manifestation of 'tribalism', as Cole's narrator ironically does in *Every Day*, we can read the presence of this trope as another moment of ambivalence. While it is often used to express fear of the 'other', who has now become a fellow Nigerian – as if creating distance and erecting a border within Nigeria – along with other tropes such as the fear of unwanted pregnancy for women who

---

[36] Janet Remmington, *"It's a Passport!" My Inner Voice Yells'. Review of Lola Akinmade Åkerström's Due North* (2017) <https://africainwords.com/2017/06/15/its-a-passport-my-inner-voice-yells-review-of-lola-akinmade-akerstroms-due-north/> [accessed 15 September 2017].

[37] Ní Loingsigh, *Postcolonial Eyes*, p. 174.

emerge into the nation, it is also often used by writers either to express their hope that the so-called cannibals can become fellow 'civilised' Nigerians, or that the reader or speaker of such a trope can overcome their 'tribalised' beliefs; it may extend hope for re-humanisation of the other, even as it dehumanises in the present moment. It is itself, therefore, a metaphor at a crossroads, standing for potential and change, at the same time as it is a metaphor of the other and of distance.

Few southwest Nigerian travel writers consider themselves to be responding to a homegrown Nigerian travel writing canon – instead, as we have seen, some contemporary writers especially bemoan the lack of Nigerian travel writers, or look to the West as the founders of the genre they are working with. In doing so, they appear to be looking, in different ways, for the 'internal gaze' as a form of what Mary Louise Pratt would term 'autoethnography': a travel writing tradition that engages with the terms of the broader colonial and postcolonial travel writing tradition.[38] But the picture that has emerged throughout this book is one of much greater ambivalence and complexity in the texts' and their writers' relationship with the genre of 'travel writing' as it is known in the West – as epitomised by Samuel Àjàyí Crowther's travel writing, which both adopts and 'exceeds' autoethnography and the travel writing genre, as Ọlákúnlé George puts it.[39] The Lagos travel writers of the 1920s and 1930s, meanwhile, were travelling self-confidently and seemingly on their own terms, without explicit reference to Western literary and travel writing cultures – but at the same time they were highly embedded in Lagos's creole culture and they did engage some of the tropes of the colonial encounter. By the late twentieth century and early twenty-first century, by contrast, some travel writers look to model their work much more closely on the Western canon, adopting a narrower definition of the genre.

Earlier models of African literary criticism suggested that European forms, particularly the novel, were melded with African orality to create the African novel. Concerns about travel writers writing through 'Western eyes', or about the genre needing 'new stories', retrace similar assumptions about a Western genre being infused with African content and style. But contemporary literary criticism has tended to consider the emergence of genres and forms in a more complex way, examining the processes of production, circulation and reception through which genres are created and evolve. Travel writing in southwest Nigeria sometimes has close connections with the Western genre of 'travel writing', but is also intimately connected with what Abíọlá Irele calls the 'Yoruba tradition of literary expression', particularly the work of D. Ọ. Fágúnwà and Amos Tutùọlá, and also with local historical circumstances, such as the growth

---

[38] Pratt, *Imperial Eyes*, p. 7.
[39] George, *African Literature*, p. 64.

of print culture.[40] Other forms of travel and narrative have an even longer and more popular history – to the extent that town histories universalise travel, placing migration and origins elsewhere at the heart of their histories of Yoruba towns and their peoples. The texts discussed in this book have a complex and ambivalent relationship with the Western genre of 'travel writing', weaving in and out of it, sometimes choosing to invoke it closely and at other times being more concerned with other modes of travel and writing.

The stories of travel told by the writers discussed in this book, and the literary, cultural and social crossroads at which they frequently picture themselves standing, are just some of the many stories of travel that circulate in southwest Nigeria and beyond. As well as formally published travelogues, diaries, letters, newspapers, fictional texts, autobiographies, blogs and oral narratives are brimming with narratives of travel, beyond the few that I have had space to examine in this book. Beyond Yoruba and English, and the southwest Nigerian region, Nigeria's other regions and languages offer much scope for research into both the history and the breadth of writing about travel by Nigerians, as do accounts of international travel by Nigerians.

In looking for the 'new stories' that African travel writing has the potential to tell, it is easy to seek a reversal of the colonial gaze, rendering Africans the subjects of the travel narrative, rather than objects of the traveller's gaze. But at the Africa Writes literary festival in London in 2014, Noo Saro-Wiwa argued that travel writing will thrive if it makes space for multiple voices and perspectives. Indeed, southwest Nigerian travel writers do sometimes reverse the colonial gaze on Africa, but they also do many other things besides, both in terms of their accounts of travel and in terms of literary genre. To be able to read these stories and to be open to the longer history of writing about travel in southwest Nigeria beyond its present exciting wave of writers, we must be prepared to look beyond the reversed or rejected colonial gaze, to forms of writing and textual sources that resonate in the region's literary and print culture, and to the many, sometimes contradictory, always intriguing and varied, voices to which such writing has played host. By reading southwest Nigerian travel writing in this way, we can see Pèlú Awófèsọ's claim that 'Nigeria is my playground' as having historical depth: it becomes a statement not just of aspiration, of laying claim to 'new stories', but also one that can be applied to over a century of travelling and writing by southwest Nigerian travel writers in Nigeria and the spaces and communities within it.

---

[40] Irele, 'Tradition and the Yoruba Writer'.

# Bibliography

Newspapers cited

*Akede Eko*
*Daily Service*
*Eko Akete*
*Eleti-Ọfẹ*
*Independent*
*Lagos Standard*
*Lagos Weekly Record*
*National Concord*
*Nigerian Chronicle*
*Nigerian Observer*


Abimbola, Oluwaseun Adeniyi, 'The Legend of Ajala's Travels and Transnational Backpacking in Africa' (unpublished MA dissertation, University of Ibadan, 2016).

Adams, Percy, *Travel Literature and the Evolution of the Novel* (Lexington, KY: University Press of Kentucky, 1983).

Adebanwi, Wale, *Nation as Grand Narrative: The Nigerian Press and the Politics of Meaning* (Rochester, NY and Woodbridge: University of Rochester Press/ Boydell & Brewer, 2016).

Adéẹ̀kọ́, Adélékè, 'Writing Africa under the Shadow of Slavery: Quaque, Wheatley, and Crowther', *Research in African Literatures,* 40.4 (2009), 1–24.

——, *Arts of Being Yorùbá: Divination, Allegory, Tragedy, Proverb, Panegyric* (Bloomington, IN: Indiana University Press, 2017).

Adegbija, Efurosibina, *Multilingualism: A Nigerian Case Study* (Trenton, NJ: Africa World Press, 2004).

Adejunmobi, Moradewun, 'Provocations: African Societies and Theories of Creativity', in *Rethinking African Cultural Production*, ed. by Kenneth W. Harrow and Frieda Ekotto (Bloomington, IN: Indiana University Press, 2015), pp. 52–77.

Adekanla, Olabisi. *Imesi-Ile: The Ancient Kiriji Camp* (Ibadan: Peetee Nigeria, 1999).

Adenekan, Shola, 'Transnationalism and the Agenda of African Literature in a Digital Age', *Matatu – Journal for African Culture and Society* 45 (2014), 133–51.

Adeniyi, Dapo. *Expedition to the Mount of Thought (The Third Saga)* (Ile-Ife: Obafemi Awolowo University Press, 1994).

Adesanmi, Pius, 'Redefining Paris: Trans-Modernity and Francophone African Migritude Fiction', *MFS Modern Fiction Studies,* 51.4 (2005), 958–75.

Adesanmi, Pius and Chris Dunton, 'Nigeria's Third Generation Writing: Historiography and Preliminary Theoretical Considerations', *English in Africa* 32.1 (2005), 7–19.

——, 'Everything Good Is Raining: Provisional Notes on the Nigerian Novel of the Third Generation', *Research in African Literatures,* 39.2 (2008), vii–xii.

Adéyẹmí, Lérè, 'Magical Realism in Contemporary Yoruba Novels', in *Texts and Theories in Transition: Black African Literature and Imagined Tradition*, ed. by Charles Bodunde (Bayreuth: Eckersdorf, 2010), pp. 91–102.

Adichie, Chimamanda Ngozi, *Half of a Yellow Sun* (London: Fourth Estate, 2006).

——, *Americanah* (Lagos: Farafina, 2013).

Adler, Judith, 'Travel as Performed Art', *American Journal of Sociology,* 94.6 (1989), 1366–91.

Adogame, Afe, '*Aiye Loja, Orun Nile* – the Appropriation of Ritual Space-Time in the Cosmology of the Celestial Church of Christ', *Journal of Religion in Africa,* 30.1 (2000), 3–29.

Afejuku, Tony E., 'J. P. Clark's Romantic "Autotravography"', *Literature Interpretation Theory,* 4.2 (1993), 137–44.

Agbetuyi, Olayinka, 'Representing the Foreign as Other: The Use of Allegory in Fagunwa's Novels', in *The Foundations of Nigeria: Essays in Honour of Toyin Falola*, ed. by Adebayo Oyebade (Trenton: Africa World Press, 2003), pp. 333–44.

Agbro Jr, Joe, *Served ... Memoirs of a Youth Corps Member* (Lagos: Grasshill Books, 2012).

Ajala, Olabisi, *An African Abroad* (London: Jarrolds, 1963).

Ajayi, J. F. A., *Christian Missions in Nigeria: The Making of a New Elite, 1841–1891* (London: Longman, 1965).

Ajenifuja, Damilola, *They Will Eat Me in Calabar ... the Story of a Youth Corper* (Ibadan: Freedom Press, 2000).

Akamisoko, Duke, *Samuel Ajayi Crowther in the Lokoja Area* (Ibadan: Sefer Books, 2002).

Åkerström, Lola Akinmade, *Due North: A Collection of Travel Observations, Reflections, and Snapshots across Colors, Cultures, and Continents* (Stockholm: Geotraveler Media Sweden, 2017).

Akinyele, I. B., *Outlines of Ibadan History* (Lagos: Alebiosu Printing Press, 1946).

Akpabli, Kofi, *A Sense of Savannah: Tales of a Friendly Walk Through Northern Ghana* (Accra: TREC, 2011).

Akpabli, Kofi, *Tickling the Ghanaian: Encounters with Contemporary Culture* (Accra: TREC, 2011).

Alkali, Zaynab, *The Virtuous Woman* (Ikeja: Longman, 1987).

Allfrey, Ellah Wakatama, *Safe House: Explorations in Creative Nonfiction* (London: Cassava Republic Press, 2016).

Anderson, David, *Surveyor's Trek* (London: Faber & Faber, 1940).

Anderson, Benedict, *Imagined Communities: Reflections on the Origins and Spread of Nationalism*, 3rd edn (London: Verso, 2006 [1983]).

Andrade, Susan Z., 'Representing Slums and Home: Chris Abani's Graceland', in *The Legacies of Modernism: Historicising Postwar and Contemporary Fiction*, ed. by David James (Cambridge: Cambridge University Press, 2011), pp. 225–42.

Animasaun, Kayode, *A Gift for the Corper* (Ibadan: Kraft Books, 2008).

Appiah, Kwame Anthony, *The Ethics of Identity* (Princeton: Princeton University Press, 2005).

Ash, Louis, and John Turner, *The Golden Hordes: International Tourism and the Pleasure Periphery* (London: Constable, 1975).

Atanda, J. A., 'Editor's Introduction', in *William H. Clarke, Travels & Explorations in Yorubaland (1854–1848)* (Ibadan: Oxford University Press, 1972), pp. xi-xxxvii.

Atta, Sefi, *Everything Good Will Come* (Northampton: Interlink Books, 2004).

——, *A Bit of Difference* (Northampton, MA: Interlink Books, 2012).

Awẹ, 'Débọ̀, *Kọ́pà*, 2nd edn (Ileṣa: Elyon Publishers (2009 [1990]).

Awofeso, Pelu, *A Place Called Peace: A Visitor's Guide to Jos, Plateau State, Nigeria* (Lagos: Homestead Publications, 2003).

——, *Tour of Duty* (Lagos, Homestead Publications: 2010).

——, *Nigerian Festivals: The Famous and Not So Famous*, 2nd edn (Lagos: Homestead Publications, 2013 [2005]).

Awofeso, Pelu, ed., *Route 234: An Anthology of Global Travel Writing by Nigerian Arts and Culture Journalists* (Lagos: Homestead Publications, 2016).

Awolowo, Obafemi, *Path to Nigerian Freedom* (London: Faber & Faber, 1947).

Ayandele, Emmanuel Ayankanmi, *The Missionary Impact on Modern Nigeria, 1842–1914: A Political and Social Analysis* (London: Longmans, 1966).

Azikiwe, Nnamdi, *My Odyssey: An Autobiography* (London: C. Hurst, 1970).

Azubuike, Chibuzor Mirian, *The Girl Who Found Water: Memoirs of a Corps Member* (Lagos: Easy Voucher, 2014).

Babalọla, Adeboye, 'Yoruba Literature', in *Literature in African Languages: Theoretical Issues and Sample Surveys*, ed. by B. W. Andrzejewski, S. Piłaszewicz, and W. Tyloch (Cambridge: Cambridge University Press, 1985), pp. 157–89.

Bamgboṣe, Ayọ, *The Novels of D. O. Fagunwa* (Benin: Ethiope Publishing Corporation, 1974).

Bamisaiye, Remi, *Service of the Fatherland* (Lagos: Macmillan Nigeria, 1985).

Barber, Karin, 'Popular Arts in Africa', *African Studies Review,* 30.3 (1987), 1–78.

——, I *Could Speak until Tomorrow: Oriki, Women and the Past in a Yoruba Town* (Edinburgh: Edinburgh University Press, 1991).

——, 'African-Language Literature and Postcolonial Criticism', *Research in African Literatures* 26.4 (1995), 3–30.

——, 'Time, Space, and Writing in Three Colonial Yoruba Novels', *The Yearbook of English Studies,* 27 (1997), 108–29.

——, 'Translation, Publics, and the Vernacular Press in 1920s Lagos', in *Christianity and Social Change in Africa: Essays in Honour of J. D. Y. Peel*, ed. by Toyin Falola (Durham, NC: Carolina Academic Press, 2005), pp. 187–208.

——, ed., *Africa's Hidden Histories: Everyday Literacy and Making the Self* (Bloomington, IN: Indiana University Press, 2006).

——, 'Introduction – Hidden Innovators in Africa' in *Africa's Hidden Histories: Everyday Literacy and Making the Self*, ed. by Karin Barber (Bloomington: Indiana University Press, 2006), 1–21.

——, *The Anthropology of Texts, Persons and Publics* (Cambridge: Cambridge University Press, 2007).

——, 'I. B. Akinyele and Early Yoruba Print Culture', in *Recasting the Past. History Writing and Political Work in Modern Africa*, ed. by D. Peterson and G. Macola (Athens, OH: Ohio University Press, 2009), pp. 31–49.

——, *Print Culture and the First Yoruba Novel: I. B. Thomas's 'Life Story of Me, Ṣẹgilọla' and Other Texts* (Leiden: Brill, 2012).

——, 'Experiments with Genre in the Yoruba Newspapers of the 1920s', in *African Print Cultures: Newspapers and Their Publics in the Twentieth Century*, ed. by Derek Peterson, Emma Hunter and Stephanie Newell (Ann Arbor: University of Michigan Press, 2016), pp. 151–78.

Batubo, Henry, *The NYSC Experience* (self-published, 2015).

Bhabha, Homi K, 'Introduction: Narrating the Nation', in *Nation and Narration*, ed. by Homi K. Bhabha (London: Routledge, 1990), pp. 1–7.

Borm, Jan, 'Defining Travel: On the Travel Book, Travel Writing and Terminology', in *Perspectives on Travel Writing*, ed. by Glenn Hooper and Tim Youngs (Aldershot: Routledge, 2004), pp. 13–26.

Bould, Mark, 'Africa Sf: Introduction', *Paradoxa,* 25 (2014), 7–15.

Brantlinger, Patrick, *The Reading Lesson: The Threat of Mass Literacy in Nineteenth-Century British Fiction* (Bloomington, IN: Indiana University Press, 1998).

Bryce, Jane, 'A Life on the Women's Page: *Treena Kwenta's Diary*', in *Writing African Women: Gender, Popular Culture and Literature in West Africa*, ed. by Stephanie Newell (London: Zed Books, 1997), pp. 47–66.

Carretta, Vincent, *Equiano the African: Biography of a Self-Made Man* (Athens: University of Georgia Press, 2005).

Clark, J. P., *America, Their America* (London: Andre Deutsch, 1964).

Clark, Steve, 'Introduction', in *Travel Writing and Empire: Postcolonial Theory in Transit*, ed. by Steve Clark (London: Zed Books, 1999), pp. 1–28.

Clarke, William H., *Travels & Explorations in Yorubaland (1854–1848)* (Ibadan: Oxford University Press, 1972).

Clifford, James, *Routes: Travel and Translation in the Late Twentieth Century* (Cambridge, MA; London: Harvard University Press, 1997).

Coates, Oliver, 'Narrative, Time, and the Archive in an African Second World War Memoir: Isaac Fadoyebo's *A Stroke of Unbelievable Luck*', *The Journal of Commonwealth Literature* 51.3 (2015), 371–86.

Coetzee, Carli, 'Sihle Khumalo, Cape to Cairo, and Questions of Intertextuality: How to Write About Africa, How to Read About Africa', *Research in African Literatures,* 44.2 (2013), 62–75.

Colclough, Stephen, *Consuming Texts: Readers and Reading Communities, 1695–1870* (Basingstoke: Palgrave Macmillan, 2007).

Cole, Teju, *Every Day Is for the Thief* (Abuja: Cassava Republic Press, 2007).

——, *Open City* (New York: Random House, 2011).

Conrad, Joseph, *Heart of Darkness* (London: Penguin, 1973 [1902]).

Cooper, Brenda, *A New Generation of African Writers: Migration, Material Culture and Language* (Woodbridge: Boydell & Brewer/James Currey, 2008).

Coplan, David B., 'Eloquent Knowledge: Lesotho Migrants' Songs and the Anthropology of Experience', *American Ethnologist* 14.3 (1987), 413–33.

Cousins, Helen, and Pauline Dodgson-Katiyo, 'Editorial: Leaving Home/Returning Home: Migration and Contemporary African Literature', in *African Literature Today: Vol. 34 Diaspora and Returns in Fiction*, ed. by Helen Cousins and Pauline Dodgson-Katiyo (Woodbridge: James Currey/Boydell & Brewer, 2016), pp. 1–11.

Crowther, Samuel, *The Gospel on the Banks of the Niger: Journals and Notices of the Native Missionaries Accompanying the Niger Expedition of 1857–1859, by Samuel Crowther and John Christopher Taylor* (London: Church Missionary House, 1859).

——, *Journals and Notices of the Native Missionaries on the River Niger, 1862* (London: Church Missionary House, 1863).

——, *Niger Mission: Bishop Crowther's Report of the Overland Journey: From Lokoja to Bida, on the River Niger, and Thence to Lagos, on the Sea Coast, from November 10th, 1871, to February 8th, 1872* (London: Church Missionary House, 1872).

——, *Journal of an Expedition up the Niger and Tshadda Rivers Undertaken by Macgregor Laird in Connection with the British Government in 1854*, 2nd edn (London: F. Cass & Co, 1970).

——, *Journals of the Rev. James Frederick Schon and Mr. Samuel Crowther, Who, with the Sanction of Her Majesty's Government, Accompanied the Expedition up the Niger, in 1841, on Behalf of the Church Missionary Society*, 2nd edn (London: F. Cass & Co., 1970).

Cruz-Gutiérrez, Cristina, '(Re) Imagining and (Re) Visiting Homelands in Looking for Transwonderland: Travels in Nigeria by Noo Saro-Wiwa', *Atlantis. Journal of the Spanish Association for Anglo-American Studies*, 38.2 (2016), 141–60.

Curtin, Philip D., *Africa Remembered: Narratives by West Africans from the Era of the Slave Trade* (Madison: University of Wisconsin Press, 1967).

Danmole, H. O., 'The "Ta'līf Akhbār Al-Qurūn Min Umarā' Bilad Ilūrin": A Critique', *History in Africa*, 11 (1984), 57–67.

Dasylva, Ademola O., and Remy Oriaku, 'Trends in the Nigerian Auto/Biography', *History Compass*, 8.4 (2010), 303–19.

Dekobra, Maurice, *A Frenchman in Japan; Travels* (London: T. Werner Laurie, 1936).

Delano, Isaac, *The Soul of Nigeria* (London: T. Werner Laurie, 1937).

——, *An African Looks at Marriage* (London and Redhill: United Society for Christian Literature (Lutterworth Press), 1944).

——, *Notes and Comments from Nigeria* (London and Redhill: United Society for Christian Literature (Lutterworth Press), 1944).

——, *Aiyé d'Aiyé Òyìnbó* (London: Thomas Nelson, 1955).

——, *L'ójó Ojó Un* (London: Thomas Nelson, 1963).

Doortmont, Michel, 'Recapturing the Past: Samuel Johnson and the Construction of the History of the Yoruba' (unpublished PhD dissertation, Erasmus Universiteit Rotterdam, 1994).

Eades, Jeremy, *The Yoruba Today* (Cambridge: Cambridge University Press, 1980).

Echeruo, Michael, *Victorian Lagos: Aspects of Nineteenth Century Lagos Life* (London: Macmillan, 1977).

Edwards, Paul, 'The Farm and the Wilderness in Tutuola's *The Palm-Wine Drinkard*', *Journal of Commonwealth Literature*, 9.1 (1974), 57–65.

Ekwensi, Cyprian, *Jagua Nana* (London: Hutchinson, 1961).

Emecheta, Buchi, *In the Ditch* (London: Barrie and Jenkins, 1972).

——, *Second-Class Citizen* (London: Allison and Busby, 1974).

Equiano, Olaudah, *The Interesting Narrative of the Life of Olaudah Equiano: Or Gustavus Vassa, the African* (London, n.p.: 1789).

Ezeife, P. C., and A. T. Bolade, 'The Development of the Nigerian Transport System', *Transport Reviews*, 4.4 (1984), 305–30.

Fabian, Johannes, *Time and the Other: How Anthropology Makes Its Object*, 3rd edn (New York: Columbia University Press, 2014 [1983]).

Fadoyebo, Isaac, *A Stroke of Unbelievable Luck* (Madison: African Studies Program, University of Wisconsin-Madison, 1999).

Fafunwa, A. Babs, *History of Education in Nigeria* (London: George Allen & Unwin, 1974).

Fágúnwà, D. O., *Irinajo, Apa Kini* (London: Oxford University Press, 1949).

——, *Igbó Olódùmarè* (Ibadan: Nelson Publishers, 2005 [1949]).

——, *Ìrèké-Oníbùdó* (Ibadan: Nelson Publishers, 2005 [1949]).

——, *Ìrìnkèrindò Nínú Igbó Elégbèje* (Ibadan: Nelson Publishers, 2005 [1954]).

——, *Ògbójú Ọdẹ Nínú Igbó Irúnmọlẹ̀* (Ibadan: Nelson Publishers, 2005 [1950]).

——, *Àdììtú Olódùmarè* (Ibadan: Nelson Publishers, 2005 [1961]).

Fagunwa, D. O. and Wole Soyinka, *The Forest of a Thousand Daemons* (Walton-on-Thames: Thomas Nelson and Sons, 1982 [1968]).

——, *In the Forest of Olodumare* (Ibadan: Nelson Publishers, 2010).

Falola, Toyin, 'Yoruba Writers and the Construction of Heroes', *History in Africa,* 24 (1997), 157–75.

——, *Yoruba Gurus: Indigenous Production of Knowledge in Africa* (Trenton: Africa World Press, 1999).

——, 'Èṣù: The God without Boundaries', in *Èṣù: Yoruba God, Power and the Imaginative Frontiers*, ed. by Toyin Falola (Durham, NC: Carolina Academic Press, 2013), pp. 3–37.

Falola, Toyin, and Ogechukwu Ezekwem, *Writing the Nigeria–Biafra War* (Woodbridge: James Currey/Boydell & Brewer, 2016).

Falola, Toyin, and Matthew M. Heaton, *A History of Nigeria* (Cambridge: Cambridge University Press, 2008).

Faoseke, John Olu, ed., *The ABC of Travel and Tourism* (Lagos: Keystone Tourism Promotion Publications, 2000).

Faoseke, John Olu, *Travellers' Guide to Nigeria* (Ikeja: Africa Pilgrims' Books, 1997).

——, *Travel and Tourism: The Road Ahead in Africa* (Lagos: Keystone Tourism Promotion Publications, 2001).

Farias, Paulo Fernando de Moraes, and Karin Barber, 'Introduction', in *Self-Assertion and Brokerage: Early Cultural Nationalism in West Africa*, ed. by Paulo Fernando de Moraes Farias and Karin Barber (Birmingham: Centre of West African Studies, 1990), pp. 1–10.

Fátànmí, D. I., *Kórimálẹ Nínú Igbó Adimúla* (Lagos: Thomas Nelson and Sons, 1967).

Frank-Wilson, Marion, 'African Travel Writing', *African Research and Documentation,* 92 (2003), 27–38.

Fussell, Paul, *Abroad: British Literary Traveling between the Wars* (Oxford: Oxford University Press, 1982).

Geider, Thomas, 'Early Swahili Travelogues', *Matatu – Journal for African Culture and Society,* 9 (1992), 27–65.

George, Olakunle, *Relocating Agency: Modernity and African Letters* (Albany: State University of New York Press, 2003).

——, *African Literature and Social Change: Tribe, Nation, Race* (Bloomington, IN: Indiana University Press, 2017).

Gikandi, Simon, *Maps of Englishness: Writing Identity in the Culture of Colonialism* (New York: Columbia University Press, 1996).

——, 'Tutuola, Amos', in *Encyclopedia of African Literature*, ed. by Simon Gikandi (London and New York: Routledge, 2005).

Gilroy, Paul, *The Black Atlantic: Modernity and Double Consciousness* (London, Verso, 1993).

Goody, Jack, *The Myth of the Bagre* (Oxford: Clarendon Press, 1972).

Griffin, Farah J., and Cheryl J. Fish, *A Stranger in the Village: Two Centuries of African-American Travel Writing* (Boston: Beacon Press, 1999).

Griswold, Wendy, *Bearing Witness: Readers, Writers, and the Novel in Nigeria* (Princeton, NJ: Princeton University Press, 2000).

Gualtieri, Claudia, *Representations of West Africa as Exotic in British Colonial Travel Writing* (Lewiston: Edwin Mellen Press, 2002).

Guignery, Vanessa, 'Landscapes Within, Landscapes Without: The Forest and Other Places in Ben Okri's *The Famished Road*', *Études britanniques contemporaines,* 47 (2014), <http://ebc.revues.org/1974> [accessed 4 April 2019].

Gujba, H., Y. Mulugetta, and A. Azapagic, 'Passenger Transport in Nigeria: Environmental and Economic Analysis with Policy Recommendations', *Energy Policy,* 55 (2013), 353–61.

Gyasi, Kwaku A, 'Writing as Translation: African Literature and the Challenges of Translation', *Research in African Literatures* 30.2 (1999), 75–87.

Habila, Helon, *Measuring Time* (London: Hamish Hamilton, 2007).

——, *Oil on Water* (New York: W. W. Norton & Co., 2010).

Haile, Maskarm, *Abyssinian Nomad: An African Woman's Journey of Love, Loss, & Adventure from Cape to Cairo* (n.p., 2018).

Hallemeier, Katherine, 'Literary Cosmopolitanisms in Teju Cole's *Every Day Is for the Thief* and *Open City*', *ariel: A Review of International English Literature,* 44.2 (2014), 239–50.

Harris, John, 'Libraries and Librarianship in Nigeria at Mid-Century', Occasional Paper No. 2 (Accra: University of Ghana Department of Library Studies, 1970).

Hart, Jennifer, *Ghana on the Go: African Mobility in the Age of Motor Transportation* (Bloomington, IN: Indiana University Press, 2016).

Hitchcott, Nicki, 'Travels in Inhumanity: Veronique Tadjo's Tourism in Rwanda', *French Cultural Studies* 20.2 (2009), 149–64.

Hofmeyr, Isabel, *The Portable Bunyan: A Transnational History of the Pilgrim's Progress* (Princeton: Princeton University Press, 2004).

Holland, Patrick, and Graham Huggan, *Tourists with Typewriters: Critical Reflections on Contemporary Travel Writing* (Ann Arbor: University of Michigan Press, 2000).

Iduma, Emmanuel, *A Stranger's Pose* (Abuja: Cassava Republic Press, 2018).

Ike, Vincent Chukwuemeka, 'A Critique of the Problems of the Book Industry in Nigeria', in *Culture and the Book Industry in Nigeria*, ed. by Sule Bello and Abdullahi Augi (Lagos: National Council for Arts and Culture, 1993), pp. 129–47.

Ikiddeh, I., 'The Character of Popular Fiction in Ghana', in *Readings in African Popular Fiction*, ed. by Stephanie Newell (London: International African Institute, 2002), pp. 76–80.

Ipadeola, Tade, *The Sahara Testaments* (Lagos: Hornbill African Poet, 2012).

Irele, Abiola, 'Tradition and the Yoruba Writer: D. O. Fagunwa, Amos Tutuola and Wole Soyinka', *Odù: Journal of Yoruba and Related Studies,* 11 (1975), 75–100.

Isichei, Elizabeth, *A History of Nigeria* (Harlow: Longman, 1983).

Iweala, Uzodinma, *Our Kind of People: Thoughts on the Hiv/Aids Epidemic* (London: John Murray, 2012).

Jaekel, Francis, *The History of the Nigerian Railway*, 3 vols (Ibadan: Spectrum Books, 1997).

Johnson, Samuel, *The History of the Yorubas* (Lagos: CMS (Nigeria) Bookshops, 1921).

Jones, Rebecca, 'How to Be a Writer in Your 30s in Lagos: Self-Help Literature and the Creation of Authority in Africa', in *Routledge Handbook of African Literature*, ed. by Moradewun Adejunmobi and Carli Coetzee (New York: Routledge, 2019).

Julien, Eileen, 'The Extroverted African Novel', in *The Novel*, ed. by Franco Moretti (Princeton, NJ: Princeton University Press, 2006), pp. 667–700.

July, R. W., *The Origins of Modern African Thought* (London: Faber & Faber, 1968).

Kay, Jackie, *Red Dust Road: An Autobiographical Journey* (London: Picador, 2010).

Khair, Tabish, Justin D Edwards, Martin Leer, and Hanna Ziadeh, *Other Routes: 1500 Years of African and Asian Travel Writing* (Bloomington, IN: Indiana University Press, 2005).

Khumalo, Sihle, *Dark Continent, My Black Arse* (Cape Town: Umuzi, 2007).

——, *Heart of Africa: Centre of My Gravity* (Cape Town: Umuzi, 2009).

——, *Almost Sleeping My Way to Timbuktu: West Africa on a Shoestring by Public Transport with no French* (Cape Town: Umuzi, 2013).

Killingray, David, *Fighting for Britain: African Soldiers in the Second World War* (Woodbridge: Boydell & Brewer, 2010).

Kirk-Greene, Anthony, and Paul Newman, *West African Travels and Adventures, Two Autobiographical Narratives from Northern Nigeria* (New Haven: Yale University Press, 1971).

Klancher, Jon P., *The Making of English Reading Audiences, 1790–1832* (Madison: University of Wisconsin Press, 1987).

Knowles, Sam, *Travel Writing and the Transnational Author* (Basingstoke, Hampshire: Palgrave Macmillan, 2014).

Korte, Barbara, *English Travel Writing: From Pilgrimages to Postcolonial Explorations*, trans. Catherine Matthias (Basingstoke and New York: Palgrave, 2000).

Kpomassie, Tété-Michel, *L'Africain Du Groenland* (Paris: Flammarion, 1981).

——, *An African in Greenland* (London: Secker and Warburg, 1983).

Krishnan, Madhu, *Contemporary African Literature in English: Global Locations, Postcolonial Identifications* (Basingstoke: Palgrave Macmillan, 2014).

——, 'From Empire to Independence: Colonial Space in the Writing of Tutuola, Ekwensi, Beti, and Kane', *Comparative Literature Studies,* 54.2 (2017), 329–57.

Kunene, Daniel, 'Journey in the African Epic', *Research in African Literatures* 22.2 (1991), 205–23.

LaPin, Deirdre, 'Story, Medium and Masque: The Idea and Art of Yoruba Storytelling' (unpublished PhD thesis, University of Wisconsin-Madison, 1977),

Larkin, Brian, 'Indian Films and Nigerian Lovers: Media and the Creation of Parallel Modernities', *Africa,* 67.3 (1997), 406–40.

——, *Signal and Noise: Media, Infrastructure and Urban Culture in Nigeria* (Durham, NC and London: Duke University Press, 2008).

Law, Robin, 'Early Yoruba Historiography', *History in Africa* 3 (1976), 69–89.

Lawuyi, Olatunde Bayo, 'The world of the Yoruba taxi driver: an interpretive approach to vehicle slogans', *Africa* 58.1 (1988), 1–13.

Lindfors, Bernth, 'Amos Tutuola's Television-Handed Ghostess', *ARIEL: A Review of International English Literature,* 2.1 (1971), 68–77.

——, 'Form, Theme, and Style in the Narratives of D. O. Fagunwa', *International Fiction Review* 6.1 (1979), 11–16.

Lindsay, Lisa A., *Working with Gender: Wage Labor and Social Change in Southwestern Nigeria* (Portsmouth, NH: Heinemann, 2003).

Lisle, Debbie, *The Global Politics of Contemporary Travel Writing* (Cambridge: Cambridge University Press, 2006).

Livsey, Timothy, 'Imagining an Imperial Modernity: Universities and the West African Roots of Colonial Development', *Journal of Imperial and Commonwealth History,* 44.6 (2016), 952–75.

Maake, Nhlanhla, '"I Sing of the Woes of My Travels": The Lifela of Lesotho', in *The Cambridge History of South African Literature*, ed. by David Attwell and Derek Attridge (Cambridge: Cambridge University Press, 2012), pp. 60–76.

Mabanckou, Alain, *Lumières De Pointe-Noire* (Paris: Le Seuil, 2013).

Maja-Pearce, Adewale, *In My Father's Country: A Nigerian Journey* (London: Heinemann, 1987).

——, *How Many Miles to Babylon? An Essay* (London: Heinemann, 1990).

——, *The House My Father Built* (Lagos: Kachifo 2014).

Mama, Amina, 'Is It Ethical to Study Africa? Preliminary Thoughts on Scholarship and Freedom', *African Studies Review,* 50.1 (2007), 1–26.

Marenin, Otwin, 'Implementing Deployment Policies in the National Youth Service Corps of Nigeria: Goals and Constraints', *Comparative Political Studies,* 22.4 (1990), 397–436.

Mars-Jones, Adam, 'A Family of Acrobats: Review of *Every Day Is for the Thief,* by Teju Cole', *London Review of Books,* 36.13 (2014), 21–3.

Matory, J. Lorand, *Black Atlantic Religion: Tradition, Transnationalism, and Matriarchy in the Afro-Brazilian Candomblé* (Princeton, NJ: Princeton University Press, 2009).

Mbembe, Achille, 'Afropolitanism', in *Africa Remix: Contemporary Art of a Continent* ed. by Simon Njami (Johannesburg: Jacana Media, 2007), pp. 26–9.

McKenzie, P. R., *Inter-Religious Encounters in West Africa: Samuel Ajayi Crowther's Attitude to African Traditional Religion and Islam* (Leicester: University of Leicester, 1976).

Meek, C. K., '*The Soul of Nigeria* by Isaac O. Delano', *Journal of the Royal African Society,* 37.146 (1938), 119–22.

Mills, Sara, *Discourses of Difference: An Analysis of Women's Travel Writing and Colonialism* (London: Routledge, 1991).

Mortimer, Mildred P., *Journeys through the French African Novel* (Portsmouth, NH: Heinemann, 1990).

——, 'African Journeys', *Research in African Literatures,* 22.2 (1991), 169–75 (p. 171).

Muniz Improta França, Nara, 'Producing Intellectuals: Lagosian Books and Pamphlets between 1874 and 1922' (unpublished PhD thesis, University of Sussex, 2013).

Mwangi, Evan M., *Africa Writes Back to Self: Metafiction, Gender, Sexuality* (Albany, NY: Suny Press, 2009).

Nas, L., 'Postcolonial Travel Accounts and Ethnic Subjectivity: Travelling through Southern Africa', *Literator* 32.2 (2011), 151–71.

Newell, Stephanie, 'Introduction', in *Readings in African Popular Fiction,* ed. by Stephanie Newell (London: International African Institute, 2002), pp. 1–10.

——, 'Devotion and Domesticity: The Reconfiguration of Gender in Popular Christian Pamphlets from Ghana and Nigeria', *Journal of Religion in Africa,* 35.3 (2005), 296–323.

——, *West African Literatures: Ways of Reading* (Oxford: Oxford University Press, 2006).

——, 'Corresponding with the City: Self-Help Literature in Urban West Africa', *Journal of Postcolonial Writing,* 44.1 (2008), 15–27.

——, 'An Introduction to the Writings of J. G. Mullen, an African Clerk, in the *Gold Coast Leader*, 1916–19', *Africa,* 78.3 (2008), 384–400.

——, 'Newspapers, New Spaces, New Writers: The First World War and Print Culture in Colonial Ghana', *Research in African Literatures* 40.2 (2009), 1–15.

——, *The Power to Name: A History of Anonymity in Colonial West Africa* (Athens: Ohio University Press, 2013).

Newmarch, David, 'Travel Literature (South Africa)', in *Encyclopaedia of Post-Colonial Literatures in English*, ed. by Eugene Benson and L. W. Conolly (London: Routledge, 1994), pp. 1595–8.

Ney, Stephen, 'Ancestor, Book, Church: How Nigerian Literature Responds to the Missionary Encounter' (unpublished PhD thesis, University of British Columbia, 2010).

Ní Loingsigh, Aedín, *Postcolonial Eyes: Intercontinental Travel in Francophone African Literature* (Liverpool: Liverpool University Press, 2009).

——, 'African Travel Writing', in *The Routledge Companion to Travel Writing*, ed. by Carl Thompson (London: Routledge, 2016), pp. 185–95.

Nkambwe, Musisi, 'Intranational Tourism in Nigeria', *Canadian Journal of African Studies,* 19.1 (1985), 193–204.

Nnodim, Rita, 'Configuring Audiences in Yoruba Novels, Print and Media Poetry', *Research in African Literatures,* 37.3 (2006), 154–75.

Nolte, Insa, 'Colonial Politics and Precolonial History: Everyday Knowledge, Genre, and Truth in a Yoruba Town', *History in Africa,* 40.1 (2013), 125–64.

Nwapa, Flora, *One is Enough* (Enugu: Tana, 1981).

Obono, Oka, and Koblowe Obono, 'Ajala Travel: Mobility and Connections as Forms of Social Capital in Nigerian Society', in *The Social Life of Connectivity in Africa,* ed. by Mirjam de Bruijn and Rijk van Dijk (New York: Palgrave Macmillan, 2012), pp. 227–41.

Ochiagha, Terri, *Achebe and Friends at Umuahia: The Making of a Literary Elite* (Woodbridge: James Currey/Boydell & Brewer, 2015).

Ọdunjọ, J. F., *Kúyẹ̀* (Ibadan: African Universities Press, 1964).

Ofeimun, Odia, *London Letter and Other Poems* (Lagos: Hornbill House of Arts, 2000).

Ògúndélé, J. Ògúnsínà, *Èjìgbèdè Lọ́nà Ìsálú Ọ̀run* (London: Longmans Green and Co., 1956).

——, *Ibú Olókun* (London: University of London Press, 1956).

Ogunsanwo, Olatubosun, 'Intertextuality and Post-Colonial Literature in Ben Okri's *The Famished Road*', *Research in African Literatures,* 26.1 (1995), 40–52.

Ogunsina, Bisi, *The Development of the Yoruba Novel 1930–1975* (Ibadan: Gospel Faith Mission Press, 1992).

Oha, Obododimma, 'The Rhetoric of Cross-Cultural Engagement and the Tropology of Memory in Remi Raji's America-Travel Poetry', in *Iba: Essays on African Literature in Honour of Oyin Ogunba*, ed. by Wole Ogundele and Gbemisola Adeoti (Ile-Ife: Obafemi Awowlowo University Press, 2003), pp. 137–50.

Okediji, Moyo, *The Shattered Gourd: Yoruba Forms in Twentieth Century American Art* (Seattle: University of Washington Press, 2003).

Okome, Onookome, 'Nollywood, Lagos, and the Good-Time Woman', *Research in African Literatures,* 43.4 (2012), 166–86.

Okri, Ben, *The Famished Road* (London: Jonathan Cape, 1991).

Okùbọ́té, Moses Bótù, *Iwé Ìtàn Ìjẹ̀bu* (Ibadan: Third World Information Services, 2009).

Okunoye, Oyeniyi, 'The Margins or the Metropole? The Location of Home in Odia Ofeimun's London Letter and Other Poems', *Tydskrif vir letterkunde,* 43.2 (2006), 107–21.

Olagbemiro, Ibukun, *A Corper's Diary* (Abeokuta: IDOL Media Services, 2015).

Olaniyi, Rasheed, *Diaspora Is Not Like Home: A Social and Economic History of Yoruba in Kano, 1912–1999* (Muenchen: Lincom Europa, 2008).

Olaoluwa, Senayon, 'Ethnic; or National: Contemporary Yoruba Poets and the Imagination of the Nation in *Wa Gbo …*', *Journal of Literary Studies,* 28.2 (2012), 37–57.

Olukoju, Ayedele, 'Maritime Trade in Lagos in the Aftermath of the First World War', *African Economic History,* 20 (1992), 119–35.

Olukoju, Ayodeji, *The 'Liverpool' of West Africa: The Dynamics and Impact of Maritime Trade in Lagos, 1900–1950* (Trenton, NJ: Africa World Press, 2004).

Olukotun, Ayo, 'At the Barricades: Resurgent Media in Colonial Nigeria, 1900–1960', in *The Foundations of Nigeria: Essays in Honour of Toyin Falola*, ed. by Adebayo Oyebade (Trenton: Africa World Press, 2003), pp. 237–39.

Omiunu, Francis G. I., and Andrew Godwin Onokerhoraye, *Transportation and the Nigerian Space Economy* (Benin City: University of Benin, 1995).

Omobowale, Ayokunle Olumuyiwa, *The Tokunbo Phenomenon and the Second-Hand Economy in Nigeria* (Bern: Peter Lang AG, 2013).

Omotoso, Kole, 'The Nigerian Federation in the Nigerian Novel', *Publius,* 21.4 (1991), 145–53.

Ọmọyajowo, J. Akin, *Adégbẹ̀san*, 2nd edn (Lagos: Longman Nigeria, 1979 [1961]).

Omu, F. I. A., *Press and Politics in Nigeria, 1880–1937* (London: Longman, 1978).

Ondaatje, Michael, *Running in the Family* (London: Victor Gollancz, 1983).

Onyeama, Dillibe, *The Return: Homecoming of a Negro from Eton* (Isleworth: Satellite Books, 1978).

Osei-Poku, Kwame, 'African Authored Domestic Travel Writing and Identity: A Returnee Soldier's Impressions of Colonial Life in Takoradi (Gold Coast)',

*Coldnoon: International Journal of Travel Writing and Travelling Cultures,* 6.4 (2018), 22–48.

Osinulu, Damola, 'Painters, Blacksmiths and Wordsmiths: Building Molues in Lagos', *African Arts,* 41.3 (2008), 44–53.

Osundare, Niyi, 'Yorùbá Thoughts, English Words: A Poet's Journey through the Tunnel of Two Tongues', in *Kiss & Quarrel: Yorùbá/English Strategies of Mediation,* ed. by Stewart Brown (Birmingham: Centre of West African Studies, 2000), pp. 15–31.

——, *Thread in the Loom: Essays on African Literature and Culture* (Trenton, NJ: Africa World Press, 2002).

——, *If Only the Road Could Talk: Poetic Peregrinations in Africa, Asia, and Europe* (Trenton, NJ: Red Sea Press, 2017).

Otun, Temitayo A., *The Pregnant Corper* (Lagos: Moonlight Publishing, n.d.).

Oyeyemi, Helen, *The Icarus Girl* (London: Bloomsbury, 2005).

Page, J., *The Black Bishop* (London: Simpkin, Marshall, Hamilton, Kent & Company, 1910).

Peel, J. D. Y., 'Olaju: A Yoruba Concept of Development', *Journal of Development Studies,* 14.2 (1978), 139–65.

——, 'The Cultural Work of Yoruba Ethnogenesis', in *History and Ethnicity,* ed. by Maryon McDonald, Elizabeth Tonkin, and Malcolm Chapman (London: Routledge, 1989), pp. 198–215.

——, 'For Who Hath Despised the Day of Small Things? Missionary Narratives and Historical Anthropology', *Comparative Studies in Society and History,* 37.3 (1995), 581–607.

——, *Religious Encounter and the Making of the Yoruba* (Bloomington, IN: Indiana University Press, 2000).

Pettinger, Alasdair, *Always Elsewhere: Travels of the Black Atlantic* (London: Weidenfeld & Nicolson, 1998).

'Pilgrimages', in *African Cities Reader: Mobilities and Fixtures,* ed. by Ntone Edjabe and Edgar Pieterse (Vlaeberg: Chimurenga and the African Centre for Cities, 2011), p. 42.

Pitman, Thea, *Mexican Travel Writing* (Bern: Peter Lang, 2008).

Plaatje, Solomon, *Mhudi* (London: Heinemann, 1978 [1930]).

——, *Native Life in South Africa* (Johannesburg: Picador Africa, 2007 [1916]).

Pratt, Mary Louise, 'Arts of the Contact Zone', *Profession* (1991), 33–40.

——, *Imperial Eyes: Travel Writing and Transculturation* (New York; Abingdon: Routledge, 2007).

——, 'Modernity, Mobility and Ex-Coloniality', in *Travel Writing: Critical Concepts in Literary and Cultural Studies,* ed. by Tim Youngs and Charles Forsdick (London and New York: Routledge (2012 [2002])), pp. 118–33.

Quayson, Ato, *Strategic Transformations in Nigerian Writing: Orality & History in the Work of Rev. Samuel Johnson, Amos Tutuola, Wole Soyinka & Ben Okri* (Bloomington, IN: Indiana University Press, 1997).

Raban, Jonathan, *For Love and Money: Writing, Reading, Travelling, 1968–1987* (London: Collins Harvill, 1987).

Raji, Remi, *Shuttlesongs. America: A Poetic Guided Tour* (Ibadan: Bookcraft, 2001).

Ravi, Srilata, 'Home and the "Failed" City in Postcolonial Narratives of "Dark Return"', *Postcolonial Studies* 17.3 (2014), 296–306.

Remmington, Janet, 'Solomon Plaatje's Decade of Creative Mobility, 1912–1922: The Politics of Travel and Writing in and Beyond South Africa', *Journal of Southern African Studies,* 39.2 (2013), 425–46.

Rettová, Alena, 'Sci-Fi and Afrofuturism in the Afrophone Novel: Writing the Future and the Possible in Swahili and in Shona', *Research in African Literatures* 48.1 (2017), 158–82.

Ribeiro, António S., 'Translation as a Metaphor for Our Times: Postcolonialism, Borders and Identities', *Portuguese Studies,* 20 (2004), 186–94.

Ropero, María Lourdes López, 'Travel Writing and Postcoloniality: Caryl Phillips's *The Atlantic Sound*', *Atlantis* 25.1 (2003), 51–62.

Saro-Wiwa, Ken, *Sozaboy* (Port Harcourt: Saros International Publishers, 1985).

Saro-Wiwa, Noo, *Looking for Transwonderland: Travels in Nigeria* (London: Granta, 2013).

Sawada, Nozomi, 'The Educated Elite and Associational Life in Early Lagos Newspapers: In Search of Unity for the Progress of Society' (unpublished PhD thesis, University of Birmingham, 2011).

Shadeko, Babatunde A., *The Magic Land of Nigeria: A Surveyor's Scintillating and Thoughtprovoking Account of His Wanderings in Nigeria* (Lagos: Nationwide Survey Services, 1980).

Shittu, Ayodeji Isaac, and Anya U Egwu, '"Third-Worlding" the Colonial Metropolis: Post-Colonial Travelogue, Identity and a Tale of Two Cities in Odia Ofeimun's London Letter and Other Poems', *Covenant Journal of Language Studies,* 2.1 (2016).

Soetan, Lape, *How to Be a Single Woman in Your 30s in Lagos* (Lagos: n.p., 2015).

Soyinka, Wole, *The Road* (London: Oxford University Press, 1965).

——, *Myth, Literature and the African World* (Cambridge: Cambridge University Press, 1976).

Soyinka, Wole, *You Must Set Forth at Dawn* (New York: Random House, 2006).

Spurr, David, *The Rhetoric of Empire: Colonial Discourse in Journalism, Travel Writing and Imperial Administration* (Durham, NC: Duke University Press, 1993).

Stewart, Garrett, *Dear Reader: The Conscripted Audience in Nineteenth-Century British Fiction* (Baltimore: John Hopkins University Press, 1996).

Strong, Krystal, and Shaun Ossei-Owusu, 'Naija Boy Remix: Afroexploitation and the New Media Creative Economies of Cosmopolitan African Youth', *Journal of African Cultural Studies,* 26 (2014), 189–205.

Sudarkasa, Niara, *Where Women Work: A Study of Yoruba Women in the Marketplace and in the Home* (Ann Arbor: University of Michigan, 1973).

Tadjo, Véronique, *L'ombre D'imana: Voyages Jusqu'au Bout Du Rwanda* (Arles: Actes sud, 2000).

——, *The Shadow of Imana: Travels in the Heart of Rwanda*. trans. Véronique Wakerley (Oxford: Heinemann, 2002).

Thompson, Carl, *Travel Writing* (London: Routledge, 2011).

Tiamiyu, Muta, 'Prospects of Nigerian Book Publishing in the Electronic Age', in *Issues in Book Publishing in Nigeria: Essays in Honour of Aigboje Higo at 70*, ed. by Festus Agboola Adesanoye and Ayo Ojeniyi (Ibadan: Heinemann Educational Books Nigeria, 2005), pp. 143–57.

Toivanen, Anna-Leena, 'Uneasy "Homecoming" in Alain Mabanckou's *Lumières De Pointe-Noire*', *Studies in Travel Writing,* 21.3 (2017), 327–45.

Touati, Houari, *Islam and Travel in the Middle Ages*, trans. Lydia G. Cochrane (Chicago and London: University of Chicago Press, 2010).

Trager, Lillian, *Yoruba Hometowns: Community, Identity, and Development in Nigeria* (Boulder; London: Lynne Rienner Publishers, 2001).

Triulzi, Alessandro, and Robert McKenzie, *Long Journeys: African Migrants on the Road* (Leiden and Boston, MA: Brill, 2013).

Túbọ̀sún, Kọ́lá, *Edwardsville by Heart* (St Leonards-on-Sea: Wisdom's Bottom Press, 2018).

Turner, Victor, 'Liminality and Communitas', *The Ritual Process: Structure and Anti-structure,* 94 (1969), 130.

Tutuola, Amos, *The Palm-Wine Drinkard; and, My Life in the Bush of Ghosts* (New York: Grove Press, 1994).

Uche, Luke Uka, *Mass Media, People and Politics in Nigeria* (New Delhi: Concept Publishing Company, 1989).

Unigwe, Chika, *On Black Sisters' Street* (London: Jonathan Cape, 2009).

Urry, John, *The Tourist Gaze. Leisure and Travel in Contemporary Societies, Theory, Culture & Society* (London: Sage Publications, 1990).

Viana, Larissa, 'The Tropics and the Rise of the British Empire: Mungo Park's Perspective on Africa in the Late Eighteenth Century', *História, Ciências, Saúde – Manguinhos* 18.1 (2011), 33–50.

W. F., '*The Soul of Nigeria* by Isaac O. Delano', *Geographical Journal* 90.2 (1937), 177.

wa Mungai, Mbugua, and David A. Samper, '"No Mercy, No Remorse": Personal Experience Narratives About Public Passenger Transportation in Nairobi, Kenya', *Africa Today,* 52.3 (2006), 51–81.

Wainaina, Binyavanga, 'How to Write About Africa', *Granta* 92.1 (2005), 92–5.

——, *One Day I Will Write About This Place: A Memoir* (Minneapolis: Graywolf Press, 2011).

Watson, Kelly L., *Insatiable Appetites: Imperial Encounters with Cannibals in the North Atlantic World* (New York and London: NYU Press, 2015).

White, Judy Anne, 'Quest for Selfhood: The Female Hero in Amos Tutuola's *The Brave African Huntress*', *Contributions in Afroamerican and African Studies,* 187 (1998), 131–42.

Wilkinson, Jane, 'Between Orality and Writing: The Forest of a Thousand Daemons as a Self-Reflexive Text', *Commonwealth: Essays and Studies,* 9.2 (1987), 41–51.

Wiwa, Ken, *In the Shadow of a Saint: A Son's Journey to Understand His Father's Legacy* (New York: Doubleday, 2000).

Yai, Olabiyi Babalola, 'In Praise of Metonymy: The Concepts of "Tradition" and "Creativity" in the Transmission of Yoruba Artistry over Time and Space', *Research in African Literatures*, 24.4 (1993): 29–37: p. 30.

Yemitan, Ọladipọ. *Gbọbaníyì*, 2nd edn (Ibadan: University Press, 1987 [1972]).

Youngs, Tim, *Travellers in Africa: British Travelogues 1850–1900* (Manchester: Manchester University Press, 1994).

Youngs, Tim, and Peter Hulme, *Talking About Travel Writing: A Conversation between Peter Hulme and Tim Youngs* (Leicester: The English Association, 2007).

Zachernuk, Philip S., *Colonial Subjects: An African Intelligentsia and Atlantic Ideas* (Charlottesville and London: University Press of Virginia, 2000).

——, 'Critical Agents: Colonial Nigerian Intellectuals and Their British Counterparts', in *Agency and Action in Colonial Africa*, ed. by Chris Youé and Tim Stapleton (Basingstoke: Palgrave Macmillan, 2001), pp. 156–71.

Zeleza, Tiyambe, 'The Political Economy of British Colonial Development and Welfare in Africa', *Transafrican Journal of History,* 14 (1985), 139–61.

# Index

Note: Page numbers in italics denote illustrations.

# AFRICAN
# ARTICULATIONS

ISSN 2054–5673

## Previously published

*Achebe and Friends at Umuahia: The Making of a Literary Elite*
Terri Ochiagha, 2015    Winner of the ASAUK Fage and Oliver Prize 2016

*A Death Retold in Truth and Rumour: Kenya, Britain and the
Julie Ward Murder*    Grace A. Musila, 2015

*Scoring Race: Jazz, Fiction, and Francophone Africa*    Pim Higginson,
2017

*Writing Spatiality in West Africa: Colonial Legacies in the Anglophone/
Francophone Novel*    Madhu Krishnan, 2018

*Written under the Skin: Blood and Intergenerational Memory in
South Africa*    Carli Coetzee, 2019

*Experiments with Truth: Narrative Non-fiction and the Coming of
Democracy in South Africa*    Hedley Twidle, 2019

## Forthcoming

*African Literature in the Digital Age: Class and Sexual Politics in New
Writing from Nigeria and Kenya*    Shola Adenekan, 2020

*Cinemas of the Mozambican Revolution*    Ros Gray, 2020